The True Intrepid

SIR WILLIAM STEPHENSON AND THE UNKNOWN AGENTS

Bill Macdonald

RAINCOAST BOOKS

Vancouver

First published in 1998 by Timberholme Books

This edition published in 2001 by

Raincoast Books
9050 Shaughnessy Street
Vancouver, B.C.
CANADA
V6P 6E5

www.raincoast.com

Cover and text design: Ingrid Paulson

Cover Portrait of William Stephenson: Kathleen Taylor

1 2 3 4 5 6 7 8 9 10

NATIONAL LIBRARY OF CANADA CATALOGUING IN PUBLICATION DATA

Macdonald, Bill
    The true Intrepid

    Includes bibliographical references and index.
    ISBN 1-55192-418-8

    1. Stephenson, William Samuel, Sir, 1896– 2. World War,
1939–1945—Secret service—Great Britain. 3. Spies—Canada—Biography. I. Title.
D810.S8S8 2001   940.54'8641'092   C2001-910850-8

Raincoast Books gratefully acknowledges the support of the Government of Canada, through the Book Publishing Industry Development Program, the Canada Council for the Arts and the Department of Canadian Heritage. We also acknowledge the assistance of the Province of British Columbia, through the British Columbia Arts Council.

Printed and bound in Canada

To the memory of William S. Stephenson,
to the people who worked for him and
for the family he left behind.

Table of Contents

Foreword by Thomas F. Troy..1

Preface..7

Introduction..13

Section I — The Life of William Stephenson

1 A Boy from the Prairies 21

2 Wartime Hero 31

3 International Success 44

4 Assignment: New York 61

5 The Secret Expansion 65

6 The Transatlantic Link 82

7 Clandestine Success..88

8 A Final Case 100

9 Island Retirement...104

Section II — Out of the Shadows

10 "A Mysterious Millionaire" 121

11 A Man Called Intrepid 130

Section III — The Unknown Agents

12 BSC Recruits — "No, he wasn't the rabbit; he was the magic." 153

13 "Cynthia" and Marion — "It's absolutely true ..." 172

14 Bill Ross Smith — "He was a very, very, very great man." 187

15 Betty Raymond — "They hated him." 211

16 Astley and the Service — "We had no idea how to approach the
     Americans." 226

17 Roald Dahl — "Anything to do with secrets
     Fleming would like to 'use' himself." 237

18 Grace Garner — "The carnage ... the terrible things." 252

19 Benjamin de Forest "Pat" Bayly — "And that was kind of
     an important job, where all these subs were." 285

Epilogue 337

Appendix 341

Glossary and Cast of Characters 360

Notes 367

Bibliography 398

Index 403

"It was impossible not to like Bill Stephenson." That comment was made to me in 1972 by a former high official of the Roosevelt administration in an interview about Stephenson's activities in the United States in World War II. The comment itself did not surprise me, because I had already experienced the likeability of Stephenson in our first meeting a few months earlier.

What did surprise me was the author of the comment. It was the late Assistant Secretary of State Adolf A. Berle, Jr., who served Roosevelt as his liaison with both American and foreign intelligence services. In that capacity Berle had been particularly lynx-eyed in watching but not always successfully hobbling those British agents he and J. Edgar Hoover of the Federal Bureau of Investigation suspected of violating American laws. Thus in 1941 he warned Under Secretary of State Sumner Welles that Stephenson's organization, British Security Coordination (BSC), was "rapidly evolving" into "a full size secret police and intelligence service." Thought was given to having him and all his agents ousted from the United States. That such a vigorous foe of Stephenson eventually came to find him irresistibly likeable struck me as high tribute.

While Berle first encountered Stephenson as a slippery suspect, I first met him as a man of mystery, which, interestingly enough, is what Bill Macdonald did when he came to write this book. Bill is a native of Winnipeg (where Stephenson was born) and a journalist who knows how to go about researching the life of a local hero. He soon discovered, however, that William Stephenson was a surprisingly unexpected man of mystery, as the reader also will soon be fascinated to discover. But to return to my story, Stephenson's alleged greatness became my job as a staff officer in the Central Intelligence Agency (CIA), to prove or disprove. The assignment came about in the following fashion. In the mid-sixties, in the course of lecturing CIA personnel on the nature of foreign intelligence and the history of the CIA, I found myself parroting what had become the received tradition inside the agency on how it came to be. It began with a man who had been a legendary American and CIA figure long before Stephenson's name percolated beyond the elite business circles in which he quietly moved. This man was the late Maj. Gen. William J. ("Wild Bill") Donovan whose postwar fame as the head of the Office of Strategic Services (OSS) trumped his pre-war popularity as the head of New York's "Fighting Sixty-Ninth."

The tale I was telling centered on the two trips that Donovan had been asked by President Roosevelt in 1940-41 to take to London and then to the Middle East and the Mediterranean area to assess the survivability, in the face of Nazi attacks, of Britain and her allies, real and potential. As a result of those trips Donovan recommended to the president that he should quickly establish a "service of strategic information," a vehicle in effect for conducting and coordinating American secret intelligence activities overseas. Out of this recommendation came first the Coordinator of Information (COI) in 1941, then its successor OSS in 1942, and finally the CIA in 1947. It was all so simple and so convincing.

But was it true? By me it was never even questioned, that is, until I read *The Quiet Canadian* by H. Montgomery Hyde, a prolific English biographer. This book, which was published in 1962, made little impact on anyone other than myself. It hit my tale hard, because it contradicted so much of what I had been parroting as gospel. It largely undercut the exclusively creative role long credited to 'Big Bill' Donovan and transferred it to an unknown man, a former lightweight boxing champion, Donovan's friend and collaborator, "Little Bill" Stephenson. It claimed that Stephenson, representing British secret intelligence, had resumed a friendship with Donovan, sold him on the idea of intelligence, engineered the trips of 1940-41, originated the idea of a new American intelligence organization, pushed the idea in Washington, and even engineered Donovan's appointment as the head of the new COI. Such a breathtaking story could not be ignored.

To my surprise, however, not a trace of Bill Stephenson could I find at CIA, even though I searched diligently. Let me say here that the reader will soon discover how diligently, and productively, Bill Macdonald, himself, had to search for the origin of Bill Stephenson. For him there were many missing pieces. For me, there was not a news clipping, a document or a book in the library's special intelligence collection that spoke of him. There was no one in the halls who had been around in the formative years who had ever heard of him. Nor was anything found in the agency's rich secret files. Of course something and somebody might have been missed, but it was not for want of seeking. Alerted to the existence of the missing and mysterious William S. Stephenson, my superiors decided that in the interest of resolving contradictory versions of agency history I should talk with the man himself. Hence it was that in February 1969 I first met the likeable and really great Bill Stephenson in Bermuda, where he lived in retirement with his American-born wife.

Stephenson, then 73, showed the effects of a stroke: a cane, shuffling feet, a slightly closed left eye, a curled upper lip, slightly slurred speech, and the years had made him heavier than the lightweight of old. But he smiled readily, his handshake was firm, his eyes were bright, his voice was strong, and his mind was active. Proof of his relative well being? On that first visit we and his wartime deputy sat in undisturbed lively conversation for fully four hours.

Thereafter, in his last 20 years, we developed a personal friendship, which caused me often to recall Adolf Berle's comment about him. In those years I visited him several times and we exchanged innumerable letters, cables and telephone calls. Meanwhile I was pursuing the truth of CIA's origin in the usual scholarly fashion — in other interviews, correspondence, archival research, and collateral reading. The fruit of this effort, which I will shortly summarize, will be found in my writings, especially Donovan and the CIA: *A History of the Establishment of the Central Intelligence Agency* (1981) and *Wild Bill and Intrepid* (1996).

Long before Stephenson had made his mark in intelligence and international affairs he had chalked up a string of notable accomplishments. His boxing title quickly followed winning medals as a fighter pilot in the first World War. In 1922 the London Daily Mail credited him as a "brilliant scientist" with a leading role in the revolutionary transmission of wireless photography. In 1924 a South Carolina paper quoted him as foreseeing "moving pictures on [the] way ... may soon be possible to 'see-in' as well as 'listen in' at one's home." By this time, nearing age 30, he was on his way to being a millionaire. His companies included General Radio, Sound City Films, Earl's Court, Alpha Cement, and Pressed Steel. In 1934 one of his General Aircraft planes won the King's Cup Race. Well before the outbreak of World War II he was recognized in business circles in England, Canada, the USA and as far abroad as Pakistan and India as a leading inventor and industrialist.

However, as often happens to great men, notably Bill Donovan, the imminence of war propelled Stephenson into a new and more rewarding work. The rise of Hitler made Stephenson's ownership of Pressed Steel, among other assets, a vital source of information about German rearmament, information that he began feeding secretly to Winston Churchill, then in his "wilderness years." Stephenson's familiarity with steel, as well as his service to Churchill, was surely instrumental in his involvement early in 1940 in British efforts, later aborted by timidity in Whitehall, to sabotage the shipment to Germany of much needed Swedish iron ore. Within weeks, however, he was asked by Churchill and the head of the Secret Intelligence Service to undertake work that would prove to be the source of public fame. This was the revitalisation of the moribund British secret intelligence station in New York, in the still neutral United States.

What he took over was a handful of people which, under his energetic direction and often at his own expense, was soon transformed into hundreds of people. These made that station, appropriately camouflaged as BSC, the largest clandestine foreign intelligence station ever established in the United States. It was not number alone, however, but its boldness that made it also distinctive. Stephenson audaciously, and often close to illegally, waged covert political warfare in the United States against all sources of Axis strength and support here and throughout the Western Hemisphere and just as covertly helped bring the American people and government into the war as a British ally. At the same time, however, he had first to contend with American officials, like Adolf Berle and J. Edgar Hoover, who had the quaint notion that no foreign intelligence service, whatever its motives, should be allowed to operate in this country without government's authorization, and second, to avoid any operational fiascos that might imperil if not shatter Anglo-American relations and thereby defeat the aim of the enterprise. In the event, Stephenson so successfully carried water on both shoulders that he and his station operated in New York for five years, until the end of the war. That success was fundamental in the establishment of the Anglo-American intelligence collaboration that has been an abiding factor in international affairs ever since.

While it is thus obvious that Stephenson rendered outstanding service to Britain, to Canada, the United States, and the entire Allied cause as well, it is not sufficiently well known that he made an especially unique contribution to the structure of the American government. That gift brings us back to my effort to reconcile the claims of "Big Bill" Donovan and "Little Bill" Stephenson to the establishment of CIA. That effort has largely documented the creative role played by Stephenson in leading Donovan to propose, propagandise, and finally head FDR's new secret intelligence agency, the COI. At the same time it has documented Donovan's success in making that organization and its successor, notably CIA, a much larger, more diverse, and especially more enduring creation than the temporary "dirty tricks" service envisioned by Stephenson. That CIA recently observed the 50th anniversary of its establishment proves the fruitfulness of the collaboration of "the two Bills."

For his services Stephenson was honoured at war's end by both governments. The United States acknowledged his "exceptionally meritorious conduct in the performance of outstanding services to the United Nations" and awarded him the Medal for Merit, its highest civilian award. For one government to be so appreciative of another's secret agent was an unusual tribute, perhaps unknown in intelligence history. Britain conferred knighthood upon that same secret agent, but in doing so felt compelled to identify him discreetly as "employed in a department of the Foreign Office." Nevertheless, Britain named him "Sir William S. Stephenson," a title by which he will always be respectfully remembered.

In the mid-seventies a new title made him doubly famous as "a man called Intrepid," which was the title of a new bestselling biography. So well known did it make him that he was constantly besieged by generals, admirals, senators, as well as journalists asking for interviews. So great was the almost universal interest in him that I did not learn of his death on January 31, 1989, until three days later. Then his adopted daughter called and apologised for not calling me sooner. She explained that her "Pops" had instructed her to withhold news of his death until after the funeral because otherwise it was likely to be turned into a media event beyond tiny Bermuda's capacity to handle. As it was, fewer than 20 people were on hand. It was a fitting end for the man whom I had first encountered as "the quiet Canadian."

For those new to the story of "the quiet Canadian," Bill Macdonald's book will be a fascinating introduction and an irresistible incentive to pursue the subject. For those long familiar with it, the breathtaking discoveries of The True Intrepid will surely prove to be remarkably fresh, challenging and quite persuasive.

—Thomas F. Troy
Former CIA Staff Historian
2001

This book retraces the life of World War II spymaster William Stephenson and the organization he created, British Security Coordination (BSC). Yet it didn't start out that way, and its course was predicated by a number of twists, some unique to the world of espionage.

Stephenson, known widely as the man called Intrepid, died in Bermuda on January 31, 1989. His war efforts were celebrated in his lifetime in two major books, but subsequently some observers questioned certain aspects of his career and others attempted to discredit his reputation or reduce his role in history. He died relatively forgotten. Stephenson's obituaries said he was a Canadian, born in Winnipeg in 1896, a graduate of Argyle High School, and the son of a lumber mill owner. An interesting life come to a close. Rest in peace.

However, there were no lumber mill owners named Stephenson in Winnipeg at the turn of the century. No one with his parents' names lived in the city then. Manitoba Vital Statistics has no record of the ex-spy chief's birth. There was no Argyle High School. So began the difficult task of trying to learn about the life of William Stephenson.

Basic facts about Stephenson's life were incorrect, but gradually his biographic puzzle pieced together and helped blaze a trail elsewhere. As this project evolved, curiosity about the real details of Stephenson's life and career also led to questions about why the wrong information appeared in the first place, and why it remained the recorded history.

Obviously a partial answer to the mystery around Stephenson's background is his occupation. In espionage lingo a "legend" is a fake biography of a spy used to provide him or her with a cover. Stephenson, an important clandestine agent during World War II, was in a position where relatives, business associates and friends could be possible targets for blackmail, kidnapping, or reprisals. They could provide clues to the agent's whereabouts, motives, modus operandi, and how to stop him. Stewart Menzies, Winston Churchill's World War II MI-6 chief, is said to have destroyed his personal papers when it appeared Britain could be invaded. Stephenson did more than that — becoming essentially a man without a factual background. Untraceable. A perfect spy. A larger, perhaps unanswerable question is why the misinformation was continued long after the war, and in two biographies.[1]

Accurately following Stephenson's life on the Canadian prairie through to his undercover activities in the World War II was a daunting challenge. It was possible to get answers from the two major books written on Stephenson and his career, but some reservations remained. Both British-born authors seem to have had some "cloak and dagger" experience, and both knew Stephenson prior to writing about him. Harford Montgomery Hyde who wrote the first book, *The Quiet Canadian* (1962), worked for British Intelligence during the war. Obviously he had to deal with certain restraints of Britain's Official Secrets Act. William Stevenson, who wrote *A Man Called Intrepid* (1976) and *Intrepid's Last Case* (1983), admits to having some experience in "operational intelligence."[2] Both Hyde and Stevenson depict a fictitious life in Canada for Stephenson, so it is difficult for a neutral observer to determine exactly at what point to start believing his story.

The books left a rather strange wake. The events leading to their publication, and the posse of criticisms they stirred up, are interesting in themselves. For example, Stephenson wanted Hyde's book published, and then he stifled it. He didn't want a second edition published and he quashed attempts to dramatize his story in film. Stevenson's *A Man Called Intrepid* portrays the ex-Winnipegger as a behind-the-scenes influence on many of the war's events and a confidant of Roosevelt and Churchill. Yet Stephenson and his organization are not mentioned in many, perhaps most, general histories of the war. One reviewer labelled the book, "from start to finish utterly worthless." At least one critic said Churchill didn't even know Stephenson, his North American intelligence man.

The aftermath of the books, especially the Stevenson tomes, was not only recognition for Stephenson but confusion about his career. Close associates, former employees and some writers have found the life and work of William Stephenson somewhat baffling. The American author and historian Joseph Lash, who published the Churchill–Roosevelt correspondence, wrote, "It is impossible on the basis of material available to American scholars to establish what is true, inflated, or deliberately distorted in William Stevenson's *A Man Called Intrepid*."[3] Following Stephenson's death, his friend for more than thirty years, Derek Bedson, still wanted to know, "What was it he was appointed to, exactly, in New York?" Former wartime personnel of Stephenson's also have trouble distilling his story. "It's a murky world, isn't it? It's hard to separate truth from fiction," said Patsey Sullivan, who was employed in Stephenson's inner office. Another BSC employee, the writer Roald Dahl, thought any author would have trouble retracing Stephenson's life and should face the fact that his ex-boss was an enigma. "And it had nothing to do with the Secret Service. It was the man himself."

The organization Stephenson headed used deception to conceal and influence, and in many instances the truth was never recorded, or will not be released. Information at the intelligence agency was on a need-to-know basis, and staff seldom knew what was transpiring in the next room. Another potential roadblock to a spy biographer is obtaining an unbiased overview: some books in the espionage genre are suspect. If intelligence work is "secret service," it is somewhat incongruous that there are books that reveal the inside stories of secret service agencies.

These literary oxymorons are often written by people with some inside knowledge of the operation of an intelligence organization — either previous employees, or those who have had access to informers of the agencies. Many are written by people using pseudonyms, and they often contain pages of non-footnoted information. Virtually all major books on diplomacy, the history of war, and politics are footnoted and well annotated. Books in the espionage genre, which for the most part have been written by people with academic credentials, often appear without much, if any, supporting material.

A retired KGB colonel, Mikhail Lyubimov, wrote that there was widespread belief in the former Soviet Union that such books were orchestrated by intelligence agencies.[4] The writer Bradley F. Smith has expressed similar conclusions about certain books. In 1968 Stephenson called Kim Philby's Cold War memoirs, *My Silent War*, "just another piece of Soviet propaganda designed to denigrate and ridicule the intelligence services of the Western powers."[5] Any reviewer of the genre who attempts to use such books as background information should maintain a certain amount of skepticism and keep in mind many files are closed, and a primary objective of some operations is to misinform.

Unfortunately in Stephenson's case facts verified in available documents may not be true. Stephenson himself is quoted as saying, "Nothing deceives like a document."[6]

There is some information relating to Stephenson and BSC in American archives. There were a few Canadian documentaries done decades after the war in which a few of the participants spoke. The Central Intelligence Agency's former staff historian published a new history in 1996, which included information on Stephenson. The British are not as forthcoming. During the course of my research they withdrew material relevant to Stephenson's career. The previously available files of Montgomery Hyde were closed to the public by the British government after his death, partially reopened and closed again after this author went through the heavily weeded remains. [See photo insert.] For Britain's Foreign Office it seems the less that is known about Sir William Stephenson, the man Churchill said was "dear to his heart," the better.

BSC's papers were destroyed at the conclusion of the war, but a summary of some of the organization's undertakings was compiled in Canada and completed in 1945. Still considered "Top Secret," sections of this elusive document, nicknamed the "Bible," were made available to this author by a person who wishes to remain anonymous.

Although espionage sources can sometimes be suspect, some basic information proved helpful during this project:

- There is an old spy adage: "Espionage is a combination of information and disinformation. Loyalty and betrayal. Believe nothing. But remember everything."
- In certain academic modern history courses, some of the reference books related to spying on reading lists are fiction. It is said a few books of fiction portray espionage more accurately than any text book. The author John Le Carré (former intelligence officer David Cornwell), for example, for years submitted his work to the British government for vetting.[7]

• During the course of this research, it became apparent that at least one ancient Chinese manuscript was still used for reference by military and defence organizations, sometimes word for word. Sun Tzu's *The Art of War*, from approximately the sixth century, says: "Let your plans be dark and impenetrable as night, and when you move, fall like a thunderbolt." Tu Yu quotes a saying of T'ai Kung that has passed into a proverb: 'You cannot shut your ears to the thunder or your eyes to the lightning — so rapid are they.' Likewise, an attack should be made so quickly that it cannot be parried."

The most important source of information about Stephenson and his career proved to be the people around him during the war. My attempts to retrace Stephenson's path unexpectedly led to new information about the war, and that there were actually four jurisdictions contributing to the behind-the-scenes manoeuvring of the Western Allies: Britain, the United States, Canada and the Stephenson organization.

Although they were called British Security Coordination, the Stephenson people were very much a law unto themselves. They made many separate deals with other countries and distributed information amongst the three Western Allies. They controlled many of the secrets of the three countries, including ULTRA and MAGIC, and also had communication influence in the South Pacific and Asia. There were a number of British appointments at BSC, but essentially, Stephenson contacted his friends, put them to work, and had them find staff. They recruited thousands, mostly Canadians. Stephenson worked for no salary and financed many of the undertakings himself. The important work these people accomplished during the war has never been fully explored.

This book begins with a chronicle of Stephenson's life, attempting to verify the factual. The second section details stories of people who were with him at the time of crisis, what they did, and what they had to say. For the most part they have never before discussed their war work. From the totality of their stories one can surmise the enormity of Stephenson's undertaking and his accomplishments. What began as research into locating the house of a Canadian prairie spymaster became a strange journey back to what has been called the greatest event in human history, World War II.

Since the first publication of this book I have been fortunate to meet many more former friends and employees of William Stephenson — intelligence professionals and legendary intelligence figures such as the late Svetlana Gouzenko. Some of their stories have been added to this edition. They helped confirm that this strange journey was a trip worth taking.

In view of recent events in the United States, it seems even more remarkable that no major acts of sabotage or Fifth Column terror- ism occurred in the western hemisphere during World War II. It was Stephenson's contention that the first line of defence for democracies was intelligence. During a critical period in world history he was suc- cessful in implementing and coordinating what Bill Donovan called "the greatest integrated secret intelligence and operations organization that has ever existed anywhere."

William Stephenson was perhaps the greatest unsung hero of the twentieth century. As best as I could ascertain — this is his story.

— Bill Macdonald
Winnipeg, Manitoba
2001

Churchill's Spymaster:
A Search for the "Real James Bond"

William Stephenson? Although Stephenson was from my hometown of Winnipeg, Manitoba, I knew little of the World War II spy chief. I read Stephenson's obituaries in the local paper and in *Maclean's* magazine with passing interest, but there seemed to be next to nothing in other media. It was Stephenson's death notice in the British *Manchester Guardian Weekly* that eventually set wheels in motion. The headline read: "Churchill's Spymaster — A Model For Bond."

> "Sir William Stephenson, the wartime spymaster whom Churchill called INTREPID has died (January 31, 1989) in the home he retired to in Bermuda, aged 93.
>
> ... Fleet Street had almost forgotten this remarkable figure until the publication of a biography (*A Man Called Intrepid*) in 1976, when [intelligence writer] Chapman Pincher was moved to call him "the nearest thing to James Bond, Callan, and 'M' rolled into one." In fact the Anglo-American show Stephenson ran in New York, British Security Coordination, has been described by another historian of the spy trade as "the largest integrated intelligence network enterprise in history."
>
> ... Ian Fleming was one to serve under him, and there's not much doubt that elements in Bond's make-up were derived from Stephenson, not least his love for fancy gadgetry.[1]

The obituary went on to say Stephenson was a decorated pilot in World War I, the winner of a King's Cup air race, and a onetime European lightweight boxing champion. He was notorious for his martinis served in huge glasses. The obituary concluded "born Winnipeg, 1896, son of a lumber mill owner."

With this information, I decided to research and write a freelance piece on the former Manitoban's childhood house and neighbourhood. It turned out not to be a simple undertaking.

Two Stephenson biographies, *The Quiet Canadian* (titled *Room 3603* in the United States), by Harford Montgomery Hyde (1962), and *A Man Called Intrepid*, by William Stevenson (1976), were consulted. The foreword to *Room 3603*, written by Ian Fleming, played up the James Bond theme. Bond was a "highly romanticized version of the true spy," Fleming wrote, and Stephenson was the "real thing." Neither of the books lists a Canadian address for Stephenson, and they display an ignorance about Winnipeg, where Stephenson spent the first decades of his life. They state that Stephenson was from Point Douglas, "just outside Winnipeg," and "near Winnipeg." Actually Point Douglas is regarded as "inner city," about ten blocks from the geographic centre of Winnipeg.

The books give Stephenson's birth date as January 11, 1896. Microfiche of the major newspaper of the time, the daily *Manitoba Free Press*, had no birth announcement within months of this date. Of course not everyone puts birth announcements in newspapers. Tracing the date through Manitoba's Department of Vital Statistics turned up no record of a William S. Stephenson born January 11, 1896. However, government records could have been incomplete.

Although *A Man Called Intrepid* said the day Stephenson was born was "the coldest day in recorded history in that bleak part of the American continent,"[2] according to the paper's weather report it was a typical winter day in Winnipeg.

Both books and Stephenson's obituaries say the former spy chief's father was a descendant of Scottish settlers and a lumber mill owner. His mother, *A Man Called Intrepid* says, was of Norwegian ancestry. Winnipeg's *Henderson's* directories of streets, families and businesses of the late 1800s indicate there were no lumber mill owners named Stephenson in Winnipeg at that time. According to the residential street index, no couple with Stephenson's parents' names — William

Victor and Christine Stephenson — lived in the city. The directories seldom listed the children of the house, so there was no sign of a young William S. Stephenson living in Winnipeg around the turn of the century.

Stevenson's *A Man Called Intrepid* includes excerpts from Stephenson's high school report card and quotes one of Stephenson's schoolteachers. Records from the time were sparse, so there was little chance of finding a class list or a report from Stephenson's alma mater, Argyle High School. This led to my discovery there was no Argyle High School. At the time an Argyle Elementary School existed, but it was strictly for younger students, and didn't go higher than grade eight.

Hyde's *The Quiet Canadian* indicates Stephenson returned to Winnipeg for a short time from Europe after World War I, and the *Henderson's* directories reveal that there was a Wm. S. Stephenson living at 175 Syndicate Street in 1920. He worked for the Franco British Supply Company. Syndicate Street is in Point Douglas.

The woman living at 175 Syndicate Street when I was researching Stephenson had been at that address for about forty years, and she didn't know anything about William Stephenson or the history of her house. She recalled that two elderly women she didn't know had visited her place and told her the house had been the home of a prominent relative. On another occasion, many years before, a woman in a local historical society told her she lived in the house of a famous person. Eventually I located the amateur historian.

"He wasn't a Stephenson," Elly Heber said. "They just took him in."

Heber said Stephenson was born into another family but was raised by the Stephensons after his natural family could no longer afford to care for him. She learned about the Stephenson family from a now deceased elderly Point Douglas resident she interviewed. She also recalled once meeting an elderly man named Gislasson who knew the Stephenson family.

When he was located, Ragnar Gislasson said his father was a friend of Stephenson's adoptive father, Vigfus. Gislasson visited the Syndicate Street house during and following World War I with his father, and he frequently met Stephenson. The former Sergeant-of-Arms at the Manitoba legislature recalled once seeing a picture of the young Stephenson returning to the European conflict in a Winnipeg newspaper in about May 1918. Every page of every edition of the May 1918 *Manitoba Free Press* was consulted. Finally a picture of Stephenson was found, headlined "Wins Military Cross." The picture was the same as a photo in *The Quiet Canadian*. The newspaper photo and caption underneath proved where Stephenson lived, and that his parents' names were different than those recorded in his biographies.[3]

The Manitoba legislature has information files on prominent Manitobans and the Stephenson file consists of a few local newspaper clippings. The clipping file indicated Stephenson covertly visited Winnipeg in the summer of 1980 and was escorted around his old neighbourhood by Derek Bedson, a Winnipeg friend. When contacted, Bedson said he met Stephenson in the 1950s in New York, when he was working for Canada's Department of External Affairs. He knew very little about Stephenson's war career, and although he showed him around town he knew nothing of Stephenson's Winnipeg background. But once he met someone who seemed to know a lot about Stephenson's early life — Manitoba's then Lieutenant Governor George Johnson. Why would he know?

"Do you know his racial background?" Bedson asked.

"It sounds quite WASPish."

But Johnson wasn't a WASP.

"He's pure Icelandic. That's the secret of them," Bedson said. "That's the secret of the Icelanders. They suddenly get you. You think you've got another WASP, and you've got an Icelander."[4]

Johnson knew of the Stephenson family because of the close ties within Manitoba's Icelandic community. William Stephenson's adoptive parents were not Scottish immigrants or from Norway: they were Icelandic-Canadians.

George Johnson, then the Queen's representative in Manitoba, was a retired doctor. Some of Stephenson's relatives were patients of his, he said, and he knew the family. Christine Stefansson of Selkirk, Manitoba, was the sister of Stephenson's adoptive mother, Kristin. She saved a newspaper clipping from a small Icelandic paper that named Stephenson's natural parents, and gave a conflicting year of birth.

Eventually the provincial Department of Vital Statistics located a copy of the birth certificate of William Samuel Clouston Stanger, born January 23, 1897. Stanger later became better known as William Samuel

Stephenson, a man called "Intrepid," born January 11, 1896.

William Stephenson's unlikely Canadian roots. Ethnic background — wrong. Parents' names — wrong. Parent occupation — wrong. Birth date, day and year, — wrong. Birth name — wrong. School — didn't exist.

Obviously a number of questions came up during this stage of my research. Two popular biographies had been written, and most of the information on the first twenty years of the subject's life — his formative years — was bogus. Stephenson's relatives indicated they mysteriously stopped hearing from him in the 1930s, when he was in England, and for the most part never heard from him again. There hadn't been a "falling out" or arguments in the family.

With the Winnipeg research more or less completed, I located a former wartime employee of BSC. Molly Phair was the only Winnipegger who had worked for Stephenson's top secret organization who still lived in the city. Phair was still somewhat reluctant to talk about her war work, but she said she worked in BSC's Japanese section, relaying coded messages. Such a department is not mentioned in the books on Stephenson.

Records of who worked for Stephenson's BSC were destroyed following the war. Former employees who attempted to have seniority recognized were told there was no record of them ever working there. Phair said that a few years before I contacted her, a meeting of former employees took place. There was a "spy reunion" in Toronto in 1986, organized completely through word of mouth and mutual friends. The BSC alumni in Toronto helped point the way to people in other Canadian cities, and to contacts in Europe and the United States. Although they were sworn to secrecy, they were all eager to learn more about the life of William Stephenson.

The world of espionage and spymasters often does not lend itself to conventional biography. Stewart Menzies' biographer said his character was such as it would baffle anyone who tried to take his measure — especially the enemy. William Shirer said of the Abwehr's Wilhelm Canaris, "He was so shadowy a figure that no two writers agree as to what kind of man he was or what he believed in." Stephenson fit a similar mold.

It soon became evident there were many people who had strong views about Stephenson one way or the other. Books about him have been called unreliable. As a result of the books, small details of his career, such as the dates he may have met certain people for dinner, came into question decades later.

Verbatim accounts help circumvent author interpretation and trivial detail. Most of the employees interviewed in the Section III of this volume have never previously talked in detail about their wartime experiences. Their opinions and contributions deserve an airing. BSC's records were destroyed, so their recollections are a unique oral history. For the most part, I have attempted to step back and leave the facts as I found them.

I

The Life of William Stephenson

"The truth is incontrovertible. Panic may resent it; ignorance may deride it; malice may distort it, but there it is."

— Winston S. Churchill

"The truth is always less believable."

— William Stephenson

1 A BOY FROM THE PRAIRIES

"I'm a Winnipegger."
— William Stephenson, *Globe and Mail*, May 20, 1982

Where do spymasters come from? During World War II a prominent Allied trio rose to power and established a symbiotic relationship which helped smooth the road to victory. Stewart Menzies (b. 1890) was born in London and raised in Scotland, where his family owned Europe's second largest distillery. His family controlled Hallyburton castle and estate, with the surrounding twelve farms, near the Royal Grounds at Balmoral. Menzies was raised an English gentleman. Ludgrove, Eton, the Life Guards, the Beaufort Hunt and White's Club.

William "Wild Bill" Donovan (b. 1883) was born in Buffalo, New York, the son of Irish immigrants. Donovan attended Catholic schools and his education was partially financed by a local Bishop. He attended university in Niagara Falls and Columbia, and became a successful and prominent Wall Street lawyer.

And then there was William Stephenson from Winnipeg, Canada.

Winnipeg, the capital and largest city of Manitoba, lies midway between the Atlantic and Pacific Oceans in the heart of Canada. The town sprang up around the junction of the Red and Assiniboine Rivers, about a hundred kilometres north of the American border. To the west and south stretch thousands of miles of prairie. To the east and north is the rocky, lake-studded wilderness of the Canadian Shield.

The Inuit, Dene, Cree and Assiniboine people have inhabited Manitoba for about 5000 years. The first Europeans established an outpost on the Hudson Bay coast in 1682. Eventually French traders arrived inland to the south from the east, and farmers from Scotland and Ireland began to settle the plains in the early 1800s.

The first immigrants from Iceland arrived in Manitoba in 1875. Many of the settlers fled the island nation because of a series of ravaging volcanic eruptions and severe winters. In 1883, among the Icelandic immigrants were Karitas Gudmundsdottir and her family. Karitas, widowed twice in Iceland, emigrated to Canada with her adult children: three sons, Thorarinn Gudlaugsson, Gudmundur Gudlaugsson, Kristjan Gudmundsson, and two daughters, Gudrun Gudmundsdottir and Kristin Gudlaugsdottir. They sailed for North America, visited relatives in North Dakota, and then moved north to Manitoba. Kristin (b.1858) was pregnant and came to Canada with her new husband, Vigfus Stephenson (b.1857).

By 1886 Vigfus and Kristin Stephenson were living in Winnipeg. Kristin's brothers and Vigfus worked in a Point Douglas lumber yard, Brown and Rutherford. The brothers later farmed in rural Manitoba near Rosser, and then moved to Lundar in the Interlake area north of Winnipeg. Vigfus, Kristin, young daughter Johinna and son Gudlauger ("Lou," b. 1883) Stephenson continued to live in Winnipeg on the banks of the Red River, in the Point Douglas area, with a half dozen other families. Vigfus worked at a variety of labour jobs, and by 1893 the family saved enough for a house in Point Douglas on Syndicate Street.

There were many other Icelandic immigrants in the neighbourhood, and Kristin became good friends with Sarah Johnston. Sarah was also born in Iceland, and was the widowed daughter of John and Sarah Johnston. On April 7, 1894, at the age of 25, Sarah remarried to William Hunter Stanger, who was 39. Stanger was born in the Orkney Islands, but had been in Canada since 1869. Supply vessels of the Hudson Bay Company often stopped at the Orkney Islands on their way to Canada to pick up workers. It is likely Stanger was previously employed by the Hudson Bay Company at Fort Garry. At the time of his marriage to Sarah Johnston, Stanger worked at Ogilvie Flour Mills as a labourer, fireman and carter.

Around the turn of the century, much of Winnipeg had a high infant mortality rate. Typhoid and smallpox were rampant and there were many medical complications caused from drinking the muddy water of the Red River. The Stangers' first child together, Gloria Elizabeth Stanger, died at the age of eleven months in December 1895 from peristalsis.[1] On January 23, 1897, their second child, William Samuel Clouston Stanger, was born. The Stangers later had another daughter, Mary Isabella, (b.1899), and a son, Andrew James Christie (b.1901). The young couple moved frequently in the Point Douglas area of Winnipeg, from 195 Gomez in 1895, to Higgins Street in 1896, to 180 Stephens Street two years later, and finally to 136 Angus. In 1899, William Stanger began suffering from a muscle disorder, likely brought on by a lifetime of labouring. On November 26, 1901, he died of progressive muscular atrophy.

The Stangers were not wealthy, and Sarah Stanger was left on her own with an infant, a two-year-old and a four-year-old. For a time she worked as a charlady for Dr. Charles Jamieson on Pacific Street, but it soon became evident she didn't have the financial resources to raise three children on her own. She approached her friend Kristin Stephenson, who once lived a street behind her, about what to do. Sarah Stanger could not afford three children. It was decided she would give her son William to the Stephenson family to care for. The young William Samuel Clouston Stanger eventually became William Samuel Stephenson.

"His mother was a very special friend of my aunt's," remembers Bina Ingimundson, William Stephenson's cousin. "When her husband died, she had three children. There was no way she could support them. So she gave Bill to my aunt."

Point Douglas historian Elly Heber says when the young William Stanger became the young William Stephenson, the process was not similar to modern adoptions. "It was not straightforward at all," Heber said. "There was nothing done about adopting him."[2] It is not known what happened to Sarah Stanger and her children. By 1903 they had left the house on Stephens Street, and there is no indication from Winnipeg street directories that they remained in the city. Relatives of the Stephenson family believe that Sarah and her children may have moved to Chicago.

One of Vigfus Stephenson's friends, Hjalmar Gislasson, immigrated to Winnipeg from Iceland in 1900, and he also started working at the Ogilvie Flour Mill in Point Douglas. Hjalmar and his son Ragnar frequently walked across the Louise Bridge from Newton Street to Syndicate Street to visit the Stephensons. Point Douglas was an area full of new immigrants, Ragnar remembers, and they frequently socialized and helped each other out. "All the Icelanders were together there. They gathered in the same places," he said. The Red River was only metres from the Stephenson's Syndicate Street house. Park area, with trails through the woods worthy of a young boy or girl's explorations, surrounded the river. Gislasson, born in 1906, remembers Kristin Stephenson as generous and kind, and she filled him full of cookies and milk whenever he went over. He often visited with William, who was nine years older than he but the youngest in the Stephenson family. "He wasn't a big guy," Gislasson remembers. "He was a good-looking kid."

Stephenson was a very quiet child who kept to himself when he was little, Elly Heber remembers being told. He was studious and a bit of a loner. "I don't think he ever bragged. He kept things to himself," Heber says. William Stephenson had a photographic memory, Irv Stefansson, a second cousin, remembers hearing his relatives say. He could walk into a room, walk out, and when questioned afterwards, he could remember every object that was in it.

The Stephenson family spent many summer holidays on the Breckman farm near Lundar, and Bill helped in the store and learned to ride a horse.[3] He became close friends with Harold Stephenson, his brother Lou's son. Harold was an excellent athlete and both he and William Stephenson liked watching boxing. Following a night of boxing at Winnipeg's Amphitheatre, Stephenson nicknamed Harold "Bun," after one of the boxers.[4]

Stephenson's adoptive father, Vigfus, worked as a labourer in the nearby Brown and Rutherford lumber yard. [Vigfus was not a common name at the time. Enumerators for *Henderson's* directories had a few problems with the spelling, listing him as Wigfus (1896, 1898), William (1900), Vadfus (1901, 1902), Vegfos (1913), Vegos (1914, 1916), Vitfus (1919, 1920,) and Vikfus (1918).] Kristin stayed at home and raised the children. Gudlauger (Lou, b. 1883) and Gudmindur (Mindy, b. 1891) became successful plumbers. Julianna (b.1894) was a secretary. Johinna (Jennie, b.1884) married William Hodgkins and raised a family in Winnipeg.

William Stephenson attended the nearby Argyle Elementary School, which was built in 1895 at the cost of $30,000 and considered very contemporary. The school incorporated many features considered up-to-date including slate blackboards, cloak rooms running the width of classrooms, and "new-fangled electric bells."

Children were not legally required to attend school in Manitoba until the Compulsory Attendance Act was passed in 1916. Argyle was a grade one to eight school, not a high school, and Stephenson completed grade six. Stephenson's foster brother Lou Stephenson is quoted as saying young William's six-year scholastic career was "undistinguished," but "he was a tiger-cat for debate."[5]

After completing grade six, William Stephenson left school, perhaps out of economic necessity, and started to work for the Sprague Lumber Yard. Later he worked as a telegram delivery boy for the Great North West Telegraph company on Main Street. After a few years with the firm he eventually did some "keying." "People didn't have a chance to get an education all the time," says Bina Ingimundson, "and I don't think Uncle Vigfus and Auntie Steena really had the money. Julianna was a private secretary, and Mindy and Lou both learned their plumbing, what you call apprentices, somewhere. In later years, Lou and Mindy were successful plumbers, but the Stephensons weren't well off. He delivered telegrams for the telegraph company. That's what he did for a long time."

It is difficult to hypothesize if any events in William Stephenson's early life helped prepare him for a career in espionage. Many years later Stephenson said his only prerequisite experience was reporting on German military industrial build-up during the 1930s. He did not undergo extensive formal training or work his way up Britain's Secret Intelligence Service (SIS) hierarchy. However, it is likely at least two events in pre-war Winnipeg may have remained with an impressionable youth endowed with a photographic memory.

The Stephenson's residential district went into decline as he grew up. When it was first established, Point Douglas, encircled by river on three sides, was a desirable residential area, and many of the founders of the city had homes there.[6] But in the 1880s, Canadian Pacific's main rail line bisected the neighbourhood and the area began to transform. Factories and sawmills gradually moved in to be close to the train, and the area became a less desirable housing district. Montreal-based Ogilvie Milling Company, where William Stanger and many Icelandic immigrants worked, finished their large flour mill on Higgins Street in 1882, just up the street from where Stephenson was born. A typhoid epidemic swept the area in 1904 and 1905, and there were frequent cases of smallpox. Numerous health problems occurred due to contaminated drinking water until 1919, when an aqueduct piped in fresh water to Winnipeg from Shoal Lake, near the Ontario border. To compound the problems of the neighbourhood, Point Douglas became Winnipeg's red-light district.

Tagging along with Winnipeg's fast growth and prosperity came social problems and vice. When the city was incorporated in 1874, the new city council quickly received complaints calling for the removal of "houses of Ill Fame." In 1883, an association of church ministers and citizens petitioned city hall about the houses of ill repute. The city responded by creating segregated areas for prostitution, and instituting regular police patrols in those areas. Unfortunately for the Stephensons, prostitution was sequestered into two small streets, Rachel (renamed Annabella) and McFarlane in Point Douglas, the streets next to Syndicate Street and only metres away from where the Stephensons were bringing up their family. By 1909, there were a hundred bawdy houses in Winnipeg.[7] In the spring and summer of 1910, living on the west side of Syndicate Street was similar to having a seat at an outdoor peep show. On McFarlane, blinds were seldom drawn and the business of the houses sometimes spilled out into the backyards, and could be easily viewed from Syndicate.[8] Syndicate Street residents protested to City Hall.

"It was the red-light district," remembered Ragnar Gislasson. "On Annabella Street there were prostitutes in all the houses. It was considered a pretty tough area." Syndicate Street had become the proverbial "wrong side of the tracks."

Similar social problems were occurring all over North America, and American groups such as the National Vigilance Committee and the Alliance for the Suppression and Prevention of the White Slave Traffic expanded to Canada. A lobby group, the Moral and Social Reform League, formed in Winnipeg in 1907, consisting of a number of community and religious groups, including the Icelandic Lutheran Synod. The League started a campaign to rid the city of the prostitution in Point Douglas and produced a report entitled *The Problem of Social Vice in Winnipeg*, penned by a prominent clergyman, Reverend Dr. F. DuVal. The paper emphasized that there was tacit approval of prostitution and segregated vice from the city's police and elected politicians, and it chastised them for shirking their duties.

Winnipeg politicians ignored the clergyman's report and groups such as the Board of Trade stayed out of the issue completely, in effect lending silent approval to the status quo.[9] But in November of 1910, the situation changed when the Toronto *Globe and Mail* interviewed the head of the Moral and Social Reform League, the Reverend Dr. J. G. Shearer, and publicized the problems in Winnipeg. Eastern headlines read "SOCIAL EVIL RUNS RIOT IN WINNIPEG, VICE DISTRICT GROWING, EVERY DEN AN ILLICIT LIQUOR DIVE."[10] The Toronto reports fuelled the topic in Winnipeg, and Point Douglas vice became an issue in the next civic election. The *Manitoba Free Press* reported that Winnipeg City Council thought the Toronto stories were simply part of the election campaign of reform-backed mayoralty candidate E. D. Martin.[11] Eventually the vice issue became more obscure, and the focus was diverted from social problems in Point Douglas to a defence of Winnipeg's reputation. The incumbent mayor, Sanford Evans, did not comment publicly on remarks to the Eastern press, but editorials in the Winnipeg newspaper *The Telegram*, owned by Evans, labeled Reverend Shearer a "monomaniac" and a "liar, and a slanderer."[12] With the vocal and strongly partisan support of *The Telegram*, and the less active support of the *Free Press*, the mayor succeeded in pushing the issue of the large residential red-light district into the background, and replaced it with the issue of defending Winnipeg's "good name."[13] The reformers were even forced to defend their integrity. At one meeting the Reform League-backed candidate Martin had to defend himself against charges that he was a candidate of foreign agitators.[14]

Evans won the election and the status quo prevailed. Brothels on Annabella and McFarlane streets operated for another thirty years, but the Stephensons didn't stay around to watch. Following World War I, they moved out of the neighbourhood to Winnipeg's West End, and rented out their Syndicate Street home. The anti-prostitution Point Douglas residents and the reformers saw their cause rise and fall through the media.

There was an incident in young William Stephenson's life that must have stayed with him over the years: he became embroiled in the manhunt and capture of a bizarre and infamous Manitoba criminal of the time.

Tranquillity in the rural village of Plum Coulee, Manitoba, was shattered the afternoon of December 3, 1913, when the local bank manager, H. M. Arnold, was shot and killed during a robbery by a disguised man. A twenty-one jewel watch later found in a getaway car was traced through a Winnipeg pawnshop's records to belong to John Krafchenko. Krafchenko had a lengthy criminal record and was rumoured to have been seen in the vicinity of the bank. "He has a genius for robberies requiring desperate action," the *Manitoba Free Press* reported.[15]

At the time Krafchenko was 33 years old and recently released from Stony Mountain Penitentiary north of Winnipeg. His criminal activity began when he robbed a bank manager who was transporting funds between Plum Coulee and Winkler, in southern Manitoba. Krafchenko escaped across the American border on a bicycle, and he was later traced to Romania, southern Europe, South America, Montana, and Prince Albert, Saskatchewan, where he was captured and sentenced to two years in prison. Krafchenko escaped and fled to Winnipeg. He was eventually recaptured, and after his release from prison he worked as a machinist under an assumed name in the St. Vital area of the city. Krafchenko was said to have worked as a civil engineer and locksmith, and he was supposed to have had a working knowledge of 15 different trades and five languages. He also toured different parts of Canada as a wrestler named Pearl Smith. He was described as "one of the most cultured men imaginable. He knows more about police work than most of the force." Krafchenko reportedly idolized William Miner, a renowned bank and train robber known as the Gentleman Bandit, or the Grey Fox.[16] Following the Plum Coulee murder-robbery, photographs and descriptions of Krafchenko were sent across Canada and the northern United States. Posses were organized and sent out to scour the surrounding rural districts for him.

Less than two weeks later, the manhunt was successful. "KRAFCHENKO, DESPERADO, CAPTURED BY POLICE IN WINNIPEG HOUSE" screamed a headline of the December 11, 1913, *Manitoba Free Press.* The accused was holed up in a rooming house on College Avenue, with two loaded revolvers and blood-stained Bank of Montreal money. Reportedly he was planning to leave Winnipeg disguised as a woman. Krafchenko was first sighted in Winnipeg on William Avenue, where he had moved into a rooming house, posing as a doctor named Fairchild. The landlord there said Dr. Fairchild frequently talked about his medical cases and the operations he had performed and even treated one of the lodgers for a toothache. A witness later said Krafchenko moved from the William Avenue house to College Street because he was afraid that he was "spotted" but precise details of Krafchenko's identification and apprehension were not released.

According to Bina Ingimundson, young William Stephenson was instrumental in Krafchenko's capture. His delivery job for Great North West Telegraph took him all over the city, and he identified the fugitive master of disguise. "He was delivering on a bicycle, and he saw him. He notified the police," Ingimundson says.

Because of the mystique surrounding Krafchenko in the community, secrecy was used as a shield for informers. Newspaper reports said police "seemed unwilling ... to give out the exact details of how they found Krafchenko." They said that certain persons had to be covered, or some of Krafchenko's friends would be liable to cause the "stool pigeons" to be missing some morning and another mystery might be added to the annals of Winnipeg police history.[17]

Winnipeggers excitedly crowded the court house to get a glimpse of Krafchenko, and later, near the police station where he was held, at least 300 people filled the street. But the accused thief and murderer treated his preliminary hearing with a bored annoyance. "Oh, get through this thing so I can go rabbit shooting in the spring," he said in court.

The court was told that when Krafchenko was captured, amongst his possessions was a fountain pen that was possibly filled with explosive nitroglycerin. When this was announced, "it caused every man in the audience to sit bolt upright with ears strained forward to catch this latest and remarkable phase of Krafchenko's craftiness." After his arrest, Krafchenko asked for his possessions and notified police about his pen. He advised that the fountain pen be emptied into a nearby sink. Police slowly emptied the liquid into a full basin of water. The police officer who emptied the pen said the nitroglycerine looked a lot like ordinary ink, but nevertheless he was in a hurry to get rid of it, and Krafchenko looked relieved when the pen was emptied. He said it was a load off his mind. "If one of the officers had let it drop, it would have blown them all to pieces."[18]

Following the preliminary hearing, on January 9, 1914, Krafchenko was committed to trial on murder and robbery charges. The next morning he escaped from his third floor prison cell. Police said Krafchenko was provided with a revolver, a skeleton key, and rope to break out from a window, about thirty feet above ground. Newspapers speculated about accomplices "under the spell of his fascinating personality" and called him the most dramatic and magnetic character in the history of Manitoba crime. There were even some indications Manitobans were actually rooting for the charismatic criminal. "DESPERADO'S SENSATIONAL ESCAPE APPEALS STRONGLY TO WOMEN OF WINNIPEG," said a headline in *The Telegram*. This brought letters of protest and condemnation from many local women, including Nellie McClung, the famous Canadian suffragette. McClung called such comments "idiotic driveling that discredited women as a class." A Royal Commission was created by the provincial government to investigate the escape, while editorial cartoons portrayed Krafchenko in a forest, hunting rabbits.[19]

One person likely not enthused with Krafchenko's breakout and his popularity was young William Stephenson, a possible "stool pigeon." "He was just a kid on a bicycle," Ingimundson remembers.

The Royal Commission investigating the escape met in secrecy, and there was a prevailing sense of shock, urgency and tension surrounding the proceedings. Even police constables appeared edgy. Some were reluctant to be identified publicly after they testified, and others used false names when questioned by newspaper reporters. A mysterious eavesdropper was detained for covertly listening to the proceedings through a partition door.[20]

On January 18, 1914, Krafchenko was recaptured in a Winnipeg block. Within 24 hours, five other men were taken into custody for aiding his escape, including his attorney, a legal clerk, a former building trade official and a prison guard. Krafchenko was eventually found guilty of robbery and murder. He was hanged in Winnipeg in the summer of 1914.

The observant young man on the bicycle who turned in a desperate criminal and was labeled a "stool pigeon" by a sensational press became anonymous. Secrecy and discretion entered William Stephenson's life at a young age. One wonders if Stephenson remembered the charismatic, athletic and cultured Krafchenko in future discussions with his friend and neighbour in Jamaica, Ian Fleming.

2 WARTIME HERO

When World War I started in 1914, Stephenson was working for the Great North West Telegraph company on Winnipeg's Main Street, but by the winter of 1916, he decided he wanted to contribute to the Great War. He enlisted in the 101st battalion, Winnipeg Light Infantry on January 12, 1916.[1] Stephenson's incorrect birth date, January 11, 1896, appears in his enlistment papers,[2] and his occupation is listed as telegrapher. His medical description at the time said that Stephenson had brown eyes, dark hair, and a dark complexion. He was five foot two inches tall with a 32-inch expanded girth. The medical officer who examined the young recruit wrote "passed as bugler," under cause for unfitness. He was then sent to train at unluxurious, frigid facilities near Winnipeg. Stephenson complained about his lot in a postcard to his friend Harold ("Bun").

> *Dear Harold*
> *We arrived in this forsaken dump and had to sleep in the cold with nothing on the first night because the blankets were held up. I was sorry I didn't see you again Saturday — It was because the car I was in got a blow-out. Give my regards to everyone*
> *Bill*
> *I'll be in town soon I think.*

Back at a family gathering in Winnipeg, Stephenson became irritated when he found out that his cousin, Bina Ingimundson's foster brother,

Joe Breckman, joined an army group that was used for recruiting and wasn't going overseas. "I remember when Joe joined the 108th battalion, Bill was very upset," recalled Ingimundson. "He said Joe should have never have joined that battalion. But Joe never went overseas, but became quite a good trombone player."

Stephenson sailed to Britain on the SS *Olympic*, arriving on July 6, 1916. Upon arrival he sent Harold an army issue, mass-printed generic postcard to say he was there safely. For security reasons, it revealed no details.

Somewhere in England.
Safe at port of disembarkment.
Nothing unusual to relate, and daily drill, physical exercises,
games and music all added to the pleasures of the journey.
Will send letter on arrival at headquarters.
Bill
Cpt W. Stephenson
No. 700758
101st Overseas Battalion (WLI)
Canadian Expeditionary Forces
c/o Army Post Office, London

Soon after arriving in England, Stephenson was transferred to the 17th battalion, and he likely was sent to France in mid July, 1916. He was wounded and gassed less than a week later and returned to England to convalesce at Shorncliffe. It took him about a year to recover. During that time he trained near Oxford and at Exeter College, taking courses in the theory of flight, internal combustion engines, communications and navigation.[3] While at the school of aeronautics, the former telegraph operator set a speed record for wireless communication.[4] He also canoed, trained with various weaponry, and did some instruction.

It is conceivable that during this time Stephenson met William Donovan, the future head of the America's Office of Strategic Services (OSS) for the first time. *A Man Called Intrepid* tells of a meeting between Stephenson and Donovan during World War I, but it has also been written that Donovan didn't remember meeting Stephenson before 1940. However, according to a biographer of Donovan, he wrote in a letter to his wife Ruth that he met an unidentified Canadian in London during the war and they dined together.[5]

Stephenson was promoted to acting Sergeant in September of 1916, and later became a full Sergeant. In April of 1917 he joined the Cadet Wing of Royal Flying Corps for flight instruction.[6] Stephenson trained near Denham and received his wings at an RFC field at South Carlton, Lincolnshire. In February of 1918 he went to France with the RAF.[7]

When he reported for duty with the 73rd Squadron, the orderly officer was another Canadian, Thomas Drew-Brook. Drew-Brook said later that as a result of the gas attack, Stephenson still looked pale and rather delicate. He took one look at the novice pilot and "with my usual perspicacity" privately advised his flight commander that "we should let A Flight have him." It was to no avail. They were stuck with the diminutive Canadian flyer. Tommy Drew-Brook later became Bill Stephenson's best friend.[8]

During the war Stephenson began to box competitively, and he participated in service competitions as a featherweight. In France, he made friends with a burly American heavyweight, Gene Tunney. "He was an excellent boxer and won the featherweight championship of the Inter Allied Games [at Amiens]," Tunney said in a 1960s radio documentary. "Everybody admired him. He was quick as a dash of lightning. He was a fast, clever featherweight ... he was a fearless and quick thinker."[9] Two decades after meeting Tunney, Stephenson counted on his friendship to covertly open doors in the United States.

Stephenson was evasive about his boxing weight in later years. He cabled William Stevenson in 1974 during the writing of *A Man Called Intrepid* to say that he boxed in a heavier division.

ANY REFERENCE BOXING IT IS LIGHTWEIGHT NOT REPT NOT BANTAM BUT NOT TOO IMPORTANT ONE WAY OR OTHER STOP[10]

In the beginning, according to Drew-Brook, Stephenson did nothing spectacular in 73rd Squadron, but he was where he should be. This changed during March of 1918, when Stephenson's Sopwith Camel was attacked by two enemy aircraft and severely damaged. He landed out of control and was nearly killed. Stephenson emerged from his plane "as mad as hops," Tommy Drew-Brook remembered in a letter to Montgomery Hyde. "He immediately got into another machine and the first thing we knew there was a report that he shot down two Germans. He never stopped going from then on, until his career was ended by a Frenchman."[11]

Stephenson was awarded the Military Cross in April 1918, and the Distinguished Flying Cross in August 1918.

There has been some controversy over exactly how many enemy aircraft were shot down by Stephenson. According to an authority at *Cross & Cockade International*, a World War I Aviation Society, Stephenson shot down a total of 12 aircraft. Following his disappearance in 1918, when Stephenson was a prisoner of war, the French paper *Avion* reported that he had previously shot down 18 aircraft and two kite balloons.[12] It is not known how many he shot down the day he was taken prisoner. Other reports say he shot down as many as 26 aircraft. In any event, he became a highly regarded fighter pilot. The French paper *Avion* mourned his disappearance.

When Captain W. S. Stephenson, M.C., D.F.C. C., de G. was reported "missing," it wrote:

> The brief notice printed above is from the French casualty list and brings a sorrowful message to Aviators on every Allied Aerodrome. France too has good reason to cherish the memory of this brilliant young Canadian pilot and to pray that he descended alive.
>
> It appears that on the afternoon of July 28th, Captain Stephenson decided to make a lone patrol of the line. Regular Scout patrols had been canceled for the day owing to stormy weather.
>
> About four miles within the Bosche Lines, just over F——, one of our reconnaissance machines was being attacked by seven Fokker Biplanes which had been hiding in the dense clouds a few hundred metres above. According to American balloon observers, a British machine of the pattern Stephenson flew (which later proved to be Stephenson) suddenly dived out of the clouds and without hesitation attacked the leader of the enemy formation, shooting him down in flames. There followed a terrific battle in which the daring captain made excellent strategic use of the clouds and succeeded in shooting down another German machine, while a third went spinning to the ground out of control. The others then disappeared in the clouds and Stephenson was seen turning sharply

toward the French reconnaissance machine and rapidly overtaking it. When just alongside the French machine, the British scout suddenly sideslipped and dropped in a series of nose-dives and stalls, as if the pilot was unconscious or the controls had been shot through. The observers then lost sight of the scout and nothing further has been heard of the courageous and dashing pilot. Previous to this engagement, Captain Stephenson had destroyed two enemy kite balloons and 18 aeroplanes … It is said of him that at the battle of Chateau-Thierry he "lived in the air" over the River Marne and helped in great measure, with thousands of well placed machine gun bullets, to prevent enemy engineers from rigging their pontoons. As remarked by a Canadian, Tommy, who knew the horrors of the Front Line : "You can always know when 'Steve' is over. He comes right down to say hello and never forgets the boys on the ground when things are hot."

His pilots are searching keenly for the remains of his machine. They will be pleased to learn — as will all of France — that Captain Stephenson, a pilot of superlative skill and courage, a sound flight commander and good sportsman, has now been awarded the Croix de Guerre avec Palme by the President of the French Republic. It is sincerely hoped that this gallant Canadian is unhurt and, at worst, a prisoner.[13]

Tommy Drew-Brook, in a letter to Montgomery Hyde, recalled the end of his friend's fighter pilot career. "The unfortunate French observer saw this machine out of the corner of his eye, spun his gun and fired a burst into Bill, which killed his engine and put one bullet through his leg. He landed just in front of the German front line, crawled out of his machine, and headed for our lines, but unfortunately a German gunner hit him again in the same leg and that stopped him and resulted in him being captured. Bill did not bale [sic] out over German territory. We didn't have parachutes."[14] Back in Winnipeg following the war, Ragnar Gislasson remembers Stephenson described a somewhat less exotic capture. "He remembered the plane hitting the ground and then he lost consciousness."

Stephenson was taken prisoner and interned at Holzminden. He found confinement very boring and to keep busy he started stealing small items from the guards. Stephenson and other prisoners later held informal contests to see who could steal what. A fellow Winnipeg prisoner, John Huggard, didn't like Stephenson's tactics, as he even stole from a deceased officer. Later Drew-Brook also became a prisoner of war and he was hospitalized at Holzminden. One day an excited Bill Stephenson came to visit him and furtively showed him a tin opener he had stolen from a guarded room, where canned goods were stockpiled. "He was full of delight at the success of his theft, but then when I failed to see any significance beyond this, he showed me the can opener had been patented in 1915, which meant that the Germans had been unable to patent it in any other country than Germany, Austria and Turkey." Stephenson told Drew-Brook he planned to escape from the camp as soon as possible, and he was going to take the can opener with him, and patent it in every other country in the world. "He did escape and took the can opener with him, and I think he did patent it and I believe was successful in making considerable money out of it. I think Bill is still a little sensitive about this story."[15]

Stephenson was more than a little sensitive about it. He later called the story apocryphal.[16] An editorial missive from Stephenson, cited in a June 23, 1962, letter from Ellis to Hyde, said "All references nonexistent tin opener must be eliminated."[17] There is no reference to the can opener in either *The Quiet Canadian* or *A Man Called Intrepid*.

Stephenson escaped the prisoner of war camp — there are no recorded details of his escape — shortly before the end of the war, and by 1919 he was back living in Winnipeg with his parents on Syndicate Street. The young veteran couldn't forget his European experience. He kept a stolen picture of the POW camp commander for years. He joined the Aero club of Manitoba, and he often talked of desperate situations of the war to his family and friends. He didn't, however, talk about himself and his heroics winning medals. Ragnar Gislasson, a frequent visitor to the Stephenson home, remembers quite clearly Stephenson's stories of the war, but didn't know he had won any medals.

Unsuccessful Entrepreneur

He still had his can opener. Stephenson set his sights on the business world. He and a friend, Charles Wilfrid Russell, started a company called Franco-British Supply. The company became the patentees and manufacturers of the can opener, which they called the Kleen Kut.

The can opener Stephenson took from the German camp was a twin-handled, clamp-style manual can opener still used today. When it opens a can, it leaves a smooth edge. Before the Kleen Kut, can openers were quite primitive and lids of cans were basically hacked off, leaving a jagged surface. The firm was also agent for hardware, stainless cutlery, the Duntley Magneto Break Timer and automotive accessories. Working out of a seventh floor office on Winnipeg's Main Street, the duo hired staff and advertised all over North America. The sky seemed the limit.

Irvin Stefansson, a second cousin of Stephenson's, remembers being told his relative was an energetic businessman who had an active mind and was very inventive. He devised a new type of mousetrap around this time and took samples out to Lundar to convince the Breckman brothers to sell it in their store.

Bina Ingimundson recalls her cousin Bill was seldom idle. "He was always busy at something. He had a wonderful convertible. He always seemed to have money because he delivered telegrams for a long time." Ingimundson remembers as a confirmation gift from her parents in 1919, she was given a trip to Winnipeg from her parents, and she stayed with the Stephensons on Syndicate Street. Cousin Bill acted as the perfect host and showed the fourteen-year-old and her sister the town. "I'll never forget Bill had a convertible car. And he took my sister and I for a drive. All over City Park, and the whole of Winnipeg. The whole evening he just spent driving around, showing us the city, and just entertaining us. It was marvelous. He was so nice to us, and it was the same in the home. Always treated us like … well, like cousins."

In some accounts it is reported Stephenson lectured following World War I at the University of Manitoba. Although this is possible, it is unlikely. The University has no record of him being on staff, and none of Stephenson's living relatives believe this to be the case or can recall that Stephenson had any special educational expertise. "He was selling pots and can openers," his cousin Bina says. "I don't think so. As far as I know he quit school when he was in grade six. Started to work, delivering telegrams, at first on bicycle. All his education is what he's picked up on his own."

Bill Stephenson moved out of troubled Point Douglas district later in 1919, and he rented a house at 988 Ingersoll Street, in Winnipeg's West End. The Stephenson family moved in with him shortly afterwards.

In the 1920s the Stephenson family moved to the Verona apartments on Victor Street, close to their church, First Lutheran, at 580 Victor. They rented out their Point Douglas house until 1931, when Vigfus sold it to his son-in-law, Bill Hodgins.

In September of 1919, Stephenson took part in Winnipeg's social event of the year, and a man who would have a direct influence on his later activities, the Prince of Wales, officially decorated him with the Distinguished Flying Cross. Stephenson and over 160 others were awarded their war decorations by the future King Edward VIII, later the Duke of Windsor, at a large presentation at the University of Manitoba campus, and a reception followed at the new provincial legislature building. The City of Winnipeg dressed up for the function and spent a thousand dollars on flags and bunting. The mayor appealed to the citizens of Winnipeg to decorate their own premises in a manner befitting the "unique event" in civic history.

British flags were flown on all light standards on Portage Avenue and Main Street to greet the royal foreigner, and double streamers stretched across the streets at various intersections. The Canadian Pacific Railroad decorated the train station, and the Royal Alexandra Hotel, creating "a blaze of colour and illumination." A large stage displaying royal standards bearing the Prince's coat of arms was constructed in front of City Hall. Carpeting was extended from the stage to the curb, surrounded by palms and others plants supplied by the city's parks board. Electric lights were strung all over Winnipeg's City Hall to spell out "The Prince. God Bless Him."[18]

Stephenson's association with the Duke two decades later was covert, less formal, and not ensnared in such festive subservience.

Stephenson attended a reception and dance at Government House for the Duke with Margaret Farquar. "I don't think that he was any particular boyfriend, but it was a big event, and they all attended, and she went with him," says Margaret Jamieson, Margaret Farquar's daughter. Stephenson's date came from a family of ten, and he was a good friend of one of Margaret's brothers, Charlie Farquar.

Stephenson and Russell formalized their business relationship in January 1921, filing incorporation papers. The company moved to 57 Victoria Street, and the young entrepreneurs went about raising more capital. According to Ragnar Gislasson, Vigfus Stephenson contributed a large amount, and he became one of his son's company's shareholders.

Bill Stephenson also canvassed other relatives and many in the Icelandic-Canadian community for loans.

The new company, Stephenson-Russell Limited, was incorporated February 2, 1921, "to carry on the business of Manufacturers Agents, Exporters and Importers of hardware goods, cutlery, auto accessories, groceries, timber, and goods, wares and merchandise of every description." It was also created to apply for patents and trademarks, and to sell stock. William Samuel Stephenson and Charles Wilfred Russell were the corporation agents. James Francis Pike, a broker, and Clive Jeffrey Macleod and John Campbell Broadfoot, two Winnipeg lawyers, were the other directors of the new company. The amount of capital stock was to be $30,000, divided into 300 shares of 100 dollars each. The directors each took one free share.

The two businessmen bought a couple of vehicles, and Russell spent a lot of time on the road trying to market company goods through stores in rural communities. Stephenson-Russell made contact with some of the pioneers of radio, such as Radio Distributing and Radio Technology Laboratories of Newark, New Jersey, and Haynes Radio of New York. Stephenson took a lot of merchandise to his relatives in Lundar, and he and G. K. Breckman tried to set up a hardware store. Breckman eventually became a shareholder in Stephenson-Russell. John Huggard, who was in the same prisoner-of-war camp as Stephenson, also became a shareholder.

But Stephenson's attempts to set up a new hardware store in Lundar using his stock was unsuccessful. "That didn't work out. The town was too small for a hardware store there," his cousin remembers.

Unfortunately very little worked out for Stephenson-Russell. Although Stephenson's poached can opener was a revolutionary product, he and Russell had trouble selling them in western Canada. The entire region suffered from a recession since the beginning of World War I. Freight rates increased and commodity prices plummeted, stifling the agriculture sector. The opening of the Panama Canal in 1914 compounded the local recession, as Winnipeg's role as a transportation centre began to slowly decrease. Economic problems and social strife culminated in the Winnipeg General Strike of May 1919. It was a tough time to start a new business in Winnipeg.

The company fell behind on their taxes and couldn't pay their rent. On August 13, 1922, a little more than a year after incorporating,

Stephenson-Russell filed for bankruptcy. "All I heard about that company was they lost their shirts," Ragnar Gislasson remembers. Ninety-seven creditors all over North America were owed money. By August of 1924, when the final company disbursements occurred, only 11 were reimbursed money they were owed. Eighty-six other suppliers, companies, and individuals were paid only four and a half cents on their dollar.

According to the Stephenson-Russell bankruptcy papers, Wilf Russell, one of the company owners, was paid for selling his corporation stock. He was the only shareholder to be compensated at the demise of the company. According to Margaret Jamieson, an unfortunate fire consumed the struggling business' effects, when Wilf Russell was away and Bill Stephenson was in charge. "My father described a mysterious fire that took place one time, when Wilf was out on the road. The business failed after that, and the partnership split up," Jamieson remembers. "But Wilf and Bill Stephenson seemed to get together again."

Bill Stephenson became a difficult person to find following the bankruptcy. Winnipeg's *Henderson's* directories list him as living with his parents in a Victor Street apartment in 1923. But legal bankruptcy papers of August 1924 still have his official residence as 988 Ingersoll Street. However, in reality, Stephenson didn't linger long in Winnipeg to field inquiries from creditors. He left town quickly and headed for England. An August 28, 1923 article in the *Manitoba Free Press* said Stephenson arrived in Britain "just over a year ago," which corresponds with the bankruptcy date of Stephenson-Russell. There was no formal farewell. "He left in a rather bad odour," said Joan Morrison, Bun Stephenson's daughter. "He got money from many people in the Icelandic community, and didn't pay it back. Then he left town in the dark of the night."

Margaret Jamieson remembers hearing that Stephenson's business activities not only sped his departure from the city, they delayed his return. "My father said he didn't think that William Stephenson would ever come back to Winnipeg, because he thought that there might be a warrant out for his arrest. I think that he lived by his wits, and had to learn to do so early in his life, and I just think that he was a con man, as we would call it today."

But the fiscally challenged entrepreneur's wits served him well in England. Incredibly, by the end of 1922, Bill Stephenson, the unsuccessful

Winnipeg can opener salesman, was being hailed as a "brilliant scientist" by the *London Daily Mail*. By mid-1923 there were more accolades for him in the British Press: "This young man has come to his Mother country from the far Canadian west and in a remarkably short space of time has established himself as a brilliant scientist and as a leader of industry. A rare combination."[19]

Conversations

Rosalind "Robbie" Hyde, *author Montgomery Hyde's widow*

The Quiet Canadian tells a false version of Stephenson's early life in Canada. Montgomery Hyde died in 1990, and his widow Rosalind was amazed that her husband's biography was so inaccurate.

"My husband was a historian," she said. "There's no money in it. Everything is checked and rechecked. One of the few joys is pointing out mistakes in another's work. What you're saying is incredible."

William Stevenson, *Stephenson biographer*

William Stevenson's *A Man Called Intrepid* describes the subject's fictitious life in Canada. It also quotes an Argyle High School teacher of Stephenson's, and cites a passage from his high school report.

"He was restless and inquisitive," recalled an Argyle teacher Jean Moffat. "A bookworm, we always thought, except he loved boxing. A wee fellow, but a real one for a fight. Of course, y'see, he was the man o' the house since the time he was a toddler." (p. 4)

This is rather surprising as Stephenson didn't complete junior high or high school, and there was no Argyle High School. He grew up with two brothers, and none of the relatives remember Stephenson boxing as a child. I was able to reach the author by phone in Bangkok, Thailand, where he was living in a hotel. Stevenson, a naturalized Canadian, still speaks with a noticeable English accent.

"There's not a great deal I can help you with," he said, "because I just accepted his account of his life. I said in the book he was adopted, [the book doesn't say that] and I gave the names of the parents he described as his, and I had no reason to question he was telling me the truth."

"How about this teacher you interviewed? Moffat?"

"In the book?"

"Yeah."

"I don't know. I don't recall the details in the book at this point."

"Because you quoted some teacher."

"In the book?"

"Yeah."

"I really honestly don't recall."

"And what she says isn't really true. Or doesn't jibe with what I found anyway."

"Did you speak with her?"

"No. I'm wondering if she exists. Because she talks ..."

"I think the teacher I do recall was one who came down to Bermuda and was introduced by him to me."

"Oh. Because she mentions he was the only boy of the house and he wasn't. He had two brothers."

"Uh, huh."

"And stuff like this."

"Look you've caught me [in the middle of things]. I'm actually late for an appointment."

Winnipeg radio report at the unveiling of the Stephenson plaque in Winnipeg, 1983:

Radio Reporter (Delores Haggerty) : "Considering he lived here so long ago do you think it's really appropriate that there should be a plaque to him here today ?"

Stephenson's relatives at dedication (Norma Feller, niece; Steena Stefannson, cousin; Margaret, niece; and Reg Rimmer): "He was brought up here. In this community." "He was raised here. He didn't grow up in Gimli or anything. He was raised here."

Haggerty : "But do you think the people of the community really associate the fact that William Stephenson did grow up here ? Do you think that would give them a sense of pride ?"

Relatives: "I don't think there's anyone left who would have any connection or know anything about the Stephensons. They've been gone for so long." "I bet there's only a handful now here that would know him."

Haggerty : "That's the part that I think is strange — why the plaque is here."

David Stafford and J.L. Granatstein, authors of Spy Wars

"In Canada, reception for the claims for A Man Called Intrepid was eager and enthusiastic. Long accustomed to the prosaic image of Mackenzie King being upstaged by Churchill and Roosevelt, Canada suddenly appeared to have its own wartime superstar to equal those of its allies."

Telephone calls to the new *Argyle High School,* Stephenson's alma mater on March 10, 1989 drew a blank on any memorial.

"No. There is no William Stephenson at the school." The receptionist/teacher's aide (Darcy Furber) assumed the inquiry was for a student, and had searched through the school's enrollment list. Furber said he would see if there was a Stephenson memorial. A follow-up call a half-hour later also drew a blank. "No. I checked around. I couldn't see anything. I asked the principal and he didn't really know anything either." "So no one's even heard of him before?" "Not really. No."

Hugh Trevor Roper, author of "Death of an Intrepid Fraud"

"Only a brave man would dare to stand in the way of such a triumphal juggernaut, especially in Canada … As for the success of the myth in Canada, perhaps the best explanation was given to me by a Canadian lady who flatly refused to believe any criticism of Sir William, however well documented. Canada, she said was a country without a national hero. Now at last it had found one, and invested in him, and he must not be devalued."

Ragnar Gislasson, Stephenson family friend

"He (Stephenson) was knighted, but that doesn't mean anything. Except that he had money — that he worked with the people that were influential in the Government. I mean knighthoods were bought and sold long before he ever came on the scene ... Of my own experience I know that he was no model for James Bond or any other person … That's all bullshit."

INTERNATIONAL SUCCESS 3

Bill Stephenson set off for Britain in mid-1922 and travelled quickly, stopping in Toronto to see Tommy Drew-Brook for only about half an hour. One of the first people Stephenson looked up in England was his friend Charles Farquar, a Winnipegger, who stayed in London following the Great War. Although Stephenson-Russell was bankrupt in Winnipeg, surprisingly Bill Stephenson still seemed to have money. The company also apparently regained some life, as a Stephenson-Russell surfaced in 1922 at 28 South Audley Street in London.

Through his Winnipeg company Stephenson gained some knowledge of the manufacture and distribution of radios and this is an area he decided to pursue. He invested in the General Radio Company and Cox Cavendish Electrical Company Limited. These firms were early manufacturers and distributors of radio sets in Britain and were also involved in research. Through those investments he met and worked with photo-telegraphy expert T. Thorne Baker. Baker was well known for an apparatus used to send photos over telephone lines, and he was working on wireless photography for the London *Daily Mail*.

It appears Bill Stephenson, although he had no formal educational background in electronics, was somehow able to assist Baker. The *Daily Mail* had been conducting research into wireless photography since 1908. Previously, the element selenium provided some success in converting light into electric currents, but it was a slow process. Stephenson devised what he later described to Hyde as a "light sensitive device" that increased the rate of transmission. He realized that if the process was sped up even further, moving pictures could be transmitted — television.

The August 28, 1923, *Manitoba Free Press*, citing British press reports, lauded his overseas achievements: "Due partly to his efforts and a tremendous advertising campaign, broadcasting was established in England on a highly efficient and comprehensive scale within a few short months and his companies were the first in England to produce a complete range of broadcasting equipment suitable for public use."

By August of 1923, Stephenson was the managing director of the General Radio Company Limited and the Cox Cavendish Electrical Company. The companies manufactured radios at Twyford Abbey Works on Acton Lane in Harlesdon and had showrooms at 105 Great Portland Street for their wireless, X-ray and electro-medical supplies.

The *Free Press* report continued, "Stephenson also devoted himself to solving the problem of the wireless transmission of photographs and television (seeking by wireless) [sic]. He has gone a long way toward the solution of these problems and has been successful in transmitting photographs by wireless suitable for newspaper reproduction."[1]

At the time, the *Daily Mail* was run successfully by Lord Northcliffe, but in the early twenties he received stiff competition from Maxwell Aitken, Lord Beaverbrook. The plucky Canadian publisher bought the low circulation *Express* in 1917 and quickly turned it into a money earner. The circulation of Beaverbrook's paper took off and eventually the *Express* achieved the largest circulation of any newspaper in the world. Rivalry between the London dailies escalated in the 1920s, and for a time both papers gave subscribers gifts, such as free accident insurance policies. It is likely during the newspaper battles of the early 1920s that Beaverbrook first met the young Bill Stephenson, as one of the press baron's subscription promotions involved unlikely giveaways. "Bewildered readers," of Beaverbrook's paper's, "found themselves offered everything from free can openers, to free radios."[2] This bewildering combination was very familiar to Bill Stephenson.

In the late summer of 1923, Stephenson returned to Canada aboard the SS *Montcalm* for a short visit and promotional trip. He landed in Montreal and then stopped in Toronto and New York. At Toronto's 1923 Canadian National Exhibition, he displayed his company's X-ray apparatus and radio sets.

Wilf Russell and Stephenson returned to England together, and it was an eventful crossing for the young entrepreneurs. Stephenson was drawn to one of the passengers, the petite Mary French Simmons. The Simmons family were wealthy tobacco growers from Springfield, Tennessee, and Mary and her sister were sailing from New York to London for business. Russell was attracted to Mary's sister. The two Winnipeggers approached the sisters together and began dating them in Britain.

In early 1924, Charlie Farquar told Stephenson he was going to bring his sister over to England for a visit, and he suggested Bill pay to bring over his sister Julianna as well. The brothers sent travel money to Winnipeg, and Julianna Stephenson and Margaret Farquar headed overland to the east and then sailed for England. On the ship across the Atlantic, Margaret realized Julianna was already out of money, and she paid for her meals. Stephenson sent over ticket money, but not spending money, and his sister was obviously not prepared for the high cost of world travel and the lengthy transit time. But the sisters received the royal treatment in Britain. The relatively wealthy Winnipeg transplants showed their siblings all over London in a new convertible. Unfortunately on the return journey Julianna was injured aboard ship. Her injuries were not treated properly, and she never fully recovered. In the summer of 1928, four years after the trip to see her brother, she died at the age of 33. Apparently there was another repercussion as a result of the English journey. Julianna was very fond of Bill and became envious of his wealthy American girlfriend and his new opulent lifestyle, a world away from Winnipeg. Bina Ingimundson remembers hearing her relatives say cousin Julianna Stephenson died of a broken heart.

Bill and Mary Simmons fell in love and were married July 22, 1924, in a small ceremony at the South Kensington Presbyterian Church in central London. None of Stephenson's relatives were present at the wedding. Wilf Russell was Stephenson's best man, and Julia French acted as a witness. Bill Stephenson's life was quickly gaining a new prominence. The August 31, 1924, *New York Times* Sunday pictorial section ran a picture of doe-eyed Mary Simmons under the caption "American Girl Weds Canadian Scientist. Simmons was married recently to Captain William Samuel Stephenson, inventor of a device to send photographs by radio," the paper reported.

A certified copy of William Stephenson's marriage certificate was obtained by Montgomery Hyde for writing of *The Quiet Canadian*, and is in his files at Churchill College, Cambridge. There are no signatures on the certificate from the General Register Office in London, and the document is full of inaccuracies. It incorrectly lists Stephenson's age at the time as 28 years. The groom's father's name is registered as William Stephenson, rather than Vigfus, and his rank or profession is "of independent means." Perhaps even more unusual is that at the time of the wedding, both Stephenson and Mary Simmons are said to be residents of 2 Hanover Terrace W2. But the London directory of postal addresses at the time indicates they did not live there. From 1923 to 1926 it was the residence of an Alfred William Thomas. On this primary document, Stephenson's age is wrong, his father's name is false, his father's occupation is inaccurate, and the couple's address is wrong. It is difficult to hypothesize why this is. Did Stephenson give inaccurate information? Could it have been altered? It is another obtuse piece of the mysterious puzzle that was the life of Bill Stephenson.

For a short time Mary ran a tobacco shop on Upper Street, London. Wilf Russell eventually married Mary's sister and later moved to Tennessee.[3] Bill's business interests continued to have remarkable success. General Radio expanded to stores on Regent Street and Baker Street. He patented the wireless photography process, with George William Walton, and it is said to have made him a millionaire before he was thirty.

Following Stephenson's death, there were two articles in London's *Sunday Telegraph*, one by a pseudonym Mandrake, and the other, citing the Mandrake editorial, by Hugh Trevor-Roper, questioning Stephenson's achievements. Montgomery Hyde, responding to skepticism that Stephenson did any work on the transmission of pictures, wrote in a letter to the editor (*Sunday Telegraph*, February 26, 1989) that Stephenson gave him a copy of his patent, "which I still possess," and that the Stephenson material was on deposit at Churchill College, Cambridge. Following Hyde's death, his papers were closed by the British government. When the file was reopened for a short period of time, many documents were withdrawn, citing Britain's national security and concerns over Crown copyright. Strangely, Stephenson's wireless photography patent, which presumably was in Hyde's file, was one of the items withheld by the British government.

Stephenson seemed to gravitate to Canadians in London and he maintained many business connections back home. He and British Columbia native A.J. Taylor formed a holding company called Stephenson Taylor, and in late 1925 they added a third partner, Amedée

Mercier.[4] By the end of the decade, Stephenson Taylor became British Pacific Trust, with Bill Stephenson as chairman. The trust company looked for investment opportunities worldwide. In British Columbia the group formed British Pacific Properties with Lord Southborough, Fred Taylor, Charles Hayward and Dominion Bridge Company of Hamilton, Ontario. Land owned by the partnership was north, across the harbour from Vancouver, and not easily accessible. Stephenson brought Guinness family interests into the syndicate to build a bridge to the new residential district. The Lions Gate Bridge, now a famous Vancouver landmark that towers over the entrance to the harbour, was eventually completed across the First Narrows, from Stanley Park to West Vancouver. Development could then begin on British Properties, an exclusive residential district in West Vancouver.

In 1934 an aircraft built by Stephenson's General Aircraft Limited won the King's Cup air race. He hired Flight Lieutenant H. M. Schofield to fly the plane, registration number G-ACTS, which won with an average speed of 134.16 miles an hour in poor weather conditions. According to Hyde, the victorious aircraft was a twin-engined monoplane that could fly and climb using only one engine, which was unheard of at the time.[5]

Stephenson travelled all over Europe and throughout the world, and he was in touch with leading bankers, financiers and industrialists. The banker Charles Hambro became a neighbour, backer and friend.[6] Stephenson controlled Alpha Cement, which was one of the largest cement companies in Britain. In the spring of 1936, Stephenson joined the board of Pressed Steel Company, which made 90 percent of Britain's car bodies.[7] Stephenson told Thomas Troy he took control of the company earlier in the decade from the Edward G. Budd Company of Philadelphia. He said it was a $13 million deal that took 13 minutes. Troy couldn't confirm the transaction.[8]

According to Bill Ross Smith, a later employee, Stephenson interests built Cramner Court in Chelsea, one of the first apartments in Britain with central heating.

In the early 1930s, possibly earlier, Stephenson formed Sound City films.[9] The company established Shepparton Studios and became home to producers such as Norman Loudon, Wainwright brothers, Embassy Pictures, Argyle Talking Pictures and Fitzpatrick Pictures. In 1934 seven features were shot at Sound City, including Alexander Korda's *Saunders of the River*. In 1935 substantial expansion took place, and by the end of the decade dozens of films were shot annually at the studios. Shepparton became the largest film studios outside Hollywood. Korda became a good friend of Stephenson's, as did many others in the film industry.

Stephenson helped form Earls Court Limited in 1935. The firm acquired from the London Passenger Transportation Board a 99-year lease of the 21-acre Earls Court Exhibition Grounds. On the site they constructed a large exhibition building. British Pacific Trust sponsored the original stock issue.[10]

Stephenson's numerous undertakings reportedly involved him with many of the great names of the 1920s and 1930s, such as George Bernard Shaw, H. G. Wells and Greta Garbo. He socialized to an extent with politicians such as Beaverbrook and Winston Churchill. It has also been recorded in British newspapers that Stephenson became an associate of aircraft designer Reginald Mitchell, and that he encouraged him to complete the Spitfire.[11] It also appears Stephenson's financial or other assistance may have helped Briton Frank Whittle's efforts to produce the jet engine.[12]

The Winnipegger, born to a family so destitute he was given away to a friend, didn't become an elitist, laissez-faire millionaire; he sought out new ideas and ways to improve society. "I believe, with Churchill, that 'the destiny of mankind is not settled by material computation,'" he said many years later in one of his few documented public appearances. It has been recorded that Stephenson actually met Winston Churchill for the first time through an association with Fabian socialists and trade union leaders.[13] Stephenson became friends with the Nawab of Bhopal and the Aga Khan. With their assistance, he helped underwrite development schemes for poor areas of the Middle East and India, to help raise the standard of living of the people there. "This he regarded from every point of view as the most rewarding field for the investment of capital overseas."[14]

In 1934 Stephenson headed a mission of technical experts to India prior to the formation of the Africa and Asia Development Company. They were looking at ways of developing the subcontinent's local natural resources. He took with him two Canadians, the renowned hydro-electric engineer Henry (Harry) Acres, and Colonel Beverly Macdonald, an expert on railway and dock construction. An American geologist, Eugene Dawson, and English chemical engineer Robin Edgeworth-Johnson accompanied the Canadians. The trip concentrated on the two predominantly Muslim states in India, Kashmir and Bhopal. The group also travelled to Afghanistan and Tibet, covering some Himalayan trails on horseback.

Stephenson's many business activities frequently took him to the continent, where he became aware of Nazi philosophy early on, and this cognizance led to his reports back to Britain about the activities of the Reich. According to Hyde, details of Stephenson's business career were fairly common knowledge at the outbreak of the World War II.[15]

Back in Winnipeg, Stephenson's activities were not well known. In the mid-1930s, the Stephenson family stopped hearing from Bill, and for the most part they had no contact with him ever again. All they knew was he'd done well in business in England. Stephenson's relatives learned of his life and espionage career from a smattering of later newspaper articles and from the books that were written about him. There was no "falling out" in the family. Stephenson's relatives are at a loss to explain why he ceased having contact. Vigfus died in 1937. Kristin, unable to support herself, moved in with one of her sons, and died in October 1940. By the late 1960s Stephenson's brothers and sisters were dead, as was his good friend, his brother's son Bun. Many remaining relatives are very saddened by Stephenson's "disappearance," and the fact that he did not even acknowledge his mother's death. By 1940, all aspects of Bill Stephenson's life were completely shrouded. Somehow the resourceful can opener salesman became involved in espionage at the highest level.

By the mid-thirties, the period when Stephenson broke with his past by severing his family ties, his corporate records are lacking in information. Shepparton Studios has no records of who owned it before the war. A history supplied by the studio quotes from Hyde's *The Quiet Canadian* that Stephenson owned the studio in 1934. The studio has a record of British Lion, run by Alexander Korda, buying most of the facilities from Stephenson in 1946. Earls Court, London's huge exhibition centre, has had an archivist since 1985, but he had no information about directors or owners before 1957. Although the archivist, Victor Bryant, inherited a room full of books and trunks, he could find no records from before the war, other than papers relating to shows that were put on. "We have no record of who built it," said Bryant. "Records are very, very, scarce."[16]

At some point during the 1930s Stephenson became involved in intelligence gathering and other areas of espionage. There has been much conjecture about how and when exactly this took place. According to Hyde, Stephenson's formal introduction to Britain's Secret Intelligence Service (SIS) and its wartime head, Stewart Menzies (pronounced Mingiss), was facilitated through Sir Ralph Glyn, a Conservative backbench MP. Glyn, later Lord Glyn, was a director of British Match Corporation, which obtained some of their raw materials from Sweden, as did Stephenson's Pressed Steel. Glyn, a friend of Menzies and one of his "honourable correspondents," introduced Stephenson in 1936, according to Menzies' biographer.[17] On the eve of World War II, Menzies was promoted to chief of the SIS, known by the initial "C."

Stephenson's connections with British intelligence appear to surface in the construction and operation of the Earls Court exhibition building. Although the Earls Court archives have no ownership information, there is a record of a bankruptcy in July of 1939. The *Financial Times* of July 7, 1939, lists the directors as Sir Ralph Glyn, MP, Sir Maurice Bonham Carter, Sir Felix J. M. Brunner, Mr. F. R. Lewis (managing) and Mr. W. S. Stevenson [sic].

Glyn had connections with British intelligence. Sir Felix Brunner was prominent in the chemical business (ICI). Bonham Carter and his wife were good friends of Winston Churchill's. Lady Violet Bonham Carter wrote a book about the former Prime Minister in 1965, *Winston Churchill as I Knew Him.*

The construction of Earls Court was a huge undertaking, and even more remarkable as it occurred during the Depression. The general contractors, Hedgemen Harris, introduced construction methods not yet used in Britain. It was built at a cost of over £1.25 million and employed up to 3,600 men at a time.[18] When completed, the structure was the largest reinforced concrete building in Europe. The span of the roof over the central area was 250 feet by 350 feet, without columns, at a height of 120 feet. It provided over seven acres of exhibition space, seating for 20,000, and had four restaurants with a capacity of 4,000. "Daylight has been entirely eliminated from the building in order to give control at all seasons of the year over both temperature and light."[19]

Many delays occurred in construction of the mega project. Eight men were injured when scaffolding collapsed, and there were nearly thirty work stoppages due to strikes.[20] In May 1936, residents of the nearby Kensington mansions applied for an injunction to halt construction because of the noise levels, as extensive work was being carried on day and night. Lawyers for Earls Court argued that the company had no control over the people doing the work, and denied legal liability. Walter Monckman KC acted on behalf of one of Earls Court's contractors.[21] Monckman was a close adviser and friend of King Edward VIII. Following the Duke of Windsor's exile in late 1936, Monckman was used to courier messages to him from Winston Churchill.

Sir Ralph Glyn explained at the Earls Court building's first annual meeting in November 1936 that the greatest contributing factor to construction delays was a lack of steel. The delivery of steel had been unavoidably held up "owing to the present campaign for rearmament."[22] Stephenson, a board member with interests in the steel, aircraft and cement industries, would be well aware of supply and demand situations.

Earls Court Grounds Ltd. controlled the fair grounds on which the exhibition building was constructed. Before the facility was built, from the mid-twenties until the mid-thirties, Earls Court offices were in downtown London at 55 Broadway, Westminster SW 1. The address of Britain's intelligence service MI6 (SIS) was 54 Broadway, SW 1.

Only months before war broke out in 1939, Earls Court declared bankruptcy. It was fortunate timing for war preparations. The largest reinforced concrete building in Europe, containing restaurants and with no light to the outside world, was soon converted into a factory to make and test barrage balloons.[23] It could be operated around the clock, even during blackouts.

Stephenson's business connections and other associations seem to have directed him into the world of espionage. "We were all friends, you see," Stephenson told a reporter in 1982. "Churchill and the rest. We were a group of friends who saw the war coming."[24]

According to Charles (Dick) Ellis, a career intelligence officer, Stephenson began "providing a great deal of information on German rearmament to Mr. Churchill, who at that time was not in office but was playing quite an important role in providing background information. There were members of the House of Commons who were much more concerned about what was happening than the administration seemed to be at that time."[25] Stephenson had few official contacts and his work was all done through his personal relationships with people such as Churchill and Fred Leathers.[26] Ellis was first introduced to Stephenson by Glyn near the end of 1938, while he was doing some research on German rearmament.[27]

Stephenson's European business links provided him a unique window on the activities of Nazi Germany. He may have witnessed the burning of books in May 1933.[28] According to Stevenson's book, Stephenson met with German military and aviation officials following his winning of the King's Cup air race in 1934, "while in London his friends tore up his past." At these meetings he is said to have learned more about Nazi doctrine and about the strategy of Blitzkrieg — lightning war. "The real secret is speed — speed of attack, through speed of communications," one German official reportedly told Stephenson.[29]

The meetings seem possible. According to Hyde's *The Quiet Canadian*, Britain's Air Minister at the time, Lord Londonderry, was impressed with an aircraft designed by Stephenson's company. Londonderry, a pilot, purchased one of Stephenson's twin-engined monoplanes, and Hyde flew with him in it on many occasions.[30] (Hyde worked for Londonderry as a private secretary and was researching a book on the second Marquis of Londonderry, Castlereagh.) Londonderry was also involved in the coal industry, and as a result had many connections on the continent. He was an "uncritical" admirer of Nazi Germany.[31] He met with Nazi leaders in 1935 and 1936 and Hitler associate Joachim Von Ribbentrop came to stay with him. Harold Nicolson, author and British parliamentarian from 1935–1945, referred to him simply as "Hitler's friend".[32] It is quite possible that Britain's Air Minister's plane came to the attention of German officials on one of his visits and they arranged to meet the manufacturer.

Toward the end of 1934, Desmond Morton, who supplied information to MI6, was told his first priority should be to find out about Nazi aircraft and aero-engine production.[33] Morton headed the Industrial Intelligence Centre (IIC) and was a neighbour of Winston Churchill. Frequently Morton had lunch with the Conservative back-bencher, and often, Churchill would soon afterward release figures of the Nazi rearmament to the House of Commons.[34] Stephenson's first intelligence reports likely went to Morton.

Although forbidden by the Versailles Treaty, the Nazis began an aircraft building program in 1934. On November 28, 1934, Winston Churchill warned Parliament the Nazis were building an airforce that could threaten Britain.[35] He found little support for his warnings of an impending Nazi threat and Britain's rearmament was a very slow process.

In *The Nazi Connection* (1978), F. W. Winterbotham, who worked for MI6, tries to explain the position of the British intelligence community, and why Churchill seemed to be alone in the House of Commons in speaking against Hitler. Churchill, well briefed by Desmond Morton, continually rose in the House to ask questions on German air rearmament. Winterbotham, in a book obviously vetted by the security agencies, places the blame on British Prime Minister Stanley Baldwin for not heeding the advice of the security agencies. According to Winterbotham, on at least one occasion Baldwin replied to a question saying that "he had no information on the subject" while the latest estimates that MI6 had been asked to send him were "in his pocket."[36]

In May of 1935, Baldwin began to agree with Churchill's concerns, and eventually the country began to prepare for a possible military threat. Baldwin does not credit the expert whose advice led him to that conclusion. He said in the House, referring to estimates of German air strength, "I was completely wrong; we were completely misled on that subject." The second half of Baldwin's remark was "of course untrue," according to Winterbotham, but Baldwin was determined that "somebody else should take the blame." Baldwin ordered an enquiry into the whole subject of German air rearmament at Cabinet committee level in July 1935.[37]

Placing the blame solely on Baldwin ignores many other factors of the time. *The Economist* was attacking Churchill. It stated that German arms were not approaching equality with Britain's, there were no grounds for panic, and "there was no immediate menace confronting us or anyone else." It is fairly common knowledge that *The Economist* was well connected to Britain's Foreign Office. (Kim Philby and others, for example, had no trouble securing jobs with the publication). If Britain's intelligence officialdom was concerned with the rise of Hitler and Baldwin's inactivity, it seems strange the information was not publicized through the media.

In March of 1935, Churchill attacked the German defence estimates, which had previously been presented to the House. For example, the British estimated the Nazis were producing a hundred aircraft annually, whereas according to Churchill they were producing 125 a month. If Baldwin had proper information, as Winterbotham says, why would he release wrong information? John F. Kennedy's *Why England Slept* asks many obvious questions.[38]

In any discussion of Britain's rearmament efforts, the question always arises — why did the British leaders make these appalling mistakes in regard to Germany's output? Why did Baldwin, for example, make such an error in his calculations in 1934? Why did the British continue to make them in 1935 and 1936? These mistakes were fatal, as the British planned their own production in accordance to what they thought Germany's. Were they misinformed? Were they merely over-confident? Was their attention so concentrated on their immediate domestic concerns that they slept undisturbed by warlike preparation on the continent?"[39]

Simply blaming Baldwin seems a rather simplistic answer. Baldwin may have been "looking for somebody to take the blame," but there certainly seemed to be numerous worthy candidates.

Following Baldwin's 1935 confidential enquiry, in which people such as Desmond Morton presented reports, Lord Londonderry was forced to resign as Air Minister. Winterbotham was present at the enquiry, but the former intelligence agent does not mention any specifics that caused Londonderry's removal. Instead Winterbotham raves at the seventh Marquis's ability to throw a party. "Poor Lord Londonderry had been Baldwin's scapegoat. A most delightful man, I'd always felt that he was far too sensitive to be in the hurley-burly of politics in the thirties: he was much more suited to his role of brilliant political host at Londonderry House. Here he and his wife gave glittering parties for diplomats, politicians, writers and artists; he performed to perfection the delicate job of intermingling the various sections of national life."[40] Winterbotham doesn't mention Lord Londonderry's affinity for the Nazis.

Lord Londonderry wrote to Ribbentrop in February 1936: "As I told you, I have no great affection for the Jews. It is possible to trace their participation in most of those international disturbances which have created so much havoc in different countries."[41]

It is generally accepted that Bill Stephenson fed German rearmament information to Desmond Morton and Churchill. This was first made public in 1951. *The Quiet Canadian* was released in 1962, when Churchill was still alive, and was syndicated in newspapers around the world, including the *Sunday Times of London*. Stephenson's activities during the thirties were never questioned, yet his contribution is not mentioned, even in passing, in Winterbotham's book or

H. H. Hinsley's pre-war history of Britain's intelligence services.

The Canadian businessman had a myriad of information sources, especially in Scandinavia and Switzerland. As time passed, Stephenson wanted to utilize more than personal contacts to publicize the Nazi buildup, as he was not sure his material was being properly used. He became frustrated at the apathy and haphazard response of Britain to the rise of Hitler. Later he said Bickham Sweet-Escot's book *The Baker Street Irregulars* was a prime example of how "little Englanders had no idea what planet they were orbiting on," and why in some cases, "they had to be hurriedly removed even from lower echelons as stupid misunderstandings comprising largely hot air have tendency [to] float to higher altitudes." After rereading the book, which deals with the thirties and the formation of the organization which eventually became Special Operations Executive (SOE), Stephenson said he congratulated himself "on what magnificently icy self-control I must have had to exercise on such occasions."[42] Eventually Dick Ellis opened new channels for Stephenson in British intelligence.[43]

There are indications that in the late 1930s, Stephenson may have plotted to assassinate Adolf Hitler. According to Stewart Menzies' biographer, Stephenson and Colonel F. N. Mason-McFarlane, Britain's military attaché in Berlin, both offered to shoot Hitler with high-powered sporting rifles at a rally.[44] Stephenson, in correspondence to William Stevenson, said there were "suggestions in 1938 for averting the impending calamity." He believed the most practical plan was one put forth by a Calcutta lawyer, Rahman Siddiqui, which involved arming a "young English crackshot with high powered telescopic sighted rifle."[45] The plans to stop Hitler were vetoed by Britain's foreign secretary, Lord Halifax, who "didn't want to use assassination as a substitute for diplomacy."[46]

It has also been documented that Stephenson was involved in a plan to disrupt the transporting of Swedish iron ore to Nazi Germany through subversive means.[47] The plan was one of his own suggestion and okayed by various intelligence authorities in Britain. There was a breach of security, however, and some of Stephenson's allies in Sweden became nervous. According to Dick Ellis, the King of Sweden contacted the King of England and asked that any sabotage plans be stopped, as he feared a German invasion. The British Foreign Office, who "had some idea of what was going on," feared a Russian invasion of Scandinavia, as they were already at war with Finland. Stephenson returned reluctantly to Britain.[48] In any event, Stephenson's espionage activities attracted the attention of Winston Churchill.

Apparently Stephenson's first consequential "martially orientated" meeting with Winston Churchill was in early 1938, brought about by Fred Leathers, the co-founder of Alpha Cement. In a discussion with Leathers about another company, William Cory & Sons, Stephenson related his concerns about German political developments and their effects on fuel, coaling and general shipping. Stephenson told Leathers he thought war was imminent. At the meeting at the Alpha Offices, in the ICI buildings on Embankment, Stephenson said Britain was "woefully unprepared" to meet what he knew to be a mightily prepared German threat. "We were a sitting bird if we did not make a sensible, most urgent, effort to spread our wings," he recalled later. Leathers told Stephenson he was holding forth just as Churchill did, and, as he was lunching with him that day at the Cory dining room, he asked Stephenson to join them. "We had a delectable lunch and a most animated discussion, as Winston and I found ourselves to be on the same wavelength, sometimes of ultrahigh frequency," Stephenson remembered. "And indeed it remained so to the end, despite some outside efforts to disrupt the unbroken close liaison. Thereafter we met together at every opportunity."[49]

Adolf Hitler came to power in 1933, with plans for a thousand-year Reich. Hitler occupied the Rhineland in March 1936, and the Nazis marched into Austria in March 1938, the Sudetenland in the autumn of 1938, and much more of Czechoslovakia in March 1939. Other areas of the world were in turmoil. Italy annexed Ethiopia. The Soviet Union and Finland were at war. There was a civil war in Spain, and Japan had invaded China. The League of Nations appeared powerless.

There was little public outcry concerning the fascist invasions in British establishment circles, or in Western democracies in general. When Hitler marched his troops into the Rhineland in 1936, Britain's future ambassador to the United States, Lord Lothian, seemed unconcerned. He commented, "After all, they are only going into their own back-garden." According to Winston Churchill, this was the representative British view at the time.[50]

Joachim von Ribbentrop, then the German ambassador to Britain, justified the invasions by saying nations large and small have the right to colonies and "Germany must formally reject every form of argument which seeks to dispute this right with her."

The United States Ambassador in England, Joseph Kennedy, seemed to hold similar views. In 1938, after Hitler's troops had occupied the Rhineland, Austria, and Czechoslovakia, Kennedy said in a speech that he thought democracies should learn to live with the Nazis and not attempt "to widen the divisions now existing between them, by emphasizing their differences."

Fortunately for Britain, American president Roosevelt was concerned about global developments. He saw the fascist invasions as crimes rather than a "right to colonies" issue. "It seems to be unfortunately true that the epidemic of world lawlessness is spreading," he said in an October 1937 speech in Chicago.

In early August of 1939, Albert Einstein, who fled Germany to escape Jewish persecution, wrote to Roosevelt and warned him of the possibility of an atomic bomb. On September 1, 1939, Hitler invaded Poland, triggering World War II. Ten days later, Roosevelt began corresponding privately with Winston Churchill, who had become First Lord of the Admiralty.

In London, Joseph Kennedy soon determined the island was a lost cause, and he considered aid to Britain fruitless. He consistently warned Franklin Roosevelt "against holding the bag in a war in which the Allies expect to be beaten."[51]

Later Lord Beaverbrook thought Fifth Column activity could be used to help convince the United States that Europe's problems were a concern. He wrote to Winston Churchill suggesting Scandinavian-Americans be urged to demonstrate, collect money and protest the German and Russian threats to their homelands. But Beaverbrook didn't think the demonstrations would occur through osmosis. "... If the Scandinavian demonstrations were successful the movement should extend to the Czech population, and also to the Poles ... the responsibility for the project must not rest with the Foreign Office or any other Government department. If there is any difficulty, there must be complete and absolute repudiation." He concluded in his letter that "a competent man should be urged to go to the United States."[52]

At the time the United States had no comprehensive intelligence service. There was no Central Intelligence Agency or National Security Agency. With world instability rising and possible war looming, Roosevelt asked Churchill for assistance in setting up an American intelligence service. A small clique that advised Churchill on intelligence matters (Desmond Morton and a few others) appointed Bill Stephenson to the job.

"There were three or four people that were Churchill's advisors on intelligence matters, and they were the ones who appointed Stephenson to the job of educating OSS [Office of Strategic Services]," said Benjamin Deforest (Pat) Bayly, Stephenson's wartime communications head, when interviewed for this book. "Roosevelt had requested this, and Stephenson was appointed for this job. But it wasn't through MI6. So there was always a funny feeling there. Nobody quite knew where his authority came from. Or ended."

Britain's lack of military preparation for World War II is well known. But the contribution (or lack) of Britain's intelligence services, both MI5 and MI6, to the state of unpreparedness has been subject to somewhat less scrutiny. Beginning in 1979, an official intelligence record, the multi-volume *British Intelligence in the Second War*, edited by Sir Harry Hinsley, was released. This voluminous narrative doesn't really specify why the deep thinkers of British officialdom weren't more suspicious that Adolf Hitler was up to something during the 1930s. It seems non-officials, businessmen such as Bill Stephenson, were supplying intelligence to those wanting to publicize the military buildup of the Nazis. Why this state of affairs occurred, and or why warnings continually fell on deaf ears has never been fully delineated. When asked in 1964 why the Secret Service had a reputation of having done little or nothing during the war, Stewart Menzies, its wartime head conceded, "I think we were rather badly beaten in the beginning."[53] According to the author R. G. Grant, Admiral Sir Barry Domville, a former head of British Naval Intelligence, found Hitler "absolutely terrific" and was jailed during the war. The Earl of Cottenham left MI5 as he could not accept a war with Germany, and Frederick Winterbotham, the head of MI6's air section and a post-war author, would have preferred Britain and Germany unite against Russia.[54]

There is evidence this was a general feeling among Britain's establishment at the time. Alvin Finkel's and Clement Leibovitz's well-documented 1997 book, *The Chamberlain-Hitler Collusion*, asserts that in 1938 Neville Chamberlain made a deal with Hitler that gave the dictator control of central and eastern Europe in return for assurances Western Europe, Britain and the Empire would not be attacked. This would eventually rid the elites of Europe of the Communist threat. The plan fell apart when Hitler decided democracies in Britain and France could not be relied upon to keep pro-Nazi leadership in power in their respective countries. In the words of the authors, "Hitler had more faith in British and French democracy than the rulers of Britain and France themselves."[55]

In any event, it appears MI6 was circumvented somewhat when Roosevelt requested intelligence assistance.

From the diary of permanent undersecretary for the Foreign Office, Alexander Cadogan, who was part of the inner machinations of the time, it is possible to obtain a somewhat uncensored view of the desperate situation in England at the start of the war. At the end of the decade, during Britain's greatest crisis, it appears elements of the British Foreign Office and the intelligence services were in a state of confusion and disarray. In fact, it's difficult to tell which side some people were on.

Excerpts from Cadogan's diary :[56]

"Tel from Washington, which seems to give us time on the leaks of the last two years. Fear someone in the office has been compromised. Saw Haskin, Admiral's Vysyo (?) about it. Very unpleasant."— September 4, 1939.

... Report (belated) from SIS that our secret documents were communicated in July and Aug. from the Central Dept. to the German Government! I can trust no one. Must look into the whole thing. [The diary does not show the result — Dilks, ed.] — January 26, 1940.

"... saw Kleffens with H before cabinet. K in good heart — a nice fellow, and he doesn't look like capitulating. Things never looked blacker." — May 14, 1940.

"G. Lloyd at 3.30 with H [Halifax]. He agreed to try and overhaul SIS which wants it badly !"— May 25, 1940.

"Tape says Hitler and Musso are meeting to decide on terms. What a nightmare !" — June 17, 1940.

"'C' came round with what looks like an indication of Germans being ready for a mass attack on the 5th. But ... he is a rather nervous babbler." — September 3, 1940.

Fortunately for democracy in Europe, the week "things never looked blacker," Winston Churchill became Prime Minister of Britain. Churchill began casting lifelines to North America. He gave a rope to Bill Stephenson.

4 ASSIGNMENT: NEW YORK

I went up to my father's bedroom. He was standing in front of his basin and was shaving with his old fashioned Valet razor. He had a tough beard, and as usual he was hacking away.

"Sit down, dear boy, and read the papers while I finish shaving." I did as told. After two or three minutes of hacking away, he half-turned and said: "I think I see my way through." He resumed shaving.

I was astounded, and said: "Do you mean we can avoid defeat? (which seemed credible), or beat the bastards?" (which seemed incredible).

He flung his razor into the basin, swung around, and said: "Of course I mean we can beat them."

Me: "Well I'm all for it, but I don't see how you can do it."

By this time he had dried and sponged his face and turning around to me, said with great intensity: 'I shall drag the United States in.'"

—Randolph Churchill remembering
the morning of May 18, 1940[1]

Bill Stephenson began his North American sojourn in the spring of 1940. He contacted Gene Tunney, the celebrated American boxer, who was a friend since World War I. The former heavyweight knew J. Edgar Hoover well, and he was asked to forward a letter to him. The missive from Stephenson was quite unexpected, Tunney remembered.

"Quite to my surprise I received a confidential letter that was from

Billy Stephenson, and he asked me to try to arrange for him to see J. Edgar Hoover, the head of the FBI. I found out that his mission was so important that the Ambassador from England could not be in on it, and no one in official government. So Mr. Hoover said to me, 'All right, I'll make him my first appointment.'"[2]

Stephenson wanted his meeting with Hoover to be covert. "Sir William did not want to make an official approach through well-placed English or American friends; he wanted to do so quietly with no fanfare," Tunney wrote responding to a request for information from CIA historian Thomas Troy in 1969. "It was my understanding that the thing went off extremely well."[3]

In his correspondence Tunney doesn't specify why British authorities were not to know of the Stephenson–Hoover encounter. In fact, decades later, Tunney questioned whether divulging this information would cause trouble to himself and Stephenson. When he responded to Troy, the former boxer sent a copy of his reply to Stephenson in Bermuda. In his letter to Stephenson, Tunney wrote, "Let's hope that neither of us will lose his head now that the war has been over for twenty-five years."[4]

Stephenson's first meeting in North America with Hoover is thought to have occurred in April 1940. There is no precise record of what took place, but obviously it dealt with cooperation in intelligence matters. According to Hyde, Hoover told Stephenson that any liaison between the SIS and the FBI could be interpreted as contravening American neutrality laws, and he would only contravene the policy if he had a direct order from the White House. Also Hoover stipulated that if there was to be a corroboration, he wished it to be through Stephenson and himself only, and no other U.S. government office should be informed of it.[5] It is also recorded that Stephenson revealed to Hoover that communication between Roosevelt and Churchill was turned over to the Germans by a code clerk in the American Embassy in London, the domain of defeatist ambassador Joseph Kennedy.[6] (It is interesting to note that the FBI later transmitted BSC messages to Britain, so it is likely communications security was discussed at an early stage). In any event, Stephenson agreed to Hoover's conditions, and he went about getting presidential approval.

The intermediary chosen was likely Ernest Cuneo, a lawyer from New Jersey and a friend of Stephenson's. Cuneo worked for New York

City Mayor Fiorello La Guardia and had expertise in international law. He had also done work for the Democratic National Committee, which gave him presidential connections. He eventually became ambassador plenipotentiary, with direct access to Roosevelt and Churchill day or night.[7] Cuneo later became the president of the large news service, North American Newspaper Alliance (NANA), and editor-at-large of the *Saturday Evening Post*. Cuneo had numerous contacts in the media, and he was a friend of, among others, Walter Winchell.[8] Stephenson later called him the leader of "Franklin's brain trust."[9]

In the spring of 1940, Cuneo met with Roosevelt and reported back that the president wanted "the closest possible marriage between the FBI and British Intelligence."[10]

Stephenson returned to Britain following the meeting. He was unsure of where and how he should try and help the Allies, or what his role should be during the war. He was offered the position of Passport Control Officer in New York City, which was a cover occupation for SIS representatives abroad. He would replace Sir John Paget in the United States. Paget reportedly was removed reluctantly by the head of British Secret Intelligence Service, Menzies ("C"). Winston Churchill was insistent that Stephenson get the job.[11] Stephenson, an independent operator, was reluctant to accept any government posting, especially if it meant answering to what he often referred to as "that gang on Broadway." He consulted many people to help decide his course.

In early May 1940, he attended a gathering at Beaverbrook's Stornoway House, with Churchill, Boom Trenchard, Lord Southborough, Duff Cooper, Lord Leathers, Billy Hughes, a former Prime Minister of Australia, and General Maurice Gamelin of France.[12] Following the dinner, his task was decided. Stephenson remembers Churchill, who became Prime Minister on May 10, 1940, took him over to a draped window and said:

"'You know what you must do at once. We have discussed it most fully, and there is a complete fusion of minds between us. You are to be my personal representative in the United States. I will ensure that you have the full support of all the resources at my command. I know that you will have success, and the good Lord will guide your efforts as He will ours. This may be our last farewell. Au revoir and good luck!'"[13]

Stephenson travelled back to the United States in mid to late May. The new Passport Control Officer and Britain's ambassador, Lord

Lothian, met with Franklin Roosevelt at the White House and, according to Stephenson, they discussed "in most warm and friendly terms all aspects [of] the oncoming wave of developing horror that was then Nazi moving venomous entrapment."[14]

Stephenson sent word to Britain that Roosevelt wanted a close relationship between the FBI and British intelligence. "The fact that this cooperation was agreed upon is striking evidence of President Roosevelt's clarity of vision. The fact that it has to be kept secret even from the State Department is a measure of the strength of American neutrality. It is an essential first step towards combating enemy operations, but it is insufficient to meet the demands of the situation. The Nazis in America are already well organized and well entrenched. They realize the extent of British dependence on American material aid, and so direct their subversive propaganda towards buttressing the wall of traditional isolationism by which the president is encompassed."[15]

Stephenson flew back to Europe, and he and his wife prepared for the move to New York. He contacted General Hastings (Pug) Ismay, Churchill's Chief-of-Staff; Colin Gubbins, later head of Special Operations Executive (SOE); the banker Charles Hambro; Fred Leathers (Stephenson's business partner, a shipping and transportation expert who joined the British cabinet); Lord Selborne (future Minister of Economic Warfare) and others.

Stephenson saw himself as Churchill's alter ego en mission to the Western Hemisphere to implement "his wishes" and to "establish favourable attitude to assure supplies flowing eastward and any other steps required to keep British ship of state afloat from Dunkirk onwards."[16] His assignment, according to the secret BSC history, was "To do all that was not being done, and could not be done by overt means, to assure sufficient aid for Britain, and eventually bring America into the war."[17]

5 THE SECRET EXPANSION

Stephenson and his wife Mary flew to Paris, and then to Genoa, and from there set sail for New York.[1] On June 15, 1940, British ambassador Lord Lothian heralded the formal arrival of a new Passport Control Officer in a letter to U.S. Undersecretary of State Sumner Welles.

> His Majesty's Ambassador presents his compliments to the Secretary of State and had the honour to inform him that Captain Sir James F. Paget, Bart. RN, has been succeeded as British Passport Control Officer in New York by Mr. W. S. Stephenson, and that the latter is expected to arrive at New York in the SS *Britannic* on or about the 20th of June next. Lord Lothian would be grateful to the authorities of the Port of New York might be requested to accord to Mr. Stephenson on his arrival in this country such facilities as be considered appropriate.[2]

Bill and Mary Stephenson arrived in New York on June 21, 1940. He gave the Waldorf Astoria hotel as their address, and described their length of stay in the U.S. as indefinite.[3] On his admission papers Stephenson said he had been in New York and California previously in 1940.

For many years the British Passport Control Office was located in a small room in the British Consulate, at Exchange Place in downtown Manhattan. There was one assistant staff, a clerk and a secretary. Stephenson took one look at the cramped office, decided it was unsuitable, and set up shop elsewhere. In the early stages, he worked out of an apartment at Hampshire House, overlooking Central Park.[4] He lived not at the Waldorf, but at the St. Regis, which was owned by Roosevelt's friend Vincent Astor. Stephenson had the help of career intelligence officer, Australian-born Charles (Dick) Ellis, in getting the organization off the ground. Churchill, Ellis recalled decades later, asked Stephenson "to go to New York realizing what a task he was faced with, and knowing Stephenson, as he did very well, he picked the right man to do this job. Firstly, he was Canadian. Secondly, he had very good American connections ... he had a sort of fox terrier character, and if he undertook something, he would carry it through."[5]

Another Australian, Bill Ross Smith, and two Britons, John Pepper and Walter Bell, ostensibly with British Passport Control, were also early staff. The new spy chief recruited his Canadian friends A. J. Taylor and Tommy Drew-Brook, and the organization grew. Apart from liaison and lobbying of influential Americans, the beginnings of his espionage organization were fairly unproductive. "I started from scratch," Stephenson said later. "I had no experience. I was a businessman and in the early days of the job, I got plenty of bangs on the head."[6]

"I needn't enlarge too much upon what my principal concerns were upon arrival in New York," Stephenson told journalist Shaun Herron in a radio interview. "Obviously the establishment of a secret organization to investigate enemy activities ... To institute adequate wartime security measures in the Western Hemisphere, in relation to British interests in a neutral territory, were of importance and the American assistance in achieving this objective was essential."[7] To help implement this they established contacts with foreign language groups. They also made connections with Visiting Nurses, the Salvation Army, Traveler's Aid, the Greater New York Fund, the Maritime Union and the International Institute. Stephenson also sought to obtain destroyers, aircraft, military supplies and equipment, as the British had left much of their weaponry behind at Dunkirk (May/June 1940).

Obtaining supplies for the embattled island was not a straightforward task for Stephenson as there was a conflicting picture on what was about to transpire on the continent. America's eyes on Europe, the ambassador to France, William Bullit, and the ambassador in London, Joseph Kennedy, both thought Britain had little chance of survival, and no leadership. Bullit had "no use for Chamberlain and almost none for Churchill," it was reported to Roosevelt. "There are no real leaders, as we see it, in all England in this time of grave crisis."[8] Former British Prime Minister Neville Chamberlain wrote in his diary in early July 1940: "Saw Joe Kennedy who says everyone in the U.S.A. thinks we shall be beaten before the end of the month."[9] Kennedy later cabled Roosevelt to say he was delighted to hear that the president said he was not going to enter the war because, "to enter this war, imagining for a minute that the English had anything to offer in the line of leadership, or productive capacity in industry that could be the slightest value to us, would be a complete misapprehension ... It breaks my heart to draw these conclusions about a people I sincerely hoped might be victorious, but I cannot get myself to the point where I believe they can be of any assistance to the cause in which they are involved."[10]

In the United States there was a general apathy towards Europe's problems and Japanese expansionism. A policy of nonintervention was an aftermath of World War I. "After World War I, there was a surge of isolationism, a feeling there was no reason for getting involved in World War I," said Averell Harriman, Roosevelt's roving ambassador years later. "We made a mistake and there were a lot of debts owed by European countries. The country went isolationist."[11] Not even Roosevelt could be sure the aid to England would not be wasted under the circumstances.

"The procurement of certain supplies for Britain was high on my priority list," Stephenson recalled, "and it was the burning urgency of this requirement that made me instinctively concentrate on the single individual who could help me. I turned to Bill Donovan."[12]

Donovan

Bill Donovan was a successful lawyer of Irish American background, a decorated soldier from World War I. It is not definite when Stephenson first met Donovan. They may have met in Europe during World War I. The two may have met in the thirties during the deal for Pressed Steel handled by Donovan's New York law firm, Donovan, Leisure, Newton and Irvine. In any event, Stephenson usually referred to the Republican lawyer as an old friend, and people who knew them both also believe there was a pre-war relationship.[13]

According to one of Donovan's biographers, Stephenson telephoned Donovan upon his landing in New York, in late June 1940, and met with him within the hour.[14] Donovan helped arrange a meeting with Secretary of the Navy Frank Knox, Secretary of War Henry Stimson, and Secretary of State Cordell Hull, where the main topic was Britain's lack of destroyers and the possibility of finding a formula for transfer, without legal breach of U.S. neutrality, and without affront to American public opinion, of fifty "over-age" destroyers to the Royal Navy.[15] Stephenson suggested that Donovan should visit Britain "with the object of investigating conditions at first hand and assessing for himself the British war efforts, its most urgent requirements, and its potential chances of success."[16] Through Frank Knox, the owner of a Chicago newspaper, who was a good friend of Beaverbrook's, Donovan's trip to appraise Britain's chances for survival was organized. Stephenson says he arranged that he be afforded every opportunity to conduct his inquiries in Britain. "I endeavored to marshal my friends in high places to bare their breasts."

There has been some speculation on Stephenson's actual involvement in setting up Donovan's trip, but part of the conjecture may be a reluctance to admit the foreign manipulation of events that occurred in a neutral country. "One wonders whether Donovan felt some indelicacy in detailing Stephenson's pre-COI assistance," concludes CIA historian Troy, who conducted what is referred to as "official research" into that time period.[17] Desmond Morton, a member of Churchill's inner circle at the time, seems to reveal the precariousness of the situation in a September 1941 letter. Morton wrote: "... Another most secret fact of which the Prime Minister is aware, but not the other people concerned, is that to all intents and purposes U.S. Security is being run for them *at the President's request* by the British. A British officer sits in Washington with Mr. Edgar Hoover and General Bill Donovan for this purpose and reports regularly to the president. It is of course essential that this fact should not be known in view of the furious uproar it would cause if known to the isolationists."[18]

Dick Ellis said afterwards that the planning of Donovan's trip was done by Stephenson. "Stephenson was able, through his contacts in Washington, to obtain results on a number of matters that would have been quite impossible at that time done through the Embassy. For instance, he persuaded, through Donovan, for Mr. Hanniman [sic, Harriman] to be sent to London just after Dunkirk. Harriman and Donovan came over to London, Stephenson made all the necessary arrangements through Mr. Churchill. They saw, with their own eyes, what the military picture was in England. And when they returned to Washington and reported that in their opinion this country (Britain) could hold over, provided certain equipment was made available, that, I think, was the biggest effort that he undertook — and it could be undertaken by a man in his position who was independent. And I think possibly because he was a Canadian. Right throughout the war the more confidential channels of communication between the Prime Minister and the President ran through Stephenson's office."[19]

Other indications of Stephenson's role in the trip can be found in OSS records. In 1944, when Donovan read an OSS statement that "Lord Lothian ... arranged for Donovan to see Churchill himself," Donovan struck out Lothian's name and wrote "Bill Stephenson" in the margin.[20]

General Donovan left for Britain by air from Baltimore, via Bermuda and Lisbon, on July 14, 1940. Stephenson later called the trip one of the most momentous missions ever undertaken by any agent in the history of Western civilization.[21] The American Embassy in London was bypassed, and Donovan's itinerary was arranged through other channels. U.S. Ambassador Joseph Kennedy had been wired previously by Cordell Hull about the possibility of a Donovan junket. Kennedy was against the idea. "Our staff, I think is getting all the information that possibly can be gathered, and to send a new man here at this time is to me the height of nonsense and a definite blow to good organization." Kennedy later stressed the trip would "simply result in causing confusion and misunderstanding on the part of the British."[22] The Ambassador was ignored. Donovan was in England about two weeks. He saw as many people as he could and developed ties with influential figures in British public life and, according to Stephenson, representatives of all classes in Britain. He visited industrial areas and military training centres. He met with American foreign correspondent Edgar Mowrer and other journalists. He met with embassy officials, unbeknown to Kennedy, such as military attaché Brig. General Raymond Lee. Lee wrote in his diary: "He [Donovan] is really over here to gain firsthand knowledge of how the Conscription Law is working and what sort of legislation is required successfully to operate a counter-espionage organization. He expects to be heard by Congress on these two things. He feels we will have conscription soon and, as he phrases it, 'Our attitude toward it will be a test of our soul.'"[23]

Britain lost most of the country's military equipment on the beaches of Dunkirk in the summer of 1940. Their ally, France, had capitulated. The island faced triumphant Germany alone in Europe, virtually unarmed. Donovan was to say later, "They could not have fought off a properly trained battalion." Hitler himself anticipated an easy conquest and the British were measuring their prospects in terms of a last ditch stand against impossible odds. Donovan established headquarters at Claridges and every effort was made to learn all possible from the British war experience.[24] He and his entourage flew back to the U.S. in early August 1940. The American lawyer returned to the United States with at least four deep convictions: (1) That the British would fight to the last ditch; (2) they could not hope to hold the last ditch unless they got supplies at least from America; (3) that supplies were of no avail unless they were delivered to the fighting front — in short, that protecting the lines of communication was a *sine qua non*; (4) that Fifth Column activity was an important factor.

When Donovan returned he wrote a series of articles dealing with German Fifth Column activities, which appeared in major newspapers and were broadcast on a nationwide hookup. It was the first broadcast to the entire United States by any speaker other than the president. The Secretary of the Navy and Donovan pressed for the Destroyers for Bases deal with the president, despite strong opposition from below and procrastination from above.[25]

On August 22, 1940, Stephenson reported to London that the destroyer deal was agreed upon. The agreement for transferring 50 aging American destroyers, in return for the rights to air and naval bases in Bermuda, Newfoundland, the Caribbean and British Guiana, was announced September 3, 1940. The bases were leased for 99 years, and the destroyers were of great value as convoy escorts. Following the Destroyers for Bases deal, Stephenson thanked Donovan on behalf of His Majesty's government, "whilst thinking that many of my fellow Canadians might be saved from a wetting in the cold North Atlantic as the result ..."[26]

According to Lord Louis Mountbatten, who became the British Chief of Combined Operations, the destroyers were a result of Stephenson's lobbying. "We were told that the man primarily responsible for the loan of the 50 American destroyers to the Royal Navy at a critical moment was Bill Stephenson; that he had managed to persuade the president that this was in the ultimate interests of America themselves and various other loans of that sort were arranged. These destroyers were very important to us. I was at sea at that time, because we were very short of escorts for our convoys against the unrestricted U-boat warfare, and although they were only old destroyers, the main thing was to have combat ships that could actually guard against and attack U-boats. That was absolutely vital until such time as the United States themselves came into the war."[27]

Stephenson said later that the deal would not have happened without the assistance of Donovan, and he described his work with him as covert diplomacy.[28] Other supplies that Stephenson was instrumental in obtaining for Britain, with assistance from his American friends, included a hundred Flying Fortresses for the RAF coastal command, and over a million rifles for the newly formed Home Guard. Later they were able to obtain kayaks, landing craft, sub chasers for blockade running, wireless equipment, radio valves, parachute outfits, passports and war material for the Middle East.[29]

"I believe too that he (Stephenson) was the man who persuaded President Roosevelt to declare that the Persian Gulf and the Red Sea were no longer combat areas within the meaning of the American Neutrality Act," remembered Mountbatten, "so that it was possible for the Americans to send war material to the British in the Middle East Theatre, and the ships the whole way escorted by American ships."[30]

BSC is also said to have set up 24-hour security patrols on rail lines, terminals and docks where goods were being prepared for Britain, supplied weekly figures to London on oil production in occupied Hungary and Romania, passed on production figures of Japanese industry, hired a psychic to make "controlled" predictions, and fabricated numerous phony documents at Canadian Station M with the assistance of the RCMP.[31]

To achieve this level of success, Stephenson quickly set about expanding the New York SIS establishment, and he decided to move to Rockefeller Center on Fifth Avenue. Lord Southborough, a co-director of Stephenson's British Pacific Trust, was familiar with the complex, as he had been involved in the development of the Center's International Building, and had discussed the construction with Nelson Rockefeller. Stephenson also contacted John Harris, of the construction company Hedgeman Harris, who worked on the complex, and on Stephenson's Earls Court, and Harris also recommended that Stephenson set up his headquarters in the building. Nelson Rockefeller was contacted and he approved of the initiative. Rockefeller leased the area inexpensively, as a contribution to the U.S. war program.[32]

Stephenson also began to contact friends. A. J. Taylor helped recruit personnel, and Taylor's daughter Kathleen became one of Stephenson's first secretaries. Stephenson's friend since World War I, Tommy Drew-Brook, who was a stockbroker in Toronto, also helped with staffing. They sought out Canadians. Canadian business executives, newspaper people, Canadian Broadcasting Corporation officials, technical experts and police authorities were approached. Drew-Brook recruited a University of Toronto professor, Benjamin de Forest (Pat) Bayly to handle communications. Herb Rowland, a Toronto investment dealer, did much of the recruiting in Canada.[33] Saskatchewan native Grace Garner, then a journalist in Toronto, eventually became the organization's head secretary. Tom Hill, from Portage La Prairie, Manitoba, who was editing an engineering publication in Toronto, was brought in to write reports and help in the day-to-day office activities.[34]

The general population was recruited as well. An advertisement was devised and put into a number of Canadian newspapers:

To Work For Britain

A Department of the British Government in New York City requires several reliable young women, fully competent in secretarial work and matriculation or better educational standing. The chief need is for expert file clerks and for typists and stenographers able to take one hundred and twenty-five words per minute. Dependable character and satisfactory background essential. Those selected can expect to serve for the duration of the war. Wages and working conditions are good. Travelling expenses to New York will be paid. Apply in your own handwriting, stating your age, education, and parentage with full details of your business experience and enclosing a recent snapshot. Also give two responsible references. Address your application to Box 1087 Telegram.

Following an interview and a security check by the Royal Canadian Mounted Police, successful candidates became members of Stephenson's organization. Many of the staff were hired through newspaper ads — at least 800 people, mostly women.[35]

Although BSC has been called an important part of Canada's war effort, it is difficult to discern this from the books written about Stephenson by British-born authors.[36] Hyde, in *The Quiet Canadian*, devotes a half paragraph to the Canadian contribution. (The English writer even refers to Stephenson as Bill Donovan's "closest British friend.")[37] *A Man Called Intrepid* mentions a handful of Canadians in passing, and stretches the contributions of the Canadian recruits to about two pages.[38] But, for the most part, the *Intrepid* author presents a rather solitary show, with Stephenson darting all over the globe, doing everything for the organization except serving the coffee and running out for donuts.

BSC's records were destroyed following the war, and there are few references to the Canadian contingent in papers that have surfaced since. Following the war, most press reports about the Stephenson organization refer exclusively to what the *British* were doing in America. Even the American CIA historian Thomas Troy refers to Stephenson as "one of several very influential but relatively unpublicized Britons" sent to the United States.[39] Five decades later, just exactly what over a thousand Canadians were doing in New York City during the war remains largely unknown. Stephenson, once asked why so little had leaked out from his wartime associates replied, "with a twinkle in his eye, 'that is because most of them were 'quiet Canadians' too."[40] The organizational secrecy Stephenson sought to establish held firm until after his death.

The Isolationists

"Immediately after the collapse of France, not even the President himself could be assured that aid to Britain would not be wasted in the circumstances," remembered Stephenson. "I need not remind you of the diplomatic dispatches from the United States ambassadors in London and Paris, that Britain's stand was hopeless and the majority of the cabinet in Washington were inclined to the same conclusion. All of which found vigorous expression in organized isolationism."[41]

British Security Coordination took aim at the isolationists.

American isolationism was organized in groups such as the America First movement and various German-American Bunds. Prominent individuals such as Charles Lindbergh spoke out against the folly of joining Europe's wars. By the spring of 1941, BSC estimated there were 700 chapters and nearly a million members of American isolationist groups.[42] Britain's Ambassador reported that nine out of every ten Americans were determined to keep America out of the war. Some, like the American Nazi Party, were determined to aid the Axis.[43]

BSC agents were dispatched all over the country to attend meetings, to keep track of members, and design and instigate effective counter-propaganda.[44]

Stephenson declared "political warfare" on Britain's enemies in America, and he sought out sympathetic journalists and media moguls. The publisher of the *New York Post*, George Backer; Ralph Ingersoll, the editor of *PM*; Helen Ogden Reid, who controlled the *New York Herald Tribune*; Paul Patterson, publisher of the *Baltimore Sun*; A. H. Sutzberger, president of the *New York Times*; Walter Lippmann; Walter Winchell and several other columnists eventually became important allies.[45]

There were attempts to woo the owners of hostile papers, such as Roy Howard, the president of the Scripps-Howard chain, but if that failed, there was a plan to put anti-British papers out of business. For example, it was discovered the Hearst newspaper chain owed a Canadian paper mill over $10 million in the form of demand notes, which were renewable every six months. Stephenson sought to buy the notes and call for payment, but the British treasury vetoed that idea and refused to provide the money.[46]

A New York-based radio station with a powerful shortwave transmitter, WRUL, was subsidized by BSC and became a propaganda vehicle. The Stephenson organization "recruited foreign news editors, translators, and announcers to serve on its staff. It furnished it with news bulletins, with specially prepared scripts for talks and commentaries."[47]

Isolationist groups were monitored, targeted and harassed. When isolationist Senator Gerald Nye spoke in Boston in September 1941, thousands of handbills were handed out attacking him as an appeaser and Nazi lover. Following a speech by Rep. Hamilton Fish, a member of a front group, the Fight For Freedom, delivered him a card which said, "Der Fuhrer thanks you for your loyalty," and photographs were taken. An attempt was made to disrupt an America First rally at Madison Square Garden by printing phony tickets.

Americans were approached to join the cause and help report on the isolationists. For example, soon after Donald Downes joined the Free World Association, a New York-based group organized by statesmen and refugees from a variety of Axis-occupied countries, he was approached by a "Mr. Howard" from British Security Coordination. "Howard" told Downes, "Our primary directive from the PM [Mr. Churchill] is that American participation in the war is the most important single objective for Britain. It is the only way, he feels, to victory over Nazism." "Howard" told Downes they believed groups such as America First were actually fronts for the Nazis, and asked for Downes' assistance in proving it. The American agreed to help, but his relationship with BSC was to remain covert and nebulous. If Downes were caught, "Howard" stressed to him, "we have never heard of you!"[48]

In the next four months, through Downes and his contacts alone, BSC gleaned information on German consulates in Boston and Cleveland, the Italian consulate in New York, the German embassy, a number of pro-Axis American politicians, a country house where *Scribner's Commentator* was published, the Bund headquarters in Yorkville, a German biology instructor, a bakery frequented by a German Embassy secretary, a retired American general and two export officials from General Motors. Downes sought and received assistance from groups such as the Jewish Anti-Defamation League, the CIO, and U.S. army counter-intelligence.

Downes eventually discovered there was Nazi activity in New York, Washington, Chicago, San Francisco, Cleveland and Boston. In some cases they traced actual transfers of money from the Nazis to the America Firsters.[49] Downes later became an important OSS operative working for William Donovan.

After the Americans joined the war in December 1941, BSC didn't need to focus on swaying American opinion any more. Stephenson remained active within the new parameters. He is regarded as the midwife of Donovan's wartime espionage organizations.

The Coordinator of Information (COI) and Office of Strategic Services (OSS)

Franklin Roosevelt wanted an all-encompassing intelligence service with an international scope that could report on the Nazis and Japanese expansionism. In mid-1940, the situation regarding security and intelligence in the U.S. was, in the words of Dick Ellis, "far from satisfactory." There was a great deal of competition between various services such as naval intelligence (ONI), and military intelligence (G-2), and each had limited operations.[50] Following the fall of France, Dunkirk, and the possibility Britain would be invaded, large intelligence-gathering problems loomed for the Americans due to a lack of a coordinating body. Because of inter-service rivalries it seemed unlikely one of the services would assume a leadership role and the others would offer to subordinate their activities to it. To help prepare for possible war, Roosevelt set up the Coordinator of Information (COI) on July 11, 1941, to help centralize the myriad of intelligence sources and named Donovan its head.[51]

Roosevelt put Bill Donovan, an outsider, in place as America's first combined intelligence chief. He had numerous personal attributes (a decorated soldier, lawyer and public servant) which commanded respect. "He had great power in Washington because he was a friend of the president," remembered Stephenson years after the war. "A close personal friend of the president, and [he] was constantly in contact with him. In addition, there was a practical advantage, from the president's point of view, in keeping Donovan actively engaged upon his side, because he was very close to what might be described as the opposition at the time. He was a Catholic and an Irishman. Republican."[52]

Although Donovan was a worthy choice as an intelligence head, in reality, in the early months it was an uphill struggle. He had little to contribute to the intelligence net that would justify his position. It was only a matter of time before he would be squeezed out of existence, according to Ellis. Stephenson knew this, and he supplied Donovan with product that he could distribute. To complement his own channels, Stephenson made numerous quick trips to London, created a direct link with censorship and security in the Caribbean, and established closer relations with Canada's External Affairs and the RCMP. He gave Donovan almost everything, according to Ellis. He also organized training. "By providing D [Donovan] with training facilities for his officers, S [Stephenson] was able to shorten the time needed for COI to stand on its own feet."[53]

Stephenson helped plan the organization necessary to carry out Donovan's functions as coordinator. He aided the task of consolidating the activities of scattered intelligence units into a single organization and set up the framework of the headquarters and field operations. He made available experienced British officers and arranged for members of COI staff to receive administrative and fieldwork training at

British schools. Hundreds of COI and OSS were trained before and after the American entry into the war.[54]

Much of the training was done at a secret Canadian location. With the assistance of Tommy Drew-Brook, a parcel of farmland outside Toronto was purchased and converted into North America's first spy school. The exact startup date of the camp is the point of some contention. In the early days Gladstone Murray of the CBC helped disguise the purpose of the property purchase. Later Canada's Department of External Affairs, the RCMP and the FBI provided assistance.[55] At Special Training School 103, known as Camp X, groups of North American agents were versed in self defence, lock picking, safe blowing, second story entry, map reading, explosives and incendiaries, radios, listening devices, and codes and ciphers. Stephenson's contacts in the film industry were put to use at the camp. Zoltan Korda, the brother of Alexander Korda, was at Camp X, and he supervised the design of mockups of various Nazi locations that were to be approached by parachuting SOE and OSS recruits. Zoltan, according to Stephenson, was an expert in reproducing the various points of entry and exit from plans usually provided by Colin Gubbins.

Alexander Korda and his wife Merle Oberon were part of what Stephenson called his "private army" who performed as far afield as Hollywood. Stephenson had influence in numerous spheres. As strange as it seems, he apparently arranged to have a Noel Coward tour of South Africa rescheduled, as the actor and author appeared tired and Stephenson thought a postponement would cause less trouble in the long run than if Coward was to break down midway through it. Stephenson sent Coward on a forced holiday.[56] According to Coward, Stephenson's men later met him in Jamaica and Natal.

The Ontario camp also became a communications centre linking Washington, Ottawa, New York and London, organized by Pat Bayly. It also carried messages from further afield and couriers were employed to supplement the system. T. D. Ingall was a courier between the radio transmitter at Camp X, called HYDRA, and Washington, Ottawa, Toronto and Montreal. "During that time I became well aware that BSC was a very extensive and worldwide organization," Ingall recalled in a letter.[57]

According to Donovan, Stephenson was responsible for satisfactory cooperation between the COI (and later OSS) and the British intelligence service. He accompanied him to Britain and established the necessary contacts with the heads of British naval and military intelligence, and other agencies. In addition, he took the necessary steps to provide Donovan "with a regular flow of secret information from sources available to his own organization, including highly confidential British censorship material not normally circulated outside British Government departments."[58] From August 18 to December 7, 1941, Donovan was in touch with Stephenson on at least 36 occasions.[59]

Stephenson set up a Washington office to keep in touch with COI, and Donovan set up a New York office in Rockefeller Centre to keep in touch with BSC. On August 9, 1941, Stephenson indicated to London that the Donovan office was functioning.

On October 24, 1941, Franklin Roosevelt informed Winston Churchill about Donovan's new post and told the Prime Minister he was setting up a London office. FDR's letter to Churchill said the Coordinator of Information had "the most helpful cooperation from the officers of His Majesty's Government who are charged with direct responsibility for your war effort."[60]

Donovan asked Stephenson for the services of experienced officers to help lay down the framework for his headquarters and to help establish field operations. Ian Fleming, who visited North America with the director of British Naval Intelligence, Admiral Godfrey, left notes for use of the new organization, but his role in laying the groundwork for the agency is greatly exaggerated, according to Ellis.[61]

Donovan was totally dependent on BSC until several months after Pearl Harbour, and Stephenson did much of the propping up of Donovan on his own, without the knowledge of intelligence officials in Britain. According to Ellis, there was not hostility towards COI on the part of "BI" (British Intelligence), but they were skeptical about passing information to the new American service. Ellis says this was because "There was little knowledge of the U.S. conditions or of the leading personalities in the U.S. scene; some of the old hands had memories of the last war, and of some aspects of the aftermath, and felt that close cooperation would be difficult to achieve and sustain. S [Stephenson] faced this situation by forming his own judgment, as the man on the spot, and took the steps that I have described above. It is quite possible that certain officers of BI would have suffered attacks of apoplexy had they been aware of the extent of collaboration already achieved with the emergent U.S. organization, the passing of information and advice, and frank discussions of technical matters etc."[62]

In *The Ultra-Magic Deals*, writer Bradley F. Smith emphasizes the unique situation, with the United States and Britain, along with Canada, sharing decrypts, intercepts and top secret information. But indications are that Stephenson, and possibly others, were giving British information to the Americans anyway without going through formal channels. In October 1941, the U.S. military attaché in London noted a dispatch he was sending to Washington regarding the Russian campaign contained information from the "British Intercept Service" and therefore needed to be kept secret "even from the British mission."[63]

According to Ellis, by June of 1942, the British agencies were accustomed to dealing with their U.S. counterparts. "BSC had evolved the machinery for maintaining liaison, and members of both British and U.S. service had been in personal contact with each other."[64]

Journalist Sidney Morrell reported BSC "covered every area of intelligence activities, from detecting enemy agents, to counter-intelligence, to protecting British and American installations throughout the Western Hemisphere. As far as I know it was the only case where a great many secret activities, which were functioning in different organizations and under different control in other countries, were under one control in this hemisphere ... where all of his [Stephenson's] efforts were given to not just bringing America in but to helping the Americans gear themselves for the struggle."[65]

Stephenson made numerous trips, perhaps as many as 43, to Britain during the war, but few are documented. Even when trips were made public, names were changed. For example, on December 6, 1940, Bill Donovan left on a trip to the continent. Travelling under the name Donald Williams, he was recognized by reporters as William Donovan. It is not known how the reporters were tipped off to Donovan's trip, but the *New York Times* reported that Donovan spoke to two passengers en route, a Mr. Desgarges from France and a Mr. O'Connell. According to Donovan biographer Richard Dunlop, "Mr. O'Connell" was William Stephenson.[66]

The Pan Am Clipper landed in Bermuda and was held up there because of bad weather. CIA historian Thomas Troy says the two men spent eight days in Bermuda and Stephenson showed Donovan the extensive operation on the island where mail, passengers and goods were checked by British censors before continuing in transit across the Atlantic. Some of the letters were checked for secret ink and it was at the Bermuda intercept station that the first micro-dot was discovered. The unit was very efficient. Following the war, Nadya Gardner of the Bermuda unit analyzed and evaluated Nazi documents from Frankfurt station while working for TOD in Washington, and she reported to Stephenson, "It was most gratifying to see that we, in Bermuda, had missed almost nothing."[67]

The intercept work was extensive and tedious. A July 21, 1941, mail intercept report from Jamaica to Montgomery Hyde reported on five days at the beginning of July when 3,727 letters were examined out of 12,320. Of these there were 32 submissions sent to the consulate in New York.

Donovan proceeded to Lisbon and then Britain, where he met with Churchill on December 18, 1940. According to some reports, Churchill told Donovan of Hitler's planned attack on the Soviet Union the next spring, which was determined from ULTRA decrypts. Donovan proceeded to the continent and to Yugoslavia. The unofficial version of events of Donovan's secret but publicized trip is that subsequently documents were stolen from him in Belgrade by German agents that were following him. Donovan's papers were phony and were prepared in New York, according to Dick Ellis.[68] Donovan's conversations with Air Force General Dusan Simovic led to a change of thinking in the Balkans, away from the Nazis, and a revolution followed in late March of 1941. Hitler was outraged at the turn of events and diverted many of his forces away from the eastern front and into Yugoslavia. The official version seems to be that Donovan had no formal position with the American government at the time, so nothing of the sort happened.

In a cable that has never been footnoted, Churchill is said to have written Roosevelt that "Stephenson and Donovan carried out the single outstanding intelligence coup of the Second World War when they delayed the Nazi invasion of Russia."[69] Through ULTRA decrypts the Allies knew that Hitler was massing forces for an attack on the Soviet Union. For Hitler, according to Churchill, the Yugoslav coup came "out of the blue," and a blow to Yugoslavia had to be struck with "unmerciful harshness."[70] Churchill quotes the German general Keitel as saying, "The decision to attack Yugoslavia meant completely upsetting all military movements and arrangements made up to that time. 'Marita'

[Greece] had to be completely readjusted. New forces had to be brought through Hungary from the north. All had to be improvised."[71] The Yugoslav diversion delayed the Nazi invasion of Russia by many weeks. By December of 1941 some German units were suffering 40 percent frostbite casualties, and the temperatures were as low as 38 degrees below zero with strong winds. As a result Hitler's forces were held up and eventually defeated by the Soviet forces and the Russian winter.

Churchill mentions in passing Donovan's trip to Belgrade in his *History of the Second World War*, but there is no suggestion he had covert plans. However, he does leave a possible clue that other factors may have been involved in the turn of events. Oddly enough, at the conclusion of his chapter on Yugoslavia, following the Nazi assault, Churchill mentions that the zoo in Belgrade was damaged during the Nazi bombing and the inhabitants escaped. He refers to the activities of a particular animal. "A bear, dazed and uncomprehending, shuffled through the inferno with a slow awkward gait down towards the Danube. He was not the only bear who did not understand." The bear is the symbol of Berlin.

At least two other Stephenson trips are documented. In June 1942, Donovan, Jim Murphy and Preston Goodfellow went to New York where they picked up William Stephenson, continued to Montreal and left for Britain the next day. The OSS records also record a Stephenson trip to Europe in August of 1942, with Lettice Silverston and Walter Wren.[72] This is the approximate time (August 19, 1942) of the ill-fated Canadian–British assault at Dieppe.

THE TRANSATLANTIC LINK 6

It is not known what exactly Stephenson did in Britain during the war. Obviously he met with various department heads of the British war effort, and he reported on the situation in the Western Hemisphere. Who else he met with, and if he had larger influence, will probably remain a mystery. "It is doubtful he had any direct influence over intelligence matters in Europe after 1939, other than through his close connections with Donovan's OSS," concludes the writer Mary Lovell.[1] However, this judgement is quite broad. Donovan's OSS were sending people all over Europe, and Donovan is quoted as saying, "Bill Stephenson taught us all we knew about foreign intelligence." Stephenson was also the North American representative of Special Operations Executive, which trained foreign nationals and organized numerous drops into occupied Europe.

Many of the activities of the SOE, the OSS, and resistance forces were of immense importance even before the invasion of Europe. For example, in Scandinavia, Danish physicist Niels Bohr, a nuclear expert, was slipped out of Europe to the Manhattan Project, away from the Nazis. In Norway, the trained resistance blew up the Norsk heavy water plant and later destroyed the last supplies. It appears Stephenson helped provide equipment for resistance activities. Following the war, the former head of SOE, Colin Gubbins, wrote to William Stevenson:

We arranged in Denmark for Niels Bohr to be smuggled out by resistance to Sweden in a fishing boat thence onto the U.K. The fast torpedo boats were I believe classified officially as submarine chasers — that's what we called them anyway. We also had two from Bill which were used on the Shetland–Norway run putting in and picking up agents. They were an absolute Godsend. Up till their arrival at Scalloway (our Shetland base) we had been working with Norwegian trawlers and crews for years or more using the methods of stealth and disguise but latterly had unbearably heavy losses — German air activity, fewer and fewer local boats fishing in Norwegian coastal waters and fearful storms — how we and our Norwegian crews blessed "Little Bill."[2]

In the files of William Stevenson is an illustrated paper with a description of the location of a message hidden in a key for Niels Bohr. The note was to be sent to Justitbraaden, a Danish government department.[3]

Gubbins, in an undated foreword, said Stephenson's activities could be best described as "a series of brilliant individual coups against Axis powers in the true tradition of secret intelligence with modern embellishments which in fact had an influence on military operation in the main theatres … We who were in SOE owe a profound debt to Stephenson and to all who worked in cooperation with him in so many vital aspects of inter-allied achievement."[4]

It seems likely Stephenson at least had knowledge of major intelligence events taking place in Europe and the planning they entailed. It also appears Stephenson provided valuable assistance to the proceedings.

Since Churchill saw American assistance as Britain's salvation, and Stephenson was ostensibly appointed by Churchill, he obviously met with the Prime Minister in London on occasion. In the files of Montgomery Hyde is an account of a meeting between Ernest Cuneo, Stephenson and Winston Churchill that Stephenson arranged.[5] Cuneo helped coordinate public policy and was appointed as an ambassador Plenipotentiary with a priority of direct access to the prime minister night or day, which Cuneo says "on emergency occasion we used."[6] According to Cuneo, "No small part of our conversations dealt with coordinated public policy of our countries, in which both Winchell and Beaverbrook were factors with whose efforts we were enabled to coordinate effectively."[7] Cuneo is also quoted as saying, "Stephenson was the only man who had the unqualified support of both Franklin Roosevelt and Winston Churchill."[8]

Colin Gubbins also indicates that Stephenson played an important intermediary role between the two world leaders. Years after the war Gubbins, the war time head of SOE, contacted Dick Ellis as he heard the former intelligence officer was writing a book on the Donovan/Stephenson collaboration. Gubbins called Stephenson's conduit role vital, and said he "played in the very highest quarters — at the top level in fact — in the Downing Street/White House 'affaire' which led to such splendid results ... I moved only rarely in the rarefied atmosphere of the top circles where the two Bills had their stomping ground but Bill Stephenson's slightest wish is to me more than a command."[9]

Any look at Stephenson's possible influence in the European theatre should not totally disregard his business interests. He had a full-time secretary, Miss A. M. Green, in England looking after his affairs. Although he was occupied in North America, his European businesses didn't disappear. As mentioned earlier, Earls Court was converted to the manufacture of barrage balloons. The cement industry (Alpha Cement) was obviously involved with fortifications and airfields. Stephenson was involved with aircraft manufacture, and Pressed Steel was surely transformed to suit the rearmament program. At the beginning of World War II, his Shepparton studios were requisitioned by the War Office and the craftsmen were directed towards the war effort. The workshops were used for the manufacture of Wellington bombers, and decoys — fake guns, aircraft and landing strips. On the studio's reservoir the Barnes-Wallace bouncing bomb was tested.[10]

In available files there is little pertaining to Stephenson's activities in Europe during the war, but there are indications he had influence there. On June 15, 1942, Montgomery Hyde wrote "Harrington" a letter from New York. In it he says, "WSS has gone to London with Bill Donovan for three weeks. His [little Bill's] presence is long overdue there."[11]

While Stephenson was away in Europe, back in New York it seems his friends continued the wining and dining of American officials. In the files of Montgomery Hyde is an invitation to a dinner party at A. J. Taylor's flat (Stephenson's business partner) at The Moorings in New York. The Canadian had invited to the June 1942 gathering John McCloy, the U.S. Assistant Secretary of War; Vilmar Stefansson, the famous Icelandic Canadian arctic explorer, who was working for the U.S. Navy;

Hyde; Lawrence Whiting, of the U.S. Army & Navy War Department, and Frank Hopwood, a director of the Asiatic Petroleum Company and the son of Lord Southborough.[12]

Hyde also met with Hoover on occasion on behalf of BSC, and they exchanged information.[13] According to his book, *Secret Intelligence Agent*, Hyde also visited the Bahamas to meet with the Duke of Windsor.

Censorship

British Security Coordination received suspicious mail coming and going from the United States and the Caribbean. The British Censorship Bureau had an office in New York at 15 Broad Street, headed by Charles Des Graz, whom Stephenson consulted. In early October of 1941 Des Gras sent Stephenson by safe hand a report of Japanese postal and telegraphic censorship and interception during World War II. The information flowed both ways. On October 14, 1941, BSC sent Des Graz an MI5 report on the movements of European art treasures that was ascertained through post censorship intercepts.[14]

There were glitches in the flow of information. Des Graz "accidentally" uncovered a major flaw in the autumn of 1941. BSC was supposed to secure ports and watch for saboteurs in the Western Hemisphere, but the organization was no longer receiving the intercepted correspondence of known security risks. On October 30, 1941, Des Graz reported to Montgomery Hyde in a letter marked SECRET that Bermuda sent letters to or from persons on the "General Security Black List" to London unopened. "It seemed to me that this was a very questionable practice as, if the persons in question are in North or South America, their correspondence seems primarily a question for your office." The instructions to forward the letters had come from London in January 1941. Des Graz assumed the London edict was misinterpreted in Bermuda. He wrote, "Bermuda Sorters took this I think wrongly as an instruction to forward them unopened. Des Graz immediately changed the practice and if the contents might interest your office you can receive early information and a photostat if necessary." On average this amounted to 40 letters a week, Des Graz reported. Soon afterwards Stephenson created a BSC mail intercept capability.

On November 27, 1941, when U.S. negotiations with the Japanese appeared headed nowhere, Stephenson asked the Director General of Postal and Telegraph Censorship, Edwin Herbert, for general information from Hong Kong and Singapore intercepts to relay to the Americans. "We are very anxious to satisfy them at this present time." He expressed interest in German and Japanese activities in the Far East and the Americas and reports on political developments in Japan and China. Stephenson then requested all the intercepts from the Asian colonial city-states. "I feel however it would be more satisfactory to have all intercepts from Hong Kong and Singapore as we now have adequate arrangements for dealing with them here."[15]

BSC added censorship to its various departments. Dorothy Hyde was an expert in mail intercept and forgery, and gave instruction to the FBI. Later she was joined in the department, known as Room 99, by Betty Raymond.

But dealing with intercepted mail involved more than the mechanics of covert opening and closing. To contend with intercepted correspondence many avenues had to be covered. Not only were they looking for possible spies and saboteurs, BSC had to stem any possible flow of strategic resources, and monitor potential supplies. In the wartime files of Montgomery Hyde is a list of books that were ordered, including language dictionaries for Dutch, Portuguese, Chinese and Japanese. There were dictionaries of engineering and chemical terms; directories of Norway, Italy and Central Europe, and telegraphic addresses for France and Italy. They ordered a Banker's Almanac that listed the banks of the world, as well as Katzaroff's patent dictionary and books on trade and finance. The Imperial Chemical Industries chemical catalogue, the ICI catalogue of names and uses of chemicals, and various Who's Who directories were ordered, as well as Lloyd's shipping supplements. Subscriptions to *Time, Newsweek, Life*, the *Sunday New York Times* and a daily New York paper flowed into the offices.[16] In Hyde's files are overdue notices for some of the above material from New York libraries. (As Pat Bayly said later, "We were breaking every law in the book.")

BSC employed many linguists to translate intercepts and financial people who understood the flow of capital and resources. Colonel Louis Franck, a descendant of a series of governors of Belgian Central Bank, was considered a bullion expert.[17] Other business people joined the organization, such as Richard Coit, Ingram Fraser, David Ogilvy, Ivor Bryce and Herbert Sichel. British journalists joined the organization, such as Sydney Morrell and Christopher Wren. Roald Dahl, who became a children's writer during the war, worked for the organization in Washington. Paul Dehn, who later wrote the screenplays for a few early James Bond movies, was an instructor at Camp X. Playwrights Benn Levy, Eric Maschwitz and Giles Playfair worked for BSC. There were also a number of university dons, such as Gilbert Highet, A. J. Ayre, Ken Maidment and F. W. Deakin.

The Stephenson organization was multifaceted and crisscrossed many diverse spheres. "BSC was not just an extension of SIS," wrote CIA historian Thomas Troy, "but was in fact a service which integrated SIS, SOE, Censorship, Codes and Ciphers, Security, Communications — in fact nine secret distinct organizations. But in the Western Hemisphere Stephenson ran them all."[18]

CLANDESTINE SUCCESS 7

Bsc created a small Washington office to act as a home base in the American capital, and Stephenson was, of course, in contact with the British embassy in Washington. The first ambassador he dealt with was Lord Lothian, Philip Kerr. Lothian died under somewhat strange circumstances in December 1940, and he was eventually replaced by Lord Halifax. Stephenson was not a big Halifax fan. "Edward the holier than thou type — a poor choice to follow Lothian but it got him out of Winston's way and into mine dammit."[1]

When the United States was still neutral, Axis and Vichy embassies and foreign missions became unique windows on continental activities. The activities of Jean-Louis Musa, a French Vichy official, were closely monitored. His phone calls were tapped and meeting rooms bugged. According to the BSC history, a number of embassies were penetrated.

Elizabeth Thorpe, code-named "Cynthia," may have obtained valuable Italian naval ciphers. In the spring of 1941 she also discovered through Italian Admiral Alberto Lais that Italian ships were going to be scuttled in American harbours. Subsequently, Lais was asked to leave the United States. Later, in May 1941, "Cynthia" was asked to concentrate on the Vichy embassy. She posed as a newspaper woman and became romantically involved with the Vichy press attaché Charles Brousse. Eventually she secured copies of nearly all the telegrams to and from the French embassy and was instrumental in obtaining the

French naval cipher. Brousse started supplying more and more material, memorizing conversations and passing on notes he took at briefings. BSC also had two other informants relaying information from the embassy. In the summer of 1941 the SI division of BSC compiled a comprehensive report on the Vichy French in the United States with an appendix of photostatted documents and transcripts of recorded telephone conversations. According to the BSC history, Stephenson took it to London in July 1941 and arranged for a copy to be given to Roosevelt. The American president is said to have called it "the most fascinating reading I have had in a long time — the best piece of comprehensive intelligence work I have come across since the last war."[2]

Stephenson leaked parts of the report to the *New York Herald Tribune* at the end of August and beginning of September 1941, and the paper published a series of articles linking the Vichy embassy in Washington to Nazi interests. "VICHY FRENCH EMBASSY IN U.S. SHOWN AS HEADING CLIQUE OF AGENTS AIDING NAZIS" one headline read. The U.S. Secretary of the Treasury, Henry Morgenthau, congratulated the paper for the journalistic feat.

There were also embassies penetrated in Mexico, Colombia and other South American countries. BSC had contacts inside the Japanese Embassy in Washington and Japanese Consulates in New York and San Francisco. There was also some success in direct penetration of the Saburo Kurusu mission that travelled to the United States shortly before the Pearl Harbour attack. BSC was able to obtain information on Spanish intentions and ciphers through the Basques in the United States and around the world. Most Basques remained loyal to President Aguirre, who had been forced to flee after Franco's victory. The janitor at the Spanish embassy was used to relay information.

According to Hyde's *The Quiet Canadian* and the BSC history, there was reason to believe the Vichy French were tapping Western Union trans-Atlantic cable, possibly using the French islands of St. Pierre and Miquelon as a base, and passing convoy information to the enemy. BSC agents were sent to the islands off Newfoundland and through surveys found 97 percent of the population were pro-de Gaulle.[3]

BSC also kept track of a number of international business people and celebrities. In the files of Montgomery Hyde there are a number of clippings on the Swedish industrialist Axel Wenner Gren, who was thought to have had pro-Nazi sympathies. Elsa Schiaparelli, a prominent dress designer, was also thought to have worked against the Allied interests. BSC believed many people's pro-Vichy sentiments — including Schiaparelli's — were inspired by avarice and a determination to prosper in the world irrespective of whether or not it was Nazi-ruled.

Stephenson kept abreast of scientific developments on both sides, such as the robot bombs, through Charles Lindemann at the British embassy in Washington. He was the brother of Frederick Lindemann, Viscount Cherwell, a physicist, who performed a similar function for Churchill. Cherwell's brother was deputied to Stephenson so he "could pass on information of such importance it would warrant informing FDR personally."[4] Stephenson also conferred with atomic scientists Chaim Weizmann and Albert Einstein.[5] Weizmann met dissident German chemist Willstatter in Zurich in 1939 and began to work in London tracing those who could help the Germans build atomic bombs.[6] Weizmann saw Stephenson early in 1944, and Einstein and Stephenson discussed scientific and political matters during long walks through Central Park. Stephenson says the physicist was escorted by Shaun Herron, who later became a novelist/journalist in Winnipeg. Herron had to accompany Einstein from Princeton to assure that the "lamb entered the train at Princeton Junction bound for New York and not opposite direction."[7] Stephenson is said to have provided protection in 1940 (John Hart, formerly of the RCMP) for Henry Tizard. The British scientist brought many of the besieged island's scientific secrets to the U.S. for development, such as radar and the jet engine.[8]

As BSC expanded, the files they collected became immense. Numerous filing clerks were employed, and a filing expert from Canada's Royal Canadian Mounted Police was loaned to BSC to set up a quick access system. The historian Gilbert Highet and his associates constantly added to BSC files. Highet, later of Columbia University, thought the advance of history could be studied not only through class movements or competing nations, but through the progress of individuals and their families. He set up large card files for personalities, German and other, throughout South America that would "enable our office to predict how in such and such an area, a segment of the population or an individual might react as the war took one turn or another." He collected information about individuals, about their right- and left-hand men, their families, habits and their backgrounds. After the direct military threat became less crucial in South America, BSC concentrated on the industrial threat and possible relationship chains or flows of capital. Highet's card system also tried to identify people who could be susceptible to blackmail. "This is really one of the purposes of espionage," he explained later. "Every human being has his weaknesses. In war, or in a very tight political struggle, both sides try to discover and then play on these weaknesses. If you have cards which indicate weaknesses of that kind reaching so deep into a man's personality structure, you can clearly become aware that the enemy will attempt to play on such weaknesses and take what steps you see fit to counter play."[9]

Problems with the Americans

In early 1941, Stephenson's vocation was officially renamed. A January 21, 1941, letter from His Majesty's Chargé D'affaires to the U.S. Secretary of State announced "Mr. W. S. Stephenson, hitherto British Passport Control Officer in New York, has been appointed to the position of Director of Security Coordination in the U.S."[10] However, his job description was still rather vague and not widely advertised. Stephenson was the representative of MI6, and SOE in the Western Hemisphere, and in late October of 1942 he was made MI5 rep in the Western Hemisphere. According to a coded message sent to the West Indian Colonies, this was a result of "greatly increased importance of security measures in Caribbean and West Indian waters and improved coordination with the Americans."[11]

It was impossible for Stephenson's expanding espionage and public relations (propaganda) organization not to draw some attention to itself. To be effective BSC had to deal with a number of American departments and various individuals. But, at least when they started, they were a foreign intelligence network working in a neutral country, so they had to be covert. Churchill said that in wartime the truth was so precious it had to be surrounded by a bodyguard of lies. Stephenson had a convoy encircling BSC. He also kept quite silent about the scope of his activities.

Hoover obviously knew Stephenson, but this knowledge didn't extend far down the bureaucratic ladder. A Treasury Department report of February 6, 1941, from special agent Bannerman, indicates others in the bureau had little idea what was going on or were keeping quiet. Bannerman said Stephenson "is not known to any of the Federal officials or agencies in New York that deal with anti-sabotage, nor have any of the federal agencies ever heard of him ... Many of the British officers in New York did not know Mr. Stephenson and did not know of his new position ... As yet Mr. Stephenson is not known to either the New York police or the New York office of the FBI," and "Mr. Stephenson has so far refused to reveal the exact whereabouts of his office and the entire matter has been handled with the utmost secrecy."[12]

According to a defining memo from the British embassy, Stephenson's employees were simply watching ships.

"The duties of these [BSC] officers are two-fold:

(a) to enforce security regulations on board British and British-controlled ships coming into port.

(b) to report either to the Director of Security Coordination, Mr. Stephenson, or to the local United States authorities with whom Mr. Stephenson is in contact, any circumstances which appear to menace the security of the British or British-controlled shipping."[13]

By the spring of 1941, the American State Department was concerned about what appeared to be occurring. A March 31, 1941, letter from Assistant Secretary of State Adolph Berle reported to Sumner Welles that "the head of the field service appears to be Mr. William S. Stephenson ... in charge of providing protection for British ships, supplies etc. But in fact a full size secret police and intelligence service is rapidly evolving ... (with) district officers at Boston, New York City, Philadelphia, Baltimore, Charleston, New Orleans, Houston, San Francisco, Portland and probably Seattle." It said Stephenson employed both regular secret agents and a much larger number of informers, and Berle urged his activities be curtailed.[14]

Berle was worried that Stephenson's network was going to cause problems. "I have in mind, of course, that should anything go wrong at any time, the State Department would be called upon to explain why it permitted violation of American laws and was compliant about an obvious breach of diplomatic obligation ... Were this to occur and a Senate investigation should follow, we should be on very dubious ground if we have not taken appropriate steps."

The situation came to a head with the possible implementation of the McKellar bill in the winter of 1942. People such as Adolf Berle wanted foreign agents expelled, or else registered and kept under tight reins. In a February 5, 1942, lobbying letter from Berle to FDR, he wrote that British espionage and counterespionage was under the misleading title of Security Coordination. He urged the registration of foreign agents and questioned why other country's spies should be in the U.S. "Logically, why have it?"[15]

In his diary at the time, Berle wrote about the lead-up to the bill's fate. "Security Coordination intervened with the embassy, but the embassy said they could do nothing about it. Thereupon they intervened with Bill Donovan who promptly put in a memorandum to the president asking him to veto the bill, which was on his desk. I am impressed with Donovan's courage, though I don't think much of it in terms of national wisdom. Why should anyone have a spy system in the United States? And what will it look like a little later when someone finds out about it?"[16] Berle seemed to think he was up against an organized lobbying clique. He later wrote "the lend lease boys called me last night."

Stephenson obviously wanted the McKellar bill to disappear, and he lobbied influential people to see that it did. For example, Robert Sherwood, a Roosevelt speech writer and a friend of Stephenson's, wrote the president and said, "This bill is a hangover of isolationism" and "would seriously hamper our numerous activities abroad."[17]

Roosevelt vetoed the bill February 9, 1942, but Stephenson's public relations problems were far from over. Later that month he reported to London that an anti-British feeling was on the increase in the U.S., "amounting almost to hostility" outside the strictly military sphere. The cause arose from a desire to put the U.S. in fighting order, on a nationalistic basis, Stephenson's report concluded. The day the McKellar bill was vetoed, Stephenson asked his staff for ways to improve Anglo-American relations.

Later in the month Stephenson had more problems. On February 13, 1942, Berle's diary reported that a Mr. Tamm of the FBI called "with a piece of information which is at once amusing, disturbing and irritating." A BSC agent, Dennis Paine, was supposedly trailing Berle and trying to get "the dirt" on him. However, all he discovered out of the ordinary was that Berle had twin tubs in his bathroom. Stephenson was called on the carpet by U.S. government officials, and Paine was expelled from the United States. There is another version to the story. According to former BSC operative Bill Ross Smith, the episode was a FBI public relations exercise. The FBI knew Paine worked for BSC, and to help prove their vigilance in the U.S., they pounced on him.[18]

At the end of the month, a meeting took place between Attorney General Francis Biddle, Adolf Berle, J. Edgar Hoover, Admiral Wilkinson and General Raymond Lee "about Stephenson working under the title of Security Coordination." Biddle concluded BSC's existence "may have been arranged by an informal agreement between Churchill and the President before the war." He thought some of the undercover men were "irresponsible" and the informants BSC used were "unscrupulous." "There are at present ninety names registered with the state department and it is believed over 300 agents are working." Biddle was also concerned that several thousand coded messages a month were being sent and received by BSC through the FBI radio in Maryland.[19]

On March 5, 1942, Biddle; the British ambassador, Lord Halifax; a British minister, Ronald Campbell; FBI head Hoover and Adolf Berle met to discuss limiting BSC's activities to liaison only and Biddle's conclusion was that British intelligence "probably needed a different type of man to head it." The British Ambassador, Lord Halifax, told the meeting Stephenson did nothing without the permission of the FBI, and that they exchanged results. When Hoover was called in, he said that didn't correspond to his impression at all. Stephenson sometimes reported afterwards what he was doing, and frequently not even then. When Hoover was bluntly asked whether he thought Stephenson was the man to head the organization, "Mr. Hoover responded that he had no quarrel with Mr. Stevenson [sic] and had pleasant personal relations with him. They did not, however feel that they were on terms of such confidence with the organization or with Mr. Stevenson as to make close relations possible. Specifically, they were never sure whether they were getting the whole story; and they knew that in many cases they were not." Certain instances were discussed in which BSC had tapped wires and shanghaied sailors and the matter was being reported to the Attorney General. Lord Halifax said that his "mental structure" was altered when he learned that there was not a close working relationship between Hoover and Stephenson.[20]

Five days later Berle wrote with some alarm that FBI radio was sending two or three hundred messages a week "in secret code from the British Intelligence here to the British Intelligence in London ... *and no one knew anything about it.*" He was told they were secret messages between Roosevelt and Churchill, but Berle decided, "Somebody has been doing some tall lying here." He figured it was Stephenson. Berle concluded the Canadian had probably transferred a considerable number of agents in the country to Donovan's payroll, on the excuse that they were to be used in "recruiting personnel" for some overseas work in which Donovan was engaged.[21]

Years after the war, Berle said he admired Stephenson "greatly," according to David Ogilvy, who met the American bureaucrat in the 1960s. However, Berle thought some of Stephenson's staff took too many risks before Pearl Harbor. Berle, according to Ogilvy, "felt it was his duty to prevent them causing public scandals which would have played into the hands of the Irish Congressmen and other isolationists."[22]

For his part Stephenson explained, "Adolf Berle was slightly school-masterish for a very brief period due [to] misinformation," but the former Under Secretary of State, "could not have been more helpful when factual situation [was] clarified to him."[23]

American bureaucratic checks on BSC continued, although they received only limited response.[24] Throughout the war BSC was required to give lists of employees and job descriptions as various U.S. departments tried to keep tabs on their activities.

There seem to have been a few attempts to get rid of the Canadian spymaster. On June 18, 1943, Canadian diplomat Tommy Stone wrote to Stephenson to say he heard from the British High Commission in Ottawa that G. C. Denham was going to take over BSC. In fact Denham took over MI5 in the United States, not the whole show. According to Hyde, he had only a hazy conception of what his new duties involved.[25] But Stone knew that even if Stephenson was not Britain's representative, he would not be leaving his post. The Canadian representative wanted the details of the "new organization you are going to build up in Washington. Would appreciate a line or two on these matters or would you rather give it to me verbally."[26]

South America

Stephenson sent numerous agents and support personnel throughout Central and South America. According to Dick Ellis, the intelligence establishment in England didn't recommend this; it was brought on by a request from the FBI. "They had no trained officers, they had nobody with any knowledge of languages or of Latin America, and they came ... and they said, 'Will you help us?'"[27] Stephenson's schemes in South America caused a certain amount of apprehension in London, where intelligence felt Central and South America were American areas. Stephenson operated largely on his own. Some of the contacts were through the British embassies and trade missions but others were not. The American diplomat Spruille Braden, in his book *Diplomats and Demagogues*, gives a firsthand account of a Stephenson agent using American resources.

In May of 1941, on a train to New York, Braden, the American ambassador in Colombia, complained to journalist Ulric Bell about a lack of intelligence in South America. Bell told Braden about Bill Donovan and said Donovan's trips to Europe were to study Nazi Fifth Column activity. Bell worked for Donovan and arranged a meeting. Donovan explained to Braden a theoretical series of subversive operations which could occur, involving propaganda, sabotage and espionage, and Braden thought similar activities were already taking place in Colombia. Toward the end of their meeting Donovan asked Braden if he wanted to meet "the head of British Intelligence," a "Mr. So-and-So."

Braden met Bill Stephenson at the Metropolitan Club in New York, and Stephenson told Braden that he was reorganizing his intelligence service in Colombia and would send a man named Stagg down to meet with him. "I'll put him under your orders," Stephenson told the ambassador. Stagg was instructed by Stephenson to act as a playboy and to report to Braden, who was to use Stagg as his own agent. "Of course, Stephenson knew that the British minister and his legation staff were phlegmatic," Braden recalled. "They didn't even know his organization existed."[28]

Stagg and his wife arrived in Bogota from Ecuador. He played polo, he played tennis, he loved to dance, go to parties and entertain. "It was perfectly obvious he was just a frolicsome dilettante." The ambassador gave Stagg priority when he appeared at the embassy, and his staff could not understand why. However, Braden found Stagg very efficient, with a quality organization. On one occasion Braden reported to Stephenson's agent that there was a large meeting at the German Legation and the street was full of cars. Ten minutes later Stagg arrived with one of his men and his wife. The couple walked down the street past the German legation at a normal pace and Stagg's agent memorized the licence numbers of every car — over two dozen altogether. Because of the memory feat they were able to trace that every car owner was tied into the Nazi movement.

One day Stagg brought the Colombian Ambassador a copy of a letter that was purported to be from Major Elias Belmonte Pabon, the Bolivian Military Attaché in Berlin, to the German minister in La Paz, telling of a plot to overthrow the government of Bolivian President Penaranda. Stagg told Braden that they had intercepted a transcript of the letter and wanted the original, and he asked if the Americans could intercept the diplomatic pouch. The State Department reported back that they would have nothing to do with the interception of diplomatic mail. Weeks later Braden heard the Bolivian government had received information about a possible coup and a Major Belmonte was involved. The same letter Braden had seen in his office was read over the radio word for word. The Bolivian government sent the German minister out of the country and broke off diplomatic relations. (Bolivia was a major source of wolfram, used in steel and arms manufacture.)

When Braden congratulated Stagg on the interception of the letter, he was surprised to learn BSC had not intercepted the letter; they forged it. Early in 1941 Stephenson received information from J. Edgar Hoover that Belmonte was in touch with Nazi elements in Bolivia. He sent Hyde down to Bolivia to survey the situation and cabled people to be on the lookout for a German diplomatic bag. Stephenson took the letter to Hoover, who took it to Hull and then to Roosevelt. The circulated letter was forged, Stagg told Braden, and having forged the letter, Stephenson had to devise the appearance of authenticity.[29] In *The Quiet Canadian*, Hyde writes about his trip to South America and the Bolivian situation, but he says the Belmonte letter was intercepted on an elevator in Buenos Aires.[30] Braden calls Hyde's account "the classic 'amalgam,' the combination of truth with falsehood that is of all snarls the hardest to unravel."[31]

According to the BSC history, in August of 1940 the possibility was explored of staging a French coup in Martinique, which would help release gold, ships and aircraft. In the files of Montgomery Hyde are a number of South American maps showing among other things, the location of raw materials, oil refineries and radio stations. There are also wartime New York newspaper clippings of Axis activities in the Southern Hemisphere. The organization seems to have kept close tabs on the flow of money and smuggling of industrial diamonds, platinum and wolfram.

During the course of the war, Stephenson represented Britain's

MI6, MI5, the Political Intelligence Department, Special Operations Executive, the Office of Naval Intelligence, the Security Executive and the Special Branch of Scotland Yard. His BSC office was the liaison for similar organizations in the United States and Canada. According to Ernest Cuneo, Stephenson engaged in covert diplomacy, supplied intelligence to Britain, monitored the flow of people, mail and commodities to and from Europe, conducted intelligence operations, propaganda and political warfare against isolationists, established a hemisphere port security system and Ship's Observer scheme, built and operated the Camp X training centre and established a covert communications system.[32] But due to the nature of the activities, the exact extent of BSC's operations will probably never be known. For example, following the publication of Hyde's *The Quiet Canadian*, Sir Bede Clifford, the governor of Trinidad and Tobago during the war, wrote to Hyde and said he knew of William Stephenson at the time. He recalled taking a Spanish diplomat for a drive on the island and for lunch at Government House, "while Stephenson's agents went through his baggage."[33]

1945

As the war progressed and gradually swung in favour of the Allies, Stephenson was given some recognition for his contribution. In 1944, following the D-Day landings, he was knighted, and it was publicly proclaimed on January 1, 1945. The announcement in *The Times* of London herded him into a list with over 40 others ("William Samuel Stephenson employed in a department of the Foreign Office"). At the end of March 1945, J. Edgar Hoover discovered Stephenson had been knighted. "It certainly is one [honour] that is both well earned and well deserved," the FBI head wrote. "In years to come you certainly can with great satisfaction look back to the very worthy contribution which you have made, not only to your own country, but to those of its Allies in this world conflict. When the full story can be told, I am quite certain that your contribution will be among the foremost in having brought victory finally to the United Nations' cause."[34]

Soon after D-Day, Donovan wrote to President Roosevelt and the Joint Chiefs of Staff recommending Stephenson be awarded the American Distinguished Service Medal.[35]

The extensive experience of the British Government in the fields of secret intelligence and special operations was made available to this country largely through the efforts of William Samuel Stephenson. Without his help it would not have been possible to establish the instrumentalities for these purposes in time to aid the American war effort. He not only enabled the United States to borrow on British experience, but he helped to secure and train the personnel initially required for this undertaking. At every step in the creation of these instrumentalities, he contributed assistance and counsel of such value that his services may be considered exceptionally meritorious both to the Government of the United States and to the entire Allied cause.

Stephenson wasn't awarded the medal, and he received no public recognition from the Americans until the end of 1946. Oddly enough, the British held up the presentation of the American award to Stephenson — a key figure in the survival of the British Isles. Over a year after the end of the war, on the letterhead of his law firm, Bill Donovan wrote to Alexander Cadogan to say he was "much perturbed to learn there appears to be some delay by the Foreign Office in returning formal approval" of the Medal of Merit to Stephenson. Donovan explained in the letter that Stephenson had already received the Medal of Merit in a ceremony after the war anyway, without their permission. He wrote that the medal was the highest civilian decoration awarded by the president, and Stephenson's case was unique, as for the first time it was presented to a foreigner. "I felt sure that you personally would be pleased with the implications of the blanket approval of the operations of the British secret organization in the United States during the war (all of which were under Stephenson)."[36]

· · ·

Donovan and Stephenson were together May 7, 1945, when word reached them Germany had signed for peace. The following day Stephenson wrote to those who worked for him, from senior officials to clerks, and thanked them for their service.

A FINAL CASE 8

At the end of the war, the files of British Security Coordination were packed onto semitrailers and transported to Canada. Stephenson wanted to have some record of the activities of the agency, "To provide a record which would be available for reference should future need arise for secret activities and security measures for the kind it describes."[1] That purpose had been "advanced to the point of immediacy ... with the advent of atomic weapons," he wrote in the foreword. The archives were collated, summarized and destroyed at Camp X. BSC's chief secretary, Grace Garner, got the papers ready, assisted by Eleanor Fleming, and filing head Merle Cameron. Stephenson wanted Garner, a former editor, to try writing the history. "He wanted me to have a stab at it, but I couldn't do it," she remembered. "I made the files quite cross referenced and the stuff was handed over to them complete."[2] The result was a history of the organization written by Tom Hill, Gilbert Hyatt, Roald Dahl and Montgomery Hyde.

Like most of the activities of BSC, the process was conducted in secret. The history was put together at Camp X and shuttled in army vehicles at night to be printed at an Oshawa, Ontario, print shop. "We had a couple of security people to carry this stuff back and forward to the camp," Hill recalled. "My wife and I lived in the hotel. We were both picked up in the daytime." The final editing was done by Giles Playfair in New York. Hill stayed at the camp and did the final checking and printing. There were 20 copies of the book printed. Hill put ten into a safe in Montreal and ten went to Stephenson for distribution. "One went to Churchill," Hill remembered, "and one had to go to each of the heads of security intelligence organizations, and SOE, and Lord Beaverbrook, Minister of Aircraft Production during the war, and he probably sent one to Lord Leathers of Transport."[3]

Hill was to be the guardian of the remaining copies. "I put them in a safe, left them for a year, and then Sir William didn't want them anymore," he remembered. "I took them out to my wife's family farm in Quebec and burned them. All ten spare copies." Hill, who worked with Stephenson following the war, regretted not keeping a copy for himself, as the history of BSC has become an elusive publication. None of the remaining ten copies has ever surfaced publicly for more than a few hours. It is often referred to as "the Bible," and it is still classified as "Top Secret" by Britain's MI5.[4] The account of Stephenson's secret organization has been called "one of the most astonishing documents in history" by the former British MP and intelligence writer Rupert Allason, who writes under the name Nigel West.[5]

Chroniclers of BSC, Montgomery Hyde and William Stevenson, were given access to the secret history by Stephenson. "Place Bible in safekeeping of 'Bill'," Stephenson cabled Stevenson in 1973.[6] Some sections of the BSC history are very similar to Hyde's accounts in *The Quiet Canadian* — almost word for word.

Gouzenko

In early September of 1945, Stephenson was on his way to see Canadian Prime Minister Mackenzie King at the Seignory Club, outside Ottawa. King couldn't make the meeting as he was ill, so Stephenson proceeded to the home of the Under Secretary of State in Canada's Department of External Affairs, Norman Robertson. At Robertson's he heard details about Igor Gouzenko, a Soviet Embassy cipher clerk who was looking for assistance. Gouzenko was 26 at the time and working for the GRU, Soviet military intelligence. "During my residence in Canada," he wrote after his defection, "I have seen how the Canadian people and their government, sincerely wishing to help the Soviet people sent supplies to the Soviet Union, collected money for the welfare of the Russian people, sacrificing the lives of their sons in the delivery of supplies across the ocean — and instead of gratitude for the help rendered, the Soviet government is developing espionage activity in Canada, preparing to deliver a stab in the back to Canada — all this without the knowledge of the Russian people."[7] Reportedly Gouzenko committed a minor breach of security and he and his pregnant wife Svetlana were supposed to return to the Soviet Union. They decided to stay in Canada instead.

Stephenson was amazed to learn that Gouzenko was not in safe custody and that the young couple were still roaming Ottawa. The Soviet Union was regarded as an ally, and the disgruntled embassy employee soon found no doors were widely opened for him. "Nobody would listen to him," Stephenson said later. "The Prime Minister himself, Mackenzie King, had said that he thought it was too hot a potato ... to interfere in this case." King apparently thought suicide would be a possible recourse for the defector. "If suicide took place, let the city police take charge ... but on no account let us take the initiative," he recorded in his diary.[8] Stephenson got in touch with Tommy Stone, who worked for Robertson and was later Canada's Ambassador to the Netherlands, discovered where Gouzenko was, and may have even driven to the defector's apartment. Stephenson recommended the RCMP take possession of him as soon as possible, or at least post guards. Gouzenko was taken into protective custody. Later Jean Paul Evans and Peter Dwyer, British-trained BSC employees, were sent to interview him. Eventually Gouzenko was shuttled to Camp X near Toronto, where he and his wife lived in guarded seclusion.

Stephenson controlled the overseas distribution of Gouzenko's revelations and the documents he took with him following his debriefing. The Canadian and British High Commission transmission links had been compromised, so BSC New York provided a secure communications link to Britain.[9]

Gouzenko and the material he took with him revealed a large Soviet espionage network in Canada and the U.S. His information also led to the arrest of the "atom spies" Klaus Fuchs and Alan Nunn May in Britain. He also implicated American government officials Harry Dexter White and Alger Hiss. His knowledge of codes and cover names likely aided the decrypting done in the U.S. of VENONA.[10] He is regarded as the most important defector of the era, and his revelations are often regarded as the beginning of the Cold War.

The defection of Gouzenko was not known publicly until February 4, 1946, when the American journalist Drew Pearson reported on a large Soviet espionage network operating in North America. Stephenson

may have prompted the publicity. "IT WAS THROUGH DREW PEAR-
SON THAT WE FORCED ACTION LIFT DIPLOMATIC FEARS LIKELY
ENSUE FROM THE GREAT MONSTER IN GOUZENKO AFFAIR AS YOU
WILL RECALL," cabled Stephenson.[11]

Following the debriefing of Gouzenko, the Canadian government
arrested a dozen suspects and set up a Royal Commission in 1946 headed
by Robert Taschereau and R. L. Kellock to deal with the charges. The
inquiry was closed to the public and many details were still secret years later.

Gouzenko was known for being touchy with journalists and others who he thought defamed him. He disliked the word "defector"
and frequently threatened people with lawsuits. According to Gouzenko
lawyers Nelles Starr and Alan Harris, he was trying to protect his reputation. He thought that before the Soviets would try to kill him, they
would try to destroy his credibility to the point of ridicule.[12]

After Stephenson's death, John Bryden questioned, in *Best Kept
Secret*, whether Stephenson was actually involved in the Gouzenko
affair. But in the period between his defection and his death in 1982,
Gouzenko, living under an assumed identity, made his presence known
to many journalists in and around Toronto, including Peter
Worthington and William Stevenson, the author of *A Man Called
Intrepid*. Worthington, the only person other than family at Gouzenko's
funeral, wrote Stephenson "probably saved Gouzenko from being
returned to the Soviets."[13] From correspondence between Stevenson
and the ex-spymaster in Bermuda, it appears Gouzenko and his wife had
no doubt Stephenson was instrumental in providing a safe haven in
Canada. "They asked to be remembered to you," Stevenson wrote
Stephenson in 1976, "and said again that they feel they owe their lives and
those of their children to you."[14] Stevenson's final book about the former
spychief, *Intrepid's Last Case*, dealt loosely with the Gouzenko incident.

Decades later, Svetlana Gouzenko still remembers her flight to
freedom. She is incredulous at the West's naiveté to the espionage that
was taking place. "Why do you think they sent over all those personnel [to Soviet Embassies]? To have cocktail parties?" Mackenzie King
wanted her husband and her returned to the Soviet authorities, she said.
It was later decided the documents Gouzenko brought with him could
be stolen before the couple was turned in. This is when Stephenson
intervened and demanded the Gouzenkos be given a safe haven. "He
saved our lives," she said.

From 1946 to early 1951, Stephenson lived in semi-retirement in Montego Bay, Jamaica, while maintaining a residence in New York on East 52nd Street. His British business was looked after by Miss A. M. Green in Carshalton, Surrey. But Stephenson's financial interests were moving from Europe to the Western Hemisphere. In 1946 he began to wind down his involvement in the film business. Stephenson sold 74 percent interest of Sound City Films for £380,000 to British Lion, which was controlled by his friend Sir Alexander Korda, and the studio went through a large expansion and renovation program.

The Stephensons were known for entertaining during the war, and they continued to attract a wide variety of personalities to their various homes. Stephenson's friends, Noel Coward, Beaverbrook and Ian Fleming, bought residences in Jamaica. Among Stephenson's friends after the war were Louis St. Laurent, Brooke Claxton, Dana Wilgress (former Canadian High Commissioner in London), the Aga Khan, Henry R. Luce (editor-in-chief of *Time* Inc.) and the British newspaper barons Kemsley, Camrose and Rothermere. He frequently used the telex machine in his house and looked forward to his regular correspondence with Lord Louis Mountbatten. In his later years Stephenson bought a satellite dish to keep in touch with world events.

Following the death of Brigadier Richard Malone (1985), the former publisher of the Toronto *Globe and Mail*, Stephenson recalled in a letter to the paper a Jamaican dinner at his house in 1946 with Malone,

Canadian politicians J. L. Ralston and C. D. Howe, "Max" (Lord Beaverbrook), Beaverbrook's houseguest, *Time-Life* founder Henry Luce, and Stephenson's own house guests, "Fred" (Lord Leathers, British Minister of War Transport) and "Pug" (Lord Ismay, Churchill's right-hand military man).[1]

According to journalist Mackenzie Porter, Stephenson surprised many famous guests by inviting them to visit a neighbour who turned out to be a local farmer with whom he chatted for hours. He also played host to scores of "obscure people" he met and liked during his travels. He sometimes hired local people to sing to his friends, and every Christmas he threw a party for between four and five hundred. In Jamaica, he provided funds for a new church in the neighbourhood. For many years, Stephenson rose each morning at five. Following the war, he reportedly ate like a bird and lost his taste for French wine. The couple maintained a house in Montreal, often vacationed on Prince Edward Island, read a lot and collected paintings and books.[2]

In 1951 the Stephensons sold their house in Jamaica, "Hillowton," to the Reynolds Aluminum Company, and they began living in New York.[3] The apartment took up an entire floor of the building. The Stephensons' neighbours above were the publisher of *Time* and *Life*, Henry Luce, and his wife, and below them lived the century's most famous recluse, Greta Garbo.

Later in 1951, Stephenson was appointed chairman of the Newfoundland and Labrador Corporation, a Crown company, by the new Canadian province's first premier, Joey Smallwood. He helped attract new industries and investment during 1952 to the tenth province, and his success was said to have "kept Joey Smallwood busy for the next three years." In October of 1952, Stephenson resigned as the chairman of the corporation because he thought it should have a local head. Newfoundland's premier accepted the resignation with reluctance and regret. "You achieved a magnificent result in a very short space of time, and I and the Government and people of Newfoundland must ever be grateful to you," Smallwood wrote.[4] He asked that Stephenson continue to act as Newfoundland's representative in the United States.

Stephenson later helped in organizing some of the financing for the huge Churchill Falls hydro development in Labrador, through his business contacts in Britain, notably Edmund de Rothschild.[5]

"He is a great Canadian and has done more than any other man to bring Canada's enormous potential to the notice of international investors," John Pepper was quoted as saying in a magazine story (1952). Pepper, who worked in Stephenson's inner office during the war, became one of the first presidents of the British American Canadian Corporation, and later Stephenson helped set him up in the Newfoundland pulp and paper business.

Stephenson was one of the originators and mainsprings of the British American Canadian Corporation, which changed its name to the World Commerce Corporation. The company, at 25 Broad Street, New York, tried using barter agreements and dollar guarantees to get around currency restrictions that slowed world trade. They also helped develop poorer countries. The *Christian Science Monitor* quoted an Italian businessman as saying: "If there were a hundred World Commerces there would be no need for the Marshall Plan." *Time* magazine reported that long before Truman called for the export of U.S. knowledge and capital to other nations of the world, "the same idea had occurred to a small forward-looking group of U.S., British and Canadian capitalists."

The company had its ups and downs. Many of the organizers were formerly in British Security Coordination or the American Office of Strategic Services. "The idea was to take advantage of the organization and international contacts that were set up during the war," Tom Hill remembered. "The goal was to set up various companies, mostly in Central and South America." David Ogilvy arranged business in the United States. George Merton, who eventually joined the CIA, organized South America, says Hill. The University of Manitoba graduate, who helped edit a western intelligence bulletin during the war, was the secretary, and believes he was asked to be involved because of his engineering background. Others joined, including Sir Charles Hambro (banker, former head of SOE), Russell Forgan (Glore Forgan group of bankers, successor to David Bruce as head of OSS Europe), Lester Armour (formerly OSS London), Sidney Weinberg, W. K. Eliscu (former OSS operatives) and Rex Benson (SIS). Nelson Rockefeller, J. J. McCloy, Richard Mellon and Sir Victor Sassoon also had an interest in the company. Joseph Grew, the ex-U.S. ambassador to Japan, Trans-America Corporation and Atlas Corporation were also said to be involved.[6]

The company didn't do too well. Frank Ryan became World Commerce head and Stephenson reportedly arranged contacts for him in London: Lord Leathers (wartime transportation minister); Sir William

Rootes (auto manufacturer); Richard Coit (stockbroker, who worked for SOE in North America); Sir Alexander Korda (film producer); Moir Mackenzie (Federation of British Industries); Lord Selborne (Economic Warfare Minister); Beaverbrook (from the newspaper business); Ian Fleming (British Naval Intelligence, Foreign Department head at Kemsley Press); Sir Campbell Stewart (director of the *Times*); Sir Ralph Glyn (politician and businessman); Fred Hudd (Canadian High Commissioner) and bankers such as Charles and Olaf Hambro. Later Ryan family interests, which were involved in international textiles, sold a controlling interest in the company and about two-thirds of the World Commerce staff were let go.[7] To expand WCC's political influence, former U.S. Secretary of State Edward Stettinius joined the company. "He brought with him a few people," Hill remembered, "Donovan was our lawyer, and ultimately the company wasn't doing well, and wasn't making a profit, so they brought in the bankers that put up the money." Hill eventually parted with the company and Stephenson arranged for him to move into the cement business.

Hill thought Stephenson was not too enthusiastic about the switch back to the business world. "He was drinking with Donovan at this point, but was able to rally around when needed."

One of the successes of WCC was helping bring a cement industry to Jamaica. Sir John Huggins, the governor of Jamaica, approached Stephenson for assistance, and he began a lengthy association with the Jamaican cement industry in the early 1950s. Before his involvement, all of Jamaica's cement was imported. Stephenson became the chair of the board of the Caribbean Cement Co. Limited, and Sir William Wiseman, the British Passport Control Officer during World War I, served on the board. In a speech Stephenson gave to shareholders in the spring of 1961, the company declared a profit of over £600,000, and he said that since 1952 the total savings to the country as a result of domestic production were over £3 million.[8] He remained involved with the cement industry for many years.[9]

During the sixties, he continued to be an active promoter of the Caribbean. In 1961 the cement plant began a large expansion and the *Kingston Daily Gleaner* headline September 28, 1961, proclaimed "SIR WILLIAM STEPHENSON BACKS JAMAICA." Later that year the paper reported on a Stephenson New York address in which he described the stable political climate in Jamaica following a referendum.[10]

The retired spychief also turned his attention to his home province. One of the main connections was through Derek Bedson, whom he met in the fifties when Bedson worked for Canada's Department of External Affairs at the United Nations. He and Stephenson met regularly, and Bedson visited Bermuda on numerous occasions. In the fall of 1953, Stephenson helped organize a New York agenda for Ron Turner, Manitoba's Minister of Industry and Commerce, when Turner was on an industrial development tour. Stephenson's assistance enabled Turner to meet with New York's top industrialists and investment people. Turner and the deputy minister later travelled with Hill to Britain, where Stephenson made sure doors were opened for them.

Soon afterwards Stephenson became the honorary chairman of Manitoba's economic advisory board, which helped funnel investment to the province. In December 1954, his position was formalized when he was named to the province's Economic Advisory Council. Stephenson got two Englishmen to join him on the board: Wiseman and Lord Semphill. Wiseman, formerly New York Passport Control, was the retired president of the investment bankers Kuhn Loeb. Semphill was the former chairman of the London Chamber of Commerce and involved in the British car industry and various technical bodies.[11] The group gave the Manitoba government accelerated access to the highest levels of world finance. "The very fact that he [Stephenson] agreed to have his name used working with the reconstruction period or anything of that kind would be very prestigious," Douglas Campbell, Manitoba's premier from 1950 to 1958, said later.[12]

In the early sixties, Stephenson suffered a serious stroke. It greatly affected his speech and slowed him down. His Bermuda doctor, Maurice Fulton, called the stroke a "devastating vascular accident," but with the constant help of his wife, Stephenson "fought back with as much tenacity and bravery as ever shown on the field of battle or the field of international espionage."[13] In the seventies Fulton was quoted as saying, "Sheer willpower has kept him going for the past quarter century."[14] Following the stroke, Stephenson and his wife left New York for good and retired to Bermuda for what has been described as "self-imposed exile."

Roald Dahl saw his former boss in New York before the move to Bermuda and was amazed at the stroke's effects and the deterioration of Stephenson's speech. The writer was impressed with the work of a British neurosurgeon, Kenneth Till, who had treated Dahl's son following a traffic accident, and Dahl recommended he visit Stephenson in Bermuda. It is not known whether Till's stay in Bermuda improved Stephenson's medical condition, but years later Dahl wrote to Stephenson to tell him the doctor was well. "I believe that some how his contact with you and the generosity you have shown towards his family has given him a tremendous boost," Dahl wrote.[15]

During the 1970s Stephenson continued to press for the development of tidal power, especially for power generation in the Bay of Fundy.[16]

In the early 1980s, Stephenson donated $100,000 to the University of Winnipeg, and through the auspices of the Winnipeg Foundation the capital is used to provide annual student scholarships. At the time, it was the largest amount of money that had ever been donated to the university. Ironically, the first person to win a scholarship was a Breckman, a great-great-nephew of Stephenson. In a roundabout way Stephenson returned to the community some of the money lent to him that launched his business career nearly six decades before.

One of Stephenson's good friends in later life was David Young, Air Canada's head in Bermuda from 1982 to 1986. Young brought Stephenson various Canadian newspapers about every two weeks, and he was introduced by Stephenson to visitors such as Canadian politician Eric Nielsen, the journalists General Richard Rohmer, Bill Stevenson and Peter Worthington, and Dr. Rodney Hunter from Winnipeg. Nielsen, the brother of actor Leslie Nielsen, was married in Stephenson's house.

Pauline McGibbon met Stephenson in the mid-1970s, while she was the Lieutenant Governor of Ontario. When she visited Bermuda, she heard that Stephenson would like to see her. "I would never have called on him myself, but I heard that he wanted to see me," McGibbon recalled. "It was one of those magic things when two people meet and they click." She returned to Bermuda every year.

By this time, Mary Stephenson was terminally ill with cancer. She was at their Paget, Bermuda, home but confined to her bedroom, and attended to by a full-time nurse, Elizabeth Baptiste. Mary died in 1977 and was buried in a private ceremony. Baptiste and her son Rhys remained in Bermuda and looked after Stephenson. In 1983, he adopted her as his daughter.

Stephenson long had a reputation for preparing hearty dry martinis. Some people (David Ogilvy, Tom Hill) believe he developed a drinking problem after the war, while others believe this wasn't the case. Excerpts of Noel Coward's diary indicate the actor-playwright imbibed while with Stephenson: "Lunched with Bill Stephenson," Coward wrote March 21, 1949, "Too many martinis. Slept in the afternoon. More martinis."[17] After the Stephensons moved from Jamaica, Coward saw them less often, and it appears Stephenson became disappointed with the post-war decade and world events of the time. "I lunched at long last with Bill Stephenson on Thursday," Coward wrote in 1956. "We reminisced about the war years and discoursed gloomily on the present crisis in the Middle East and Hungary. The world is so idiotic," Coward continued. "There is so much superstition, graft, greed and general stupidity that I cannot feel any impulses to do anything about it whatever, even if I could."[18]

Similar post-war sentiments are echoed by Stephenson in *A Man Called Intrepid*, in which he says, "'The springtime of our hope was 1945. If the world had fully grasped the essence of the devastating experience we'd survived, we might by now have dispensed with secret intelligence and stopped the creation of terrifying weapons.' He paused again, lost in thought ..."[19]

But Stephenson remained concerned with the future and seemed to keep in touch with modern developments "The farseeing James Schlesinger utters a word of warning with reference to danger of U.S. entering an era of neoisolationism," he cabled to William Stevenson. "It's dangerously bringing up to today the fear that Winston expressed in his book *Triumph and Tragedy*. 'And as the great democracies triumphed and so were able to resume the follies that so nearly cost them their life.'"[20]

Until late in life Stephenson had sources that could give him quick results of such things as political conventions before they were available through regular channels.[21] He frequently sent messages using his telex all over the world to people such as Louis Mountbatten, who apparently visited him in Bermuda in March 1975.[22] In the late sixties Stephenson may have still been involved in some type of intelligence activities. Thomas Troy, who was with the CIA at the time, says Stephenson wanted him to join "Olds," a line of communication that was monitoring activists.[23]

Apparently Stephenson's opinion was sought on Western intelligence and defence matters, and he received official visitors from Canada and the United States until his death. Reportedly he cabled the Israeli Prime Minister following the rescue of hostages from Entebbe, and he knew of the operation beforehand.[24]

Stephenson became disappointed at the turn of events in Washington during the early 1970s and thought Canada had the potential to fill the moral vacuum that paralyzed the American leadership. Cables of questions and answers dealing with preliminary work on *A Man Called Intrepid* with the author were interrupted by what Stephenson referred to as "tears over Washington telephones." At about the time of Richard Nixon's resignation (as a result of the Watergate scandal) Stephenson cabled to say:

WHAT A SAD DAY STOP THE WORLDWIDE ANSWER NOW LIES SQUARELY UPON THE STRONG SHOULDERS OF CANADA STOP THIS IS NOT THE SUGGESTION TO GRASP LEADERSHIP STOP IT IS THE MOMENT OF DECISION THAT ONLY A NATION WITH A REAL SOUL AND COMPLETE FLUORESCENCE OF PER ARDUA AD ASTRA COULD ABSORB OPEN ITS MIND WIDELY TO ENCOURAGE ENCOMPASS AND ACHIEVE ITS GREAT DESTINY STOP WELCOME YOUR VIEWS STOP. [25]

Stephenson's anti-fascist stance, his lobbying and brokering on behalf of both Britain and the U.S., his attempts at post-war reconstruction and assisting the developing world could only be described as internationalist in nature. Yet he remained patriotic toward Canada. In *Roosevelt and Hopkins*, Robert Sherwood wrote: "There was established by Roosevelt's order and despite State Department qualms, effectively close cooperation between J. Edgar Hoover and British Security Services under the direction of a quiet Canadian, William Stephenson." Stephenson later said he considered the simple designation of being a "quiet Canadian," a higher accolade than the British and American honours he won for his war work.[26] He made it the title of the first book about his espionage career.

A *Toronto Star* 1979 interview asked Stephenson if he felt "like the prophet who is without honour in his own land," as Britain, the U.S., France and Belgium had honoured him, but Canada had never recognized him with the Order of Canada or any other major honour. "My personal balance sheet with Canada is much in Canada's favour,"

Stephenson replied. "It does not bother me. I am too preoccupied with the fate of the whole Western world."

Instead Stephenson used the occasion to warn of the Soviet threat. The "cold warrior" told the reporter he thought Washington should be vigilant in the armaments race, and he quoted one military analyst who said, "There are tanks ready for action as far as the eye can see and what do we have? Without the neutron, they will plough through us as a knife through butter."[27] He also advocated that the best insurance against surprise was a close-knit, coordinated intelligence service that was continually on the alert in every part of the world and could report accurately and quickly.

But according to many of his contemporaries, the lack of recognition from his home country did bother Stephenson. In Canada's centennial year, 1967, the government created the Order of Canada in recognition of exceptional achievement in any field, and a quarter century after the conclusion of the war an informal campaign began to see that it was bestowed on Stephenson. Some of Stephenson's friends helped lobby politicians in Ottawa for the country's highest civilian honour, the Companion of the Order of Canada (CC).

In October 1972 journalist and writer William Stevenson drafted a letter to Canadian Prime Minister Lester Pearson outlining Stephenson's career.[28] Pearson died later that year so was in no position to lobby. (Pearson should have been well aware of Stephenson's career, as he acted as a BSC contact person in a number of spheres, and he became Canada's ambassador to the United States during the war.)

Over a year later, in December of 1973, Derek Bedson presented the case for Stephenson in Ottawa. The same month Peter Worthington wrote two columns in the Toronto *Sun* citing Stephenson's credentials for the award. In the second column he wrote, Stephenson should be honoured "not for Sir William's sake, but for Canada's."[29] Stephenson commented on the editorial afterwards in a cable to William Stevenson: "Perhaps some indication at long last CC may be forthcoming."[30]

Six months later Worthington wrote about "The Forgotten Canadian" and said Stephenson was "isolated, forgotten, ignored." He said the former intelligence head, although he resided in Bermuda, was still a Canadian citizen and "is proud of his nationality and goes about his business expressing neither dismay or rancour at being unrecognized in his own country."[31] A year later the *Sun* ran an editorial which said Stephenson's intelligence feats won the Battle of the Atlantic, and in August of 1975, Worthington wrote a column which stressed, "our survival today hinges on Stephenson's activities then."[32] No award for Stephenson was forthcoming from the government of Pierre Trudeau.

The shortlived Conservative government of Joe Clark finally presented Stephenson with the Order of Canada in 1980. Due to Stephenson's failing health, it was bestowed away from Canada for the first time. The then Governor General, Edward Schreyer, travelled to Bermuda, and Stephenson was named a Companion of the Order of Canada. Stephenson appears to have borne no grudges for the long delay. The cover of *A Man Called Intrepid* features a photograph of the numerous medals Stephenson was awarded from various countries. The front cover of *Intrepid's Last Case* depicts only one, his Order of Canada.

In September of 1983, Stephenson was awarded the William J. Donovan medal. It is bestowed on an individual who has rendered distinguished service in the interests of the democratic process and the cause of freedom by the veterans of the OSS. The presentation took place on the aircraft carrier *Intrepid*, which is permanently moored in New York. Stephenson appeared and spoke at the dinner, although at the time he was barely able to walk. U.S. president Ronald Reagan sent a letter for the occasion.

> *The White House*
> *Washington*
> *September 12, 1983*
> *Dear Sir William:*
>
> *I was delighted to hear through Bill Casey that you would be the recipient of the William J. Donovan Award. I can think of no person more deserving. What an extraordinary life you have led in the service of freedom. Your career through World War I, World War II, and the post-war years adds up to one of the great legends, one of the great stories of personal valour and sacrifice for the sake of country and fellow men.*
>
> *All those who love freedom owe you a debt of gratitude; but we, as Americans, are particularly grateful to you for all the warmth and friendship you have always shown to our nation. We want you to know that the friendship is reciprocated tenfold; and*

I want to assure you that as long as Americans value courage and freedom there will always be a special place in our hearts, our minds, and our history books for the 'Man Called Intrepid.'

Your accomplishments need little embellishment from me: they are your monument; they remain our inspiration. On behalf of the American people, I send you our warmest congratulations, our deepest gratitude, and our sincere wishes for many years of friendship and service together.

Sincerely,
Ronald Reagan

Despite his strong feeling for Canada, throughout his later years Stephenson remained completely separate from his relatives in Winnipeg. For the most part, they heard nothing from him since about 1935. Stephenson returned to Winnipeg for a final time privately in 1980 and stayed at the Fort Garry Hotel.[33] Derek Bedson drove him around his old Point Douglas neighbourhood, but news of his trip home came out only after he departed, and while in the city he looked up none of his relatives. A radio interviewer, years later, remarked to family members, "This is almost as mysterious as his life was. Why did he come to see his birthplace and not contact you people that he grew up with?"

That question is difficult to answer. "They'd be talking and he didn't want too many people knowing about it," Reg Rimmer replied. Rimmer, the husband of Stephenson's niece, believed there was no chance of seeing Stephenson in Bermuda, and Stephenson's relatives had false assumptions about his security on the island. According to Rimmer, "You'd have to get through the Mounted Police ring to get to him."[34] Bina Ingimundson, Stephenson's cousin, had similar opinions. She was under the impression Stephenson lived on a separate island, away from the main island of Bermuda, which "was guarded very closely. Nobody went to that island except by invitation. What he was afraid of, or whether he was afraid of something, I don't know. But there were guards there all the time. There was no way anyone would go to the island without being invited."[35]

Other relatives believe Stephenson moved to Bermuda for security reasons, although none of the family are sure where the information came from. "He was afraid of things that might happen to him, because of what he has done, you know, during the war. Being in the espionage and everything," Irv Stefansson said. "This is what is making us think that he's erased all of his past that he possibly could. That's what made us think that he didn't want anything to happen to anybody here because of his doing things ... I don't know. It's just a supposition."[36]

According to people who knew him after the war, the ex-spychief was concerned about his safety. Mackenzie Porter, the first journalist to interview Stephenson, thought the former espionage head was excessive in his anxiety about security. "I thought, oh, he's retired, he's out of it, he's finished. He's drinking heavily, this is some mistake. Some mistaken idea he's got. Some bug he's got in his mind. That's what I thought."[37]

Tom Hill, who knew Stephenson during and after the war, said, "I always thought the stuff about his paranoia for security after the war was a bit phony myself. It's one way of showing how important you are to people. At one point he went down to Jamaica and got the Managing Director to meet him at the airport with a gun, and so on. I don't think there was any threat to him at that point in history. I think he was merely trying to impress the MD, who would then pass it on to the other directors how important he was."

David Young, Stephenson's friend in later life, says he was very concerned about being assassinated. He often mentioned to Young how easy it could be, pointing out the case of the Bulgarian who was killed in London by poison injected from an umbrella tip.[38] Stephenson covertly visited a Toronto hospital in the 1970s for his wife Mary's cancer treatment. According to Dr. Philip Hall, who was working at the Toronto hospital at the time, there was security with the ex-spy chief — "a big burly fellow."[39]

Any information about Stephenson's security concerns that filtered back to Winnipeg possibly came through Lillian Stephenson, his stepbrother Mindy's widow. Stephenson's sister-in-law was able to contact him. According to Lillian's son Gerald, Stephenson secretly visited Winnipeg in 1944 en route to elsewhere. Lillian Stephenson died in 1989, soon after Stephenson, and her son doesn't recall her opinion of Stephenson's low profile and the phony backgrounds in his biographies. Ironically the only record the family has expresses concern about publicity Stephenson had received.

608 Fifth Avenue
Suite 607
New York
January 14 1955
Dear Lillian,

We have just returned here from Washington. This is a brief note to acknowledge your nice card and to reciprocate your good wishes. I agree with you that there has been a lot of publicity and as much as I dislike publicity, I am afraid it is an inevitable consequence of agreeing to assist the province in development.

There was only one article that was irritating and inaccurate in the FP [Winnipeg Free Press]. You will know the one to which I refer. I hope to get settled long enough in one spot in order to catch up on personal correspondence more fully. I will write to you at greater length. Love and best wishes to you both.

Yours, Bill

Derek Bedson said Lillian once got in touch with him before he was travelling to Bermuda to visit Stephenson. "I was going down there. I don't know how she knew."[40]

If Lillian had a way to contact Stephenson, no other relatives could. A cousin, Margaret Mack (nee Breckman) visited Bermuda and tried to see him, but was told she couldn't. Irv Stefansson, the son of Stephenson's cousin, was surprised that media people such as Winnipeg radio talk show host Peter Warren could contact Stephenson "and we could never seem to get through. My mom sent a birthday card because she knew when his birthday was, and it was returned."[41]

Following the publication of *A Man Called Intrepid*, the author William Stevenson was in Winnipeg and appeared as a guest on a radio talk show in the spring of 1977. Stephenson knew of the broadcast and requested a transcript of the Eric St. John show be sent to him in Bermuda. He was perhaps seeing what the reaction was in his hometown to the phony Winnipeg background depicted in the book. There was little other publicity of the author's trip to Stephenson's old stomping grounds. "I did not see an article about him in the paper though, as was expected," wrote the show's producer Carolyn Rickey.[42]

It is difficult to deduce the raison d'etre of such a private person. Two biographers of the man didn't even find out his parents' names.

Bedson, a friend for over thirty years, knew nothing of Stephenson's Winnipeg background, and had little idea about the espionage work that made his friend so famous.

The public account of Stephenson's life records only one major speech. It was organized by a press friend, Charles Vining, for a May 31, 1954, presentation to the Periodical Press Association in Toronto.

Stephenson's address was entitled "The First Line of Defence." In it he says the first true line of defence is information. He talks about the importance of intelligence services and gives examples. Napoleon, he said, was long regarded as a military genius and of having mysterious foresight. But historical research debunked the intuition idea and revealed he had good political intelligence and even had agents on the enemy staff. "You will recall that Hitler was supposed to have miraculous intuition," Stephenson's speech continued. He also talked of the value of code breaking during the war and of the fear of the unknown. Fear of the unknown or the incomprehensible doesn't always produce a sense of panic in an individual, Stephenson said. Quite often it produces the opposite: apathy.

Not all of the speech to the Periodical Association was published in the media, but in the files of William Stevenson is a draft of the conclusion of his speech. In it, Stephenson talks of his love of his home country, and in a way, he echoes the thoughts of two of his pre-war contemporaries, H. G. Wells and George Bernard Shaw.[43] Stephenson wrote:

> To my regret, circumstances have kept me in other lands for more years of my life than I have spent in Canada but it may be this condition of exile has given me a sharpened appreciation of the good fortune one has in being Canadian and of what our country can mean to all mankind. In her institutions of law and order with freedom, in the character of her people, in the great endowment with which providence has blessed her.
>
> In a troubled world, Canadians have increasing reason to be proud and thankful. We also have increasing reason to recognize the obligations and responsibilities which are meant to accompany good fortune, whether of men, or nations. Of these things I have become more and more aware with the passage of time.
>
> I have no patience with those who seem to look upon the scientific age of our 20th century as a kind of Greek tragedy, catching all mankind in an inexorable finale of doom and destruction.

[He concluded his speech by talking about his convictions.]

We Canadians have not the habit of speaking easily with each other about divine providence and the human soul, although I have heard in this respect one does not need to feel quite as diffident in the city of Toronto as in certain other communities. At any rate, putting diffidence aside, I beg to give you my belief that the most powerful force in the world remains what it has always been: the human soul attached by faith to its creator.

I have faith in providence. I believe with Churchill that "the destiny of mankind is not settled by material computation." I also believe that faith must be practical. That to receive the help of providence man must so conduct and exert himself as to deserve and earn that help.

Stephenson died January 31, 1989. He was buried in Bermuda in a secret ceremony at St. John's Church. According to his wishes, his funeral took place before his death was made public. He told his adopted daughter Elizabeth, "I don't want people to know that I am dead until I am buried."[44] Some local police acted as pallbearers. There was only a handful of people at his funeral. Elizabeth, his adopted daughter and her son Rhys, Stephenson's doctor, his physiotherapist and Manitoba-born undertaker Brian Graham. The media reported he had no family in Winnipeg.[45]

Conversations

George Johnson, former Lieutenant Governor of Manitoba
"And I said to Derek [Bedson]. You know if you're talking to Sir William. Tell him I've heard these stories of his origin, and I know the Breckmans and Stefannsons. And three days before he died, I got an acknowledgment thanking me for my greeting."

II

Out of the Shadows

"The Truth is never pure and rarely simple."
— Oscar Wilde

10 "A MYSTERIOUS MILLIONAIRE"

Although Stephenson's achievements during the war appear considerable, decades later his accomplishments were ridiculed. Following his death he was tagged the "Spymaster who wasn't," "an Intrepid Fraud," and "from start to finish a liar." However, the criticisms are not based on research or interviews, but on the books that were written about Stephenson, especially *A Man Called Intrepid*. Stephenson's public persona became defined by a few articles, books and reviews, which warrant closer examination.

The first details of Bill Stephenson's espionage career became public in a 1952 feature story in the Canadian magazine *Maclean's*. It was written by British-born writer Mackenzie Porter, who learned of Stephenson during the war and initiated the story. "I found out where he lived and got at him," the retired writer, now living in Toronto, remembered.[1]

Stephenson was wary of reporters and publicity in general, Porter says. Before the interview was arranged, he contacted the journalist a number of times for personal information and references. Porter said to him, "Well, one guy I know that you know, is Ian Fleming." Prior to the war, Porter worked for the British paper *The Daily Sketch*, and during the last two years of the conflict he was with the Political Warfare Executive (PWE) in Rome, Athens and Vienna. After completing his PWE work, Fleming was one of Porter's editors, and eventually the writer moved to Canada and started working for *Maclean's* magazine.

Stephenson contacted Fleming about Porter and received a long telegram in response. Later he showed Porter the biographical information on him. Fleming's report concluded "Mackenzie Porter is a good second-class journalist." "I never quite forgave Fleming for that," Porter said.

The *Maclean's* interview took place at Stephenson's New York apartment on East 52nd Street, and pictures were taken by *Maclean's* photographer Ronnie Jacques. The accompanying photograph of Stephenson on his balcony, with the United Nations in the background, is one of the few pictures of Stephenson publicly released. Porter also talked to some of BSC's former secretarial staff in Toronto and New York, Ernest Cuneo and Tommy Drew-Brook. Cuneo is quoted in the story as saying Stephenson was the only man who had the unqualified support of both Franklin Roosevelt and Winston Churchill, which later became a point of contention for some historians. "If I said Cuneo said that, Cuneo said it," Porter emphasized.

The Biggest Private Eye of All appeared in the December 1, 1952, edition of *Maclean's* and revealed for the first time some of the exploits of a "mysterious millionaire from Winnipeg." The article opened:

> This is about a mysterious middle-aged Canadian millionaire who during the Second World War became the mastermind of British intelligence throughout the Americas. His New York staff of more than a thousand handpicked Canadian men and women spoke of his doorkeeper as "Peter," of his secretary as "Gabrielle" and of him as "God." Only a handful of them knew him by sight.[2]

So began the public story of William Stephenson and British Security Coordination. The article credited BSC with training hundreds of Canadian and American parachutists for jumps into occupied Europe, helping to detect enemy submarines by pinpointing their radio signals, delaying Hitler's attack on Russia by six weeks with a few calculated indiscretions; neutralizing a vast Nazi sabotage ring in Central America; contributing to the smashing of dummy corporations and helping to sustain the American faith in British victory after Dunkirk. The article also marvelled at Stephenson's observation skills and his speed-reading ability.

The narrative concluded by mentioning that although Stephenson received a knighthood for his war service, he was more proud of the fact that it was conveyed by Churchill himself, with a written comment beside his name. The note was "in green Churchillian ink on a list of candidates of honours that was submitted to George the Sixth. It read 'this one is dear to my heart.'" Porter remembers seeing the document. "I saw that, yes," he said, "I'm sure he showed it to me — that note from Churchill."

In Manitoba, people who befriended Stephenson in his childhood and relatives read the story of long-lost Bill with great interest. At least one contacted *Maclean's* to obtain his address, but early the next year was told it could not be given out for security reasons. "It is probably a safe assumption to conclude that even eight years after the war it was discreet for Sir William to be cautious. Even in times of peace, life can be endangered through the actions of revengeful self-appointed assassins," W. J. Lindal later wrote.[3]

No letters from Manitoba relatives were published by the magazine; in fact, no letters to the editor at all were published about the Stephenson revelations. It later was written that this was an indication there was little interest in the piece, as most long articles for the magazine received a few letters.[4] However Porter says he received good response to the story and wished to pursue it further. It is possible Stephenson had some influence internally at the magazine, and public discussion was suppressed. Napier Moore, the managing editor of *Maclean's* for nearly twenty years, often commented on intelligence affairs in the fifties.[5] His wife, Marjorie Noble, worked for Stephenson during the war.[6]

Following the publication of the *Maclean's* story, Porter wanted to write a book about the spychief and BSC, and Stephenson indicated a book might be possible, but later he refused to give the go-ahead. Porter called New York twice about a future publication, but Stephenson said, "I'm afraid something has happened and we can't go into the book at this time."[7]

The Quiet Canadian

By the end of the decade Stephenson was interested in having a history of BSC written, but he chose a professional intelligence officer and colleague to write it. The actual motives behind the publication of *The Quiet Canadian* (1962) are difficult to establish. Preliminary work on the book was done by Charles Howard (Dick) Ellis, an Australian and an employee of the British service, who worked for Stephenson during the war. Ellis, one of the founding members of British Security Coordination, was awarded the U.S. Medal of Merit for his valuable help in the establishment of the OSS. Following his death, Ellis was publicly accused of being a German spy, and possibly a Soviet spy as well, by the British journalist Chapman Pincher and others.[8] The start of *The Quiet Canadian* project can be traced to an August 24, 1959, letter from Stephenson to Ellis.[9] In it Stephenson thanked the Australian for a previous letter and a copy of *Soviet Affairs*, and wrote that he was impressed with the amount of research the various articles entailed. "If you spent this kind of effort on doing a sort of 'journalist' history of 'our' war you would be adding constructively to historical records," Stephenson wrote. He proposed to pay Ellis for his expenses and then be reimbursed from the profits of the book. In the same letter, Stephenson said that *Time-Life* chief Henry Luce at one time offered him a $100,000-plus advance to tell his story, and that Mackenzie Porter offered him the first $30,000 of royalties of his book. (Porter doesn't remember discussing the figure of $30,000. "I just said I think I could make some money if you'd let me write the book," Porter said. "And I was ahead of anybody else on the research.")[10] Stephenson added at the conclusion of his letter to Ellis, "Bob Sherwood said once : When the story of BSC and related activities comes to be written it should be titled *The Quiet Canadian* as I was described in his book, *Roosevelt and Hopkins.*"

Stephenson gave Ellis access to his records and helped with the draft, but he apparently was unhappy with Ellis' literary effort. According to Ellis' letters in the files of Harford Montgomery Hyde, Stephenson was "for an all-out attack on various people and a *succès de scandale*" and he criticized Ellis' draft because it lacked "ginger."[11] "Dick Ellis was not the sort of a chap to write a red-blooded book at all," according to colleague and former BSC member Bill Ross Smith. Ellis wrote in a dull "governmentalese," Ross Smith recalled.[12] (Ellis' working book title appears to have been *Anglo-American Collaboration in Intelligence and Security: Notes for Documentation.*)[13] Eventually work on the book was passed to Harford Montgomery Hyde, who was teaching in Asia at the time.

Hyde was a politician, lawyer, former intelligence officer and historian who also previously worked for BSC. He was the son of a Belfast magistrate and was called to the bar himself in 1934. Later he lectured in history at Oxford, and he became a private secretary to Lord Londonderry.[14] When the war started in 1939, Hyde was commissioned in the Signal Corps and was an assistant censor at Gibraltar. He became a military liaison and censorship security officer in Bermuda and then worked for Stephenson's British Security Coordination as "assistant Passport Control Officer." In 1944 he was transferred to the Supreme Headquarters with the Allied Expeditionary Force. Following the war he did legal work for the Alexander Korda group of film companies, wrote, and became an Ulster Unionist member of parliament. When Stephenson contacted him about a possible book, Hyde was a history professor at Punjab University in Lahore, Pakistan.[15]

The Quiet Canadian was released with much fanfare and was syndicated in numerous newspapers around the world, including the *Sunday Times* in Britain and *Weekend Magazine* in Canada. Revelations in the book became news carried by the major news wires. Ian Fleming wrote a long preface to accompany the syndicated *Times* stories and a rendition of it was printed in the American version of *The Quiet Canadian*, which was called *Room 3603*.[16] Publicity for the book in the United States drew comparisons between Stephenson and Fleming's famous creation, James Bond. Newspaper advertisements read, "Ian Fleming says: James Bond is a highly romanticized version of a true spy. The real thing, the man who became one of the great agents of the last war, is William Stephenson."[17]

After the release of *The Quiet Canadian*, there was a desire to publicize the BSC story further in film or television, but all attempts were quashed by Stephenson and his wife. Following the publication of the book, Ellis wrote to Hyde that Stephenson reportedly was alarmed at having entered the public domain as a result of the book, "and seems to want to hide himself."[18] A May 1963 letter from Hyde's agent, International Literary Management, to Hyde conveyed the sentiments of a Claire Degener in the United States. "I certainly think Cary Grant is a good idea to play Stevenson [sic] but it is insane to go to any major star until we have a much clearer picture of specifically what would induce Stevenson [sic] to a release. Frankly I could have sold the book thirty times in the last two weeks and my heart is broken for Hyde." Degener wanted to approach Alfred Hitchcock as producer.[19] Later

Mary Stephenson cabled Hyde to urge a television program about Stephenson *not* be done and Stephenson refused to have the book reprinted after the first edition was sold.[20]

Hyde did not become wealthy as a result of the book. He was paid a £600 advance for expense money to write it, but the professorship he left in Lahore paid him £3,000 annually and it cost him £800 to move from there. To complicate his finances more, he was supporting his mother, who was bedridden in Ireland. In July of 1963, after the release of the book, Hyde wrote to Stephenson and asked if he could repay the advance money gradually.[21]

Later Ellis approached Hyde for a portion of *The Quiet Canadian* royalties money, but Hyde felt no obligation to pay him as he didn't use the Ellis draft. From letters in Hyde's file, it appears Ellis did offer some advice. In one letter Ellis urged Hyde to stress that "Anglo-American cooperation was a wartime development." He said to emphasize in the book that "not everything was started by Stephenson," and that the U.S. was bound by the neutrality act. To write otherwise "... simply plays into the hands of those elements who consider that the U.S. was seduced and lead astray by FDR and the Limeys in 1940."[22]

Ellis' financial difficulties were possibly compounded as a result of the publication of *The Quiet Canadian* and its revelations. Ian Fleming wrote in the *Sunday Times* (and in the introduction to *Room 3603*) that it was "the first book, so far as I know, about the British secret agent whose publication has received official blessing."[23] However, this does not seem to be the case. There are clear indications that British intelligence circles were upset over the publication of the book, and Ellis was removed from his intelligence work because he was connected to it. In January 1963, Ellis wrote to Hyde, "The flap has died down here but I gather 'C' (chief of intelligence) is still sore, and the F.O. (Foreign Office) show no signs of reinstating me in the IRD (Intelligence Research Department) job."[24] Hyde, in a letter to Stephenson, reiterated that Ellis' trouble was a result of the book project. He said it was because he listed Ellis' help in the acknowledgements of *The Quiet Canadian*, which was "a normal courtesy." It "got him into hot water at Broadway, not to mention the F.O., and he lost one of the jobs he was doing for them."[25] Other letters in Hyde's files at Cambridge indicate the confusion was because MI6 vetted Ellis' version of BSC's activities, but not Hyde's more detailed account.[26]

Although Hyde is said to have had access to Stephenson's files, the ex-spychief didn't help fill in details of his personal life. Hyde corresponded with Stephenson's friend Tommy Drew-Brook to receive more information. Drew-Brook wrote back, "He tells me that in his opinion, McKenzie Porter's summary of his business career is quite sufficient."[27] Hyde's available papers at Churchill College, Cambridge, have little information on Stephenson's early life, and according to Montgomery Hyde's widow, Rosalind, the biographer was unaware that Stephenson's Canadian background was fictitious.[28] For some reason, perhaps related to concealing his Icelandic Canadian roots, in March 1963 Stephenson cabled Hyde to try and halt the publication of *The Quiet Canadian* in Iceland.[29] Hyde cabled back to say the rights were a normal course of events handled by his British publisher and he could be sued for breach of contract if he didn't follow through. Hyde wondered why Stephenson objected to an English edition released in Iceland, and he replied, "There is a comie [sic] plot to handle publication and use that hotbed Reykjavik as a base to discredit us and create unfriendly relations [with] Sweden and the whole of Scandinavia through Olason ... I am beginning to regret the whole thing."[30] Some of Stephenson's critics have used this cable as evidence that Stephenson was fantasizing and he "had impaired judgment."[31]

Why did Stephenson decide a book was possible in the late 1950s, and not earlier? In a 1959 letter to Ellis, Stephenson says, "The whole story is far enough behind us to be told fairly completely," but they would "have to talk about the OSA (Official Secrets Act) aspect."[32] Stephenson was also quoted as saying he was reticent because of the possibility "the last war may not be the final one."[33] It has also been suggested that the publication of *The Quiet Canadian* was part of a Cold War propaganda campaign. In the introduction to *A Man Called Intrepid*, Dick Ellis indicates that the release of *The Quiet Canadian* was related to the defection of Soviet double agent Kim Philby. Philby knew of BSC's existence, but "was not aware of the full and far-reaching purpose of Intrepid's organization. Thus, just enough of the truth was revealed for publication to blunt the effect of any disclosures that Philby or his supporters might reveal."[34]

Before that book was released in 1976, Stephenson, in a telegram (October 20, 1975) to the author William Stevenson, commented on the Ellis passage and said the release of *The Quiet Canadian* "had nothing to do with Philby or general vetting."[35] Hyde, later quoted by the writer John Le Carré in February 1976, said if *The Quiet Canadian* was simply "sand in the Russian eyes," it was without his knowledge, and the biography had started with Stephenson.[36] Following Hyde's comments, printed in the *New York Times*, Stephenson cabled Hyde and told him to "not allow himself to be quoted stupidly by scribblers," and express "derogatory views on subjects far removed from the serious work they know nothing about."[37]

Indirectly it is possible the release of *The Quiet Canadian* might have had something to do with the defection of Kim Philby and/or boosting morale of Western security services. According to some reports, "The entire community of BSC operatives were amazed Hyde had been able to write this book ... given the security that then existed and still exists now."[38] The full extent of the damage Philby caused to Western intelligence operations will probably never be known. He nearly rose to be the head of MI6 in Britain, and he also spent a great deal of his career in the United States, liaising with the FBI and CIA. Philby first came under suspicion following the 1951 defection of Anthony Burgess and Donald Maclean, and pressure on MI6 from the Americans led to his recall from his Washington posting. In the 1950s Philby was asked to resign from the Foreign Office and was sent to Beirut to work as a journalist for the *Observer* and the *Economist*. He disappeared in January 1963, apparently after he received news from Moscow there was a CIA hit man on his trail.[39] According to Robert Ducas, who was with the *London Times* when investigative work on the Philby case was done in the late sixties, Philby knew who every CIA operative in Europe was. This provided the agency with the ultimate conundrum for their European operations. "They had to decide whether to forget the whole thing, or start again," said Ducas.[40]

When viewed in the time perspective of Philby, the shooting down of U-2 pilot Francis Gary Powers, and the Profumo affair, it is plausible that a positive story about Western intelligence services would not be regarded as a negative. Whether or not *The Quiet Canadian* was related to that realm is a point of conjecture. Recently it has been revealed that the publishing of *The Quiet Canadian* caused "a tumultuous uproar" behind the scenes in various intelligence communities, as it was much too candid.[41] A classified CIA review concluded, "The publication of this study is shocking."[42]

Stephenson's career was again in the public eye in the late 1960s when Shaun Herron, an Irish journalist and novelist who worked for Stephenson during the war, put together a radio series for the Canadian Broadcasting Corporation, *The Great Canadian Spy*. According to Herron, upon hearing Stephenson was about to retire from espionage, Churchill remarked, "The eagles have flown. Now the vultures will take over."

"I hope this book will be published as soon as practicable. I say this particularly in view of the long investigations that have been in process and promise to last indefinitely, of the operations of the CIA. The truth is that only a small fraction of the public or indeed of those who are vocal on this subject have any idea of the importance of clandestine operations."

—David Bruce (former OSS London) to Julian Muller
(A Man Called Intrepid editor)[1]

If there was the possibility of Cold War intrigue or espionage public relations involved with *The Quiet Canadian*, that likelihood was magnified with the release in 1976 of *A Man Called Intrepid*. It, too, began as a project by Dick Ellis, but the task was passed to British-born journalist William Stevenson.

Ellis, obviously using some of his previous material, began a new undertaking in the late sixties, and added to his draft. He contacted Colin Gubbins, the former head of SOE, in August of 1972 about assistance with a Foreword for his book about the Stephenson organization. Gubbins replied:

I am glad to hear you have written a book on the Stephenson-Donovan collaboration — on the vital role that Bill Stephenson played in the very highest quarters — at the top level in fact in the

Downing Street/White House "affaire" which led to such splendid results ... I moved only rarely in the rarefied atmosphere of the top circles where the two Bills had their common stomping ground but Bill Stephenson's slightest wish to me is more than a command.[2]

Gubbins concluded his letter: "I remember well your own very distinguished record 'in the Service.'"[3]

Soon afterwards it seems the Ellis book project was curtailed, but this time it wasn't because of the Australian's lack of literary flair. On September 11, 1972, Stephenson cabled Stevenson about "Dick." "His electrical potential has turned from positive to negative like an overdrawn battery by reason of the unconcerned Dracula."[4]

At about the same time British intelligence writer Chapman Pincher reports "an international authority on intelligence and defence affairs" heard negative reports about Ellis. The individual, who wished to remain anonymous, was involved in the setting up of "Interdoc, the International Documentary Center, an organization involving intelligence affairs." Interdoc wanted a London representative, and Ellis had taken on the job, but the appointment quickly came under fire from British intelligence. "In the early 1970s," wrote Pincher, "a representative of the Secret Service called on my informant (the anonymous expert) to ask if he had been responsible for recommending Ellis, because he was known to have been a spy for Germany and was suspected of being a Soviet agent too."[5]

Although, obviously, it is difficult to ascertain the validity of the accusations against Ellis, it does appear that each time he attempted to publicize the war work of William Stephenson, it didn't add to his job security. Ironically, if Ellis' imposed unemployment was meant as a punishment for selling out to the "enemy," it seemed to make him more vulnerable to foreign overtures. Ellis' trouble with his British employers — perhaps even losing his pension — made him more dependent monetarily on others. Ellis went to Stephenson for financial assistance, and when Ellis died he owed Stephenson a large amount of money.[6]

At approximately the same time, William Stevenson was conducting a number of television interviews relating to British Security Coordination. The work on the new BSC volume was eventually turned over to Stevenson. Born in London in 1925, Stevenson apparently served in the RAF during the war, and later became a journalist.

One book review says the author was Stephenson's assistant director of operations during the war, but this is not the case.[7] (As the writer was 15 when Stephenson received his New York appointment, his lofty stature in the organization is somewhat surprising — even apparently to Stephenson.)[8] His early journalistic background was similar to Mackenzie Porter. Stevenson "first received a taste for international intrigue while working for the Kemsley newspapers of London, under Ian Fleming," and he worked as a journalist in China, Africa, Canada and Bermuda.[9] At some point Stevenson became a naturalized Canadian, although this is not always indicated in his books. The jacket of his 1986 novel *Eclipse* says he "was born and bred in England" and lives in Washington.

Prior to *A Man Called Intrepid* (*AMCI*) Stevenson did two books about the Israeli military. He apparently knew fighting would start before the Six Day War took place in 1967, and he wrote *Strike Zion* soon afterwards.[10] In 1970 he wrote *Zanek!: A Chronicle of the Israeli Air Force*, with the assistance of the IAF. At the time of the *Intrepid* research, Stevenson had recently finished a book on the mysterious Nazi, Martin Bormann. Stevenson's *The Bormann Brotherhood* is dedicated, "For Intrepid". In the early seventies, he worked on a television documentary, *A Man Called Intrepid*, about Stephenson and BSC for the Canadian Broadcasting Corporation. The author-journalist refers to the *Sunday Best* documentary's interviews as the genesis of his book research. However, although the author's voice can be heard on the tape asking questions, and he can be seen in some of the interviews, nowhere in the documentary or the credits does his name appear.

From a perusal of Stevenson's papers at the University of Regina one could draw many curious conclusions about a symbiotic relationship between certain journalists and intelligence work. Amongst Stevenson's files are newspaper clippings he collected from the *New York Times* (February 18, 1976, and others) concerning revelations that newsmen were used as stringers for the CIA.[11] In 1975 he wrote to Stephenson in Bermuda explaining what he thought the *Observer's* merits were to Britain's Foreign Office. The newspaper's value "has been that it could air some of the more trendy liberal notions and win over a few influential friends in the Third World, while extracting information not for publication. But the awful fiasco with Kim Philby has made this an even more delicate operation than ever."[12] (Philby was working for the *Observer* in the Middle East.)

From reading his letters, there are a few indications that Stevenson may have been more than a casual chronicler of the cloak-and-dagger business. He said, in a letter to Stephenson, that while he was working in Zanzibar, Tanzania, he was "watching Kao Liang, the chief of Chinese intelligence in Africa and a guy I got the Indian government to expel three years earlier."[13] The Soviet defector Igor Gouzenko was an acquaintance of Stevenson's, and he kept Stephenson informed of his well-being. Gouzenko, in one Toronto meeting with the writer, complained about his treatment in the West, and this reminded Stevenson of similar treatment accorded a Chinese defector who was convinced to come to Britain. "His [Gouzenko's] chief argument is that if the West treats people like himself in the way it does, few will ever come over from the Soviet side. I know that to be true too, because we coaxed a chap out of China and having emptied out on the floor, shaken all the value out of his skull, we let him fend for himself in England on the basis that letting him live there was largesse enough. The poor fellow ... ekes out a beggarly existence without help."[14]

In the summer of 1975, Stevenson wrote to Stephenson that the *Intrepid* book could act as a springboard for his career from journalist to writer, but he didn't seem to have Hemingway's literary aspirations. "I want to make it absolutely clear that I do not depend on AMCI for financial survival, but that I do feel it opens the way to full-time writing, which I've not been able to do hitherto, and gives the opportunity to launch a counter-attack against communist and other subversive elements in the best way I know." In his correspondence Stevenson frequently brought up a perceived Soviet threat, and it is clear he was no fan of Soviet socialism. In *AMCI* he frequently transposes historical references somewhat incongruously into views on the Soviet Union.[15] The Chinese were also discussed in Stevenson's consultations with Stephenson. In a letter from the summer of 1975, the journalist thanks Stephenson for his support with his writing project. He continues: "When we lived in Asia, the Chinese Communists mounted a campaign through dupes to discredit me, and succeeded in getting me transferred to India. It's a long story but I mention these examples to reassure you about my very keen awareness of how these bastards work. I told you a long time ago that I had a tough fight on my hands and needed your support and you have responded magnificently."[16]

When asked if William Stevenson, journalist, had any background in "intelligence" work, one of his friends laughed and replied, "That's for you to dig into." He then added, "But I'll be surprised if you get that out of him."[17] As this tome is not a biography of William Stevenson, I am content to leave it at that.

Much of *AMCI* appears to have been written with the author in Toronto and the subject in Bermuda. There were numerous cables and letters between the two, which seem to show Stephenson did not know what was being written about him, and he disagreed with some passages he was shown.

Before the book was published, the writer consulted a number of people about its progress. By June of 1974, an early draft of *AMCI* was complete and Stevenson wrote to then publisher and editor-in-chief of the *Globe and Mail*, R. S. Malone, and informed him about the book. Stevenson told him he was discussing the draft with the people "directly concerned — Julian Muller who runs the trade department, and Oscar Dystel who is the president of Bantam books. Both are former intelligence officers...The publisher in London is Robin Denniston of Weidenfeld and Nicolson whose father was Alistair Denniston, the chief of Bletchley Park wartime coding etc... Much of the basic material has come from Washington and London (the CIA historian and War Cabinet diaries, for instance)." Later in the letter he says, "I may continue on from New York next week with a copy of the MSS for Sir William, depending on publishing schedules."[18]

Stevenson also contacted David Ogilvy, a former BSC employee and later an advertising mogul. Ogilvy seemed less than gung ho about Stevenson's book project. Replying to Ogilvy's concerns with the book, Stevenson wrote that he had "no wish to embarrass anyone [in the book] and do not think this is possible." Stevenson said he would use restraint in *AMCI* and could "see no way to overstate Bill's achievements. I agree Bill needs no overstated tributes." Stevenson emphasized he was receiving guidance from a number of people who had an understanding of the situation. "My publisher was with me all day yesterday discussing the first draft," he wrote to Ogilvy. "He is a former U.S. Navy intelligence officer with a tremendous admiration for everything British, and I have to restrain him ... Let me repeat that nobody [is] named in the current book who as a result would suffer embarrassment. The last difficult task of this nature was a book about the Israeli air force which placed me under the most stifling security wraps

— I survived ... I don't see how the OSA [Official Secrets Act] limits me, since my sources are documents in the public domain and men and women who have been told what can or cannot be said."[19]

A Man Called Intrepid apparently cleared more editorial hurdles than most biographies. On October 9, 1975, Stevenson wrote, "All the security people who've read this are pleased by the spiking of Kim Philby's guns ... It should be emphasized that *AMCI* has been so thoroughly vetted now that it's clean as a whistle — including the formidable lawyers on both sides of the Atlantic and sundry gentlemen of the famous bureaucracies."[20] It seems somewhat peculiar if the book was thoroughly vetted that the Dick Ellis foreword was printed. Ellis was, according to unsubstantiated reports, a known treacherous double agent by this time. It seems Stephenson did not even want the Ellis passage used, and he requested that a passage from Colin Gubbins or Ernie Cuneo be in the book. The writer responded by saying comments by the two Stephenson contemporaries were based on earlier information on *AMCI* and "had not been approved in connection to the final version of *AMCI*. The situation a year ago was we had a book more limited in scope." One might have assumed that if the book dealt with the war career of William Stephenson, his associates' comments wouldn't become obsolete or irrelevant because of changes in the book.

Later Stephenson sent the author a telegram saying, "DICK MARGARINE [Butterfield, a friend and business associate] BEGGED ME TO PASS TO YOU IN ALL SERIOUSNESS HIS SUGGESTION THAT YOU INSERT THE [David] BRUCE LETTER IN PLACE OF ELLIS IN THE SAME PART OF THE BOOK STOP. I AGREED ..."[21] Yet it is the Ellis passage that appears in the book.

The book is not footnoted and it contains a number of reconstructed conversations. Following its publication, there was a great deal of controversy in some quarters, due in part perhaps to the style and depiction of events in *AMCI*. Stevenson's book *Zanek!* contains narration from a stranger called "S" who could be in several places at once watching and listening and who could bring together several incidents that occurred on one day. "'S' could create one character out of several men whose identities had to be protected for security reasons."[22]

Stevenson's approach to *AMCI* seems similar, as the spychief seems to turn up almost everywhere. Surprisingly, he was even waiting in a desolate Scottish field one night to greet the Danish atom scientist, Niels

Bohr, after he was smuggled there in a bomb bay of a plane on a secret flight from Sweden.[23] As the chief of a huge organization based in North America, one wonders how Stephenson found the time to loiter in Scottish fields waiting for secret night flights. Did he have nothing better to do? Many point to such instances to ridicule Stephenson, and to question his honesty or mental stability.

There are references by Stephenson to the Bohr incident in Stevenson's files at the University of Regina, but nowhere does he say he waited for him in a field.[24] At some point the Bohr story was changed. Why and by whom?

In a June 4, 1973, letter to Stephenson, the writer tells him, "You have a natural role at the heart of the story and it should be told through your eyes. *This does not mean of course quoting you* [italics mine]. It means simply the main events between Dunkirk and Pearl [the chronological length of the original book draft] are recounted in relation to your activities. This requires that I reconstruct these events in the well-tried manner of other recorders of recent history ..." And, "I may have to bother you with some further questions."[25] More than a year later, after a draft of the book was complete and sent to his editor, Julian Muller, Stevenson wrote to Stephenson saying, "Julian is entirely in sympathy with the philosophical thrust of the book but wishes there were more anecdotes. He feels the density of the material demands lighter touches ... *The second look is my responsibility* ... It means scissors and paste, rejigging actions, writing tighter historical bits, *keeping you in the middle of events* ... Julian's original estimate of six weeks more work has been revised downward [italics mine]. He thinks two weeks more work by myself [working flat out that is]."[26]

Countless critics of *AMCI*, even former BSC employees, have surmised Stephenson was hallucinating about some of the escapades in Stevenson's tome. "... Stephenson is quoted verbatim as though an eyewitness. Sir John Martin, who accompanied Churchill on this unplanned visit has no recollection of his presence."[27] "It is a tragedy that so much of the stuff that was written about him [under his own inspiration] ... was such a gross exaggeration of his achievements," wrote David Ogilvy. "It was probably booze that addled his brain."[28] The second look, keeping Stephenson in "the middle of events," if composed by Stevenson, indicates such summations may not be accurate.

It appears the writer Stevenson did receive some false information about Stephenson's life in Canada. A cable from Stephenson to Herb Rowland was forwarded to the writer, and it concocts a "subject's" life with a Scottish Canadian background, which appears in *AMCI*. The "subject" learns of the death of his father in the Boer War in 1901, about the same time as the death of Queen Victoria. Winston Churchill was visiting Winnipeg at the time on a lecture tour, the Stephenson cable said.[29]

A few of Stephenson's relatives in Winnipeg who heard nothing from him for decades wrote the publishers of *A Man Called Intrepid* in New York, to report biographical errors in the book, and sent the correct information. "My mother-in-law registered the letter, and heard nothing," says Mary Jane Stefansson, who also wrote Harcourt Brace and Jovanovitch. "I heard nothing. No one ever responded to receiving it." According to Reg Rimmer, when Stephenson died a Winnipeg radio station talk-show host reported Stephenson had no rela-tives in the city. Rimmer contacted the station to report that he was a relative, but the station didn't pursue the matter.

Following the publication of *AMCI*, Stevenson met with more than the typical book reviewers in Canada and the U.S. In January of 1976, he wrote Stephenson saying, "The meeting with the chaps in Ottawa was to map out some way of using the publicity on *AMCI* to further drive home the argument that intelligence is a vital necessity, etc."[30] A few months later he reported, "Ernie (Cuneo) has arranged for me to speak to the Dutch Treat Club in New York ... before 'key figures in the communications media.' They want me to use *AMCI* as a means to defend the CIA et al today, and this I shall do along the lines already discussed." He continued, "*AMCI* makes it clear that Allied intelligence saved us once and can save us again."[31]

The book ran into some obstacles in Britain in the very early stages of publication, when there were problems with expected newspaper serialization. In mid-March of 1976, Stevenson reported to Stephenson that London's *Sunday Times* was dropping plans to publish book excerpts. "The *Sunday Times* in London is rent with strife," he wrote. "Macmillan [British publisher] is taking legal action because the *Times* dropped an excerpt on the basis of someone challenging the facts ref your World War I record. 'This smells of conspiracy,' in Julian's words, and indeed I'm quite sure we shall be smoking out those who would dismantle all intelligence apparatus and therefore launch attacks on *AMCI*. I hope you don't get any flack. I'll do my best to attract it."[32]

Stephenson's response later the same day seemed to indicate he wasn't surprised at the British controversy, and he expected more. "The *Observer* probably have half a dozen people busily writing eroding letters to the *Sun Times*, let alone the avalanche which will descend from the read [sic] enemy heard [sic]."[33]

A few months later Stevenson wrote that he thought his British publisher was subjected to outside influences. He wrote Stephenson to say, "Macmillan for a time inhibited by the attacks from Marxists and professional American haters like A. J. P. Taylor."[34]

In August 1975 Stephenson read a draft of *AMCI* in Bermuda. He disliked the "Dickensian model" of himself as a "waifish Tiny Tim" and questioned whether his house in Bermuda was accurately described. "You live only in Royal places if you consider this thing austere." He continued, "Perhaps title should have been *The Secret War*." He also distanced himself from the book. "I trust that your, repeat your project, will prove rewarding to you," he cabled the writer.[35]

Stephenson complained about the negative depiction of Sothenes Behn, the founder of International Telephone Telegraph Corporation in *AMCI*. The writer Stevenson's response was unrepentant: "The ITT story in *AMCI* makes it clear that if Sothenes had not been active in Germany, we might not have got the early indications of the ENIGMA coding machine."[36] The book also portrays Behn as a Nazi sympathizer who was involved in producing arms for the Germans, and refers to him as the "notorious Sothenes Behn."[37]

After publication, ITT was not pleased with the portrayal of their founder in *A Man Called Intrepid*. Edward Gerrity, Jr., a senior vice president, wrote to the author April 23, 1976. He complained about comments in the book, and he blamed Stephenson for the story. Gerrity set out the case for Behn, "With all due respect to Stephenson ..."[38]

Stevenson responded to Gerrity about a month later and explained that his book "was intended to demonstrate that secret intelligence accomplishes great things in the name of democracy." He concluded his response by implying he would change the text. "I am looking for some way to strengthen the reference to ITT's part in ULTRA in subsequent editions."[39] (No changes occurred.)

In fact ITT provided invaluable assistance to BSC's communication network, which is not mentioned in *The Quiet Canadian* or *A Man Called Intrepid*.

The Curious Case of Dusko Popov

There are other indications William Stephenson's opinions may, in many cases, have been different than as chronicled by the writer Stevenson. In fact, the *Intrepid* author was later quoted saying the exact opposite of what his subject told him.

Dusko Popov (1912–1981), was a Yugoslav recruited into the Abwehr as a German agent in 1940, and he was turned into a double agent by the British. Among the information passed on by Popov to the Allies was a copy of a Japanese questionnaire requesting information, including quite specific details about the American base at Pearl Harbor. When Popov travelled to the Western Hemisphere he came into contact with BSC (Popov remembered being met in Bermuda by John Pepper) and later was funnelled to the FBI.

According to Popov's autobiography, *Spy/Counterspy* (1974), and some British sources, when Popov travelled to Washington he "forced" a meeting with J. Edgar Hoover and showed the FBI chief the Japanese questionnaire. Hoover, according to the story, was abrupt with Popov and chose to ignore the Japanese information, which heightened the catastrophe of December 7, 1941. Hoover didn't like Popov's lifestyle. He believed Popov was a playboy, and the code name Tricycle was assigned to him because he liked to sleep with two women at once.[40]

The Popov story has been repeated in over 30 books, mostly written by British authors, since the death of Hoover in 1972, but it is not necessarily true. John Masterman, who helped control German agents during the war, started the tale with the publication of *The Double-Cross System* in 1972. Masterman concedes, somewhat condescendingly, "We should certainly have risked a snub and pointed out to our friends in the United States what the significance of the document might be."[41] The British author Nicholas J. Cull goes as far as to blame Stephenson for the entire disaster. Hoover, according to Cull, regarded Popov's intelligence as suspect as a result of BSC's propaganda tactics. "Stephenson had cried wolf once too often. The U.S. Pacific Fleet picked up the bill."[42]

The Popov story came somewhat to a head in 1989 when CIA historian Thomas Troy published "The British Assault on J. Edgar Hoover: The Tricycle Case" in an intelligence journal. Published accounts of the neglected questionnaire and the Popov–Hoover encounter have propagated, Troy says, as they are examples "of the cleverness of British intelligence sabotaged by American incompetence."[43] Troy lists the numerous English authors who have repeated the Popov story, and the slur against Hoover, and points out that at least three are former British intelligence officers. The Britons, Troy wrote, have been joined in the attack by two Canadians, both familiar with the career of William Stephenson, the British-born author-journalist William Stevenson and former British Foreign Office employee, historian and author David Stafford.

According to Troy and former FBI director Clarence Kelly, Popov never met Hoover. Kelly wrote to *True* magazine about an excerpt from Popov's book *Spy/Counterspy* that after a "very careful study of the entire matter," he concluded Hoover could not have warned anyone of the Pearl Harbor attack. The FBI later released over a thousand pages of documents related to Popov's visits. Troy's conclusions stemming from the papers were:

- The questionnaire had a number of other questions as well, and possibly was a case of the Germans simply updating their files.
- If the British had knowledge of the attack on Pearl Harbor, why did they not inform the Americans through other channels? Why would they rely on the persuasive abilities of a 29-year-old Yugoslav, who arrived in the U.S. with thousands of dollars in his pocket, and a desire to party?
- The documents related to Popov indicated the FBI did pass on the questionnaire to G-2 and ONI.
- Hoover never did meet with Popov.

Judging from the correspondence between Stevenson and Stephenson, it appears the ex-espionage chief wasn't impressed by Popov's exploits and in 1974 after he read Popov's book, Stephenson cabled the author to say the young Yugoslav didn't meet Hoover:

POPOV TRICYCLE APPEARS TO BE GETTING AWAY WITH HIS USUAL CUNNING AND HIS REFERENCES TALKS WITH JEH [Hoover] PURE IMAGINATION STOP HAD THOUGHT OF TAKING EWEN MONTAGU TO TASK FOR HIS AGREEDING [sic] EXPRESS FAVOURABLE FOREWORD BUT THE WHOLE AFFAIR IS OF SUCH MINOR CONSEQUENCE THAT MYSELF RELEGATE TALE TO WPB [likely war propaganda board] STOP.[44]

During the writing of *AMCI* Stephenson requested changes in a section concerning the double agent Popov, but didn't see any in the draft sent to him. Stevenson replied the changes were sent to the printer, but not to Stephenson. "When you mentioned this [Popov] to me I made the necessary amendments. Of course the clean copy you have now got from Julian did not pass through my hands, and I guess that he did not transfer to that copy, the changes I had written into the one that went to the printers. The printers have the changes." This seems to clearly indicate Stephenson didn't see the book's final draft before it went to print.[45] The former espionage head requested passages in the book reflect his impressions of Popov's character, but the writer's letter to Stephenson two days later seems to show he didn't make the amendments his subject requested. "I enclose a copy of the changes made in the Popov section. I can't very well call him a scoundrel without risking [indeed being involved in] a libel action."[46]

Strangely, after Stephenson's death the author had a completely different recollection of Popov's exploits. "Our conversation was not for publication at the time," Stevenson told the author Anthony Summers. "But he [Stephenson] was very clear. He said Popov had indeed met Hoover — he knew all about it. He thought it was a terrible failing in Hoover who had this straightlaced attitude that shut him off completely from realities. Stephenson had no doubts about Popov's credibility, and he thought the FBI had totally failed to pick up on what Popov was trying to tell him about Pearl Harbor."[47] It is somewhat peculiar that if there were such discrepancies in the telling of his career, Stephenson would allow the same author to write another book, *Intrepid's Last Case*, with his blessing. In fact Stephenson asked Hyde, and possibly others, to produce a book entitled *Intrepid's Last Case*. Hyde's account evolved into the *Atom Bomb Spies*.[48] The second Stevenson book, which deals loosely with the Gouzenko case, did not make as big a splash as *A Man Called Intrepid*. Stephenson told Canadian journalist Robert Collins, who was working for *Reader's Digest* at the time, he went ahead with the second book for two reasons. "That it would bring active Reds and pseudo-Reds from the woodwork to attack me in every possible way. And it would clear Ellis. He [Stevenson] failed in that completely."[49]

The Reviews

Despite some eroding reviews, *A Man Called Intrepid* became a best-seller — selling millions of copies. A number of Stephenson's contemporaries — people who were aware of what Stephenson actually did during the war — were less critical of some of the book's contents. On February 6, 1976, Colin Gubbins, a former head of Britain's Special Operation Executive, wrote to the author Stevenson, saying, "What a tremendous job you have done in matching up to the occasion to what Intrepid achieved. And I am so glad too for Intrepid's sake that at last everything that really matters for him has been told and what I mean that the remarkable achievements of BSC have at last been revealed, 'honour where honour is done.'"[50]

The same month Lord Louis Mountbatten wrote to Stephenson to say, "I am so glad that at last the story of all you achieved is being told in spite of your continuous cloak of anonymity up to date. It was always a great thrill meeting you and working with you and high time the world knew all about what you did."[51]

The historian Gilbert Highet wrote to say, "It was grand to see something like justice done to your magnificent career — at long last — in Stevenson's very careful book. It confirms my pride in having been associated with you at a great time in history."[52]

David Bruce, of OSS London, who later became U.S. ambassador to Britain and a NATO official, wrote to the editor, Muller, "Had it not been for Sir William's achievements it seems to me highly possible that the Second World War would have followed a different and perhaps fatal course. This is an amazing account of the influence exercised by one man on one of the great crisis [sic] of history. I am grateful to you for sending the manuscript to me."[53]

John Le Carré in the *New York Times Book Review* wrote, "I even wonder whether in our unconscious spiritual selves lies a hope that our old heroes will rise again and save us now." Until the autumn of 1942, "in the secret war the job of saving Britain was left to a Scottish Canadian and an Irish American," and he referred to Stephenson as the de facto general of Anglo-American clandestine warfare against Hitler.[54]

The Critics

A number of what have been described by the London *Times* as "distinguished figures" entered into the debate on Stephenson's career.

Their comments were seemingly not based on the historical record, personal knowledge or interviews with people who worked with Stephenson, but by the exploits described in *A Man Called Intrepid* and its sequel. Two reviewers seem to be especially vitriolic in their analysis of Stephenson and his career.

Hugh Redwald Trevor-Roper (Lord Dacre of Glanton)

The most prominent and vocal of the critics of the *Intrepid* saga is England's Hugh Trevor-Roper (b. 1914). He is an historian, author, university professor and life peer. (He was introduced to the House of Lords as Lord Dacre of Glanton in November 1979.)

Dacre obtained his BA at Oxford in 1936 and was appointed Regius Professor of Modern History there in 1957. He became Master of Peterhouse College at Cambridge University in 1980. Trevor-Roper is also a former intelligence officer who worked in Signals intelligence during the war. In 1945 he was sent to Germany to investigate the mystery surrounding the death of Adolf Hitler. His *The Last Days of Hitler* was based on secret documents and interviews, and it won Trevor-Roper international acclaim. His academic career has been somewhat controversial.[55]

Trevor-Roper is often asked by the media to comment on espionage affairs. Explaining his background in intelligence, he told the *New York Times* (April 24, 1977), "I was recruited as part of a package. A small body of which I was a member made some discoveries which were rightly regarded as of great importance; and to have them the Secret Service had to have me ..." He was an associate of double agent Kim Philby, and after the latter's defection wrote a book, *The Philby Affair; Espionage, Treason and Secret Service.*[56] He was also apparently an associate of Anthony Blunt, and in the words of Canadian journalist Peter Worthington, was "discredited" when it was revealed he may have accompanied the known Soviet agent to Europe following the war to recover letters from the Duke of Windsor to Nazi leaders.[57] [See Appendix .]

Trevor-Roper wrote in the *New York Review* that *A Man Called Intrepid* was "start to finish utterly worthless." To write such a book the author would have to understand British Intelligence, but the writer Stevenson was exempt from this precondition as "it would be like urging a jellyfish to grit its teeth and dig in its heels."

He did say in the review that Stephenson was a friend and ally of Winston Churchill. He said he was the confidential liaison officer for

ULTRA material sent to Roosevelt before the Americans were in the war. He also makes factual errors in his review.[58]

Following Stephenson's death, the *Sunday Telegraph* in England ran a Trevor-Roper story titled "The Death of an Intrepid Fraud." The story's subheadline said Stephenson "was a fraud who fooled the world into believing he was a master spy."[59] In it, Trevor-Roper, who is described by the Folio Society as "Britain's greatest living historian," wrote Stephenson was undoubtedly the source of all the anecdotes in *A Man Called Intrepid*.

"The author could be left to mug up the story of these operations elsewhere, but it can only be Sir William who put himself into them: for he had not been there before." He says a note described in the book from Churchill inviting Stephenson to his house must have been a forgery. "Such a document can only be provided by Sir William … the implications of this forgery, which Sir William has chosen to ignore are disquieting, even sinister," Trevor-Roper reports. (In fact, Stephenson said years earlier Churchill phoned and didn't send him a letter.)[60]

The success of the Stephenson book in the United States was because the CIA needed a figurehead, Trevor-Roper wrote. "To the old OSS hands and their CIA successors, Stephenson was the mythical figure who in the heroic past had stood behind their semi-mythical founder Donovan." To rob people of heroes was a cruel act, Trevor Roper continued, "like robbing children of their cosy woolly bears."

Stephenson was not the only Western espionage head who did not pass Trevor-Roper's scrutiny. Stewart Menzies, the head of Britain's SIS during the war was, at the end of his life, "suffering from delusions of grandeur," Trevor-Roper says. The historian attributes this problem to "secret service insulation from real life, which can lead, in old age, to dangerous hallucinations," and "publishers should flee from their approaches and friends should prevail upon them to be silent."[61]

He also wrote a laudatory introduction to a book critical of former West German intelligence head Reinhard Gehlen, who released his memoirs in 1971. [See Appendix .] In *The General Was a Spy*, Trevor-Roper says Gehlen's organization after 1958 declined into a series of "small failures" followed by "great failures." One of the book's major summations is that Gehlen's chronicle, "Reveals himself as a victim of an outsize [sic] ego," and "The greatest service Gehlen could have done himself would have been to preserve his silence."[62]

In the sixties, Trevor-Roper appeared on a CBC radio documentary entitled, *The Great Canadian Spy*. Oddly enough, the historian had nothing negative to say about Stephenson. Surrounded by Stephenson's contemporaries (Lord Louis Mountbatten, Montgomery Hyde, Malcolm Muggeridge and Eric Maschwitz), in a documentary that heralded Stephenson's accomplishments, Trevor-Roper didn't mention that he thought Stephenson "was a fraud who fooled the world into believing he was a master spy," as his later literary efforts stressed.[63]

David Stafford

British-born historian David Stafford (b. 1942) is a former employee of Her Majesty's Diplomatic Service in London. He served as a Third and Second secretary with Britain's Foreign Office in 1967 and 1968, and shortly afterwards, he moved to a more academic career at the University of London and became a researcher and part-time lecturer. About 1970 he came to Canada and worked as an assistant professor at the University of Victoria. Stafford has also been linked with the University of Western Ontario, Concordia University in Montreal, Cambridge, and the University of Toronto as a "research associate," "visiting associate" or as a "visiting associate professor."

Stafford's specialization is World War II and espionage. He lectured Canadian and American universities and teachers on World War II events and spy literature, and he provided commentary for a variety of media. The British Foreign Office vet was the director of the Canadian Committee for the History of the Second World War from 1981 till 1984, and a member of the American committee. He has co-edited espionage books with Jack Granatstein , the former curator of the Canadian War Museum, and Wesley Wark, a British-educated academic who frequently reviews books on intelligence for the *Globe and Mail*.[64]

Stafford researched the career of William Stephenson and British Security Coordination and published a book, *Camp X*, in 1986. Stafford stresses career achievements of William Stephenson have been exaggerated by books and films. At the end of *Camp X* in a chapter titled "Myth and Reality," Stafford concludes, "It is now difficult for the serious historian to give him [Stephenson] credit for anything."[65] Stafford says the Camp X "myth" had been embellished by Canada, "in the service of nation building." Canadians, according to Stafford, "anxious to decolonize their past, have thus rewritten their history since the war to cleanse it of imperial heritage." He doesn't mention any Canadian writers doing this purging, just English-born, RAF vet William Stevenson.

Following Stephenson's death, Stafford wrote "A Myth Called Intrepid" for *Saturday Night* magazine. The cover read "Intrepid: the Spymaster who Wasn't," and the story asserted, "the amazing exploits of our favourite spymaster turned out to contain large doses of fiction concocted in the forgetful mind of an old man." Throughout the October 1989 piece Stafford refers to Stephenson as "the old man." He also wrote that publishers of *A Man Called Intrepid* had "finally relented," and the book had been officially classified as a novel. (Subsequently *Saturday Night* magazine wrote a correction that the British paperback publisher Sphere Books had made an error on one edition in the early eighties, and that error had not been repeated. The book was not a novel).

The Stafford story on Stephenson led to the threat of legal action against the Canadian magazine. This appears to have been initiated not by Stevenson, but by the wife of the author, Monica Jensen-Stevenson, as Stevenson was away in Asia.[66]

The matter was settled out of court. A year after the story was published a handful of letters were printed by the magazine, most of which took Stafford's revisionism to task.[67] The author Stevenson responded to the article in a letter and wrote mostly about himself. He flew planes in World War II, he said in rebuttal to the story that diminished Stephenson's career. (He flew Hellcats, "modified for 'lone ranger operations' behind Japanese lines at extremely high altitude." Stevenson got around — another report puts him in the Atlantic at the end of the war, "searching for a U-boat suspected of transporting [Martin] Bormann and his Nazi treasures to Argentina.")[68] His research was extensive, he wrote in *Saturday Night*, and he was not a tabloid journalist.

Oddly enough, Stevenson doesn't mention Stafford's connection to Britain's Foreign Office, or the "Red Menace," which is so prevalent in his correspondence with Stephenson. He, too, seems to conclude that controversy over Stephenson's career was Canadian-based. Stephenson "made enemies because he cut through bureaucratic red tape and offended the Liberal government of William Lyon Mackenzie King. It is shameful that these old enmities should be served up at the earliest opportunity following his death." This is a rather confusing connection. Stafford was eight years old and living in England when former

Canadian Prime Minister King died in 1950. No Canadian residents are quoted in Stafford's *Saturday Night* story criticizing Stephenson. When Stafford's article appeared, Canada's Liberal party had been out of power for five years. In all the research and interviews with former BSC people I have conducted, there is no record of problems with the King government. (In earlier articles Stevenson has been rather non-analytical of the critics of the *Intrepid* sagas, labelling others "miserable cockroaches," "anti-Semitic," and "Canadians of convenience.")[69]

Earlier in the decade Stafford was unimpressed by another espionage celebrity with a Canadian connection, Igor Gouzenko. "Gouzenko was not a modest man and throughout his life he displayed a tragic combination of massive ego and minimal self-knowledge." Gouzenko was also made into a myth by malleable Canadians, Stafford asserts. "How has it happened that Gouzenko found in Canada an audience that was eager to transform him from a man to a myth? In part it was Canada's relative naiveté in world affairs, and Gouzenko provided a rather brutal rite of passage into that arena," Stafford wrote in *Saturday Night*.[70]

Other Intrepid Reviews

A number of other reviews did not acclaim Stephenson's war achievements but questioned the accuracy of parts of *A Man Called Intrepid*. The English historian A. J. P. Taylor, writing in the *New Statesman*, continually refers to Stephenson as Sir William Stevenson in his review, yet criticizes the book for its lack of accuracy. "Nearly everything else in the book is either exaggerated, distorted or already known," Taylor wrote. "Great play is made with the BSC papers. It is not explained what they are or where they are." He complained there were no precise references and "the only book quoted by name was *Casino Royale* by Ian Fleming."[71]

Sir David Hunt provided another negative review. He disputes whether a picture portraying a shadowy figure and Churchill surveying the bombing damage of the House of Commons could be Stephenson. The unidentifiable shadow in the photo was not Stephenson but Brendan Bracken, he said. "Stephenson is quoted verbatim, speaking as though an eye witness. Sir John Martin has no recollection of his presence and from Montgomery Hyde's book it appears he was in New York at the time." He also doubts that Churchill knew about the bombing of Coventry beforehand, which is mentioned in the book, but he admits this has also been discussed in *The Ultra Secret* and *Bodyguard of Lies.*[72] Following Stephenson's death, Hunt discounted any possibility Stephenson could have known Churchill, as Sir John Coville, Churchill's secretary for a short time, didn't remember meeting him. He continued, "I've also spoken to Alan Taylor [A.J.P. Taylor, Beaverbrook biographer] and there is no evidence Stephenson even knew Beaverbrook, let alone Churchill."[73]

For his part, Coville, who also worked for Neville Chamberlain and Buckingham Palace [1947–49] doesn't explain why he would know everyone Churchill knew, simply because he worked for him for a while.[74] If Churchill didn't know his own Intelligence Chief in North America during World War II, when his great desire was to have the Americans as Allies, his competency would have to be called into question. One would have thought someone could have told the Prime Minister what was going on over there. Coville doesn't explore this catastrophic breakdown of communication during England's greatest crisis.

On June 28, 1940, Churchill wrote to his American Ambassador Lord Lothian in Washington complaining, "We have really not had any help worth speaking of from the United States so far." In his post-war account Churchill minutes, "The rifles and field guns did not arrive until the end of July. The destroyers had been refused."[75] Bill Stephenson arrived in the United States June 21, 1940.

Weeks after Stephenson's death the *London Times* attempted to explain the "Intrepid" controversy. The conclusion ascertained from the British scholars and "distinguished figures" interviewed seemed to be that the former espionage head inflated his importance. They implied Stephenson was egotistical and loved drawing attention to himself. "The source of the information turns out to be only Stephenson himself — amplified by biographies whose authors he knew and whose writing he vetted."[76] Ironically the picture accompanying the article, which was supposed to depict Stephenson, was of someone else. The *Times* photo editors and/or the defence correspondent who wrote the story didn't know what this long-time publicity seeker looked like. (They were not alone. The *Globe and Mail* in their year-end review of prominent Canadians who died in 1989 printed a picture of William Stevenson, the author, instead of the "publicity loving" Stephenson.) The *Times* article also doesn't speculate why Stephenson, on his personal instructions, was buried before his death was publicly announced. As a result, six people attended the "megalomaniac's" funeral, and local policemen acted as pall bearers.

Other British writers such as Nigel West and Chapman Pincher have commented about questionable historical references triggered by the book *A Man Called Intrepid*. West, the pseudonym for ex-British parliamentarian Rupert Allason, has pointed out some photographs purporting to be from BSC's Station M archive are actually still pictures from a movie. He doesn't report that Station M was the BSC division in charge of false documents. The photographs from *A Man Called Intrepid* at the University of Regina have been classified "restricted" by Stevenson, and can't be viewed by researchers.

Controversial incidents described in *A Man Called Intrepid*, and Trevor-Roper's, Stafford's, and others' subsequent analyses have influenced Canadian authors as well. In his book *Official Secrets*, Richard Cleroux hypothesizes Stephenson became forgetful as he became older. "By this stage in his illness, he [Stephenson] could no longer distinguish between fact and fiction and he misled a number of people."[77] The writer John Bryden, in *Best Kept Secret*, says, "Stephenson's warped version of events has directly or indirectly influenced dozens of histories, many of them by very competent writers. From first to last however, Stephenson was a liar."[78] *Spy Wars*, which J. A. Granatstein coauthored with David Stafford, reduces Stephenson's wartime role to that of charlatan. Timothy Naftali seemed to echo the opinions of Stafford and Trevor-Roper in "Intrepid's Last Deception," published in *Intelligence and National Security*.[79]

Years after his death, this is essentially the public record of William Stephenson. A career misted in controversy, and a character so tight-lipped that two biographers did not even determine the names of his parents or his date of birth. After working tirelessly to help save democracy in Europe, his career has been reduced in some quarters to questioning dates when he had dinner nearly fifty years earlier, whether he knew his friends, or if he was an unidentifiable shadow in a photograph. Partially as a result, it was difficult to obtain a relevant grasp on the man and his accomplishments, even for those who were close to him. "What I'd like to know is what was true. And what wasn't true?" said his friend of nearly forty years, Derek Bedson. "I mean, what was he appointed to? Exactly. In New York."

Most intelligence files relating to Stephenson's British Security Coordination were destroyed, and many other intelligence records remain closed. However during the war Stephenson surrounded himself with numerous people. Many of them had similar questions as Stephenson's friends and relatives, and subsequently they also provided some answers.

A Conversation

Pauline McGibbon, former Lieutenant Governor of Ontario and a friend of Stephenson's, was interviewed on the subject of *AMCI*:

The former governor of Bermuda, Edwin Leathers, is quoted as saying, "Sir William once told me we would have to wait a long time for the official history of his wartime activities to be written. In the meantime we will have to be content with the fictional one."[80] McGibbon said Stephenson expressed similar sentiments to her.

"Let's say this, Bill [Stephenson] said the same thing. That [*A Man Called Intrepid*] was a fictionalized version and I really feel very strongly that the other Bill Stevenson did Sir William a great injustice doing that book."

"But why would he get involved with him again on the second book?"

"That I don't know. That I don't know. I also know that he turned over all his records to him. I think he was so damn mad at the things that were being said that were not true, that he wanted to make sure that somebody was going to write a true history."

Former Stephenson employees in Toronto said McGibbon once asked Stephenson why he didn't answer back against his critics. Stephenson replied, "One day the truth will come out."

"Yes," McGibbon said. "That's right. Oh yes. Bill was very, very, very closed-mouthed, and I know one time I asked him something and he just looked at me with a grin, and he said, 'I don't know, and if I did I wouldn't tell you,'" she laughed. "Oh, no. Right to his death he was a secret service person. He was very, very ... he would just never say anything."

III

The Unknown Agents

"But the leaders of the new order did not
reckon with the indomitable courage of the
individual. The urge towards freedom is
irrepressible. Multiplied many times,
it generates a force which cannot be measured
in terms of tanks or machine guns firing
hundreds of rounds a minute. Many times
in the past it has slowed the onslaught of a
tyrant and helped bring about his downfall.
Tolstoy in *War and Peace* referred to it as
the mysterious force of X. I was priveleged in
World War II to have played a role in helping this force to be generated and brought
into play."

— Sir William Stephenson

12 BSC RECRUITS

WINNIPEG
Molly Phair

Marjorie Ferguson first saw the small newspaper ad. She trundled down to Winnipeg's Fort Garry Hotel for a job interview, and when it finished, recruiter Herb Rowland was impressed. He wondered if she knew of anyone else who would move to New York "for British government war work." Marjorie told her younger sister Ruth, and she called her friend Molly Phair. Ruth would go to the hotel to apply for employment only if Phair went as well. "We were pretty young at that time," Phair remembered. Although they weren't keen on leaving Winnipeg, the duo went to the hotel for the interview. Time passed and they nearly forgot about the application completely. Then one day a friend of Phair's in the Royal Canadian Mounted Police (RCMP) turned up at her door and said, "Oh, so you're on your way to New York. I know more about you than you know about yourself." "The RCMP investigated us," Phair remembered. The trio passed their police check, and in June of 1943, a half dozen Winnipeggers left for New York City to join the Stephenson organization.

On arrival in New York, BSC provided temporary accommodation at a women's hotel where "the bedrooms were the size of broom closets." Eventually they looked for apartments, but there were restrictions on their movement and conduct. When they found a new place, the address had to be screened by the organization before they could move in. They were not allowed to go to Harlem. If the new employees needed medical attention, they were only allowed to visit doctors that had been pre-approved by Security Coordination. If they wanted an appointment with another doctor, they could only go after he was investigated and checked out by security people. "Other than that, we were quite free agents to do what we wanted to do."

But they were to keep their activities surreptitious. "I think the British security were pretty smart people," Phair says. "Three of us were living together, and none of us knew what the others were doing. They impressed us very much, but we did not talk about it."

Phair worked in BSC's communications department on the second floor of Rockefeller Center's International Building, near the statue of Atlas, and across the street from St. Patrick's Cathedral. "It couldn't be in a more public location." There was no uniformed security around the office and employees entered through an unmarked door.

The division dealt with the collation and dispersal of intercepted coded messages. Phair was in the Japanese section. Fourteen women were in her group, which contained a room full of "TK" (telekrypton) machines. They received long sheets of Teletype-like messages from an adjoining room and processed them. Phair's section counted portions of the tapes, cut them with a paper cutter, and sent them off by safe hand. Phair doesn't know where the messages originated, only that they were Japanese. "I was not involved with the decoding, just the transfers of the messages." Herb Rowland, who hired her in Winnipeg, became her boss.

Marjorie Ferguson worked on the second floor as well. Her sister Ruth worked on the 36th floor for Wing Commander Richard (Dickey) Byrd, and later she came downstairs as the secretary of Benjamin de Forest (Pat) Bayly. Much of the younger Ferguson's activities involved basic secretarial work and accounting. Many of the messages that came across her desk were in code or ciphered. She remembers there was one telex machine in the office, for important messages, that only two people were to touch — herself and Bayly. But almost all basic daily procedures were on a "need-to-know" basis, and it was difficult to obtain any type of overview of the operation. Names such as Bill Ross Smith, Dickie Coit and Cedric Belfrage were not familiar to Ferguson, although they too worked on the upper floors with Stephenson. "People ask me what I did during the war," Ferguson says. "I can honestly say, I don't know. People think I'm teasing!"

Nearly all the people working with BSC were Canadians, Phair said, although there were a few English women, and British military men around. Many of the Canadians knew each other because they were from the same cities.

The organization was known at first as the British Passport Office, but later changed to British Security Coordination. No employees revealed to anyone specifics about the organization or job descriptions. "If people wanted to believe that it was dealing in securities, or stocks and bonds, that was fine, let them think that," Phair said. "Because we didn't say what we were doing to people that we met."

When she was back in Winnipeg on holidays, a year after starting at BSC, Phair discovered people were interested in what she was doing. While at the race track, she met a friend with someone she didn't know. The stranger seemed quite aggressive, asked persistent questions, and asked her out. He came to a gathering she had the next day, as did Phair's friend in the RCMP, who knew she was working for BSC. When the Mountie arrived, he looked around the room, took Phair aside, and said, "What is that man doing at this house? Get him out!" The stranger left, and she never found out more about what had occurred. "That was sort of strange."

Contrary to some reports, Phair believes most employees were aware of who Stephenson was. "We knew he was the head; we knew what he looked like, if we saw him." Her section would see Stephenson occasionally when he would quietly slip in and out, but he kept a low profile. Every now and then a small delegation would tour the area. Noel Coward and Lord Mountbatten came through the office with Stephenson, Phair says. Bill Donovan was around, and his association with Stephenson was an important aspect of the entire operation. "I know during the war, while we were there, there was a very close relationship between him and Bill Donovan, who was the head of Strategic Services," Phair said. "Because of that relationship, the Americans worked so closely with the British."

Bill Stephenson, to the average BSC employee such as Phair, was a quiet individual who everyone held in high esteem. "He had the respect of everybody. A great deal. Certainly nobody would have criticized him. He was not the type who blew his own horn. He was the kind of person who would never talk to anybody about some of the things he had been doing." Although he didn't mingle with the personnel, his staff sensed Stephenson's covert manner. "I can never imagine him ever blabbing. He was a very, very quiet person." She thought some people made a cottage industry out of his career. "I am sure this has been done by people who are taking advantage of him."

Phair was surprised any information at all came out about BSC, let alone the saga of the international swashbuckler portrayed in *A Man Called Intrepid*. She believes the book's revelations had something to do with the defection of Kim Philby. She also thought Stephenson might have lost the ability to intellectualize and reason in his later life. Errors about Stephenson's career tarnished his reputation, which he didn't deserve, she says. "I think people are taking him at face value and that's not fair." Phair thought William Stevenson must have written *A Man Called Intrepid* in a great hurry. "He had a lot of inaccuracies in it," she said. "When he described Sir William had come from Manitoba, he said he came from Point Douglas, near Winnipeg — Nothing could be more Winnipeg!"

Phair remains somewhat reluctant to discuss her war work fifty years later. She remembers a day in June of 1943, when she started to work for Stephenson's secret organization, and the preliminary instructions that were given. "The day we arrived, we were given a talk to the effect that other countries, when a war was over, may reveal what they did. And he said you are never, ever, to reveal anything you did. And I don't think anybody that worked there ever said a word."

Some of Phair's former BSC colleagues gathered in Toronto in 1986. "We jokingly called it the 'Spy Reunion.' There were no records kept of staff or anything — afterwards everything was destroyed, so the only way the people could go to the reunion was by word of mouth." Former BSC people in Toronto sent out notices to the former employees they knew, and those people sent back names of any BSC alumni they were in touch with. Stephenson was told about the reunion, and he sent his adopted daughter Elizabeth from Bermuda to attend on his behalf, and she brought a video message from him.

Phair left BSC in October of 1945. She was asked to stay on in the accounts department but, as math wasn't her forte, she decided to return to Winnipeg. The Ferguson sisters eventually moved to the United States. Molly Phair is the only former Stephenson employee who still lives in his old home town. She enjoyed her time with the organization, she says, and "I would just like to reiterate the respect that everybody had for the man."

Station M closed down and Camp X was phased out in May 1945. BSC's 800 Canadian women went home, forever sworn to secrecy about the details of their war time work. But they would always remember with pride what they helped to accomplish — and, with amazement perhaps, the secrets they shared.

— Canadians at War

Charmian Manchee worked in BSC's inner office as one of Bill Stephenson's personal coding clerks. "It was called SIS," she remembered, "and you went through the passport control to get up to the office. There were two secretaries and two coders, and all of Stephenson's correspondence had to come through us." They were in a central area and Montgomery Hyde, a Mr. Baxter, John Pepper, and another had outside offices. She coded outgoing and incoming messages by hand from code books. "We weren't as proficient as Dorothy [Evenson]. We did it all by hand in those days." The messages, once decoded, went straight to Stephenson. A majority of the outgoing dispatches went to Britain, she remembered. "They went direct to England, to Churchill, and 'C' [Menzies]," and "they came from all over." There was an outer area where the messages were evaluated. If they were designated as confidential, they came into the inner office where Kathleen (Kay) Taylor and Manchee decoded. If the message was less urgent, it went to the outer office where they were transposed and sent to various other members such as Pepper, Hyde, Baxter, etc. "But his own personal messages were sent to us."

The coding and decoding went on around the clock, and the women worked in three eight-hour shifts. Messages had to be decoded and waiting for Stephenson each morning. She was paid $35 a week every Friday. (A good bookkeeper earned about $20 a week at the time.) There was no official record of the payment transactions, and no deductions. "It was all cash payment in an envelope. No payroll." Manchee eventually moved out of a women's hotel where she first stayed and into an apartment. The women employees paid their own rent and usually lived together.

Manchee was hired through family connections. She worked first in Washington for the British Purchasing Commission and British Air

Commission, and after about six weeks there she was moved up to New York. "When I arrived in New York I was told that I was on a very confidential job, and I was not to socialize with anybody." As a result she lived at the women's hotel and did little else, "simply walking to and from work each day," until others were sent down from Toronto and she made a few friends. For about the first two months she lived with Kathleen Taylor, who was the daughter of A. J. Taylor, the close friend of Stephenson's and one of the financiers of Vancouver's Lions Gate Bridge and British Properties.

The BSC offices expanded after the American entry into the war, and on a lower floor in Rockefeller Center a separate office opened for Stephenson. "There was a set of offices with a door that was not used very much and he would come in that door to meet various people such as Donovan and other dignitaries, or people that he was sending on missions hither and yon."

If someone asked her what she did for a living, she said she worked for Passport Control. "That was the cover." But after a period of time the name changed "publicly" to British Security. They were known by the security staff and most of the employees punched a clock.

Taylor and Manchee did the filing, coding, deciphering and distribution. Miss Elizabeth Richardson was in charge of receiving the messages and if they were marked Secret and Confidential they were sent to the inner office for decoding, and to Stephenson.

"Could you read them?"

"Well, we'd have to decode them first."

"But then you would be able to read the decoded message?"

"Oh, yes."

"Well, you would know his contacts with Churchill or whatever?"

"Oh, yes."

Stephenson "certainly did" know Churchill, she emphasized. He met with the British Prime Minister throughout the war. She and a friend in purchasing could tell when Stephenson was about to go to Europe because he ordered certain things, she said. "And we knew just from common knowledge that he must be going over ... and he certainly did go over to meet Churchill."

Another point the women could substantiate was that BSC planted propaganda in New York papers. The department was called Office of War Information (OWI). "We did in our office that, I'll remember the name of it eventually, but they did certainly curry favour, is that the right word, with the publishers of the papers and plant pro-British propaganda in the papers. You read that in all the books and it is very true ... Ralph Ingersoll and *PM Magazine*, they really worked on him."

Janet FitzGerald worked primarily for Special Operation Executive's Richard (Dickie) Coit, although the acting Western head of SOE changed from time to time. She did secretarial work and filing for four years. The files were about individuals and businesses, and agents who were sent abroad. Her immediate superior was Russian-born Alexander Halpern. She heard about the New York job through a friend, Betty Cook.

"I was working at the National Trust, and I heard about this marvellous opening in New York, so I applied in early June of '41. What I remember most is being interviewed for the job, and they wanted Canadians obviously, and you had to have a reasonably good background. We had to be investigated by the Mounties [RCMP]." Stephenson's friend, Bay Street stockbroker Tommy Drew-Brook, interviewed her. In New York she was later told by Drew-Brook the only blot on her application was that some of her family were Oxford Group (an anti-war peace movement). "It was supposedly a subversive organization. So I nearly didn't get the job. I had to convince them that I wasn't a member of the Oxford Group. My mother and my brother were. When I got to New York, there was a file 'Oxford Group' and my brother's name was in it."

There was only a small organization in New York when she started, and she worked in an outer office and remembers Stephenson vividly. She was told the cover of the operation was British Passport Control, but was well aware few travellers visited Britain in the early forties during the war. "No one thought to ask me 'who was getting a British passport in 1941?' In the middle of the war?' and I wondered about that."[1]

They were told to live at either the Barbizon Hotel or Beekman Tower, and they were given strict instructions not to speak to anyone about what they were doing.

• • •

Helen Woolley was in the records department primarily doing filing. At the time BSC was concerned with German shipping, and sailors leaving ships along the East Coast of the U.S.A. who could possibly become spies and terrorists. The organization had long lists of incoming Nazi ships and sailors to check, but she doesn't know how the information was obtained. In 1942, after the United States was in the war, Woolley moved to a new BSC office in Guatemala and did similar work. A major concern in Guatemala and Central America (of both Britain and the U.S.) was the process of sending German colonists (most of whom had married Guatemalan women) back to Germany or to detention camps in the U.S. for the duration of the war. B-17s from U.S. air bases in Guatemala, Panama and Galapog patrolled the Caribbean on the lookout for submarines.

Wooley's friend, Betty Cook, went to New York near the beginning of the war, and wrote and told her it was great working there. Later she answered an ad in a Toronto newspaper.

The women were instructed to use specific doctors and dentists, and BSC would pay their bills. One of the doctors was William Rowland, the brother of Herb, who was an office manager, recruiter and a friend of Stephenson's.

· · ·

Gwen Rollaston heard about the New York employment through her friend Margaret Mowat, who was working for the Stephenson organization and enjoying it very much. Rollaston told her she would like to work in New York, so when Mowat heard BSC was doing more recruiting, she gave Herb Rowland Rollaston's name, and an appointment was arranged.

In December 1941, she arrived in New York and worked in the Registry doing filing and clerical work, similar to the work done by FitzGerald. She remembered particularly large files on the German multinationals IG Farben and General Analine, and also on suspected Nazi sympathizers. In 1943 she moved to a Guatemala office and did secretarial work. The BSC representatives in Guatemala worked with the British. "We were with the British Legation down there, working for the so-called Civil Attaché, who was actually SIS from New York, Arthur Neal." They made reports on all the Germans in the area that were "suspect" and sent them back to New York.

BSC subagents sent coded messages utilizing pages of books, similar to coding described in *The Key to Rebecca*, a novel by Ken Follett, the women said. The agent in the field was given a novel and the office used the same one. To convey the message, references were made to words in the novel using numbers, such as the third word on the fourth line of page fifteen would be "3415." The patterns could be reversed, and certain numbers could be transposed to represent other numerals. The women received all their code training in New York.

Rollaston remembers there was a high degree of anti-British sentiment when she arrived in the U.S. "I remember going out socially and being terribly insulted. An American was terribly rude to me. He hated anything to do with Britain and these destroyers [for bases deal]. The Lend-L:ease that they were getting. It was terrible. I was shattered."

• • •

Nancy Thompson didn't go to New York until 1943. She had been working for the Royal Bank at that time and a woman she worked with knew Herb Rowland and found out about a recruiting drive. Her interview was in a hotel room at the Royal York in Toronto, but she doesn't recall a tough interrogation. "I think all you really had to do was identify a typewriter and you were in," she said. "Then they put the Mounties on you." She lived with three other girls in an apartment and they split the $125 a month rent. Thompson was a statistician. She did surveys on the time it took between when a message was intercepted, when it was relayed, when it was received in New York, and finally when it was received in England.

The clocks at BSC were on Greenwich mean time, and when Thompson first started she had a few problems. "I'm not very good about the international date line, you know, whether you go ahead, or behind, or whatever," she said smiling. "And there was no set rule whether you put the intercept station first, and then the date, and then the time. There was just this series of numbers across the top of the messages. So I would have messages received in Greenwich before they had ever been intercepted."

Thompson was nearly fired a few days after she started working for British Security Coordination, as one thing the women could not do was reveal the office phone number. "My brother was in the Navy and happened to be in New York and he knew that I was working for British Security Coordination." When he was at Admiralty House in lower New York, he mentioned that he wanted to get in touch with her, and Admiralty House gave him BSC's number. He called Thompson. "Well, we had the office manager. We had the personnel manager —

everybody in there — wondering how this person had got hold of our telephone number," she remembered. "It was a very serious offence."

Thompson says the American Navy was using BSC facilities. "The U.S. Navy right through the war used the British Intercept Services because they were apparently much more effective." The code room she worked in used three separate codes, Dumpy, Fido and Fog. She totalled numbers on an intercept page which indicated length and duration of the message and charged the Americans at a set rate. "And every time Britain lost a capital ship, I would add another $5,000 to the U.S. Navy bill," she smiled. ("I was just kidding," she said later.)

She worked on the second floor of Rockefeller Center. There was security to go through, and the department punched time clocks when they started work. She worked with a group of four and she was the only one of her group who didn't have to work in shifts. The women were to tell people they were nurses, which would explain why they came in and out of their apartment at strange hours. "We were really kept in great ignorance of what we were doing. They were very careful not to let us know."

Although the women worked, socialized and lived together, they didn't talk about their work to each other. Most have stayed completely quiet. "I've learned more tonight than I have in the years since." They signed Britain's Official Secrets Act and were cautioned not to talk about what they were doing. On one occasion a woman mentioned what she was doing in a social setting and was sent home.

· · ·

Dorothy Evenson saw an advertisement in a Winnipeg newspaper about employment interviews at the Fort Garry Hotel. She remembers the ad said the applicants had to be British subjects and one of her friends suggested they go for an interview. Evenson didn't tell her parents. Herb Rowland interviewed her at the famous Winnipeg hotel. "He basically just talked to us, and I think we were asked if we could type. But he just asked us our background and what we did." Later, in New York, Evenson asked Rowland how he screened people he interviewed and decided who to hire. He told her he sought people who could get along with other people. "I thought that was interesting."

A week later she received a phone call saying she was to start work in New York on April 16, 1943. About a dozen people left Winnipeg in the spring of 1943 to join Stephenson's British Security Coordination.

Soon after her arrival, Evenson was given an aptitude test and was asked to speak to Major Ken Maidment. He told her she was to learn a new machine because she was mechanically inclined. "I told him that I wasn't really at all," she remembered. "And he said 'yes, you are.'"

Evenson was sent to a small office and brought a small machine and box. "This was the Type X machine." She was given a manual to read, and then instructed to take the machine apart and put it together. Evenson studied the rotating drums inside and turned them to change the coding of the machine. "So I struggled through that, and finally got it down. They gradually brought down more girls from Toronto, and I taught them the machine, and then they set up a section."

The section was at the back of the large telex room on the mezzanine floor of Rockefeller Center. The messages came in via long tapes, which were sent to another section and different staff. About two dozen people worked on the machines in her department, and the machines ran 24 hours a day. They used pasting machines, similar to those of telegrams, which were separated with a preamble, time and date, and ended with a signature where they would start a new page. "And these then went in to Miss Richardson. She was a lady, a titled lady. And she was very mannish in the British sense, and no nonsense. I was scared stiff of her, but she was very kind." After Richardson sorted the pasted messages, they were sent upstairs to Stephenson.

As the messages were coded, the women didn't know their contents. But they could see where the messages were coming from. They came "from all around the world." One woman recalled seeing some from Madagascar. "Station Two was Colombo."

On some occasions the upstairs brass knew when important correspondence was going to arrive. They would get a phone call from the 35th floor and people would come down to wait for it. Periodically the communications department would get a call from Stephenson saying that he was bringing a visitor. He showed up with, among others, Louis Mountbatten, Noel Coward and Lord Beaverbrook. "All these people would come down to look at the messages. And he would walk behind, with his hands behind his back. A little wee man in a grey suit."

"And Lord Louis was up here," said Evenson, measuring his height.

"And gorgeous," said another.

"Oh, yes."

"In navy uniform ..."

Evenson was asked by Manchee if she worked on the microdot and it was obvious there was a great ignorance of what each person had done. "This was the secret of the whole organization," Manchee repeated. "Nobody knew what anybody else did."

"I think the whole thing about our organization was don't tell anybody, not even your roommate what you were doing. All we knew was what we were doing. So we couldn't tell anybody anything, because all we knew was this narrow little box that we were in every day."

However, the Stephenson organization was very discerning and knew what the employees were doing, even after work. Evenson said BSC was aware of who she was seeing socially. "They watched who you dated. Because I was going with a Bill somebody or other, and he had a car. And I was called in and asked who is he, because he was of an age to be in the forces. He was an American and he wasn't in the forces, so 'what did we talk about?', and they asked what he did. He told me, and as far as I know it was true, that he was the head of this Junior Achievement, which is still in existence in New York. And when you think about it, it is rather a funny thing for a young man to be involved in, so they told me to keep dating him. Ask him questions, and if he asks you questions, you know what to do." Evenson later discovered she was being followed. She was questioned after seeing "Bill," and BSC agents knew where she and "Bill" went for dinner the night before.

"I asked him questions. He never asked me a thing. He was just a nice young man. And then they told me to drop him."

Evenson was with the last group to leave BSC's New York offices in December 1945. She worked for British Information Services, which formed after British Security Coordination. At that time she says the Soviet Union was spreading black propaganda about British officials in New York.

"I worked with British Information Services, which was a follow-up on this. There were things going through to do with BSC through British Information Services. Because at that time the Russians were sort of blackmailing the high British people in New York and that came through our offices. That's how I got the job, they asked me then if I would work for British Information Services."

"What do you mean blackmailing?"

"Well, they were telling stories, which they always do, about high people — they would try and paint a black picture of them. At the time, even the man I worked for [Keith Fowler, head of British Information Services]. But it tied in with BSC."

. . .

Jean Peacock was a civil servant working for the Air Force in Toronto. She heard through a friend returning from New York about a variety of people with interesting jobs there. Peacock found out about a recruitment drive in November of 1943, and she was interviewed at the Royal York Hotel by Herb Rowland and a "Mrs. Shakespeare". "If you sort of looked respectable you were in." She knew of two other women who were going to work for BSC at about the same time, and the trio lived together in the Beekman Tower, which was recommended to them by the organization. Later they were free to look for their own apartments, but the new buildings had to be checked by BSC security before they could move in. "We knew that we had to be careful about what we said and who we saw. And that was okay because it was sort of exciting to be a part of it, and also it was during the war, and we were all very patriotic and we wanted to make sure that we were doing the right thing."

She did shift work (9–5, 5–1 and 1–9) the entire time she was employed at BSC, and first worked in section "Dumpy." The "Dumpy" messages had to be grouped in multiples of 15 before they were decoded. The grouped strips of paper passed through a test tube-like mechanism with liquid in it, which made perforations in them, and then the tape was pasted on another paper similar to telegrams. Peacock doesn't know where the messages were coming from, but she was told once that they were shipping messages. "I never knew a thing. It was no problem not to talk about what you were doing, because we didn't know."

The communications department usually socialized together. They went for lunch on Seventh Avenue or Broadway, or to Hamburg Heaven, which was very popular at the time and full of the rich and famous. "We used to go Child's, which was up Fifth Avenue, and we used to run into Walter Winchell up there. And he was a great fan, and I'm sure he knew what we were doing, because he used to write quite good columns concerning Canadians who were in New York."

After a period of time the Dumpy code became obsolete and Peacock was transferred to a small Type X section, which was off the main room. The main Type X department was an absolute din all the time, she said, and very hot in the summer, with salt tablet dispensers on the walls.

"So I was in this other section for a while and then after the atomic bomb fell all of a sudden everything was over and people were being fired left, right and centre."

"Fired, or laid off?"

"Same thing. Everybody was sort of anxious to get back to living again."

"Sent home."

In the late summer, Peacock's communications expertise was called on again. The top coding machine was needed to relay information about Igor Gouzenko. "I guess Dorothy [Evenson] had gone because she had moved over to that other section, but I was the only one left that knew how to run this machine and they apparently got worried that there was a message coming through, and it was about Gouzenko. So I had to stay around." They told me to go to the Beekman where I was living at that time, and to just stay there until they called me. So I stayed there and I went back to the office two or three times and then I decoded the messages about Gouzenko and I could read those messages. And that was in August or September, I guess it was in September '45.

"We didn't hear anything about that here until about January or February of 1946." (Gouzenko's defection was not made public until months after the fact.)

"So who were these messages going to then?"

"I don't know. Upstairs, but I don't know ... [they] probably had to report to Canada due to the powers that be that were holding Gouzenko."

Peacock and Thompson visited New York in August of 1989 and were surprised a section of Rockefeller Center was still called the Passport Office.

Isolationism

There were large BSC files on the America First Movement, the large isolationist organization that tried to keep the United States out of the war.

"Because that was part of the problem — to get rid of that sentiment."

"That's right."

"That's part of the reason we were there."

"So they gave stuff to the newspapers. I think that's in the BSC history."

"And Mr. Stephenson was influential in promoting the Lend-Lease, the fifty ships, the tankers, British bases."

Canadians in New York
"Did you let on that you were Canadian when you were out socially?"

"Some people thought we were from Boston."

"But you weren't told to cover up that you were Canadians?

"Oh, no."

"I didn't socialize much with Americans at all."

"We had so many of us down there, that we had a good time just with ourselves."

Communications
"And another company that was very closely involved was Commercial Cables."

"Communications?"

"I dare say. I remember they used to have a marvellous Christmas party. When you think about it, it was sort of questionable."

Colonel Bayly was in charge of communications, they said.

"He was a famous person."

"He was the one that was at Camp X too. He did something at Camp X."

"So he was the head of communications that figured out how to run this stuff?"

"Yes, he was the head ..."

"He was an agent that disappeared periodically and then came back."

Office Departments
"On the 2nd floor, it was a great big huge room with a row of desks."

"And there was a section where they parcelled things, the mailing room, and another section was kind of glassed-in where [Ken] Maidment was; I've no idea what he did."

"My part was the Registry and it was everything that came out of Sir William's office and it went to Betty Cook's desk and she sorted it under headings and then she passed it on to the correct person who handled that particular area, such as you mentioned, the IG Farben or the 'Electrolux man' [Axel Wenner Gren — see Appendix] from Sweden. And also the isolationist groups in the States."

Maclean's Magazine Article

The *Maclean's* story talks about Stephenson being a speed-reader who woke up at five in the morning to start work.

"That would be true, I'm sure."

"And that he was extra observant of things?"

"Very much so."

"In fact, the dictum was we weren't supposed to go out with anyone in the office. We had an assistant who asked me out to lunch. So we had to meet outside the office, and he took me to a French restaurant. We went back separately to the office and apparently Sir William was so smart, he caught on to the fact that we had been out to lunch together. He just smelt the garlic wafting through the office."

"How about his love for martinis?"

"Yes. I think that is true. I could be wrong. I know only one occasion. I remember a party and William was there and there were martinis."

"I think that was the drink of the time."

"Some places served only martinis."

Bill Stephenson

"Did you know he was a Canadian?"

"Oh, yes."

"We knew who he was."

"Just a few people could identify him?"

"He was a very inconspicuous man. He kind of melded into the background."

"I guess we were just told who he was."

[It says in *Maclean's*:] "*Women spoke of his doorman as Peter, of his secretary as Gabrielle and of him as God. Only a handful of them knew him by sight.*"

"Oh, that's garbage."

"Oh, well, maybe later on. But in the early days we all knew who he was."

"Noel Coward. He was a good friend of Sir William's, and I remember going to a party that Sir William and his wife gave for the opening of his play."

Stephenson's code number was 48000, Manchee said, with 48 indicating the United States.

"The Mayan Restaurant was one restaurant that we weren't allowed to go into."

"That was instant dismissal."

"At 630 Fifth Avenue."

"And we were never to take a course at Berlitz [language school]. That was another thing that we weren't supposed to do." No one knew exactly why.

A handful of Toronto ex-BSC people continued to get together after the war. That nucleus organized a BSC reunion in 1986. The guest speaker, before the publication of his book, *Camp X*, was David Stafford.

Reflections on being in wartime New York with BSC
By Jean Peacock, 1986

We were an unusual group within an unusual organization — we weren't the "Cynthia"s etc. (I think!)—Canadians because employees had to be British and we were the closest market.

We were a bit of history of World War II — a lot has been written about Intrepid's organization but not from our perspective.

The thrill for Canucks working in N.Y. during that special period. People working shifts — unusual then except for nurses and production line women, which we were—seeing another side of N.Y. life. The café society (movie stars at Hamburg Heaven, Sinatra from the Capital to the Waldorf, etc.) to Child's and Walter Winchell, and the low — all-night cafeterias like Bicks and Walgreens. Out for graveyard shift lunches at 4 a.m.

Radio City Music Hall; the Rockettes; the old Roxy. Radio shows for free if you got your tickets ahead. Fred Waring and the show he used to put on after the broadcast. Seeing the Rockettes in the AP drugstore, when a toasted English muffin order was "burn the British."

The glamour night spots which we might see if someone turned up from out of town to take us — the Stork Club, El Morocco, the St. Regis Iridium Room with an ice show, the Rainbow Room. Then there were the Zanzibar, the Copacabana, the Latin Quarter. The #5 Fifth Avenue bus all the way up to the Cloisters. Movie classics at the Museum of Modern Art; pictures at the Museum of Modern Art. The Frick Collection.

The beautiful stores and store windows — Saks, Lord and Taylor, Altman's Bergdorf; the gorgeous jewels in the window of Van Cleef & Arpel's and Cartier's.

The battle of the baritones on the radio. Secondhand clothes from the Dressing Room Shop. Lunches at the Stockholm. The Mayan in our building a no-no. St. Patrick's Cathedral; Fifth Avenue parades. Shopping at Klein's and Orbach's. Showing visitors the town. Shoes at Beck's and Kitty Kelly. Thirty-five-cent martinis. Broadway shows from the cheap seats (or even standing). The Blue Angel; Upstairs at the Downstairs. All those jazz spots on 52nd Street.

The Village; the East River; the Staten Island ferry to see the Statue of Liberty; the Automat; Jack Dempsey's. War bond drives on street corners with good entertainment. Uniforms. Central Park on Sunday afternoons; concerts at Carnegie Hall on Sunday afternoons. The itch to get home again and get on with our lives.

N.Y. — it was wonderful.

Doris Hogg

Former BSC employee Calgary native Doris (Griffiths) Hogg was recruited by Bill Stephenson's friend Tommy Drew-Brook in 1940, and did similar office work in New York as the BSC employees in Toronto. When she was working there she was unaware of which organization actually employed her. "I didn't know who I was working for," she said. In August of 1942, Hogg was moved to a division in Mexico City and she eventually married a man who was attached to the British legation there.

She said her husband's group discovered if an Axis attack was to occur on the United States, it would not be simply an attempt to storm the coasts. The attack was to come overland through Mexico. On one of her husband's covert raids, Hogg says, an actual map was discovered of a Japanese invasion plan for the west coast of Mexico.

Elizabeth Wood

One of British Security Coordination's head secretaries, Patsey Sullivan, relayed a passage describing Stephenson by the late Elizabeth Wood, another New York inner-office BSC secretary, who also worked in Washington. Wood wrote about her old boss:

To those who didn't know him, no words are adequate; to those who knew him, no words are necessary. "Intrepid" is still the greatest mystery of all; no release from the Official Secrets Act "thirty years after" will solve that one. Mercurial ... magic ... masterly ... magnificent ... these were the epithets used to describe him. Yet no one has ever properly defined him, and we cannot do so now.

His most conspicuous quality was an inherent capacity to disappear, swift as summer lightning; or if he were confined to, say, an elevator, to make himself invisible. We knew he had escaped from a German prisoner-of-war camp in World War I, but we didn't know it had been so easy for him! Like the magician's rabbit, he could melt into the mists of the night, or into the madding crowd of Fifth Avenue with the speed of a jet, without a sound, without a breath. No, he wasn't the magician's rabbit; he was the magic. Everyone felt it; no one could explain it.

Wood later wrote to Sullivan on January 6, 1987, about the BSC reunion in Toronto. "And *Stafford*! W. S. S. is *furious*, but that is *Top Secret* ..."[2]

Elizabeth Pack — "Cynthia"

During the war many agents worked for Stephenson, but the one with the highest profile was an American woman, code-named "Cynthia." Her exploits first appeared in Hyde's *A Quiet Canadian*, and a few years later he featured her in an extended, non-footnoted book entitled *Cynthia*.

"Cynthia" was born Amy Elizabeth Thorpe in Minneapolis, November 22, 1910, the daughter of a U.S. marine major, George Cyrus Thorpe, and Cora Wells Thorpe. At the age of twenty, she married Arthur Pack, a secretary at the British Embassy in Washington who was nearly twice her age. She was in Spain during the civil war and helped a number of Franco supporters to escape.

Pack began her espionage career in Poland, where she had a relationship with an aide to the Polish Foreign Secretary, Colonel Joseph Beck. Some of the information she obtained may have related to secrets of the German cipher machine ENIGMA, which the Poles were working on, and a prototype was eventually smuggled to Britain.

She and her husband later moved to South America where Elizabeth Pack, writing under a pseudonym, published propaganda sympathetic to the British cause. "It was at this time she was summoned to New York and given her code name by the highly skilled spymaster, William Stephenson, head of the British Secret Service in America."[1]

According to Hyde's account, the first major assignment for Betty Pack from BSC was to renew an acquaintance with an Italian naval attaché, Alberto Lais, who was stationed at the Italian Embassy in Washington. Her goal was to pilfer information from Lais. She is said to have discovered the Italians planned to scuttle their ships harboured in the United States in March of 1941, and warned the Americans. Her work may have led to the obtaining of the Italian naval cipher.[2]

In May 1941, Cynthia was asked to concentrate on the Vichy French Embassy. Posing as a journalist, she arranged for a meeting with the Ambassador Henry-Haye. Before the interview, she met with the embassy's press attaché, Charles Brousse, and he told her of the situation in Europe. "France's future requires cooperation with Germany," he reportedly told her. "If your car is in the ditch, you turn to the person who can put it on the road again. That is why we work with Germany." The two began a relationship, and after time, Brousse expressed a dislike of Laval, which Cynthia cultivated with guidance from BSC, and he talked more and more about Vichy affairs. In July of 1941, she told him she was an agent of the American government and he could receive money for information. She stressed this could help defeat Laval and the Nazis, and that he'd be a patriotic Frenchman. Eventually she obtained copies of nearly all the telegrams to and from the French Embassy and Cynthia was instrumental in securing the French Naval ciphers.

Published reports say one night the couple heard a guard at the embassy approaching and Cynthia quickly removed all her clothes. When the guard saw her, he decided he should leave the two alone. On at least one occasion BSC is said to have used the services of a criminal, "the Georgia Cracker," a Canadian safe expert, who helped the couple procure information. By November 1942, Vichy embassy officials in the U.S. were detained in a hotel in Hershey, Pennsylvania. Cynthia tried to join the personnel by posing as Brousse's daughter. However, Brousse's wife began to put "une and une" together and Cynthia's tryst with the Vichy French came to an end. Elizabeth Pack eventually married Charles Brousse and they retired to France.

Cynthia's exploits for Stephenson's organization are said to have greatly assisted Allied European and African operations. The Italian ciphers may have contributed to the one-sided defeat of the Italian Navy by the British in the battle of Matapan. Ellery Huntington, who headed OSS special operations for TORCH, the invasion of Africa, was quoted as saying Cynthia's work "had changed the course of the war."[3]

Hyde wrote he first met Cynthia in 1941: "I had heard (only half believing, I must confess) of some of her more astonishing exploits in Europe, and I was aware, too, that she recently engaged in some unusually strong and subtle anti-Nazi propaganda work in South America."

Hyde wasn't the only Briton "half-believing" escapades of Bill Stephenson's most famous undercover agent. The English historian Hugh Trevor-Roper (Lord Dacre) wrote following Stephenson's death that the story of Cynthia had "been proved fictitious." Noted British World War II authority Sir David Hunt not only doubted Cynthia's reported accomplishments, he questioned whether such a person ever existed.[4]

It is difficult to obtain firsthand personal accounts to confirm the exploits of Cynthia. Obviously BSC operated on a need-to-know basis, and according to Hyde's books, Cynthia and her husband Brousse died in the 1960s. Hyde died in 1990. In Hyde's book, *Cynthia*, there is a nebulous reference to a BSC liaison person who introduced Cynthia to him during the war: "She sounded so improbably romantic and fictional (and I was younger then) that I told her New York contact, whom I knew as 'Marion', that I was eager to meet her. She would arrange it and so it came about."

Marion de Chastelain

The "Marion" Hyde knew was Marion de Chastelain, mother of Canada's Armed Forces recent head, General John de Chastelain.

Born Marion Walsh, she grew up in Europe, where her father worked for Standard Oil of New Jersey in Bucharest. Her future husband, Alfred Gardyne de Chastelain, was a petroleum engineer and sales manager with Unirea de Petrol Company in Romania, which was controlled by Phoenix Oil and Transport of London.

> "... OUR MAN INVOLVED [in Romania] WAS READY COMPLETE OPERATION WAS PETROLEUM GEOLOGIST GARDINE DE CHASTELAIN WHO MARRIED ONE OF MY NY SECRETARIES AMERICAN GIRL WHO HANDLED AND TRANSLATED ALL CYNTHIA'S VICHY PRODUCT STOP THE DE CHASTELAINS NOW LIVE CALGARY AFTER UNSATISFACTORY SOJOURN AUSTRALIA.
>
> —William Stephenson to author Stevenson
> (undated, University of Regina)

Alfred de Chastelain was also involved in espionage. Early in the war he worked for British Intelligence in Istanbul, and he was in touch with various factions in Romania.

Marion and their children visited her parents in New York in November 1940, intending to stay only a short time, but her mother became ill, and she received a job offer. "I got a phone call one day asking me, in these words, would I care to do something 'for King and Country'? And I said why not? So I went down to Rockefeller Center."

She was interviewed by Alexander Halpern, a Russian-born naturalized Briton, who was in SOE, and who previously worked for the Kerensky government in Petrograd. The interview was simple and over quickly, as they knew of her through her husband. During the war British Intelligence had a tendency to employ relatives of people in the business because they were familiar with their backgrounds.

"So I was with SOE for all of maybe two weeks when Sir William whisked me upstairs to SIS and that was that. They were on a floor below us, SOE had a separate office from us, and SIS was upstairs."

De Chastelain, fluent in French, soon started working with Cynthia, who was then working on the Vichy embassy. Unlike Hyde, she had never heard of her before. She was shown her picture and sent to meet Cynthia in a Washington hotel. At the time Elizabeth Pack was separating from Arthur, her British diplomat husband.

"She was the type who revelled in espionage. She really loved it. And she came from a good Washington family so she had entree to all the embassies and places. So she circulated."

Although Cynthia was an attractive woman, her allure was something deeper, de Chastelain says. "She was tall, I would say a dark blond. She wasn't a light blond. Beautiful figure. Not terribly good-looking, but she had what I suppose Elinor Glyn wrote about years ago, and that was 'It.' Which certainly appealed to the males. She did very well for us."

"Is it true about the ciphers being smuggled out?"

"Oh, yes. It's absolutely true."

Cynthia's contact with the Vichy French, Charles Brousse, raided the embassy safe regularly and handed over the contents. Later he supplied more and more material. He memorized conversations, took notes at briefings, and pilfered telegrams that were going to and from the embassy. He forwarded the material to Cynthia, who gave it to Marion. "That was why I would have to go and collect them, and go back to New York, and translate them, and go back to Washington and give them back to her. I spent a lot of time on airways." De Chastelain usually collected the information in the morning, took the next plane back to New York, translated the papers and took them back the same day so Brousse could return them to the safe. He hauled out a variety of information, but BSC was interested mainly in the diplomatic cipher and the naval cipher. They used the naval cipher to help translate radio traffic to and from Martinique, where there were a number of French war ships. "The admiral that was there absolutely refused to have anything to do with the United States or Britain or the Allies. So we were monitoring his traffic constantly. From Vichy to Martinique."[5]

De Chastelain usually met Cynthia at the Wardman Park Hotel in Washington, which sat amidst several acres of park and had numerous entrances. She left a cab several blocks away, walked to the hotel, and would never enter or exit the same way. If the two women didn't meet at the hotel, they would arrange meetings at "strange places." BSC's Washington office was central, although it was small and located in a private house, but de Chastelain was not allowed to go there, in case she was followed. The two women met at regular intervals — at least once a week, sometimes more, depending on what Cynthia was getting from the embassy. Cynthia was finished with her work with the Italians when de Chastelain started working with her.

Stephenson didn't want Cynthia in New York meeting with people in the organization, and that was one of the reasons de Chastelain travelled to Washington, she said. Although Hyde refers to trips Cynthia made to New York on "shopping" excursions, de Chastelain doesn't remember them. "I never saw her in New York. Never. I always saw her in Washington."[6] At nearly every meeting, sometimes numerous times in a week, Cynthia asked de Chastelain if she could see Bill Stephenson. He always said no. "I think he saw her once, probably when she was recruited, but he would never see her again."

It seems Elizabeth Pack had strong feelings for Bill Stephenson. "I am already filled with nostalgia for the happiest days of my life," she wrote to Hyde in 1962. "They were packed with all sorts of emotions: the supreme desire to help the Allied war effort; anxiety lest I fail in the responsibilities entrusted to me; lonely despair when my moves went wrong; satisfaction when things took a constructive form. And in the end (it is with me still) the real anguish of wondering if, with more experience and better judgement, I could not have worked faster and done more." Hyde belonged "to that happy period that even in wartime exists for those who have a common cause and are especially united where there is a 'Quiet Canadian.' Long life to him, and to you!"[7] She later commended Hyde on his efforts: "My heart sings because at last someone has written about this remarkable man."[8]

Cynthia told de Chastelain about taking off her clothes to convince the guard she and Brousse were engaged in other undercover activity. "Of course she told me. Didn't surprise me in the slightest," she laughed.

"I got that the next day. She looked absolutely beat. She said, 'I've had quite a night,'" de Chastelain chuckled. "She told me the whole story. She was either top of the hill, or deep down in the valley. She'd look simply dreadful when I got there and she'd be so depressed. And I'd try to cheer her up." Part of the problem was Pack became very fond of Brousse, and he was living in the same hotel as she was, with his wife and children.

The safecracker used to open the embassy safe was handled in Washington, and de Chastelain didn't meet him. "That was a real James Bond sort of thing. I don't know why they had to break in. Unless, probably what happened was they changed the lock on the safe, which would be normal practice in an embassy every once in a while, no matter how much confidence you had in your personnel."

When the Vichy Embassy staff was interned in Pennsylvania, Cynthia attempted to stay at the compound in Hershey. "She was acting as Brousse's daughter, from another marriage or something," de Chastelain remembered, "to see if she could find out anything there." There were also plans for her to go to France with the embassy staff.[9]

De Chastelain left New York for England in November 1943. Although Cynthia also travelled to Britain, de Chastelain never saw her again. "By that time the thing was over." Cynthia's espionage career was finished. Some accounts say she later tried to work in Europe, but was not allowed to.

"Her cover was pretty well blown by that time, I would think," de Chastelain said. "In any event, she wanted to drop into France. But with what she knew they wouldn't let her drop."

She does not know if Cynthia was involved in obtaining ENIGMA secrets in Poland. "How true that is, I don't know. She certainly worked in one of the offices there in the intelligence department. And she may well have done. Then, there was another thing. Anybody who knew about ULTRA was not allowed to drop behind enemy lines."

Elizabeth Pack and de Chastelain got along well together, and she remembers her positively. "Well, she tried hard. And she was a very charming person. There's no question about it."

When she wasn't involved with Cynthia, de Chastelain worked in BSC's inner office and was a cipher clerk for Stephenson. She met with John Pepper, who was running the French and the Spanish section, she said. "And I had to do with him, simply because I took care of the French side of it." Grace Garner and de Chastelain had access to a safe containing one-time pads used in decoding messages from Britain and other places. "And apart from Bill himself, we were the only ones to have it."

The messages coming into the office were "Most Secret. Top Secret. Destroy-before-reading type of thing," she laughed. Once the messages were decoded they went straight to Stephenson. Grace Garner, Stephenson's chief secretary for most of the war, would be able to read what he read. Garner was usually the final link. "She would know what was transpiring from England back and forth. From any of our far-flung people in South America who were communicating directly with us."

According to *A Quiet Canadian*, BSC produced and distributed in the U.S. an anonymous booklet titled *Sequel to the Apocalypse*, which told of "how your dimes and quarters help to pay for Hitler's war." It linked North American companies to trading partners, various subsidiaries and parent companies operating in Nazi-occupied Europe. Hyde's book says the managing director of Standard Oil offered $50,000 to find out who was behind the publication. Ironically de Chastelain worked in the inner office of BSC, and her father worked for Standard Oil. She was aware BSC spread black propaganda about them.

"Of course they did. Most of the big oil companies. They all had subsidiaries abroad. You take any of the major oil companies. Same as Ford, apparently, and Baer and IG Farben."

Visitors

Stephenson received a plethora of visitors when de Chastelain worked there. The secretaries fielded all the guests and decided who advanced further. Charles Farquar, Stephenson's old Winnipeg friend, discovered he was in New York's Rockefeller Center and decided to look Stephenson up when he was there. But he couldn't get past the first secretaries. "No one could," de Chastelain said.

Mountbatten was a visitor while she was at BSC. "He was only there once while I was there. Whether he came later, I don't think so, because after '43 he was pretty well taken up with other things. I don't think he came back." Bill Donovan was a frequent visitor. Once when she was there he was nearly hit by a message projectile flung from a vacuum tube. "As Bill Donovan walked in the door with his aide, one of these things came down and shot right over my head and just missed him. He said, 'I didn't think I was too popular, but I didn't think anybody wanted to kill me.'"

Pat Bayly came by and chatted to her, and tried to show her how a few of the communication machines worked. "He was in the office for some time in New York. He was definitely fussing around with the telecommunications ... And an awfully nice man too. And last I heard of him, I gather he was sent over to England to work on some of their towers or whatever they were putting up. He was an extremely bright man and a nice man."

Bayly had a reputation for not discussing his war activities. "I can't imagine him ever saying anything to anybody about anything. He was a very quiet man, but we got along very well ... He certainly worked at Bletchley."

Tommy Drew-Brook, the Toronto stockbroker and Stephenson's friend, was frequently in the office. Eventually de Chastelain and her husband became friends with the couple.

"And Beaverbrook was in and out like a yo-yo. I always knew, if I happened to be out of the office for a few minutes, and came back in—we had a sort of a reception room off of our office and when I saw that coat with the great big fur collar and the funny hat — I knew Beaverbrook was in there ... They were interesting times."

December 7, 1941

The Quiet Canadian says Stephenson had success in penetrating the mission of Japanese special envoy Suburu Kurusu, who came to the United States to negotiate in November of 1941. One of Stephenson's men contacted a secretary of the Japanese envoy, and Stephenson sent translated transcriptions of the recordings of the conversations to the White

House daily. Hyde's book also says James Roosevelt was sent to Stephenson with a message from the President, which told him of the lack of progress in talks with Japanese Special Envoy Kurusu and Ambassador Nomura. The same day, November 27, 1941, Stephenson supposedly sent a telegram to Britain saying prophetically, "Japanese negotiations off. Expect action within two weeks."

Although she remembered meeting him, de Chastelain didn't recall James Roosevelt in the office. She was aware of many books and documentaries that conclude there was some prior knowledge of the attack.

"If they were monitoring a lot, it is hard to see how they missed it," de Chastelain said. "My opinion is that they did know, and unfortunately the poor admiral and general in Pearl Harbor took the blame. I mean such foul-ups—sending such vital news by cable. Instead of picking up the phone if necessary."

De Chastelain obviously was in a unique position, as she was working in the inner office of BSC at the time. "Now mind you, Churchill was probably just as anxious, because I remember the day it happened, Sunday the 7th and I hadn't had a day off for about a month, and I said to my father, no matter what happens, I am not going into the office on Sunday. So I was sound asleep and he banged on the door and said 'you are wanted on the phone' and I said, 'tell them I am dead!' He said, 'their last word was turn on the radio.' So I turned on the radio and of course they were blasting this thing on and on. So I got dressed and beetled into the office just as the Japanese were being removed, because they had their offices in the same building we were in, a few floors down [the Japanese Consulate]. And then finally I got upstairs, and we had champagne and we sat on our desks and chatted."

It was a pivotal time for British Security Coordination, as the Americans were then on side. "And that of course was Bill's first big job, trying to combat the isolationists."

The inner office staff and Bill Stephenson were all at work that Sunday. "He had probably been there for hours. I didn't get there till about 2:30 in the afternoon. Anyway it was quite a day. And then of course Bill Donovan was back and forth because he was setting up OSS."

"Would Donovan have known too?"

"Bill, if he hadn't known, may have guessed. Bill Stephenson. And obviously Bill Donovan too. And Bill Donovan being in Washington was very close to Roosevelt."

Europe

De Chastelain's husband visited North America in July 1943 to recruit Canadians with European ancestry for drops into the occupied continent. The scheme only met with limited success, and he himself parachuted into Romania, December 22, 1943, to help oust the pro-Nazi government. "What he wanted to do was to get the head of the peasant party to come out, but he wouldn't come." When her husband was in North America she realized she wanted to return to Europe. "I told him that I was going back, with the children being spoiled rotten by my parents and at this time a little war would do them good. Besides, I was bored." She returned to Britain in November 1943 and reported to her new espionage assignment just before Christmas. Her husband was taken prisoner on the continent and she didn't see him until after his release in 1944.

In England she worked for British intelligence in London. "I was Section 5 of MI6. That's counter-intelligence, and we were in the Charity Commissioner's office building, which dated from mid-Victorian, I guess, on Ryder Street, just off St. James Street."

At that office she dealt with numerous intercepted and decoded messages. De Chastelain was surprised that news of Britain's code breakers success, the ULTRA Secret, was released in the 1970s. "I didn't see the necessity of publishing it anyway. What was the point? That's why Churchill's books are so peculiar. 'Now we knew that this was happening.' How did you know that this was happening? I used to get piles of intercepts on my desk every morning from London to go through ..."

"From ULTRA. The German Army, the German Foreign Office. Of course you could tell from troop movements. And even orders for food that were put through. I mean a lot of it was awfully dull. A hundred tons of something or other. But then I passed them on to people who dealt with this sort of thing, and from that they could figure out troop movements in Europe. Right across Europe. So that's where it was so relevant."

The de Chastelain family moved to London in the late 1940s, as they couldn't go back to Romania. After the war "the Russians simply didn't want my husband back in, because he knew too many people, and they thought he'd be a problem ... So they ended up sending an Englishman in there. I think he was an Air Vice Marshal, who didn't have a clue. So as far as the Russians were concerned, that was just fine."

Following the war, the oil business eventually brought the family to Canada. John de Chastelain, Marion's Romanian-born son, joined the Canadian military and by the 1990s became Canada's highest ranked military officer, the Chief of Defence Staff.

Bill Stephenson

During the war, Stephenson often bore the brunt of the costs of running the organization, de Chastelain says. "His years with BSC cost him in the region of $3 million of his own money. I'm sure he paid our salaries many times because it is very difficult to get money out of SIS. Or SOE for that matter ... And of course we were paid in U.S. dollars and they were very loath to let go of U.S. dollars because they didn't have all that many of them. And they were earmarked for other things. So I'm sure that he certainly spent I would say in the region of about $3 million, which he never regretted, I'm sure."

De Chastelain remained close friends with Stephenson and his wife and visited them in New York and Bermuda on many occasions. The couple's apartment in New York was the whole floor of a building on East 52nd St. near the water. "He had one wall of the bedroom knocked out, it was all glass, so they could look at the United Nations."

De Chastelain knew nothing of Stephenson's background or work before the war. She thought his espionage career began when he reported on the Nazi build-up from Europe during the thirties. "He never talked about that sort of thing. He never talked about himself in any way. Sometimes it used to come up in conversation, something he had done in India or Germany or wherever. But never concluded, just passing remarks of that nature." She thought Stephenson may have attended university in Cambridge for a time immediately following World War I, but she knew few details. "And lord knows I spent enough time with him. But we mainly discussed present situations or things that had happened when I was there. But he never discussed anything personal. His wife probably knew the whole story, I don't know."

Stephenson's fortune evolved from the can opener and the radio business, de Chastelain said. "But he had mining interests in Yugoslavia. He was heavily involved in the movie business with the Kordas — Alexander and his brother — and knew Merle Oberon extremely well, and Greta Garbo."

She was surprised to learn most biographical information about Stephenson was incorrect. "I knew nothing about his early life. To me, he was just somebody I met in 1941. Out of the blue." Once Stephenson created his phony background, he must have made a decision to keep it. "By that time he'd certainly lived the life for so many years. It was probably second nature to him. I mean why go back and ... it was no point to it. I mean if he wanted to."

She thought it was "marvellous" that Stephenson was a difficult person to trace, and the spy hubris was maintained. "Absolutely. No, he was absolutely made for it. And a lot of these stories that he's told people, if they knew him well they'd know that he was just ... pulling their leg," she laughed. "To see how much they believed."

Elizabeth, Stephenson's adopted daughter, was upset with press people descending on her after Stephenson's death. She went to England for three months and changed her unlisted phone number. "I don't think she'd see any journalists ever."

Some reports say his house was gone over by security people searching for papers. "She didn't mention it. She was so disgusted with the whole thing anyway, that all she wanted to do was get out. And I guess she had a pretty bad time there for awhile. Until she did the right thing, and just went to England." She planned on staying in Bermuda, and at the time her son Rhys attended school there.

People visiting Stephenson at the office during the war were frightened. "He had a cold steely eye. People were petrified, actually, when they went in to see him, if they were called in. He intimidated."

Stephenson knew Churchill, she said. "Of course he knew him. And the [North American assignment] meeting I've gathered took place at Beaverbrook's house. And why Colville should know about it, well, there's no reason in the world he should know," she laughed.[10] "He's another one of these with great egos who had to know everything ... I mean the whole thing is so stupid."

De Chastelain had little time for some authors of books and articles chronicling Stephenson's war career, and she avoided reading much of it. She was surprised to receive a note from British Foreign Office vet David Stafford following the publication of his book *Camp X*, which questioned aspects of Stephenson's career. "He had the gall to send me a thank you letter for all I did for him. I didn't do a damn thing for him; I wouldn't have given him the time of day."

She refused to read *Camp X* and was "infuriated" at Stafford's "A Myth Called Intrepid" story in *Saturday Night* magazine. "I can't stand him, and anything he writes. I could wring his neck."

"Bill made a lot of enemies during his time and a lot of people would want to smear his name," she said. She also knew the historian Hugh Trevor-Roper when he was doing British government work. "He worked right above my head in London in SIS. He and ... the spy who ended up in Russia, Philby. He and Philby were up in the attic above my head."

According to Philby, Trevor-Roper was threatened with court martial during the war by the head of Section V, Felix Cowgill. Trevor-Roper was one of the "formidable Oxonian" men who "outclassed Cowgill in brain power," he wrote in *My Silent War*. Like the former British intelligence department head, de Chastelain wasn't a great fan of Hugh Trevor-Roper's either: "Hugh Trevor-Roper is a little bit of a man with a big ego." She was quite pleased when his historical expertise was called into question and the supposed diaries of Adolf Hitler he said were genuine proved to be forgeries. "That was one of the great days of my life, when they found they weren't [authentic]. And he had spent what? $400,000 of the *Times'* money?"

De Chastelain says the Stephensons' move to Bermuda had nothing to do with security or his previous activities. He moved to the island because he liked it there. "He loved Bermuda from way back, and when he had his stroke that is where he wanted to be." The couple lived in the Princess Hotel in Hamilton for two years while their house was built. He may have bought his property there during the war, as he stopped off there on a number of occasions. "Lady Stephenson didn't particularly care for Bermuda, but anything that he wanted. She was a big city girl ... Mary was just the right size for him because Bill was quite short and she was even shorter. I felt tall when I was next to her ... She loved New York and she had lots of friends. And I imagine she found Bermuda fairly boring ... And she had lots of society friends. Personal friends. And of course it must have been rather difficult for her, because Bill was not a man to socialize. You know, go to big parties. That wasn't his ..."

Although Stephenson wasn't a party person, stories about his affection for generous martinis were true, she said. "He made the wickedest martini that was ever made." But he didn't always drink them. She recalled in June of 1944 Stephenson had invited over former BSC New York people who were in London to his suite at Claridges for drinks. De Chastelain watched Stephenson all evening carry around an untouched martini. "He never drank it. He just carried it around and then watched the results. He had the same one when we left as when we arrived."

The 1989 "A Myth Called Intrepid" narrative in *Saturday Night* by David Stafford describes a doddering, seemingly senile man living in Bermuda. "He wasn't out of it at all. I don't know what he's talking about. The impression of course could be due to his speech problem. Sometimes it was extremely good. And other times it wasn't ... that would give the impression that he wasn't quite with it. But if they had listened to what he said, not the way he said it."

One of Stephenson's great interests in later life was the potential to harness the Bay of Fundy tides, she said. "That was very dear to his heart, from when I saw him after the war until he died. He still thought that would be one of the greatest, cheapest forms of electricity that anyone could have. It would be very expensive to harness but when it's done, it would produce a fantastic amount of cheap power."

Stephenson longed for some recognition from his own country, and hoped he would some day be awarded the Order of Canada, de Chastelain said. But various nomination appeals from different sources during the seventies were ignored. She thought perhaps there might have been objections to the award from then Prime Minister Pierre Trudeau. "He would never have had it from Trudeau, I'm sure. I think Bill obviously knew a lot about Trudeau, and the fact that he didn't fight in the war, and all those good things." When Stephenson was awarded the Order of Canada, it was during the short-lived Conservative regime of Prime Minister Joe Clark.

De Chastelain attended the BSC reunion in Toronto in 1986 and spoke on Stephenson's behalf. "David Stafford gave a long speech, and Grace Garner spoke on behalf of the women in communications. And she was in tears. So when it finally finished, I said about ten words. That is it. 'Sir William thanks you. He loves you. He wishes you well.' And that was it. And I think everybody was relieved."

She knew few of the BSC employees who attended. "They were all in communications except me. And Grace. And I think her name was Butler — she was a Canadian girl ... I mean communications ... We went up the stairs and that was it. I don't even know where they were located. We never saw them."

The person most knowledgeable about Bill Stephenson's war career was his former head secretary, Grace Garner, she said. "She probably knows more about it than anyone else. Because she was his secretary for the whole time. And a very good one. Although her heart was always in fashion magazines!"

"Bill Stephenson was the only man who could have done the job at the time as efficiently as he did it," de Chastelain concluded. "And keep his people reasonably in control. Because that's difficult. Especially when you have them all over the place ... South America ... He did an excellent job."

She thought Stephenson hadn't received appropriate credit. "But then there's something about Canada that doesn't like heroes. I don't know why. Can you imagine if he had been an American citizen? He would have been full of glory, and so on and so forth. And when they gave him that decoration [Donovan award], he did come to New York. And they had it on the USS *Intrepid* anchored in New York Harbor. And he was constantly having visitors from Washington. They were always coming down to see him. Right up to the end. When it probably wasn't very good for him. It was probably very tiring."

14 BILL ROSS SMITH

Britain

A.M. Bill Ross Smith's career in espionage began through his friendship with Dick Ellis. He knew Ellis for a long time in Australia and in England, and about a year before the war started, Ross Smith was invited over to Ellis's place in London for a number of stag dinners. "I didn't realize it then, but what he was doing, what the Service was doing, was recruiting," Ross Smith said. People attending the parties decided which men would be suitable for British intelligence, and in which area. When the war began Ross Smith was anxious to contribute, but as a 32-year-old Australian in Britain, he found it difficult. In June of 1940, Ellis invited Ross Smith for lunch. Ellis told him he was going to America that week, and he wondered if Ross Smith and his wife would like to go along. "That was my invitation to join SIS."

Four days later Ross Smith and his wife sailed to Canada and then travelled to New York. They met Ellis there and moved into a Madison Avenue apartment. Later Ellis introduced Ross Smith to his new boss, Bill Stephenson. "I had become one of the first four or five men and three women to start British Security Coordination."

His first assignment for BSC was to deliver $1,000 to a French woman in New York and tell her that her husband was okay. He had no idea who the woman was, as he had no reason to know. This was a basic security measure in the service. Ross Smith assumed the woman's husband was an agent in occupied France and she was being paid his sustenance, but no one told him. "Nobody said this is for that purpose, because it wasn't my business to know," he remembered. "Everything was safer that way."

Ross Smith is still unaware of the essential priorities for BSC in the early stages. There were no office meetings to plot a basic strategy for covert operations in the U.S. In fact, he was unsure what he should be doing each day. "Stephenson gave me absolutely no guidance, didn't say, here is a job, get on with it — precisely nothing." Eventually Stephenson told him they were interested in the penetration of foreign missions and whatever the Germans were doing generally, but he was too busy to orchestrate Ross Smith's daily routines, and John Pepper was immersed in economic matters. One day Ross Smith asked Dick Ellis which organization he was actually working for, and Ellis told him, "It is an offshoot of SIS London. Don't leave too many trails to the door here." He could tell his wife everything or nothing, Ellis told him, but preferably nothing. The SIS veteran said there was a lot of interesting information in newspapers, so Ross Smith bought all the New York papers each day and went through them.

The seemingly elementary reading of newspapers proved fruitful, and BSC obtained numerous leads and intelligence from them. "That was a basic thing, because there were literally thousands of eyes and ears gathering news and unusual events," he remembered. The Australian chronicled many types of information, such as arrival of ships, passengers, robberies, news of strategic elements, such as platinum, and he decided whether they were worth following up. The flow of certain elements was important because of their value to the Nazi armament industry. Platinum, for example, was needed for magnetos in aeroplane engines. Two primary sources of platinum at the time were Colombia and the Soviet Union. Before Germany attacked the Soviet Union, they relied on Russian supplies, but afterwards they were forced to buy it in small pieces wherever it could be found. As a result the price rose astronomically and illegal trade began. "There were seamen, travellers and what not, apart from the Germans themselves, organizing means of smuggling this out of the Americas into Portugal and Spain," Ross Smith said. BSC tried to stem the flow, piece by piece. Ross Smith's first major assignment related to smuggling was to contact a subagent named "Gray" and from there his activities developed mainly in shipping and Iberian liaison.

His naval contributions to the Stephenson organization began when a prominent Portuguese shipping operator, Jose Bensaude, unexpectedly approached the British Consul in New York and asked to get in touch with British intelligence authorities. A great percentage of civilian trade between Europe and the United States came on Portuguese and Spanish ships, and Bensaude said there were many suspicious travellers on board. BSC decided to keep an eye on them. "This was the actual start of what became a large organization known as the Ship's Observer Scheme," Ross Smith said. With Bensaude's assistance, at least one secret agent, and sometimes many, were put on each of his ships. Then Ross Smith began conscripting observers for other ships. The McCormick shipping line was approached through the British Consul and told about German intelligence people in North and South America and the possible threat to American ships and interests. Ross Smith then recruited most of the captains, some of the chief stewards, and others on the McCormick ships. "The bar man, if he was suitable, was a useful contact," said the Australian, with a slight grin. The recruits were told to keep watch on possible German couriers and suspicious travellers. Many supplies from South America were cut off by the British naval blockade, so smugglers were active in transporting a variety of small items that were vital to the Nazi war effort. The observers also watched for the movement of enemy ships on the high seas and in various foreign ports around the world. It developed into a worldwide reporting network of over four hundred. All of the observers were volunteers.

Information was procured in many ways. On one trans-Atlantic crossing from Lisbon to New York, a Portuguese captain announced to his passengers that there was a strong possibility the ship would be intercepted by British destroyers, so anyone with important papers or letters could deposit them in the captain's safe for posting in New York. The contents of the safe were handed over to Ross Smith, and BSC's censorship section looked at it all before it was dispersed. Another use of the observers was to spread rumours. Rumours were manufactured, usually in England, and spread throughout the world. Using ship's observers the same rumour could get back to Germany from Calcutta, Bombay or Montevideo. "It was a way of spreading rumour or black propaganda. You tell something in 'strictest confidence,' that's the best way to start a rumour," he said.

BSC was located in an unobtrusive office called Passport Control in Rockefeller Center, and the growth of the New York intelligence net required an increase in physical space. The Passport Office consisted of an entrance lobby, where the general public could obtain visas and other travel information, and had a regular passport section and staff. The annex of that eventually became a huge office area controlled by the Stephenson organization, but in 1940, BSC was a small office on one floor. Ross Smith was unaware of a special rental agreement with the Rockefellers and apparently early BSC expansion depended on the benevolence of the office neighbours. One day Stephenson said the organization needed more space, and he told Ross Smith to persuade the people in the office next door to move out. "I went to them and said we needed it for the war effort and would they be very nice and find somewhere else. And they bloody well did!" Eventually that section of the secret office took up two upper floors of Rockefeller Center, with half of one floor occupied by OSS.

With the expansion, organizing and cataloguing the immense flow of information into BSC offices became a Herculean task. Superintendent Edward Bavin of the Royal Canadian Mounted Police was a contact of Stephenson's, and as result, he borrowed a filing expert from the Mounties and had him seconded to BSC offices. "He set up the filing system, which was superb, and one should be very grateful indeed to the Royal Canadian [Mounted] Police for producing that man and the system they put in," said Ross Smith. "Because the filing system — this was before computers — is the basis of every bloody thing. You put things together — suddenly a picture emerges. If the filing system is faulty, well, you just can't do that."

The information-gathering network extended even to talk on the streets. Ross Smith found a good source of political intelligence was taxi drivers, especially in Washington, as "people will chat simply because there's a taxi driver there who's got to listen." He says he learned a lot from Washington cab drivers, especially when Congress was debating the Lend-Lease bill.

One of the major problems BSC had to confront before Pearl Harbor was the massive isolationist feeling in the U.S. According to Ross Smith, the America First movement, one of the largest organized groups, had approximately $200 million of German capital behind it. "It was a very, very clever thing, because what American could possibly argue with a thing called 'America First' — bloody wonderful." The group was used as means of promoting Nazi slogans and propaganda, such as 'England will fight to the last Frenchman,' and lobbied against pro-British U.S. decisions such as the Destroyers for Bases deal, and the Lend-Lease agreement. Isolationists were "egged on by the Germans, and the America Firsters, but they didn't realize they were being egged on."

BSC began to gauge reaction to the isolationists, and American public opinion in general, through a number of channels. David Ogilvy, who later became renowned in commercial advertising, was with an opinion research bureau in Princeton at the time, and he indicated to Ross Smith that he wanted to become more active in the war "even if it was shovelling coal into a battleship or something." He became a sub-agent of the organization, providing information on public intentions and public opinion generally. Later Ogilvy began working for BSC itself in the British Embassy, working on financial affairs and economic warfare.

In early 1941 Germans and Italians began sabotaging their ships in American harbours and were banned from them. As a result, thousands of German sailors (and nationals), many of whom were skilled men, were marooned in North America. "The Germans wanted them back." Before the Soviet Union entered the war, they were returned on Japanese ships through Russia, across Asia, to Europe. One Saturday Ross Smith received a telephone call from an observer saying there were 700 German seamen on a Japanese ship sitting in port for half an hour before sailing. "These are the buggers who were just scuttling their own ships in American harbours," the observer told him.

Ross Smith went to Stephenson in the afternoon with a suggestion. "I said how about ringing [Frank] Knox, who was Secretary of the Navy, and saying to him, 'Here are 700 men on a Japanese ship heading for the Panama Canal. They've just sabotaged their own ships in American harbours. Suppose they sabotage this one in the Gattun lock? How would you like it?'"

Stephenson contacted Knox, but the Secretary of the Navy saw the danger in possibly blocking the Panama Canal. Stephenson suggested interning the 700 men in Colon, Panama and stopping any Japanese ships from going through the canal to prevent future sabotage. Knox did, and as a result Japanese shipping had to circle Cape Horn to reach the eastern U.S. "Knox was a hell of a good man," Ross Smith remembered.

Later the German sailors began to leave from San Francisco instead of the East Coast, for the return journey. There was an agreement with Japan by which their ships would not carry Germans between 16 and 60 years of age of certain skilled categories, and the British would not molest the Japanese ships. According to Ross Smith, this came about after the HMS *Liverpool* intercepted a ship in the Bay of Tokyo and found a number of German seamen aboard. Lieutenant (later Admiral) Madden of the British cruiser interned the men in Hong Kong, but the Japanese protested. The British Foreign Office arranged for the sailors to be released and agreed not to interfere with Japanese shipping, but negotiated the agreement that only certain people would be transported. "When these 20,000 men had to be transported, well they had different thoughts," said the Australian. Japanese captains were approached in San Francisco and if skilled Germans were on board they were told the Royal Navy would intercept them in international waters, and most of the passengers would be removed. "Then the Japanese got a bit sly and they wouldn't give us a manifest to show who was on the boat at all. So we had to find ways to get that manifest, which we did on a regular basis every Thursday night." Later the Japanese complicated matters further. "They would have a manifest, but they would show 'Rudolf Hench': painter, or hairdresser, or something like that, masseur.

"These bloody, big beefy chaps were trying to ship home as hairdressers." The next step for BSC was to obtain the ship's manifest and try to discover the true occupations of the German passengers to prevent their passage back to Europe. The actual occupations were obtained through "many surreptitious means," according to Ross Smith, and sent to San Francisco. "Then we could say to the captain, 'That fellow isn't a hairdresser, he's a toolmaker working at Ford last week,'" Ross Smith smiled. "In the course of the war they got about 20,000 of those chaps off the boats and interned."

Kim Philby, in *My Silent War*, wrote that British Security Coordination and FBI head J. Edgar Hoover were sometimes at odds because of BSC's unscrupulous activities in various harbours. "He [Hoover] was incensed when Stephenson's strong-boys beat up or intoxicated the crews loading Axis supplies," Philby wrote.[1] Although obviously he was aware of many covert shipping activities in New York at the time, Ross Smith denied any knowledge of rough stuff at the docks. "I should think that was absolute bloody nonsense," he said. "At least it certainly wouldn't be organized by us. Anybody might start a fight today and blame you or me, but certainly we would never do anything stupid like that."

The activities of BSC's Dennis Paine were another point of contention with American officials. In early 1942 the FBI claimed to have definite evidence that Dennis Paine of British intelligence in New York was conducting a surveillance operation on assistant Secretary of State Adolf Berle, for the purpose of getting "dirt" on him, because he was thought to be anti-British. The FBI informed Berle that they had proof Paine had been conducting a campaign against him. The FBI wanted Paine out of the U.S. immediately, and if he wasn't out within 24 hours, they would arrest him. Berle called in Halifax and Stephenson to complain, and Paine was sent out of the country. Halifax and Stephenson were reported to have thoroughly objected to the deportation, and denied involvement, but Hoover was adamant.[2]

Dennis Paine worked for Ross Smith, and he believes Paine was set up, perhaps by the FBI, to encourage more State Department control of BSC and OSS. Paine was known to the FBI through a German-speaking American FBI informer who patrolled the dock areas of New York picking up information in bars. "Paine may have used him as an informer himself." Ross Smith says Paine was his immediate assistant on the Ship's Observer Scheme, and was not involved in any type of surveillance. Following the war Paine denied vehemently that he was involved, Ross Smith said. "The real outcome of this was that Berle was then able to put great pressure to bring all British intelligence activities to an end, and to try and bring British things under greater control. This was averted, however, by the intervention of Donovan." It was apparent to Ross Smith that if the Paine affair was not an FBI plot, it was a contrived attempt to get Berle to take action to try and get BSC under the control of the FBI.

"You see, Hoover was jealous of the contact of other services, particularly Donovan, with the British services, and that's the fact on that." Ross Smith said he spoke to *Camp X* author David Stafford about where he received his information on the Paine incident, and Stafford said he got the information out of Montgomery Hyde's book *Secret Intelligence Agent.* Hyde told Ross Smith he learned of Paine through Berle's State Department papers. "By gad they do appear in Berle's papers, as a permanent myth."

Ross Smith later learned Stephenson detailed Walter "Freckles" Wren to escort Paine out of the country. Wren called Paine and told him to pack a bag, bring his passport and meet him at Grand Central Station. The pair got on a train to Montreal and checked into a hotel, but Wren didn't stay there for long. "Freckles said 'Give me your passport,' and then buggered off to New York, leaving him there. No explanation. Absolutely nothing." Weeks went by, and Paine's bills were paid regularly, but he didn't know why he was left stranded in Montreal. Ross Smith was in South America at the time, and when he returned he wondered what had happened to Paine, who used to sit next to him in the office. "I went to Stephenson and said, 'Where's Paine?' And he said, 'You'll never see him again.' No explanation. I didn't hear about this thing until after the war. Long after."

"But that was just Stephenson. I didn't need to know. 'Get yourself another assistant,'" laughed Ross Smith. "He just says, 'Oh, you'll never see him again.' No explanation, but that was him. A few words. That's all it needed."

South America

In the early months of the organization Stephenson approached Ross Smith and asked him how many languages he knew. "Pretty good Australian, some English, a little American," he answered. "Not good enough," Stephenson said. "How long will it take you to learn Spanish?"

Although BSC was dealing with Western Hemisphere security, they didn't have appropriate linguists or agents suitable for work south of the equator. "London was sending us all sorts of chaps who spoke German, French, Dutch, Pashto, but not a chap with Spanish or Portuguese," Ross Smith remembered, "and so I learned Spanish under great pressure." He attended the Berlitz language school in New York an hour every morning for nine months. His language training paid off, as during the course of the war he travelled throughout Central and South America and established a good working relationship with Basque and Portuguese representatives.

Ross Smith's affiliation with the Basques began with a cable forwarded to him from an Admiral Burrows in Britain, which said basically, 'look up the Basques and say I said so.' In the late 1930s Burrows was captain of a British destroyer that rescued the Spanish government out of Bilbao, Ross Smith said. The spiriting away of many Spaniards who were under physical threat from Franco's forces endeared Burrows to the Basques. Ross Smith met with the Basque government delegate in New York, Manu Delasota, and discovered he was educated in Britain and was very interested in helping the Allied cause. Basque influence, contacts in the fiel, and other assistance soon proved to be invaluable to BSC and the Allies. It reached throughout South America and into mainland Europe. "They provided us with a marvellous network in Europe, guides across the Pyrenees, escape routes. They were very, very helpful." Many presidents of South American republics were of Basque descent, as were several South American bishops. Many agents in the Ships' Observers project were Basques.

In 1941 an observer on a Spanish ship reported that the captains of all Spanish ships were carrying wallets containing very heavily concealed documents, which were of such importance, if they were lost or opened, the captain could be subject to the death penalty. The captains took the secured document to a Spanish Consulate whenever the ship was in a port, to certify that the seals on the document envelope were intact. "Well, naturally I wanted to have a look at these things," Ross Smith recalled.

He told the Basque delegate Delasota of the problem, and they planned a theft. "I arranged for him to take Spanish captains out to dinner, until he could eventually get one of them sufficiently "tight," and then to telephone me." After a few weeks Delasota telephoned Ross Smith about eleven o'clock at night and said "I've got one." He was at an all-night restaurant on 58th Street and Madison Avenue, and when Ross Smith arrived he found Delasota with an appropriate Spanish captain. "It was obvious that he had a bit more wine than usual, and so I was able to extract the document from his breast pocket without him being aware of it." The document pouch had to be opened, photographed, closed and returned, all in a way that the Spanish authorities would be unable to detect and the Spanish captain would be unaware of what had been done. He called Dorothy Hyde, Montgomery Hyde's wife, who worked in Room 99, which specialized in opening and closing envelopes without detection. Ross Smith also contacted a photographer named "Hall" and the trio hastily assembled at BSC offices in Rockefeller Center at about 11:30 p.m. The document package wasn't a typical envelope. "Dorothy took one look at the documents and said 'God, this is going to be a hard one'," remembered Ross Smith. It took her an hour to open it, Hall photographed the contents, and Hyde closed it up again. Ross Smith rushed the document pouch back to the restaurant, where Delasota was still at table, plying the captain with a drink every time he woke up, and he carefully replaced the envelope pouch in the captain's pocket.

The document inside was to be opened when a radioed code word was received, and the code word was on the outside envelope. The memorandum inside, from the Spanish maritime chief, instructed the captains of approximately 700 Spanish ships to immediately sail to the nearest Axis port, as opposed to neutral, Spanish or Allied harbours. The pilfered message indicated which side the Spanish government was on. "So with this piece of information, it provided Churchill with definite knowledge of where Franco stood. Secondly, it provided our navy with the code word." If the code word on the document was radioed and intercepted, the Allied Navy could react and take action. The ships were to sail to the closest Axis port, so the Allies knew which direction the Spanish ships were to proceed and where to find them.

Manu Delasota's family owned many ships prior to Franco's reign, and at least two of the captains were still loyal to the Delasota family. It was decided he, his relative Ramon Delasota, who was chief of the Delasota clan, and Hosio Antonio Deaguirrie Quobre, the president of the Basques in exile, should record a message to broadcast to Spanish ship captains if the code word was picked up. The message, recalled Ross Smith, roughly translated, said "'Look, you've just received the word so-and-so, which told you to open the document. The document tells you to take your ship to an Axis port. But don't be a sucker, boys. Bring it into Plymouth!'"

In February of 1942, BSC discovered that the Spanish captains' documents had been changed. A wire was sent to Manu Delasota saying "happy birthday," in Spanish, which was a prearranged code word that meant new documents had been distributed. Ross Smith was instructed by Stephenson to try and obtain the new documents. But this time it was a much more difficult task, as Spanish ships were no longer going into New York, they were sailing into Buenos Aires. Ross Smith met with Delasota and told him that he could use the assistance of good men and crew in Argentina.

"He did a remarkable thing," Ross Smith remembered. "He said that the Basques are either like that (he extended his arm with the palm up), or like that," (he extended his arm with a clenched fist). Delasota gave the Australian the name of a contact in Buenos Aires and told him to say to him "Manu says ... like that" (palm up). Ross Smith and Betty Raymond, who also worked in Room 99, flew to Buenos Aires with a replica of the old document pouch to try and retrieve the new one. He met Delasota's contact, took him by the hand, and said, "My name is Miller [his pseudonym at the time], and I put my hand like that — open, and said, 'Manu says like that.'" There was an immediate kinship and Delasota's contact asked what he needed. Ross Smith told him his problem. He needed help finding out which Spanish ships were available where, and who some contacts were.

A Spanish ship that was in port for an extended period of time was soon located and Ross Smith began to follow the captain whenever he was on shore. He noticed he frequented a restaurant called the Odeon for lunch, and he was always accompanied by "two rather tough-looking henchmen." One day Ross Smith went to the Odeon wearing a military raincoat and fedora hat, and he waited for the trio about a yard inside the doors of the restaurant. When the Spaniards arrived, Ross Smith walked straight into the captain and at the same time put his hands on his breast pocket and felt for a document pouch. "Sure enough there was the document wallet there, which felt exactly the same as mine. He didn't notice a damn thing — it was over in a second." A few minutes later Ross Smith returned to the restaurant, but without his raincoat and hat, acting as a different person, and sat at a table where he could keep an eye on the Spanish sailors. After the captain ordered his lunch, Ross Smith followed him to the men's room. He noticed he took off his coat and hung it up on a peg before he went about his business, washed up, and returned to his table. "So I prayed he would be doing the same thing the next day."

The following day Ross Smith waited in the washroom. When the captain came in and repeated his routine, he was able to exchange his phony document wallet for the real one while the coat was on the peg. He took the document wallet to Betty Raymond, who had her special paraphernalia laid out in an office set up by Jim Henman, an SOE representative. Behind closed doors, away from the men, she worked on opening it. Eventually she emerged to say she didn't think it could be opened, because part of the glue seal was egg white. She left the package under treatment while they ate dinner, and when they returned Raymond was able to get it open. The document was photographed by a Basque photographer, checked with the original, and the differences were sent back to Stephenson by cipher machine. The package was then resealed and Ross Smith was able to exchange it with the replica at the restaurant the next day.

The new documents changed little from the old ones. "It confirmed they were still going to go the German way, not our way," Ross Smith recalled. "Spain didn't come into the war, so it was never done, but it was there ready to be done." He received a personal commendation from "C" in London for his work in South America.

In early 1942, because of the Berle situation and the implications of the McKellar bill, Stephenson ordered a temporary shutdown of BSC's political activities. Also around this time BSC handed over much of the Ship's Observers program to American control. Secretary of the Navy Frank Knox was present at the meeting, and he was quite surprised at the scope of the operation and the fact there were some Americans reporting from American ships. Knox wanted answers from those under him, Ross Smith remembered. "He looked at the naval intelligence intercepts and said, 'How the hell have these Limeys put all these men on your ships without you being aware of it?'"

Camp X

During the shutdown, Ross Smith asked Stephenson's permission to attend the SOE/OSS training Camp X near Oshawa. He was a student at Camp X for a month, and afterwards he instructed in most disciplines, with the exception of parachute jumping and demolitions. He was taught self-defence by the infamous Captain William Ewart Fairbairn, a co-inventor of the double-edged commando knife and founder of many close combat techniques.

Fairbairn taught his students how to board and leave a train travelling at high speed, how to break into a house, and rappelling, but his specialty was silent killing. He learned his fighting techniques in China, after a stint in the Royal Marine Light Infantry guarding the British legation in Korea. Fairbairn, sometimes referred to as Dangerous Dan or the Shanghai Buster, is said to be the first Westerner to earn a black belt in jiu-jitsu. He is often credited with bringing the martial arts to the West.

Richard Dunlop, formerly with the OSS and a biographer of William Donovan, wrote later that Fairbairn "had an honest dislike of anything that smacked of decency in fighting." Another former student of Fairbairn's was Richard Helms, one of five past directors of the CIA who were OSS recruits.[3]

Ross Smith learned at Camp X how Fairbairn became an instructor. At the beginning of the war he was a man of about sixty and had recently returned to England from the notorious Shanghai police force where there many problems, a huge population and relatively few police. "One man had to be worth ten men (in Shanghai), and he had contrived a means of fighting both physically and with knives and guns, which indeed did make one man worth ten." When Fairbairn went to the War Office in London to volunteer, they told him war was not a game for ancient gentlemen and sent him on his way. After Dunkirk, Fairbairn contacted the military again and said, "Look, we've got nothing now, most of the arms have been lost, and we've only got a few thousand men. I'll show you how to make each man worth ten men." The military brass he visited wondered how, and Fairbairn told them to bring in a couple of tough young men and he would deal with them, to show how things could be done. Two majors were brought in and told they would have to fight the old gentleman. When they protested, Fairbairn said in effect, "Don't have a worry about me. I have to convince these dunderhead generals that I, a gentleman of 62 years of age, can deal with tough young men like yourselves. I'm sorry," he added, "but I'll have to put the both of you in hospital." "Which he bloody well did in a matter of minutes," Ross Smith said. The quick and violent display impressed the military, and Fairbairn immediately began to instruct a hundred men. "That was the start of the commandos." Fairbairn taught at SOE schools and eventually was taken over by the American OSS.

Ross Smith said techniques were taught that could kill a person within seconds. Fairbairn not only taught how to kill, but the means to inflict injury on various organs and limbs. "He also had this marvellous method of shooting with handguns, and he maintained that the old-fashioned method of taking aim and firing — you're dead by that time." Fairbairn said a person had to learn to aim and shoot immediately, and the quickest way to do that was to use a gun as a pointer. "It's natural to point your finger," Fairbairn's former student remembered. "He said to point your gun as you point your finger, and fire twice. That will stop anything."

Other instruction at Camp X wasn't as deadly. Operation VIC was harassment and dirty tricks. "Just as sex was the most fun you could have without laughing, this was the greatest fun that the Resistance boys could have with the Germans without being caught." Several games were invented. If a wife of a German officer was visiting him in Paris for instance, flowers addressed to another woman would be delivered to his room. Ross Smith says there were countless variations thought up to aggravate or stress.

The Camp attempted to develop recruits mentally as well as physically. "There are other senses," Ross Smith said, "and you can learn to control them." Fairbairn and others taught that people's ability to observe their environment visually, aurally and through general sensitivity could be focussed and improved. Ross Smith eventually lectured in sensitivity to the original OSS, some of whom were FBI agents, some of whom were lawyers and engineers, and most of whom were what he calls "trained brains." The course started with simple recall and observation. Ross Smith gave the class of about a dozen a test where they were told to put their heads on their desks and not look up. The first question was, "How many windows are in this room?" Then he would move from the classroom to places the recruits saw each day. "How many windows are there in the common room? How many in your bedroom?" Many of the highly intelligent people couldn't answer seemingly simple questions about their immediate environment. But the ability could be improved. General sensitivity and awareness was not only used to increase observation skills — it could be converged to the stage where some agents could function in the dark. "Not everybody, but at least seven men out of ten could come into a jet black room, jet black, no light at all, and hit a moving target five times out of six."

The Australian also became involved in the training of 22 Yugoslav North Americans who were to be sent behind enemy lines. The Yugoslavs were men between the ages of 36 and 56. "The older men did better than the younger men in the actual services, because they have one essential of experience — judgment." Ross Smith said. "That's a useful thing to have."

They were trained in the entire syllabus of how a man operates as an undercover agent: how to handle propaganda, how to obtain information, codes, demolitions, and how to conduct unarmed combat. Following the six-week course the recruits sailed for Cairo where they were to receive final orders and instruction, but their ship was torpedoed not far from Canada and a surfaced U-boat machine-gunned them. Most of the Yugoslavs survived and were able to get to Montreal. The survivors were given the option of returning home or continuing, and they all chose to go on. Eventually the group made it to Yugoslavia.

Ross Smith was unaware of their final mission, but assumed it would be to operate various intelligence and sabotage cells under the General Tito umbrella. "We started under Mihailovic and switched over to Tito."

Donovan

At Camp X Ross Smith met oss chief Bill Donovan for the first time. Donovan was at the camp on business and was unpretentious, with a good sense of humour, Ross Smith remembered. He was given a complete tour of Camp X, including demonstrations of a plastic explosive that could take out a telegraph post or a rail line.

Later, when Donovan became more active in the European theatre, Stephenson asked Ross Smith to introduce Jose Bensaude to him. The Bensaudes were a prominent Portuguese family involved in the transportation business for many years. Jose Bensaude was a gentleman of the old schools, spoke a number of different languages and was honoured to meet the great General Donovan, Ross Smith said. He deemed the meeting a formal occasion and before the rendezvous he put on a top hat and a cut-away coat and cravat. They met Donovan in his suite at the St. Regis hotel and found him without shoes and dressed very casually. According to Ross Smith, Donovan told the surprised Bensaude, "'Take off your coat and tuck up your feet and let's get down to business.' Whereupon Donovan got up on the sofa and literally tucked up his feet under his bottom, and that was that. That was start of a long and happy association with Bensaude and the Donovan organization, and eventually they [the Americans] decorated him." Bensaude, among other things, helped transfer supplies to people in occupied territory, and paid a great deal of money to Allied agents working in occupied France through his Portuguese office.

New York

With a staff of hundreds and a payroll in cash, vast sums of money were handled around bsc, but unobtrusively. Ross Smith remembers on one occasion Beryl Phelps, who was handling the accounts section, told him to go the British Consulate and pick up $12,000 in cash, a huge sum in 1940. He and Ted Scott, a New Zealander who was a former professional boxer, a journalist and BSC contact in Panama, went to pick up the money. The two simply stuffed the bills into their pockets. "We had to be generous. The consulate weren't a bit fazed," Ross Smith smiled. "They said, 'Of course you won't give us a receipt for this.' I said, 'Hell no.'"

Stephenson received numerous requests concerning minor day-to-day operations from the British bureaucracy during the course of the war. Occasionally Stephenson showed them to Ross Smith. "Stephenson would get such telegrams as 'His Majesty's Third Secretary of the Treasury has noted, with pain and regret, that certain of your officers are using taxis to go to the Consulate in 25 Broadway, New York City, when it is known that there are other, and cheaper, forms of transportation available. Pray explain.' I ask you," said Ross Smith shaking his head, "in the middle of a bloody war!" Stephenson collected a few of the missives and returned them. "Bill would save up about four of these and then he'd wire back saying, 'There's a war on.' That was another instance of him saying everything in few words," he laughed.

"Another time he got one, 'His Majesty's Third Minister of something or other, or something or other, noted that certain of our officers are using His Majesty's diplomatic bag for purposes other than His Majesty's Mail, viz the sending of silk stockings. Pray explain.' Well, you know, Stephenson had other things to do. And he sent this marvellous cable back saying 'Not us. We only send pink elephants.'"

Ross Smith didn't have a precise job title or description, and he reported only to Stephenson. "There were no exact positions for anybody. Everybody just headed up to Stephenson, who was the one boss," he said. "He never interfered with anybody. All he wanted to know was successes." He and a few assistants coordinated the approximately 400 ships, observers and the men who contacted them at various harbours. All of the observers were volunteers but the contacts in the different ports were usually paid employees.

All of Ross Smith's office staff were Canadians. He thought one secretary, Eleanor Fleming, was particularly good, but one day he made the mistake of telling his boss. "I had found this super, superb, magnificent secretary in the Security Office, which was downtown. Stephenson said, 'You have?' I said, 'Yes, sir.' He said, 'Fine. She can come to me. You find somebody else,'" laughed Ross Smith. Eleanor

Fleming moved from his office and became one of Stephenson's inner office secretaries.

Ross Smith's final task before leaving the organization was to write the achievements of his division, which was to be compiled into the BSC history. He never saw the finished work. "I'd personally like to see at least my own section, to see whether it was accurate or not." But he did not recount everything he did for publication. "No, by no means, of course not. It's the bare bones."

Ross Smith did not see Stephenson after the war. They talked on the phone occasionally and they exchanged Christmas cards, but he never saw his former boss again. "I regret never seeing him." Montgomery Hyde and his wife saw Stephenson quite often in Bermuda, and when they returned to Britain, "Hyde would then report to us how the great man was." Ross Smith had many cables from Stephenson, particularly on the Ellis affair. He sent him strongly worded cables saying that Ellis was not a mole, and at one time he offered to sue the journalist Chapman Pincher who made the first accusations after Ellis' death.

Following the Philby defection in the early sixties, Ross Smith was contacted by Ellis about Communist activities during the war years. There were some concerns about Cedric Belfrage, who Ross Smith believes was involved with political warfare for BSC. "Cedric Belfrage was an Etonian, an elitist, very, very nice. A literary sort of chap. I never knew whether he had any Communism. It certainly was never apparent around the office, and he went to Mexico. The middle sixties, I suppose, when there was that witch hunt generally, Dick Ellis contacted me and asked whether I had any feelings about Belfrage working for the Russians during the war, and I said 'Hell no,' as far as I was concerned he was simply a normal one of the old chaps. But other than that I don't know about that at all. Except the charge laid afterwards against Ellis, which I was telling you earlier was quite ridiculous.[4]

Ross Smith was disappointed and annoyed at the bad press Stephenson had received. He believes the author of *A Man Called Intrepid* set out to make a bestselling book and as a result fleshed out the bare bones of the story, and may have added things that he may or may not have run by Stephenson. "I can't see him [Stephenson] saying certain things were true," he said. "I refer particularly to the assassination of [Reinhard] Heydrich, which I believe had nothing to do with British Security Coordination."

But other aspects of the story could be factual. It was possible, for example, that Stephenson assisted in getting Danish atomic scientist Neils Bohr over to North America, Ross Smith said.

"Anything at all was possible with Stephenson. Frankly, one never knew what he was doing, except if it happened to concern me or my own particular organization. Then I can speak with my own authority of knowledge. But what Stephenson was doing in other directions ... like anybody else in the organization, everybody was individual. One had a 'need-to-know' law. Unless you happened to be cooperating with somebody else in the next office, you didn't know what in the hell he was up to. Whether Stephenson had anything to do with getting Neils Bohr out, he may well have done so, he may not."

"How about his relationship with Churchill?"

"Again, that's very high level stuff. I feel that it would be very true."

As an example, Ross Smith remembered the Italian Naval Attaché Admiral Alberto Lais. In the spring of 1941 Admiral Lais was ordered out of the United States because Italian ships were being sabotaged and scuttled in American ports. Lais was granted safe passage out of the United States back to Europe by the Americans, who were still neutral, and they received assurances from the British that Lais would be allowed to return to Europe unimpeded. The British Embassy in Washington sent the following letter to the U.S.

> *Secretary of State Cordell Hull*
> *April 22 1941*
> *His Majesty's Ambassador presents his compliments to the Secretary of State and has the honour to acknowledge the receipt of Mr. Hull's note of April 10th regarding the return to Europe of Admiral Alberto Lais, former Naval Attaché at the Italian Embassy in Washington, and his two Italian naval orderlies, Gaetano Canepa and Giovanni Burlo.*
>
> *This matter has been referred to His Majesty's Government who have authorized Lord Halifax to give the assurance that the British authorities will not attempt to prevent the return of Admiral Lais or his orderlies to Europe.*
> *British Embassy*
> *Washington DC*
> *April 17 1941*[5]

However, according to the book *Cynthia*, BSC agent Elizabeth Pack met Lais in New York before he departed and wrote down the colour and dimensions of all his luggage. She knew the Admiral was going to be detained in Bermuda.[6] Shortly after Lais' ship departed, contrary to British assurances, it was intercepted en route, and Lais was detained in Bermuda. American agent "Beck" discovered the detention and wired the mainland:

May 1, 1941

STRICTLY CONFIDENTIAL

Understand Admiral Lais removed from Spanish steamship Marques del Comillas *on the high seas now under detention here. In addition two women, one alleged to be a Nazi agent have been removed. Will report further if necessary.*

—*BECK*[7]

Ross Smith says Lais was detained because of Stephenson's intervention. The Italian admiral was returning to Europe with a small staff and all his codes, records and files. "Naturally we wanted to have a damned good look at them." But the *Marques del Comillas*, a neutral vessel didn't go into the control of Bermuda. It was covered, Ross Smith said, by a "Navy Serve." The ship's captain was given his own specific route to cross the Atlantic, and if he detoured off the route, he was subject to arrest at sea. Ross Smith went to Stephenson before the ship sailed and said "Let's get the Navy to pick him up because he's bound to stray off, by a few yards at least, off his Navy Serve route." Stephenson agreed, and he contacted the naval chief in Bermuda and told him to intercept the *Marques del Comillas*. The Bermuda official said no. "The admiral refused," Ross Smith remembered. "'Absolutely outrageous, arresting a fellow admiral." So that's when Stephenson phoned (contacted) London direct. And the order came to the admiral, 'Do what you're asked.'" The ship was intercepted on the high seas.

"He was reputed to have a four-lane highway to Churchill and I'm absolutely certain in my bones that it's true. Because, by God, he had influence everywhere. He was a very, very, very great man."

Publicly there seems to have been confusion as to why the Italian official was incarcerated, especially since he was granted safe passage home. The Associated Press reported from Rome that the British had detained the admiral "under the apparent impression that British diplomats were being held by the Italians in Albania."[8]

"Well, what happened was very amusing, because in due course the British destroyer discovered, 'Well absolutely outrageous, the chap had strayed off his Navy Serve line!'" smiled Ross Smith. The destroyer put a party on board the crossing ship and then signalled to Bermuda. When the ships passed closer to the island, the English admiral there sent a cable for Admiral Lais aboard the *Marques del Comillas*, Ross Smith recalled, saying "he had no part in this outrageous performance and that when the ship arrived in Bermuda, he would like the admiral to be his personal guest. Well this of course alerted the admiral and the staff that they were being taken into Bermuda. So as they came up to Bermuda, five or six code books started coming out the portholes."

Fortunately for the interceptors, this was anticipated. The *Marques del Comillas* was being followed by two small boats, ready to scoop anything up from the water. "He got two naval pursers, armed with great bloody nets on each side — hand nets. They were on each side of the ship and sure enough, as soon as things were thrown out of the porthole they went 'whoop,'" Ross Smith said, as he shovelled at the floor with his hands and laughed. "So we got the entire bunch of files. Codes. Every bloody thing."

On May 8, 1941, the *New York Times* reported that Lais was to be liberated because of American requests. "The State Department made prompt representations to the British authorities for his release."[9] Five days later, American agent "Beck" cabled the end of the affair. "Admiral sailed early this morning."[10]

(According to Patrick Wilkinson, who was a codebreaker at Bletchley during the war at about the same time, codebreakers had success deciphering Italian messages as a result "of captures.")[11]

A Man Called Intrepid

Ross Smith is unsure about some of the claims in *A Man Called Intrepid*. He believes Stephenson may not have been mentally alert at the time. He was surprised that some of the pictures in *A Man Called Intrepid* were from a training film, and a soe map seemed copied from a book released in the 1960s. The Australian noted the source of the pictures in the book "bsc Station M archive." "Do you know what Station M was?" he asked ... (It was run by Eric Maschwitz, and was the manufacturer of fake documents.)

The critics of the book should be blaming the author and not Stephenson, Ross Smith said. He would have responded loudly to the critics of his former boss and the controversy when Stephenson died, but he was in Australia at the time. "You see all these chaps have the wrong end of the stick. Stephenson didn't say these things. Stevenson the author said all these things."

The simple truth, said Ross Smith, was that the real judges of BSC were the British government, the FBI, the American government, the Canadian government and Donovan. All of those groups honoured Stephenson. "Well. All these people recognized him! Well who the hell? These denigrators!"

A Man Called Intrepid begins with forewords said to be written by William Stephenson and Dick Ellis, but Ross Smith has doubts about their authenticity. He doesn't believe either man wrote them. "If you look at the so-called forewords in that book, they are so obviously not written by either Stephenson or Ellis. It is not their literary style at all. Stephenson had the ability, and invariably used it, of saying in one phrase what takes the average person three pages to do. Now I'll give you an illustration of this. On Pearl Harbor day plus five — that was a Saturday night [sic]. He called me at about two in the morning and said he wanted a 'Deal for a party at the Fat Boy's place.' It needed to be one page and on his desk by 12 tomorrow. Now, that meant to me that he wanted a plan for basing an undercover organization in the Azores — the 'Fat Boy's' place. The 'Fat Boy' being Jose Bensaude, who came from the Azores. On one page meant it would be going to either Roosevelt or Churchill."

(In what may be a coincidence, in December of 1941, after the Pearl Harbor attack, secret plans for Churchill's trip to the United States began. According to Churchill's *Grand Alliance*, escort ships sailed from the Azores and intercepted Churchill's crossing vessel. Ciphered communications were then transferred to the Azores ships for transmission, so the exact location of the crossing vessel remained secret.)

Ross Smith went immediately to work on the Azores assignment, and he completed a report shortly before noon the next day, and delivered it to Stephenson. "I said 'Look, the plan's perfect. It was originally forty pages. It's now down to eight.'" Stephenson took the pages and read them. "He picked up a pencil and wrote maybe three-quarters of a page. One page. He read it to me, and said, 'Do you want to add anything?' He said it all 'like that', in what originally took forty pages. He said it all! Now that was his nature. Not stilted, but he just said the absolute essentials. Well, if you read the thing there [the foreword]..."

"It's very long-winded."

"That's right ... The author got him to sign that thing to substantiate, saying every word in this is true. It was never in his nature to say such a thing."

"Half of spying is lying, isn't it?"

"Well, yes," he said.

William Stephenson

"He was undoubtedly a genius. And he had the tremendous ability that anybody would do anything for him. For instance, I was going to South America on another occasion. No, I think it was Turkey, to get those things. I said to Bill, 'I really think this one is an impossibility,' and he said to me, 'If it can be done, you can do it.'" Ross Smith paused. "'If it can be done, you can do it,' he said with complete confidence. So you couldn't fail after that. He had this amazing ability. No pyrotechnics. There was no such thing as a staff meeting, or anything like that — ever. There was no organization, no orders. Everybody there had to be a self-starter. Had to be a self-starter."

"But he knew what was going on?"

"Oh, by God, did he know what was going on. Did he know what was going on! For instance, he bloody well knew ... For instance, I was astounded, what I just told you, 'at our Fat friend's place.' I don't know if I ever told him he [Bensaude] came from the Azores, but he bloody well knew. Also one morning I said something, that I'd been in Harlem the previous night, and he said something which indicated that he knew exactly ... [where I had been]. We thought ... we all on earth thought that he must have a parallel organization keeping eyes on each one of us ... It seemed that way. I don't think it was so. But it seemed that way."

No one in British government commented on the controversy after Stephenson's death because, Ross Smith said, "the Service itself, and the government, never affirms or denies anything."

"Why?"

"Just tradition. You see I took it up on Ellis' part, and had many letters published in papers putting the facts right in this thing. It didn't do any good. But nevertheless, it was in."

At the time of the interview, the Russians had recently announced there was a Fifth Man in the Philby, Maclean, Burgess and Blunt chain of English traitors, and he had recently retired.

"There may be a Fifth Man," Ross Smith said. "There may be a fifty-fifth man. But one thing that's sure is that it's Russian policy to always stir up trouble, and if you can get the intelligence services diligently putting their efforts into hunting for a fifth or fifty-fifth man, it's better that than looking into what the Russians were up to."

The Australian thought the Stephenson plan to assassinate Hitler in 1938 with sporting rifles mentioned in Anthony Cave Brown's book *C* sounded far-fetched. "Consummate balls," he said. After he was shown the book, and he read the passage, he hesitated in passing a definite opinion. "Sporting rifles. It must have been in the open air, at some gathering. The choice of weapon. So much depends on where the deed is going to be done. For instance, you wouldn't want to use a sporting rifle inside a house," he said. He looked at the book again. "It says they had a plan to assassinate Hitler — I find the thing a bit more acceptable, by putting that thing [the proposed weapon] in there. But I have a feeling that Bill would have told me about that ..."

After the war Ross Smith worked for the German company IG Farben in the United States. "Which was very useful because I had a little part to do in taking them apart," he smiled. "So I went to work for them, which was very good." The Australian maintained a residence in the U.S. until 1960, but he spent a great deal of time in Britain and ended up in business there.

Ross Smith knew little about Bill Stephenson and his Canadian life, and he went through clippings, photos, cards and obituaries with great interest. He often wondered about the circumstances concerning Stephenson adopting his nurse as his daughter, and he believed his ex-boss' background contained an answer. "Extraordinary. What was done to him originally, he was [repeating]. [He] adopted this daughter and her son, as his godson. That's really repaying the kindness of the original Stephensons."

The Australian was surprised his former boss broke contact with the Stephenson family in Canada in the 1930s. "I wonder why he did that? Well, it's actually unimportant. It's the man himself," Ross Smith said. "You see, he was so remarkable, that no matter who he met, without making the faintest endeavour at all, he was the superior being. Without making any significant move. And yet everyone who met him immediately liked him. Immediate respect. But at the same time he maintained a coolness … He was really a man apart. Completely a man apart."

It didn't appear Stephenson worked his way up a MI6 ladder. "Oh no. He was undoubtedly appointed by Churchill. Well, you see, Churchill wanted a man over there. That paper's [Washington Post, 1989 story on BSC] quite right. He wanted a man who could really get together with the top rungs, and top social lines, and American thinking. There's no doubt about it. And Stephenson was exactly the right man, because he had all these terrific contacts and had this tremendous flair of … influencing people, in an incredibly quiet way. An incredibly quiet way. If he could walk into this room now, he could sit down in that chair and, without saying a word, dominate this room. I tell you he was absolutely, bloody well a genius. Inevitably he was a phenomenal fund of knowledge."

Ross Smith continued: "I bumped into him about nine o'clock once, on Fifth Avenue one night, and [his wife] Mary. He was having a dinner at the Plaza, and I said, 'the Basques had just told me the German troops were mounting at St. Jean de Luz [in southern France]. 'They think this might be a prelude to an invasion of Spain.' And he said, 'No, they haven't got nearly enough people there to do that. But discuss it with me tomorrow morning.' He knew! It was absolutely incredible."

"So he was a real James Bond-type character?"

"Well, James Bond never existed, he was a combination of one hell of a lot of people, but in reality he was no James Bond because he didn't go around killing people with his bare hands, or even with a gun. He dealt strictly with his brain and his personality. He used to start the day with 100 skips. A hundred skips in the morning. And lots of cold coffee for breakfast."

15 BETTY RAYMOND

In the 1930s Betty Raymond was working in a rural English hotel doing secretarial work when she was approached by her brother-in-law, Francis Ogilvy, about joining British Intelligence. Ogilvy, formerly with the Air Force, worked at Whitehall. He and Walter (Freckles) Wren were approached by their superiors in the intelligence community, who said they needed "two or three women of education, who they could trust," Raymond recalled, and "who would be good with their hands." Betty was interviewed by Francis Ogilvy and signed the Official Secrets Act. "I said yes blindly and signed the lot." One of her friends, Dorothy Hyde, joined about the same time. "That's how they got Harford [her husband] Hyde into it. Harford only came in because Dorothy was in it. But that's how he came into it."

Raymond began training soon afterwards, and her manual dexterity was funnelled into intercepting mail and forgery.

She learned the unique craft from an elderly man named "Webb," who began the art during World War I. William "Steam Kettle Bill" Webb devised a method of opening and then resealing envelopes without detection and controlled a large department in London.[1] "He was absolutely wonderful, and he taught us. But it was really one of the things you had to learn after that from experience." Years later when she returned to London, Raymond realized she was one of the few who had all the various skills. Mail tampering had become compartmentalized.

"Nobody was allowed to do them all. Typical. It was a rather civil servanty thing, you see. One could open some thing, and one could do another, and one could do another."

Tampering with mail so that it couldn't be detected was an acquired skill, rather than a formula. Some people were better at it than others, and improvisations could better the end product. Raymond says she and Hyde improved some aspects of what they were taught, but "dear old Mr. Webb," the teacher, remained proficient. "All his work was very good. Chamfering, for instance. If you opened a letter that you shouldn't have opened. If you cut it open, then you had to put it back together again, as if nobody had opened it. This is a very difficult procedure, which he originated. Called chamfering. It was not easy, but you could do it."

After a relatively quick training period in Britain, Raymond and Dorothy Hyde were sent to a major mail intercept station located in Bermuda. Working behind locked doors, six to eight women toiled in their Hamilton section, covertly going through mail and packages sent to and from Europe and the Americas. With practice, both of the women became experts in opening and sealing mail without detection. "Harford always said that I was Dorothy's assistant, but he didn't know very much. We were totally different, but we were a very good team. Both Dorothy and I moved up to New York, you see."

The process could be tedious, but occasionally their diligence was rewarded. In one instance an examiner had a hunch about a letter. "She didn't know to this day why she had a hunch. I can't remember her name, I wish I could. And she used to get these letters and send them off to be examined for secreting." (It was likely Nadya Gardner. According to Hyde's *The Quiet Canadian*, the letters were addressed to a cover address of the Gestapo.) In secreting, the letters could be checked for invisible ink, but nothing was found. "She was absolutely determined there was something wrong with these letters. So she went up to them one day and she said, 'Have you tried the Rd in the Indian?' … 'Oh no, we haven't tried that.'" Secret writing appeared on the letter. "Later on we had an enormous job," Raymond remembered. "We had to open up all the envelopes with gloves. We tried to get fingerprints from them and everything, and it built up, and built up. When we were in New York and they pounced on this ring." Gardner was singled out afterwards. "They honoured her with a lunch ... because of the work she'd done. But she just hit it. It was a hunch, that was all. They rounded up a lot of agents. That was one thing that was worth doing."

There were regular scheduled ships and flying boats stopping in Bermuda carrying mail, and on occasions messages were purloined from couriers. "You'd have to get a sack open and read it before the ship sailed the next day, and we'd do it all." Pictures were taken of contents of the mail considered relevant, and sometimes, if there were suspicious couriers, of the mail bag itself. A "Miss Birling" would often speak to couriers, Raymond remembered, and say, "'Oh you've got about four hours on shore. Now I will lock it up in my safe. It'll be perfectly safe.' And off they'd go, and the moment their back was turned, it was out of the safe, over to us with it." Soon the mail intercept people opened it, went through the contents, put it back together and it was ready for return. "Nine times out of ten the courier would take it, and they'd look at it with a spy glass to see if it was the exact way it was originally. They didn't trust us."

Envelopes were a complex process that involved "opening it all up and then cutting a bit away, and then chamfering it away fine, so you could join them up together so you couldn't see," Raymond said. "And the postmark would have to match. It was terribly complicated. It was terribly clever of him [Webb]. He originated that. It was very good, because there were some letters that were opened by mistake. I know there was one letter opened to a member of the Royal Family. Opened by mistake. There were panic stations. So it had to be chamfered and put back. And there were other things that were opened, and possibly had to go on. Shouldn't have been opened by censorship and rather that they thought it hadn't been looked at. All that sort of thing. We had all that coming through."

Raymond travelled to Jamaica and helped start an office there, and spent about three months in Kingston where she continued to examine mail of random people and companies, and specific individuals. "There was a man there — I knew all about him! He didn't know I knew all about him, and we intercepted all his mail and everything. We were trying to check up on people."

At the end of the summer of 1941, Raymond left Jamaica for New York, where Dorothy Hyde and her husband were already working for William Stephenson.

When Raymond arrived she stayed with the Hydes, and then moved to an unfurnished apartment on East 43rd Street, about four blocks from BSC. Raymond earned $40 a week, in cash, from the espionage business.

"It was all very lax and very happy until a very nice man, Brooks Banks, came and he was a civil servant, and he absolutely ruined it. We all had to sign on then and check out, which ruined it. Because I don't think anybody worked as hard. We were clocked in and out."

Unlike some of the women working for BSC, Raymond's movements in the city weren't restricted by the organization, she said. But her fraternizing was. BSC employees and other people were not to be combined. "I would either go with the people who had nothing to do with it, or from the office. But not mixed … supposing the Hydes had some people over who had nothing to do with BSC — I couldn't be invited, you see. Only if they were office people, or people that weren't office people — we never mixed. For instance, if you got into an elevator at lunchtime, you got in — one day Bill was there. He'd got in at the same time from the floor above, or whatever it was. You didn't recognize each other. It would be very funny. You'd be chatting away outside on the landing, but as soon as you got on the lift, you didn't know anybody. It was a very funny little trick. It was very funny, I thought. But that was it. Mind you, I was with Dorothy, so we talked together. But you didn't acknowledge anybody else to your right or left, although you worked with them. That was the sort of security they had."

She later discovered she was followed in New York. "I still don't know who by until this day." Raymond went to a dentist near Central Park and afterwards someone made inquiries to the dentist about who she was, and what she did. Her dentist later told her about it, and she reported it directly to Bill Stephenson. He didn't seem to react at all. "He didn't appear to be the least bit interested about it — so tuned out. But he then put a man on, to follow the man who was following me. For three weeks, I didn't know. I had two men following me for three weeks! It was wonderful," she remembered. "I didn't know. I didn't know! That was the art of following."

On another occasion Raymond was assigned by Stephenson to follow her friend Marjorie Wren, as it was feared one of her friends was a German agent. She and a New York photographer she knew as "Tiny" followed Wren to try and catch them together. Tiny, who was enormous, was given a miniature camera for the task. Raymond soon found it was not an easy assignment, and the tailing was made more difficult as Wren knew who she was. "There's a great art to following people, and I never knew." It took weeks to catch the two together and take the required photographs. Then they discovered "Tiny had put his thumb over every one. So you couldn't see a thing!" she laughed. The Marjorie vigil was quickly terminated when the German agent left New York, and the escapade wasn't revealed to the principals.

Raymond occasionally saw Bill Donovan, although he saw more of the Hydes. "He was really quite interested in what we were doing, because we were helping the FBI. Because they didn't know anything in those days, when we were over there. They were very new. They were very anxious to be spies. All of them very anxious, these Americans. They loved the idea of being a spy." In a Lima bar, returning from Argentina, she ran into an American agent. He said, "Here comes the opposition," when she appeared. "In a loud voice you see, so everybody there thought, 'Here comes a spy.'" Raymond said. "They had no idea! No idea at all. They learned though."

Partially because of BSC's social restrictions, Raymond didn't meet anyone but BSC people in New York. "Because you didn't. So it was really a rather lonely life, but they were all there. It was an absolute hive of industry during the week. There was Ivor Bryce, Tommy Fairly, Ingram Fraser, John Pepper, Cedric Belfrage. So many of them. Christopher Wren, Bill Gooch, Sir Alfred Ayer, who recently died. Freddie Ayer. He was the philosopher, a brilliant man. He was there. There were two Wrens. Freckles Wren, whose wife was Marjorie, who I told you about. The other one was Christopher Wren. Last I heard Christopher Wren was in the Algarve. I didn't have anything to do with him. I must admit he was there, and we said hello, and we met occasionally. But he was on the other floor 35 and 36. We were really, really separate.

"We didn't know what anybody was doing. It was all so secret. It was very funny. I didn't know how important one was, or if one wasn't. Some of the things we did were important and some of them were just routine. I think there was an awful lot of paperwork. There was a whole lot of wasted paper. There always is."

Raymond and Hyde worked behind locked doors in a small office designated Room 99. No one was allowed into the office to see what they were doing except Bill Stephenson. "Nobody else was allowed in at all. Maybe Harford, but he never bothered. Dorothy and I sat behind our locked door."

Bolivia — Forgery

In May of 1941 BSC was worried some military figures in Bolivia might attempt a coup backed by the Nazis. BSC did not have enough concrete proof to link right-wing South American elements with Berlin, so a letter was concocted from Major Elias Belmonte of the Bolivian legation in Germany to Ernst Wendler, the German Minister to Bolivia. Belmonte was, according to Hyde, a fervent pro-Nazi.[2] Hyde travelled on Stephenson's instructions to Bolivia to glean the needed details. Paper and ink usually used by the Bolivian mission in Berlin, and a suitable text, were obtained through Hyde's South American contacts. A letter dated June 9, 1941, from Berlin (written in Spanish) was put together in Canada with a typewriter that duplicated the print of one usually used by Belmonte. His signature had to be forged by Betty Raymond and Dorothy Hyde.

"A sample of it was given to Dorothy and myself, and we practised it, because you must practise, and it was a desperately difficult signature to do." After much repetition, neither of the women could match the signature accurately. "We practised for weeks and neither of us were able to do it. Until one day we found to our amazement, she could do one half, and I could do the other. Now you don't break a signature in half normally, but there does come a break in the signature, as it so happens, and we found that this was how it was. This is the absolute truth. She signed one bit and I signed the other." After the forged text of the Belmonte letter was created, there was only one copy for the women to sign. "You couldn't make a mistake. There was only one."

Hyde says he took the women's handiwork to Ottawa and it was shown to RCMP experts. The Mounties were told, "We think this is a forgery," and it was compared to an original Belmonte signature. The RCMP studied it, and concluded the signature was genuine.[3] BSC then decided it would go ahead with the ruse.

The letter from Belmonte talked about the moment approaching to liberate "my poor country from a weak government." It spoke of focal points of the proposed uprising, and said wolfram contracts with the United States must be rescinded. He hoped to "save Bolivia and later the

rest of South America from North American influence." The concocted
letter said that eventually a single supreme leader for all of South America
would be required.[4] Stephenson devised a scheme, using false rumours
and fibs, to authenticate the letter. He sent notice to Brazil and London
that a German courier was expected with incriminating documents.
Later the courier's secretary was bribed, and some details of his mission
were released. The Belmonte letter was subsequently stolen from the
courier in Buenos Aires, where a FBI agent reported the theft to
Washington. Stephenson soon afterwards handed the letter over to J.
Edgar Hoover. Both the British and American governments pressed for
its release to the Bolivians. It was widely distributed in South America,
and the letter's authenticity did not come into question — its contents
appeared genuine.

"Photostat copies of the letter, whose signature was authenticated
by the chief of the Bolivian general staff, were published in all morning papers [in La Paz]," the *New York Times* reported in 1941.[5]

"And that was done by two different hands — one signature,"
Raymond remembered. "That is unbelievable, but it is perfectly true.
Harford didn't bother to ask me, and said that Dorothy had done it.
It doesn't matter now. It's water under the bridge. But it was a much
better story, because it happened to be true ... Doing signatures is not
an easy business.

"You have to learn how to do it, and you have to practise it like mad.
Because you can not pause. You cannot hesitate on a signature.
Otherwise you are undone. Because nobody pauses on their signature. You just do it. And if there's the slightest hesitation, but the
slightest — it is a forgery."

She would usually practise two or three hundred times. "But there
were some easy ones, and they don't take any time at all."

The Bolivian letter led to the expulsion of the German minister,
the closing of the German mission in Bolivia, the arrest of Nazi sympathizers, and the harassment of German officials in other South
American countries. Wolfram continued to be exported to the Allies,
and was denied to the Nazis. The German Foreign Office called the letter "falsification in the crudest manner possible," and the Reich's
government wrote all Latin American countries to complain about
the forgery. The forged letter helped poison the climate towards the Axis
in the Western Hemisphere. On July 29, 1941, Texas congressman

Martin Dies warned that the Nazis had about a million soldiers in South America poised "to produce a diversion to prevent our aiding Great Britain."[6] German diplomatic pouches started being stolen in Argentina, "with a typical show of Wild West bad manners," a Nazi spokesman complained.

Six months later, most Central and South American countries broke with the Axis powers at a Pan-American conference in Rio and set up a common scheme for defence. That move was described by U.S. Under Secretary of State Sumner Welles as "the decision that saved New World unity."[7]

Years after the war some people suspected the Belmonte letter could have been a forgery. Montgomery Hyde admitted the document was phony to American television (CBS, Mike Wallace) in August 1979, and later in the *London Telegraph*, August 22, 1979.

Raymond says she didn't help on the letter, which was purported to help put Italy's LATI airlines out of Brazil.

On one occasion she was asked to forge the signature of Britain's ambassador to the United States. "They came along and said Lord Halifax has to sign something, and I signed it on his behalf. I don't know what it was," she laughed. The top part of the document was covered so she didn't see what she was signing. "I just busily signed it. Had a little practice and signed. You know it's awful to laugh about these things. It was probably terribly important."

Room 99 only had signatures to deal with, and never tried to forge handwritten notes. "We couldn't write letters, or anything. We could never get around to doing that." Raymond taught the tricks of the trade to four Canadians in New York, and they were sent to various places in South America.

Argentina

Raymond's major expedition during the war was to Argentina with Bill Ross Smith. The two flew south to Buenos Aires to find a Spanish ship's captain with a document package. Spanish ships no longer visited New York, so Raymond and Ross Smith flew down together to South America to try and pilfer another message packet. It was a five-day flight, as aircraft were not allowed to fly at night in South America, Raymond says. During the journey she became ill with trench mouth, so she left the plane in Peru and was nursed back to health in Lima by the British consul and a dentist, while Bill Ross Smith continued down to Argentina to find a Spanish captain.

When she arrived, one of BSC's Argentine agents, who had been to New York, saw Raymond there. "Suddenly ... cables were flashed back and forth to the New York Office, 'I've seen Betty Raymond here. What is she doing?' And all this. It was terribly secret. And we were followed everywhere. It was horrid. Very unpleasant."

After a number of days Ross Smith obtained a document package and hurried it to Raymond to open. They set up shop at a British estate agent's place, and Raymond discovered there was no envelope to open. The package consisted of one large piece of paper that had been folded and sewn up. "It was the most difficult thing I had to do in my life, because it was all closed up. All porous paper, very soft, which they sealed with dark brown glue and egg white. And they'd sewed a thin string right through it into a cross and right around and put a seal onto it." She got the package in the afternoon and worked on it until midnight, she said, as they only had it for 24 hours. "We promised this man we would get it back to him ... ha."

"Bill got the captain at long last. It was the third one they tried. He got the captain to pass it over. He said somebody had a third eye, not to worry, it was quite safe. It wouldn't be touched. He would hand it back."

(This conflicts with Bill Ross Smith's sequence of events. He said he stole the package when a captain was in a washroom. Why were their stories not the same? Later Ross Smith said he didn't tell Raymond how he actually got the package. He lied to her. It was "the need to know." She didn't need to know where the package came from. If Raymond was captured, threatened or tortured, and eventually revealed where the package came from — it would be the wrong information. Her interrogators would know no more about the actual source, and if they pursued the matter they would be aimed in the wrong direction.)

When she finally got the package open the contents were in poor shape. "Absolute shreds," Raymond remembered. "And I handed Bill this paper. They had a camera waiting. And I handed it to him, and Bill went green in the face," she laughed. "He went green ... he thought this is the end, you see." Raymond slept for a few hours while the material was photographed. When the contents were returned to be put back together again, she told everyone, "All I ask is leave me alone. Nobody come near me, whatever you do." Raymond was able to repair the package and it was returned by noon the next day.

"Spain didn't come in, but the Argentines were very pro-German. We were trailed everywhere. It was most uncomfortable. Our rooms were searched every day. It was horrible. I was very glad to get out of there." Raymond thought they were not in actual danger, but people wanted to know what they were doing there.

There was nothing suspicious to find in the hotel room. She had only a few tiny tools to take through Customs. She then bought a rubber ball at a toy store and cut it in half to get a rubber bowl. Her only other equipment was plaster of paris and some oil. The camera work was done by others. There were at least three BSC people in Buenos Aires, she said.

When the two were departing for New York, the Basques in Argentina held a dinner in their honour. "They thought we were all so splendid and they looked at us in awe," she remembered. But she was not taken with the cuisine. "A very, very funny dinner. It was, ah, octopus and deer's genitals, I think," Raymond chuckled. "It was absolutely ghastly! Bill fed me [later], but he was very noble. He ate it. I couldn't. But it was a great honour. Very sweet."

Raymond made another trip for BSC to Trinidad. A ship was expected in Port of Spain that was laden with sacks of mail they wanted to go through. Trinidad had an intercept office, but they didn't have anyone experienced enough to do it all. "We had these ruddy sacks," Raymond remembered. "I didn't want to go." She spent about three weeks in Trinidad dealing with the mail, and nothing was in them. She returned to New York. "Some weeks later we had a most excited call from the FBI. A ship was in — 'Could we possibly deal with something on it?' It was the same ruddy ship, and the same ruddy bags that I'd already done, and I couldn't tell them!" The FBI contacts didn't need to know about BSC's activities elsewhere. Raymond redid the bags under the watchful eye of the Americans. "The utter frustration. It was that sort of thing, you see. No. It was an interesting life."

Travelling from the Caribbean, through Spanish Honduras, to New York on a banana boat, Raymond thought she was drugged aboard ship. "I nearly got bumped off. One was very unimportant. But they knew who you were."

Before Raymond departed on one of her next assignments for BSC, Stephenson gave her a "gas gun" for protection. She still has it. "Well, I'll show you," she said. "I'm not supposed to have it, of course, because it is a weapon, but Bill had one, and when I was going off on my trip, I forget which one I was going on, it was given to me and the thing is ... because Bill [Stephenson] had used it once himself ... If you get into a corner and you get trapped, as he was once. He told me he was. Trapped in a corner ... you take out this little gas gun and as long as you are near the door ..."

She disappeared into her bedroom and returned with an antique-looking fountain pen and a small white box. She held the pen with two hands and feigned pulling on the clasp.

"If I shot the gun out to you, very close like this to your eyes — it would blind you ... It would ruin your eyes. But the thing is, if you're over by the door and you're getting away, you just shoot it — the place is full of gas and you're just crying, you can't see, of course, because of the gas, and the person who shoots it goes away."

(The pen seemed similar to John Krafchenko's pen. "News of the pen had caused every man in the audience to sit bolt upright with ears strained forward to catch this latest and remarkable phase of Krafchenko's craftiness." It seems Stephenson may have carried with him a reminder of the spirit of the Wild West.)

The pen saved Stephenson's life, Raymond said. "Bill used it. He used it either in Spain or in Portugal. I'm sorry I can't remember, it is many years ago, and he said he got cornered. But he said, 'It was perfectly all right. I got to the door, shot my gun, and I got away. I walked away.' You can walk away like that, because they can't see for some time. Absolutely paralyzed with this gas. And he said, 'I walked away, and I walked out of the hotel, perfectly safe.'"

Raymond said the pen made her feel quite safe but, she says, at BSC headquarters there was no security. You just walked in. "Well, I don't know what they would do to us all. We were just office people. There was nothing very much. We weren't any great problem."

She was not sure if Stephenson had extra protection. "Maybe he had a bit of security. I wasn't conscious of it. He was on the other side of the office, away from me. He was away from all of us. It was a separate bit he had so maybe he was very safe. I don't think anybody could come in from the outside or anything like that."

Eventually Raymond felt there was no longer enough work for Dorothy Hyde and herself in New York, and she wanted to go home. She returned to England before Christmas 1942. When she arrived back in London to continue her profession, she was tested and retested by MI5. She believes it was because of her connection to the Stephenson organization. "I went to the London office, and they were going to send me out to Turkey. You see, London office was very, very jealous of Bill Stephenson. Terribly jealous of Bill Stephenson," she said. "They hated him. So they put me through every hoop, to prove I couldn't do anything." She could do everything they asked of her. "Well, I was the best that they had. So that was very silly of them."

In the end Raymond wasn't allowed to go to Turkey for health reasons. She resigned from MI5, and Stephenson found her a job with the American OSS.

Raymond was employed by OSS in London for eighteen months, given a furnished flat on North Orderly Street, and was on call. But her workload was undemanding. "I never did a day's work for them. I never did a thing. But they thought it was very nice to have me, in case they needed some secret operation that I could do." She was given false American identification and once a month went to Grosvenor Street to pick up her salary in cash of £80, "which in those days was an enormous amount of money. I was on call, which was very nice, but I couldn't go away. They never called me," she laughed.

One of the few times her OSS contact, a Mr. Murphy, sought her out, Raymond was in hospital having an operation. "I got a letter from them saying, 'We don't feel very nice, but I don't think we can use you after all'. That was the end of OSS. So I never had anything to do with them."

Stephenson

Raymond was a good friend of Stephenson's during the war, especially when she was in London. "That's very funny; I say I didn't know him after 1944, '45. I never saw him again after then. Because I knew him all over here, when I came back to England, rather than New York. [In the] New York office everyone was terrified of him."

"In New York, you had this long, big office, with a desk at the far end and there was Grace guarding him," she said with a laugh. If someone wanted to see Stephenson, they had to go through Grace Garner. "One spoke to Grace and said, 'Can we see Mr. Stephenson?'. It was in those days, and Grace used to consult and see if we'd be allowed to see him."

People allowed to see the spymaster then waited outside the office. Most were intensely nervous while they were waiting. When they were called and got up to see Stephenson, they were actually physically shaking.

"So people would go along shaking. I never shook, because it was just one of those things. He used to beam at me when I came in. But I was a girl, you see. It was one of those things that was a different matter," she laughed. "I was never frightened of him ...

"They [visitors] were terrified. You see he never spoke. He sat there, and he waited for you to speak. It was a very great trick he had. He sat there just looking at you, with these hooded eyes. As I said, I thought he had a lot of 'Indian' in him. I suppose it was because he was Icelandic. He had these hooded eyes, and he just looked at you. And didn't utter. And you were pulp, you see. It was a very great trick he had."

When Stephenson did talk, he didn't say much. "He only said —" she paused, "He was very, very lean with his words. One word. Not necessarily two. If one did, he said one."

She doesn't think her former boss wrote the foreword to *A Man Called Intrepid*. "That's not Bill Stephenson," she said. "No. No, it isn't. He couldn't have done it, I don't think. No, socially he was much more talkative in Claridges (where he stayed in London).

"He did know the War Lords. I'm absolutely convinced he knew them over here. Because I remember one evening I was having dinner with him at Claridges. We'd been away for the weekend and we came back and he said, 'I've got the War Lords coming tonight. They're going to be down here to "sweep" later on.' And I said, 'I'll go back down,' and he said, 'Don't hurry, don't hurry.' He was in one of those chatty moods. Not about himself, but he was in a chatty mood and I kept on saying, 'I must go,' and he said, 'They can wait.' And he made them wait. He said Louis Mountbatten was with them ... I don't think he [would] have lied to me, I don't think there'd be much point. And he made them wait until two or three in the morning before he went down and saw them. He was a law unto himself, you see."

She also thought Stephenson met often with Churchill in London. "I'm absolutely convinced he did. I'm absolutely convinced he did. He knew them all. I'm sure he did.

"He had a really great friend called Alexander Korda. He was a very famous film producer, and Korda used to come down. Korda lived there in Claridges. Korda used to come down after dinner. And very happy evenings. He was very happy and relaxed and chatty but then it was very different, you see.

"What was his relation with Korda?"

"Just a friend, just a very good friend." Stephenson took Raymond to see Shepparton studios during the war, but she was unaware he owned it. "One weekend we went out to the studios. He had friends, obviously. He had friends there, and they used to come and see him. As I say, Korda liked him very much. I don't think he had any financial connections. He might have had. I don't think so. He was just friendly."

(As stated earlier, according to information supplied by the studio, Stephenson likely owned it at the time. Alexander Korda purchased much of it from him in 1947. During the war much of an imitation invasion force was constructed there, which was used to confuse the Nazis before D-Day.)

Stephenson came over to England every few months, Raymond said. When he was there, Miss A. M. Green, a secretary who looked after Stephenson's business concerns in Britain, came to Claridges daily. She didn't know Mary Stephenson. "But he adored her [Mary], I do assure you, absolutely adored her. He used to call her his 'Old Dutch.' His 'Old Dutch,' yes, and he was absolutely devoted to her.

"He had an iron constitution. He drank Gin and French. And you wouldn't have known he had had a drink, until one day I gather, all of a sudden, it caught up to him and he couldn't drink another drink for the rest of his days.

"But he was a very good companion. He was a lovely person to be with ... He never talked about his past, but as I say, he had a lot of important meetings at Claridges, a lot of important people. I know he did.

"Very important people, as I say. He went off on D-Day and viewed D-Day from somewhere. He did. I remember that. I don't think he knew any fear at all. I think he was fearless."

Stephenson was in London when the v-1 rockets started to attack England. "Yes. The one thing I remember about that ... v-1s. A v-1 came over; I can't remember the year. A v-1 came over and I was alone in my flat over there. And it terrified me. I saw this thing with a red flame, and Bill was over here. He was at Claridges and the only time I ever rang him. I rang him up, and it was late at night. I said, 'Bill, I'm very frightened, what is this?' He said, 'Put your head under a pillow and put the phone down,'" she laughed. "Which was typical, you see."

"It was going so slow," Raymond said. "There was a terrifying black object with flames coming out. It was the first one. I'd never seen anything like it. At night. And they were very frightening in the daytime. I'd never seen one before."

"So he had some idea what it was?"

"Oh, he knew perfectly what it was. He was in a meeting. I had disturbed him. He wasn't going to sympathize with me. 'Put your head under a pillow.'"

This was typical of Stephenson, Raymond thought. "This is how he got on so well. That was his attitude. He just put people off. He wouldn't mind. One evening we were having quite a big party in his suite at Claridges. And he was giving quite a good party, and he got a bit bored with it and he said, 'Now young lady, I think you must go home.' I said, 'Yes indeed, yes.' I was thinking I'd overstayed my welcome, how embarrassing. And he saw me out to the lift, and saw me down, and saw me to the taxi, and he never went back to his party ever. He was like that, you see. He was an extraordinary man, just left everybody there," she continued. "He didn't care. He had the oss people there and all sorts of things."

She thought one of Stephenson's major contributions to the war was alerting the Americans to the horrors of the Nazis. "Absolutely rightly. Roosevelt, as we knew, was very anxious to get into the war. He had to get in. We knew that, and Bill was very instrumental, I'm sure, in doing that. I think, in all, that he was marvellous.

"In those days you see he was only in his forties ... and he was very active and very clear, as clear as a bell, obviously, and a very active, intelligent man. He was at the height of his powers, I think, then." Raymond said she thought Stephenson remembered everything she ever told him. "Every word."

"But about Bill Stephenson, there's very little I could tell you because he never told anybody about himself. Never. I was devoted to him. I knew him very well. He used to ring me whenever he came over and I used to go over to Claridges and we had happy times together. We were in the services of friends of his a weekend or two and it was lovely. But he still never talked about himself. He was a very pleasant companion. He was absolutely charming."

"When did you see him last?"

"Well, I saw him when the war was coming to an end, and then the war came to an end. You see he kept on flying over in bombers. He used to fly over here very regularly. He came over a great deal and saw all these people. That's why I'm certain he saw Churchill. He always came to Claridges. He always had a suite."

IF *BORMANN* NOT YET SENT ASTLEY PLEASE ADDRESS TO
MRS. J ASTLEY ON XX XXXX STREET LONDON SW 3 AND
NOT REPT NOT TO FOREIGN OFFICE AS PREVIOUSLY INDI-
CATED STOP SHE WAS PRINCIPAL WARTIME ASSISTANT TO
GENERAL LORD ISMAY AND SUPERVISED PREPARATORY
ARRANGEMENTS ALL HIGH LEVEL CONFERENCES ALLIES
WINSTON ATTENDED GREETINGS INTREPID[1]
    — Stephenson to Stevenson (following the publication of
       William Stevenson's book *The Bormann Brotherhood*)

Joan Bright Astley

Stephenson's activities in Europe during the war will probably always
remain a mystery. In London, Stephenson, a conduit of secret information, was in contact with Joan Bright Astley.

Born in Argentina, Joan Bright lived in South America until the
age of three, when her family returned to England. She began her
British government career when, following in her sister's footsteps,
she started working for the Foreign Office in Mexico. She left in July
1936 and returned to London to look for a job. For a short time she
worked for Alfred Duff Cooper, helped with his book *Tallerand*, and
had opportunities to work for British embassies in Rome, Vienna and
Paris. Instead Astley moved from one temporary post to another.
During the Munich crisis of 1938, she worked in the headquarters of

the anti-aircraft unit of the territorial army.

She also had an offer from the British Consul-General in Munich to live at the home of the enigmatic Nazi leader Rudolf Hess, to teach English to his family. [See Appendix.] She later regretted not taking the post. In her book *The Inner Circle: A View of War at the Top*, Astley remembered the Nazi leader's arrival with a certain regret. "Rudolf Hess arrived in May, his parachute swinging him down mad and alone on his private peace mission. I imagined myself sent for by the Foreign Secretary. 'Miss Bright, you alone in England know this man. Go and see him. Here is your ticket for Scotland.' Yes, certainly I should have accepted to go to the Hess family in Munich in 1938."[2]

Bright found more permanent government employment when a childhood friend told her to go to St. James Park underground station at a specific time wearing a pink carnation. From there, in a roundabout way she was led to an office and interviewed by the military. She was informed of the methods of torture of the Nazis and signed the Official Secrets Act. After the interview she was led to a window and a lone figure on a street corner was pointed out. She was told he had been watching all morning and not to let him see her. "It all seemed like good clean fun and I was pleased to be joining an organization in which fact and fiction played so smoothly together."[3]

Bright began working for the most secret departments of Britain's war effort — Colonel J. C. F. Holland, Colonel Colin McVeagh Gubbins, Major Millis Jefferis and Commander Dymock Watson in the Military Intelligence Directorate of the War Office. She then worked in Section D under Colonel Lawrence Grand. "Grand's section D deeds would be done by undercover men spies and saboteurs who, if caught, would be neither acknowledged nor defended by their government," she remembered in her book.

Her responsibilities grew during the war. When Winston Churchill decided his generals needed easier access to covert information, he instructed Pug Ismay to set up a "special secret information centre" in the Office of the Minister of Defence that Commanders-in-Chief could visit whenever they came to London. Ismay got Joan Bright to run it. She became the director of the information centre that collated and distributed confidential material to Britain's war commanders. Before and during the June 1944 D-Day landings in Normandy, the Allies feigned an invasion at Pas de Calais so Nazi strength would concentrate there.

In Anthony Cave Brown's *Bodyguard of Lies,* Sir Ronald Wingate, the deputy chief of the main deception bureau of the invasion, remembers Joan Bright informing them of the ULTRA intercept that indicated Hitler still believed the deception. The Nazi leader was stopping the flow of Panzer and infantry divisions to Normandy, and sending reinforcements to Calais. As a result D-Day would be successful.

"We looked at the ULTRA — and there it was. Hitler had cancelled Case Three. We'd won, and what an astonishing moment that was! We knew then that we'd won — there might be very heavy battles but we'd won. The PM came in with Stewart Menzies and the PM said this was the crowning achievement of the long and glorious history of the British Secret Service — or something like that."[4]

Astley attended all the major Big Three conferences, and eventually she was appointed the manager of the British delegation at the Allied conferences. The cover of the American version of her book is a circular picture, as if viewed through a spy glass, of Winston Churchill in Tehran in 1943, celebrating his birthday with Joseph Stalin.

Many prominent people corresponded with Bright during this time, including General Archibald Wavell and Admiral James Somerville, and she socialized with both Peter and Ian Fleming. According to Peter Fleming's biographer, he planned to use forged correspondence between Wavell and Bright in a deception during the Allied retreat from Burma.[5] She introduced Winston Churchill to Ian Fleming following his famous "Iron Curtain" speech, and had entertained some thoughts of marrying the future spy writer. She married Philip Astley in July 1949.

Joan Bright was a friend of William Stephenson. She refers to Stephenson in her book and implies he was instrumental in convincing Bill Donovan in 1940 that the United States needed a centralized intelligence organization:

> The contact with Mr. Stephenson and this visit convinced him (Donovan) that when the United States entered the war it would be profitable to draw into one body the many intelligence agencies which worked independently of each other in the department of War, Navy, and State, and to include in the body the study and implementation of unorthodox methods of war such as were now being pursued in England.[6]

Astley and two of her friends, Walter and Katie Bell, together discussed Bill Stephenson.

Bell worked in passport control when Stephenson arrived in the United States in 1940, and was one of the first members of what became British Security Coordination. He was with the Foreign Office for most of his career, stationed in New York during World War II and then transferred to Mexico. He was also on embassy staffs in Washington and various British missions in Africa. According to one report, Bell relayed information from the chief of British Security about the 1944 assassination attempt on Adolf Hitler to OSS representative David Bruce, because he "had important contacts with the conspirators."[7] Bell and his wife were also associates of Donald Maclean, the Soviet double agent.[8]

Walter's wife Katie was the daughter of American General Carl Spaatz.[9] (Spaatz was a prominent figure during the war. Among his assignments was Berlin in May 1945. He signed, on behalf of the United States, the surrender documents that ended the military war against Nazi Germany.)

After the trio learned of Stephenson's Canadian life, they offered some of their observations.

"Well, he was just someone I met during the war," Walter Bell said. "I was just in the passport office in New York working with passports." He made a stamping motion with his hands. "This little Canadian fellow arrived, and no one knew who he was.

"David Bruce had a tremendous regard for Bill Stephenson," Bell said. "He told us how Bill took him to Cheatley (Beaverbrook's house) for tea. Bevin was there and Dalton and Bill brought Bruce. Well Beaverbrook stood up and started making all these anti-American comments. Repeatedly. Eventually Bill Stephenson just got up and said, 'Look, our guest is a distinguished American. He's a guest from a remarkable country, and I didn't bring him here to be insulted. We're leaving.' And they began to walk out. Well, Beaverbrook got up, ran after them to the door, apologized, and pleaded and pleaded with Bill. He begged them to stay. You don't do that in Beaverbrook's house without knowing him very well."

"I don't know how well he knew Churchill, but I do know this," said Astley. "If Little Bill rang up General Ismay, Ismay would clear his desk. Immediately. I think that's important. Very few people could even get in to see Ismay.[10]

"He may have seen Churchill a few times. I don't know. I don't think it matters," she added.

The consensus of the trio seemed to be it was easy to read too much into the espionage business and Stephenson's career. "We're so close to it, we know what hokum a lot of it is," Astley said.

But were there not certain security precautions and guidelines within the "hokum" such as "need-to-know"? For example, Canadian BSC women in New York couldn't go to Berlitz language schools during the war. Bill Ross Smith, when he was dealing with South American assignments, learned Spanish at Berlitz in New York. Everything was on a need-to-know basis. No one else at BSC needed to know Ross Smith was taking Spanish for South American contacts. "So no one can go to Berlitz?"

"Oh, I think that's ridiculous," Katie Bell said. "They couldn't go to Berlitz, because they might see Bill Ross Smith there? Come on."

To BSC people certain restaurants were out of bounds as well. "That's just so they don't see their bosses drunk there," Astley said. "Oh, don't get caught up in that nonsense! The war was won by the people on the front lines."

Astley said the secrecy seemed a bit much at times. Employees were to walk into her office with their heads down in a certain way, she said, and once in a while she would look up at someone she knew and shout "Boo" at them. "People read too much into this spying business, don't they, Walter?"

"Well, yes," Bell said. "But don't call it spying. It's the Service."

"What about ULTRA?"

"Oh, that wasn't espionage, really," Astley said. "You know Winston felt a little guilty about ULTRA. He was very much a man of fairness. ULTRA was a bit like cheating."

Later Walter Bell spoke about Bill Stephenson. "We had no idea how to approach the Americans," he said. "The most valuable thing he did was talk sense about the Americans. The British feeling was the Americans were just a bunch of salesmen. The disquieting thing was that they were all rich," he laughed. "Stephenson cut all that out. He said, 'That's all bullshit. They're our friends. They'll help us. And we need them if we're going to win.' Which is what Churchill thought. Of course, he was right. Absolutely ... he was an invaluable person."

Following Stephenson's death no one from British officialdom spoke up for him amid negative press reports.

"Well, British Intelligence never acknowledge anything, one way or the other," Bell said. "Never. And the government? Well, it happened so long ago who would really know, without a lot of researching.

"I submitted something for [H.H.] Hinsley's book *British Intelligence in the Second World War*, that would have refuted one of [Hugh] Trevor-Roper's criticisms. But they wouldn't put it in," Bell said. "National security, they said. National security. Nonsense.

"In many ways Stephenson was very uncouth," Bell continued. "He knocked the establishment and the rules and pretty much did what he wanted. He wasn't being paid or anything. So if he didn't like what you were doing, he'd tell you to bugger right off. I can't say I was a fan of his. I wasn't a fan of Fleming's either. All this 'James Bond.'" He shook his head. "But on the other hand, I do know this. He did an incredible job."

A biography of Jim Thompson, a British silk merchant from Thailand, stood out from the bookcase. According to *Donovan*, Anthony Cave Brown's book, Thompson was a secret OSS agent, and following the war he became the Thai contact of World Commerce Corporation, which Stephenson headed. By the end of the evening, Astley said she was *sure* Thompson worked for Stephenson. "Everyone did! Don't you see?" she said, raising her voice. "And even people who didn't, said that they did. I'm certain that one day, an aboriginal will walk out from the far reaches of the outback, and he'll say, 'Oh yes ... I was working for Sir William,'" she said in a low raspy voice. And she laughed.

A day later a message was relayed from Katya Bell to this author by Grace Garner, Stephenson's wartime secretary. "They couldn't go to Berlitz because that was where people were trained for drops into Europe."

· · ·

Astley thought any new Bill Stephenson publication should deal with his early years, and not the war. "Bill covered up his childhood. I find that so sad," she said, "and to me that's far more interesting than anything you do about the war. If you could do any kind of character sketch as to what made this man tick over. What made him into the character and the personality he became, because — why are we talking about him now? I think if you could go through such research, such as parish registers and that sort of thing, and find out what sort of man. Why? What it was in him. As a serious study of a personality, I think it would be absolutely fascinating.

"I figure about these silly old people who wonder if Dick Ellis was a spy or wasn't a spy, or whether Bill was liked by Churchill or not. I think all of that is so unimportant. But what made Bill tick? Why this lonely little fellow as a small boy —" She wondered about his mother, and other family. "He's got no brothers and sisters alive?"

Behind her computer desk, she started sifting through her files. The keeper of many of the war's top secrets retained many personal papers. "I think it would really be something to put an end to this. 'Little Bill', here's a file now." She pulled up copies of letters from Montgomery Hyde and from Edwin Leather, "who's very concerned."[11] Astley questioned if certain instances in *A Man Called Intrepid* were true, such as Stephenson being an unidentifiable silhouette in a photograph with Churchill at the bombed-out Houses of Parliament.[12]

"This is William Stevenson [the author, making the claims]. I've heard from friends and I think this is true, that Mary Stephenson was frightfully against *A Man Called Intrepid*. She didn't want it, and if she'd been alive I don't think that book would have been published."

Astley knew the ex-wife of the author Stevenson, and she saw her in Bermuda. She read *A Man Called Intrepid* while she was there as a favour. "I said, 'I promise you,' I said, 'I'm devoted to you, Glynnis, and I don't want to be mean about your ex-husband, but I'm going to settle down and very quietly read it.'"

She walked to the bookcase and retrieved a copy of *A Man Called Intrepid.* "Oh really, on the first two pages. Let's just pick any page." She started thumbing through it. "'*Area of disaster ...Coventry ... Roosevelt discussed with Stephenson the dangers of knowing too much.*' I don't believe that for a minute. '*War is forcing us more and more to play God ... I don't know what I should have done. Churchill chose one*', etc. '*Bletchley obtained the German order destroy Coventry*'. I don't believe it. And then this is the main street maps of Europe. Here, you see. SOE wasn't even formed when observer units went undercover to defend England in case of invasion."

After stressing her concerns about Stephenson publications, Astley talked about her career during the war. The surreptitious work of her office at the beginning of the conflict was brought on by Britain's crippled circumstances at the time.

Vigfus and Kristin Stephenson, pictured in 1912, took in young William Samuel Clouston Stanger and renamed him William Samuel Stephenson. (Photo: Norma Feller)

William Stanger's birth certificate. He was born January 23, 1897, but became better known as William Stephenson — the man called Intrepid — born January 11,1896.

The Stephenson family home at 175 Syndicate Street (as seen today), Point Douglas, Winnipeg. The family lived here from the 1890s until after World War I. (Photo: Bill Macdonald)

Stephenson and his family in 1920 near Lundar, Manitoba. Clockwise from far left: Kristin (Breckman) Stephenson, Julianna ("Lulu") holding Bill Hodgins, Johinna Hodgins, Lillian Stephenson, Vigfus Stephenson, Margaret Hodgins, Bill Stephenson (in fedora) and Victor Hodgins. (Photo: Norma Feller)

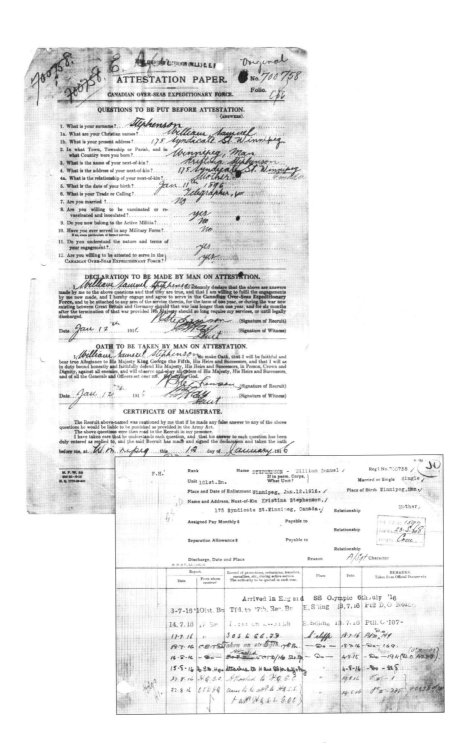

Stephenson's enlistment papers and part of his military record.

Captain William Stephenson, 73rd Squadron, RAF, awarded Military Cross, April 1918 and the Distinguished Flying Cross, August 1918. As a Sopwith Camel pilot, Stephenson brought down many enemy planes before he was shot down by friendly fire (a French aircraft) and captured by the Germans. (Photo: Feller family)

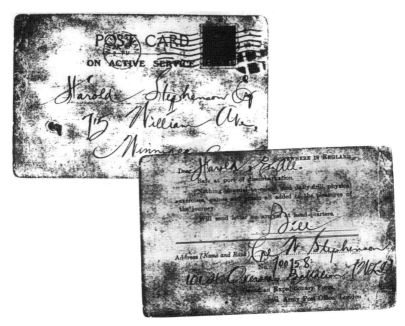

Upon his arrival in Britain in 1916, Stephenson sent this army-issue, pre-typed generic postcard to his nephew, Harold, to say he had arrived safely. For security reasons, it revealed no details.

"Icelandic Flyer" is the headline for this news item about Stephenson, printed in a May 1918 issue of *Votogorold*, an Iceland newspaper.

A new type of can opener poached from a German prisoner of war camp in World War I helped Stephenson launch his business career. Unfortunately, the Canadian company went bankrupt.

Wilf Russell, Stephenson's friend and first business partner. Russell and Stephenson started a company called Franco-British Supply, which became the patentee and manufacturer of the can opener they called "Kleen Kut." (Photo: Margaret Jamieson)

With Winnipeg friends in London, 1924. From left: Charlie Farquhar, step sister Juliana Stephenson, William Stephenson, Jane Farquhar-Olsen and Margaret Farquhar. Stephenson "recovered" from bankruptcy in London and was quickly hailed as "a brilliant scientist." (Photo: Margaret Jamieson)

The Farquars, the Olsons and Juliana Stephenson out for a spin in Stephenson's convertible, 1924. Later that year, Stephenson married Mary French Simmons. (Photo: Margaret Jamieson)

Stephenson and scientist T. Thorne Baker developed and improved a method of sending photos by wireless. On December 27, 1922, the first transmitted photo appeared in the *Daily Mail*.

Patent papers for Stephenson's improvements in wireless telegraphy. (Courtesy James Bell)

The German cipher machine, ENIGMA. The Allies' breaking of ENIGMA messages and their success with Japanese machines is said to have shortened the war by years. Stephenson's quick and unbreakable communications links — devised by Pat Bayly — were used to carry many of the decryptions and fed "raw" intercepted messages to Allied cryptography centres. (Photo: National Security Agency)

A code book obtained from the Washington Embassy of the Vichy French by Elizabeth Pack — code named "Cynthia" — Stephenson's most infamous undercover agent.

Elizabeth Pack, AKA "Cynthia."
(Photo: Mary Lovell)

Betty Raymond, 1990.
(Photo: Bill Macdonald)

Molly Phair, 1943.
(Photo: Margaret Jamieson)

Ruth Ferguson, 1943.
(Photo: Margaret Jamieson)

Molly Phair (left) and Ruth Ferguson with unidentified Canadian servicemen at Billy Rose's Diamond Horseshoe, Paramount Hotel, New York.
(Photo: Margaret Jamieson)

The largest department at Stephenson's BSC office in New York was communications, and most of the employees were Canadian women. Clockwise from left: Doris Ell, Georgie Davey, Molly Phair, Mary Grant (Pat Bayly's sister-in-law) and Mary McNeil.
(Photo: Margaret Jamieson)

Roald Dahl, who became a children's book author during World War II, worked for the British Security Coordination in Washington. (Photo: Bill Macdonald)

Benjamin de Forest "Pat" Bayly, 1959. For years after the war, Stephenson's communications genius and right-hand man could not be identified by name.

"Pat" Bayly in his home office near San Diego, 1991. (Photo: Bill Macdonald)

Office of Strategic Services (OSS) head William Donovan presenting William Stephenson with the U.S. Medal for Merit, 1946. Lady Mary Stephenson is standing next to her husband with Col. G. Edward Buxton, Assistant Director of the OSS looking on.

19 June 1944

MEMORANDUM FOR THE PRESIDENT

Attached is a proposed recommendation for award of the Distinguished Service Medal to Mr. William S. Stephenson, chief representative of the British Secret Intelligence Service and the Special Operation Service in the Western Hemisphere.

All that is said in the proposed citation is absolutely true. Just as we have been insistent on the right of our country to have an independent secret intelligence service, so I would like our British colleagues to see that we recognize and appreciate the help they gave us.

For that reason I hope that you approve such a citation.

William J. Donovan
Director

Unclassified

LRR 333/1

12 March 1991

Foreign &
Commonwealth
Office

London SW1A 2AH
Telephone: 071- 217 2049

Mr G A Calkin
Counsellor
Canadian High Commission
Macdonald House
1 Grosvenor Square
LONDON W1X OAB

Dear Mr Calkin,

Thank you for your letter of 21 February 1991. I understand that
the photocopies Mr MacDonald requested from Churchill College,
Cambridge were despatched by the College some days ago by second
class Airmail.

Unfortunately, I cannot give you a definite account of the position
regarding the Montgomery Hyde papers as there are legal aspects
concerning Crown copyright to be clarified. I will let you know as
soon as this has been done. In the meantime Mr MacDonald may like
to know that the closure of many of these papers may be only
temporary.

I apologise for any inconvenience caused to Mr MacDonald by these
closures and to you for the delay in responding to your letter.

Yours sincerely

I S Lockhart
Library and Records Department

"Unclassified" letter from British Foreign Office to Canadian High Commission
explaining the status of the personal collection of papers of Stephenson
biographer H. Montgomery Hyde. The files Hyde donated to Churchill College
Cambridge, which were previously available, were closed for viewing because of
"legal aspects concerning Crown copyright."

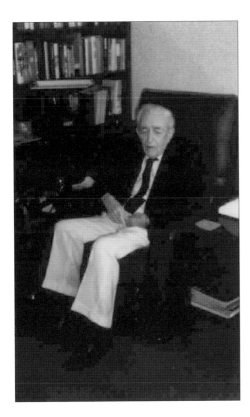

After the war, Stephenson lived
in Jamaica and New York,
then retired to Bermuda.
(Photo: David Young)

Canada Post's special Millennium
Series stamp, issued in 2000,
commemorated Stephenson.

A Winnipeg statue of Stephenson, unveiled in 1999. Originally etched to show 1896 as his birthdate, the inscription was redone, and Stephenson's correct date of birth, 1897, now appears.
(Photo: Bill Macdonald)

SIR WILLIAM SAMUEL STEPHENSON
"INTREPID"

SIR WILLIAM STEPHENSON WAS BORN IN 1896 IN THE POINT DOUGLAS AREA AND RECEIVED HIS EDUCATION IN THE CITY OF WINNIPEG.

IMMEDIATELY UPON HIS GRADUATION FROM ARGYLE PUBLIC SCHOOL IN 1914 HE ENLISTED IN THE ROYAL CANADIAN ENGINEERS. HE SERVED WITH DISTINCTION DURING THE FIRST WORLD WAR AND WAS DECORATED SEVERAL TIMES FOR BRAVERY, BEING AWARDED THE MILITARY CROSS, THE DISTINGUISHED FLYING CROSS AND THE CROIX DE GUERRE.

FOLLOWING THE CONCLUSION OF THE WAR HE JOINED THE STAFF OF THE UNIVERSITY OF MANITOBA WHERE HE TAUGHT MATHEMATICS AND SCIENCE. IN 1921 HE RETURNED TO ENGLAND ENJOYING A BRILLIANT CAREER IN HIGH TECHNOLOGY INDUSTRY AND PLAYED AN INSTRUMENTAL ROLE IN THE EARLY STAGES OF TELEVISION DEVELOPMENT.

DURING THE SECOND WORLD WAR, SIR WILLIAM WAS APPOINTED DIRECTOR OF BRITISH SECURITY CO-ORDINATION AS WELL AS PRIME MINISTER WINSTON CHURCHILL'S PERSONAL REPRESENTATIVE TO PRESIDENT ROOSEVELT. HE IS MOST POPULARLY KNOWN FOR HIS PIVOTAL ROLE IN THE BRITISH INTELLIGENCE EFFORT, AN ACTIVITY WHICH EARNED HIM THE CODE NAME, INTREPID. HIS SERVICES TO THE COMMONWEALTH DURING THE WAR YEARS WERE RECOGNIZED BY HIS BEING KNIGHTED IN 1945.

TRULY A REMARKABLE SON OF WINNIPEG, SIR WILLIAM ALWAYS EXCELLED IN EVERY ACTIVITY IN WHICH HE BECAME INVOLVED AND ALWAYS EXEMPLIFIED THE HIGHEST QUALITIES OF DEDICATION AND PATRIOTISM.

THIS PLAQUE ERECTED IN HIS HONOUR BY THE CITIZENS OF WINNIPEG AND THE RESIDENTS OF THE POINT DOUGLAS COMMUNITY WAS UNVEILED BY:

HIS WORSHIP MAYOR WILLIAM NORRIE, Q.C.

AUGUST 15TH, 1982

A commemorative 1983 plaque in Stephenson's old Point Douglas neighbourhood in Winnipeg. Interestingly, the plaque contains a few factual errors. He was not born in 1896. He did not graduate from Argyle Public School in 1914. Nor did he teach at the University of Manitoba. (Photo: Bill Macdonald)

"I was in the office before it had become SOE, a branch. It was very straightforward. The war had to be fought that way. We didn't have an army. And the decision was there were only three ways to wage the war in the beginning. By economic warfare, you know, by interception of ships, etc. And bombing. And by subversive operations, and commando raids, and that sort of thing — while the army was being built up."[13]

At the time, Astley was working on a book about former British SOE chief Colin Gubbins, but she didn't see Stephenson about him. "No, I had no business arrangements with Bill at all. We were friends. I knew him in the war and then I married, and we lost touch and that type of thing, and then when I published my book [1971] somebody must have sent him a copy, because he sent me a telegram. He was absolutely thrilled with it. And then he kept in touch every Christmas, and then after my husband died, I think I went altogether three times. He put me up at the Princess Hotel about ten days. It was always very measured. You didn't see him every day, but you would get Elizabeth or someone to ring up and could you come at 11:00 and that sort of thing." She met some of Stephenson's friends in Bermuda who were not involved in espionage, such as Derek Bedson. "He was very sensible ... You saw Walter Bell the other night. Once you've been involved with intelligence, you become very cagey." She didn't think Bell's name should be mentioned in any publication, "He's retired. Put John Brown."

Bell emphasized Stephenson was a very good liaison with the Americans. "That you could say without quoting him," she said. "That you could quote anyone saying, about that. I think that is absolutely true. Anyone who signs the Official Secrets Act. They get very angry, you know."

Astley said certain things she was careful not to put into print. There was a huge signals organization, for example, and she got wrapped up in coding of all kinds. "I am very careful in my book not to reveal the actual system. Coding can go on forever. If the key can be found. Even a hundred years after, it would be interesting."

Stephenson attended the Quebec Conferences, Astley said. "Well, sure, he was there. Very likely. It would have been very odd if he wasn't. When you say "at," there's a great deal of difference from being "at" [as] a member of the delegation, which he wasn't, and "being at," being called and coming up, or being important enough to say, 'I'd like to see you while in Canada.'"

There would be no need for Stephenson to attend the other conferences. "He was in charge of the Western Hemisphere. He wasn't a spy. He wasn't spying, really. He wasn't a spy. He ran a large organization covering from the Argentine up to Alaska. You Canadians, as well, you know."

But Stephenson was made aware of the major decisions. "Well, of course. Naturally. I don't see how you could possibly run anything, unless you had a certain number of people who have to know. You can't, of course. I mean ULTRA, very few people knew. Bill Stephenson knew. He would have had to know." Although Astley dealt with ULTRA messages, stored and distributed them, she says she was unaware of their source. "I didn't know about ULTRA. Ian Jacob, my boss, one of my bosses, he swears he didn't know. Because there was no need for him to know. He didn't need to know. Only the people who needed to know knew. So this is sensible. A lot of us juniors, we all knew the date of D-Day long before. I mean, you'd certainly find out if you did give it away. You're relying on people's honesty, confidentiality."

"You said that Ismay would make room for him?"

"Oh, always. Bill was a senior operator. If you wanted to give ranks, he would have been a Major General or an Air Marshal or Air Vice Marshal. That would be his rank, and as such result he would have entree. And Churchill he might have rung. I wouldn't know. There would be no need for him to see Churchill. He had nothing to do with intelligence matters. I mean he was Prime Minister.

"People get extraordinary ideas about things. Intelligence is not as exciting or secret as it appears to be. Intelligence is what you glean in order to mount an operation. You can't mount an operation without first finding out what type of guns the enemy have on the other side, or what the people are thinking. Therefore Bill would be gleaning the intelligence. He would be passing on what he thought was important. The same as the directors of intelligence in Washington and in Canada, and Australia, and the headquarters in India. You wouldn't tell India about the intelligence in France."

Grace Garner thought that Bill Stephenson knew Bill Donovan before the war and meeting him in North America wasn't set up in London. Astley's book suggests otherwise.

"I may have been wrong on that one," Astley said. "Well maybe I'm wrong there. Perhaps he did know him before. I'm trying to think who I talked to." She went to her files and bookcase and started to go through a few things.

"I used to lunch with him and Mary after the war," she said. "Mary didn't come over during the war. Travel was very restricted, I suppose. 'Dined with Bill and Mary. Claridges.' I often look back. I suppose he used to come into the office. I suppose he did. I had my one operations room, and wasn't privy to everything coming in. I was running my own show. How awful if I'm wrong here. I loathe being wrong." She started to read from her book to confirm her Donovan story. "It's not very polite of me to say 'At a much lower level.' *At a much lower level — at what even may be called a personal 'subversive' level — collaboration had begun between the two countries earlier in the year.*[14] I don't know who I got this from. I never met Donovan.

"As Walter Bell was saying so rightly. For example, Desmond Morton. Industrial intelligence. Bill would have been used. He was a high-up man then, and people would have said get a hold of Bill Stephenson.' You see in the years between 1930 and 1938, he was a hired man in that business."

Astley went through notes she had made while in Bermuda visiting Stephenson and watching the *A Man Called Intrepid* telefilm, which featured David Niven as Stephenson, and was loosely based on Stevenson's book. She didn't believe it was accurate. "Talks about Gubbins and ENIGMA. Poppycock.

"Gubbins shows Bill Stephenson the pill that kills. Stephenson and Gubbins who were as busy as bees in New York. The film was awful. It was all made up, wasn't it? I don't know who made it." (Lorimer Productions did.)

She looked at further notes she had made about the 1979 made-for-TV film and a telephone call she received to try and halt its broadcast in England.

"Nigel West, a 27-year-old BBC producer called as a result of Intrepid giving him my name, you see, to discuss a crime being committed by ITV. A reporter writes about a Canadian film, *A Man Called Intrepid,* in which David Niven plays Stephenson.[15] I can't remember who plays Colin Gubbins. He wonders if it could be stopped. I don't understand this. He, West, is working on a 20-minute obituary film on Stephenson.'" Then she added, "Stephenson hadn't died yet. 'I would like to see the film. I must make inquiries to doing so. I cannot see what could be done. If Colin is portrayed inaccurately, what can one do, unless it reduces him?' This is all to do with what Nigel West said."

Astley was Stephenson's guest in Bermuda in 1979 and 1981. She continued to scan her files of those visits. "Camden House, a presentation by me. Poor old Bill, it was part of his hubris at the time. Nothing there. I'm not trying to hide anything! Let me be quick to say. Nothing about Bill there! We had to listen to some of his fantasies, such as him and Colin Gubbins blowing up the heavy water ferries. In other ways his memory is perfectly okay. Chapman Pincher. He goes on and on, these old chestnuts. Pincher was very much a journalist. It's all there. Very boring."

Although some aspects of Stephenson's career may have been "very boring," years after the war Astley was still concerned about the ex-spymaster's welfare. In April 1973 Astley wrote Bill Stephenson a letter thanking "dear Intrepids" for his telegram at New Year's and for not forgetting his old friends. In it she talks about what she and her family have been up to.[16]

But the end of the letter has a completely different tone.

"I should love to see you again. I am sure you are wise enough never to come to England. But I hope, if you did, you would tell me." The last paragraph is handwritten, "And so with my love and thanks — and keep away from random and purposeful bullets. Joan"

17 ROALD DAHL

A Question of Honour

People from a variety of backgrounds and occupations worked for Stephenson's BSC. There were professional intelligence officers, secretaries, businessmen, military, police and professors. There were also writers.

Roald Dahl was born in Wales, the son of Norwegian parents, and was educated at a British private school in Derbyshire. He started working for Shell Oil in England and in 1937 was transferred to Tanzania. When the war broke out Dahl joined the Royal Air Force in Kenya. He was shot down in Libya and suffered a skull fracture, spinal injuries and a smashed hip. Eventually he moved to Washington as an Assistant Air Attaché at the British Embassy.

The novelist Cecil Scot Forester asked Dahl to jot down a few thoughts about being a combat pilot for a story he was doing. Forester, who created Captain Horatio Hornblower, was impressed with Dahl's writing and decided to submit the young Briton's notes as a story. Dahl says the *Saturday Evening Post* paid him $1,000 for his article, which he later lost playing poker with Senator Harry Truman at Washington's University Club. Dahl became a writer, and he produced an eclectic body of work. One of his short stories, 1943's *The Gremlins*, was made into a movie by Walt Disney. Eleanor Roosevelt took a liking to Dahl's work, and soon he was a regular guest at the White House and Hyde Park.

Some later British press reports say Dahl got into writing by accident.[1] However, C. S. Forester was doing a number of things during the war. He covered the Nazi occupation of Czechoslovakia in Prague and was a member of British Information Service.[2] "During World War II Forester devoted himself to writing propaganda for the Allied cause, much of it for American consumption," the *Cambridge Guide to Literature* reports.[3] During the war Dahl was an agent working for Bill Stephenson.

When Dahl was contacted about contributing to research into the life of William Stephenson, he wrote he was willing to talk about Bill Stephenson's work "while in the saddle," and he thought Stephenson's work with British Security Coordination was "outstanding." But he had some reservations. He later said he was unsure of some of the claims in the books about Stephenson, and Dahl believed in his later life, the ex-spy chief was trying to get attention. But he was interested in his old boss' background, and he was surprised people from BSC were talking.

"Aren't they worried about the Official Secrets Act?" he asked over the phone.

It was pointed out many of the people were Canadians.

"Well, *WE* do," Dahl said.

He extended an invitation to discuss the life of William Stephenson at his house, but he made a point of saying he would reveal no secrets. "You won't get any from me!" the renowned children's author said emphatically, and then he paused, and sounded more subdued, "It's a question of honour, really."

Lunch at Dahl's

Dahl sat down and immediately started talking. Before any questions could be asked, he remembered 1941.

"Bill always affirmed that he had chaps in the next hotel room to the ... I don't know what he was, the Japanese foreign minister, who came over just before Pearl Harbor to Washington. Do you know who it was? [Special Envoy Saburo Kurusu.] It was a big shot. And they were talking in this room and they had tapes of them discussing the actual date of Pearl Harbor. And he swears, he did to me, anyway, that he gave that transcription to FDR. He swears that they knew therefore of the oncoming attack on Pearl Harbor and hadn't done anything about it."

"Do you think that's right?"

"I don't know," Dahl said. "I have no way to judge, except Bill didn't usually tell stories like that. That's the end of that little story. That's all I know and heard about."

"What date would that have been?"

"Whenever that chap was visiting. I don't know, shortly before Pearl Harbor."

A number of sources imply certain officials possibly knew about the oncoming attack, but Dahl was still a bit incredulous. He wondered how the base could have been left so unprepared if they knew the situation. "FDR was a very sensible man, and I knew him well. I mean there was no way he'd let the Pacific Fleet be destroyed if he could avoid it. The whole thing doesn't make sense.

"Not with the destruction of the Fleet," said Dahl. "If you'd have been FDR or I'd have been FDR and we got hold of Nimitz and we'd said 'move most of the battleships away for Christ's sake,' the day before. And just leave one or two if you want. You don't want the whole bloody lot destroyed. There's many many ways to do it."[4]

Dahl then didn't want to talk about Pearl Harbor, he wanted to talk about Bill Stephenson.

"Much more interesting to me is this very secret man, all through the war, and he was very, very secret," said the writer. "Very private was the main thing. An extremely private man."

He remembered the wartime BSC offices, and Stephenson's relationship to staff. He didn't deal with subordinates in his office, he only talked to very few designated people and they were seldom called in to see him, "unless a big thing came up and he wanted to hear your version specifically." Some people who worked at BSC never saw Stephenson, because he didn't go through the large cluttered area in front of his office. "He was a very, very private man," Dahl repeated.

Following the focussed frenzy of the war there was a letdown and a somewhat troubling void for Stephenson. Over five years he had built up a huge organization and used all of his connections. "Then the war finished, and then although he got a knighthood, he got no publicity whatsoever. But then people in the secret service, the SIS, don't expect to get publicity.

"I think he felt he did expect to get it, myself," continued Dahl. "Even before his first stroke. And was a bit nulled by it all. And my own opinion is that he set the machinery rolling. And he did hire people to write books about him."[5]

Dahl thought Stephenson was interested in promoting himself and said that if Stephenson made a speech after the war, he sent copies of the text to "anybody he could think of. I got the bloody things. Everyone got them. He circulated them. You know of a lot of people like that, but we don't have a very high opinion of them."[6]

Books about Stephenson were full of mistakes, "Because Bill didn't bother to check them. Or he gave false information. Or his memory was at fault. Well the question is whether he made the mistake in telling us about the Pearl Harbor thing too. You know, there's other things there."

"What did you do, exactly? Or are you going to say?"

"I'm not telling you. No."

"Honour?"

"No, of course I'm not," he said smiling. "I'm not a Mr. [Peter] Wright [*Spycatcher* author]. All I'm here for is to give you my own opinions of Bill Stephenson. No. No, you won't get anything out of me on that sort of thing."

From interviews he did decades earlier one can piece together some of Dahl's work for the Stephenson organization. When he first arrived in Washington, the young RAF pilot had no idea who Stephenson was, but he soon realized that everyone in any position of power from the British Ambassador down or on the American side knew about "this extraordinary fellow up there." During the war Stephenson was a silent secret, "a kind of unknown small creature, hiding in a dark room somewhere up in New York," Dahl said. Stephenson didn't outline a job description for the former pilot. "When he hired you he expected you to know what your role would be." Dahl worked for Stephenson for over a year before he met him.[7]

One of Dahl's contributions was purloining information from prominent people. The socially active British Air Attaché became friendly with a number of Washington politicians, including then Vice President Henry Wallace. Once while visiting his friend Charles Marsh's house, Wallace left a position paper for postwar Asia, and Marsh showed it to Dahl and asked for his opinion. Dahl quickly phoned a friend who he knew was a BSC contact in Washington, and told him to meet him outside Marsh's. The BSC contact arrived within minutes and the position paper was photographed and returned as quickly as possible. While he waited for its return, Dahl hid in the basement bathroom.

The paper *Our Job in the Pacific* called for "the emancipation of colonial subjects in the British Empire countries of India, Burma, and Malaya, and the French Empire of Indo-China, and the Dutch Empire in the East Indies." The paper also outlined plans for creating an American monopoly of postwar commercial aviation. The Wallace draft is said to have incensed Winston Churchill. For the 1944 election Wallace was replaced on the Roosevelt ticket by Senator Harry Truman. It is not known exactly the extent to which BSC played a role in Wallace's downfall, but "Stephenson could be very devious," Dahl recalled to the writer Anthony Cave Brown.

Dahl later confirmed in writing that the "Wallace Affair" incident was accurate.

Wallace knew Dahl worked for British Security. After the war, Wallace wrote in his diary that Wing Commander Dahl told him of the very close friendship between Bill Stephenson, "his chief," and Bill Donovan. "He spent most of his time trying to convince me that the United States should continue the Donovan Secret Service set-up. He thinks a combined American-English Secret Service is necessary to prevent destructive possibilities of the atomic bomb." (Wallace was unconvinced and thought the agency would be under the thumb of the English.)[8]

In 1943 Dahl started working for British Security Coordination full-time and described his job as "to try and oil the wheels between the British and the American war effort. He was a frequent guest of the Roosevelts and would ask informally what FDR or cabinet members thought about a variety of subjects, and he relayed their off-the-record comments to Stephenson.

He also shared information with the prominent columnist Drew Pearson. On one occasion details of Britain's Ambassador Lord Halifax's telegrams to London about the situation in India appeared in Pearson's *Washington Post* column. The embassy didn't know the source of the leak and eventually London sent word to Stephenson to locate it. Stephenson designated Dahl to find it. Since Pearson was a friend, Dahl soon discovered the columnist's source was a person in the India High Commission. This served as an indication that future telegrams sent from Britain's Washington Embassy might not be safe and could also be compromised.

It appears Dahl may have previously discussed what he could say about the war with British Intelligence, before he was quoted in the past.

A letter from the author William Stevenson to David Ogilvy says Dahl "checked with what he regarded as the proper authorities before talking on film. I know this, not from Dahl, but from the consulted."[9]

Dahl thought Stephenson had a brilliant mind. "There's no question about that," he said. "I mean the fact he became a millionaire about the same time as Beaverbrook and at about the same age, 27 or 28. Came over here and took over Pressed Steel for Christ's sake, at that age. Which is the Morris Works in Oxford. And it was not so easy to become a millionaire as it is today. He became rich as soon as he wanted to, more or less," he concluded. "And that was it."

Stephenson was always drawn to intelligence and intrigue. It was through his company connections he saw Hitler building up militarily, and he started informing Churchill, who Dahl thought, Stephenson didn't even know at the time. "But he would have had a connection through Beaverbrook."

The connection could also have been through Desmond Morton.

"It could have been too, through there. But he didn't know Churchill personally then, I don't think. But he got the notes through. He got them through for patriotic reasons, number one, and secondly, with his absolute cleverness, he spotted Churchill as a future leader. Christ, he could have sent them to Chamberlain, but he didn't. Yes, he could have sent them to Halifax or Chamberlain. But they were both idiots, and he wouldn't have got anywhere," he said. "And he picked the right man to send them to; and Churchill, when he came to getting a chap for America, he said, 'This is the chap for me.' It was on that, I'm sure. And I think Max Beaverbrook advised him to do it, too, because they were both Canadians. He was a close friend, a really genuinely close friend of Beaverbrook. No question about that. I've been in Beaverbrook's house in Jamaica with him and they were absolutely like that," he said crossing his fingers. "A couple of Canadians, a couple of old Canadian millionaires who were both pretty ruthless."

Toward the end of the war Stephenson wondered about Dahl's financial situation, and he gave him some investment advice the writer remembered. One day they were chatting in his office. "'Do you want to make some money?' Stephenson asked. 'Well, everyone does,' I replied. 'Do you have any?' 'Not much, I've got about £3,000 saved in England.' 'Well, I'll tell you what to put it in,' said Stephenson."

The spy chief told Dahl about an entirely new type of pen his agents in Argentina had found out about. 'It's called the ballpoint,' Stephenson said. 'This is going to sweep the world.'

The rights to the ballpoint pen were owned at the time by a small British Aviation company, and he advised Dahl to buy their stock. At the time the shares were worth about three shillings, and he put all of his money into the company.

"He was absolutely right about the ballpoint pen. He couldn't have been righter," Dahl recalled. "But the trouble was this little fucking company that had the patents sold out to another company, and the whole thing was fiddled and my company disappeared," he laughed. "So I lost all my money!" and he keeled back on his chair. "The interesting thing was his intelligence was good. It must have been — it swept the world."

At the conclusion of the war Dahl was a fairly successful magazine and short story writer, and Stephenson wanted him to help write a history of British Security Coordination. Tom Hill was in charge of the operation and Grace Garner, Eleanor Fleming, Harry Smith and a few others packed up the files from the New York office and transported them in a convoy of vans to Camp X, near Oshawa. "We don't dare to do it in the United States, we have to do it on British territory," Stephenson told Dahl. The reason being security. "You're going to open these things all over the bloody place. Room after room of God knows what. And you know he pulled a lot over Hoover particularly. He didn't pull anything over Bill Donovan. But he pulled a lot over Hoover. And he didn't want any of that seen. He pulled a few things over the White House, too, now and again. It was secure, and he was protecting SIS anyway." Dahl didn't know if Stephenson pulled anything on Stewart Menzies, the head of Britain's SIS. "I wouldn't be surprised, but I wouldn't corroborate that at all," he said. "He was a schemer."

In Ontario, Dahl found the sorting and summarizing difficult. He was a fiction writer and didn't want to organize the files into a readable history. "I wrote a little bit of crap, and I said 'Christ, I'm not going to do this, it's an historian's job,'" he recalled. "And I called Bill and I said, 'I'm packing this in, I can't write.' And he said 'Okay, come on back.' And that was it. And this famous history of BSC through the war in New York was written by Tom Hill and a few other knocks."

Dahl thought the finished product was circulated to Members of Parliament and others. He had a copy for a period of time, but wasn't sure where he'd put it. He was surprised it had been leaked in the fall of 1989 to the *Washington Post* by the author Bill Stevenson.

Dahl was primarily in Washington during the war following his accident and knew the Roosevelts. He went to dinners at the White House and for weekends at Roosevelt's retreat at Hyde Park, New York. Mingling at the various gatherings, he met cabinet members such as Secretary of the Treasury Henry Morgenthau, Secretary of Commerce Will Clayton and others. The President took a liking to the young British Embassy Attaché and Dahl even drove around with him alone in his specially designed car. Security men would carry Roosevelt to the driver's seat, where he operated the gas pedal and brakes from controls on the steering wheel.

"I was just a sort of clown for him in his relaxing time ... Twenty-six or twenty-seven ... I was just a young man who he found fun to talk to, when he wasn't doing business. That's all. Exciting for me, but not for him particularly."

"And he'd tell you what to tell Bill?"

"No! Never. Never," Dahl said. "I never got anything out of FDR. Nothing at all. I don't think he even knew I worked for Bill. I was sort of an attaché at the British Embassy. That's all he knew. He didn't care, I wasn't that important."

It's possible Dahl's value was not only liaison with the U.S. officialdom, but general liaison — public relations. At the beginning of 1942 Anglo-American relations were at a low ebb and certain members of the U.S. government thought foreign espionage services should not be allowed to operate on American soil. There was also a rising feeling in the U.S. that Britain was "sitting on her rifles" in the war, and the value of British lectures on "London Can Take It" and the exploits of the RAF in Europe were wearing thin in a country greatly concerned with the Pacific conflict. Stephenson sought opinion from a variety of sources on how to improve relations with the Americans. A February 10, 1942, paper from 'V. W.' in BSC's Washington Office to W.S.S. had a number of ideas. The final suggestion:

> The appointment to Washington of a tough and invigorating personality, who would make an end of the present almost hermit-like seclusion in Washington, would be a step in the right direction, especially if he were not one of the official governing class, but more

or less a man of the people, as there is reason to believe the President would desire. But the present decline in Anglo-American good understanding would not be checked if such a change were seen to be merely a political reshuffle or if the new appointment were not supported by a drastic reorganization of Cabinet Offices at home with a thorough burning-out of all dead wood.[10]

Not being of "the official governing class," it's possible one of Dahl's Washington assignments from Stephenson was to be an 'invigorating personality.'

Dahl felt Stephenson kept everyone at arm's length in BSC, except John Pepper, and Pepper was the only person in on all of Stephenson's plans. (Pepper later denied this, but offered no elaboration.) The BSC chief often ask Dahl's opinion on things. "He used to confide in me a lot. And sit and chat. 'What will we do about this?' But I was very young, you know."

The English writer knew nothing of Stephenson's background or that he had very little formal education. "You mean he was lowly educated? Well the old mind worked all right, I'll tell you that." But he questioned many of his ex-boss's reported achievements. He doubted if Stephenson was actually involved in scientific developments in the 1920s or whether he actually won medals during World War I.

Newspaper clippings from a 1921 *London Daily Mail* that described Stephenson as a brilliant scientist, and a World War I Winnipeg newspaper clipping headlined "Wins Military Cross" were available and shown to the writer. "No! I'm an old man. I don't want to see that crap." He then said Stephenson had likely planted the telegraphy information.

"I believe it. But I'm sure he disseminated that information. I'm sure he did. Yeah, I'm sure he did."

"He'd just got off the boat from Canada."

"Yes, but you misuse the words 'brilliant scientist' because he was never a scientist ... No, he wasn't any brilliant scientist," he repeated. "You're getting yourself into —" he paused. "I'll tell you what's interesting, about what you're doing, which you should pinpoint. You'll find contradictory statements everywhere you go about this man. Don't you? You do!" he said raising his voice. "And that's interesting, you see. And that's not to do with the fact he was in the Secret Service. It's to do with the man himself, I think."

Dahl was one of the few ex-employees who remained friends with Stephenson after the war, and he often received telegrams and telexes from him. "He never wrote letters." Dahl visited Stephenson in Bermuda and stayed with him there. But he hadn't seen the spy chief since the early 1960s following Stephenson's first stroke. He was shocked, as Stephenson's speech had been greatly affected. This was around the same time as Dahl's son Theo had a traffic accident, and Dahl suggested Stephenson see his neurosurgeon, Sir Kenneth Till. The writer talked Till into going to Bermuda, all expenses paid, to treat his old boss.

Immediately following the stroke, Dahl was told Stephenson's survival was uncertain. Newspaper executive and former BSC liaison Ernest Cuneo said Stephenson appeared deathly ill after the stroke, and simply remained in bed most days, waiting to die. But one day Cuneo was at his bedside talking to him and all of a sudden, just like that, Stephenson got up and went back to work. Cuneo told him, "We need you to fight the Reds, or something like that," Dahl remembered, and then Stephenson perked up.

Dahl said he learned nothing from Stephenson, "Except what I disapprove of, the art of secrecy. He was a very secret man, like I've been saying. No, he was a totally uncultured man. Totally. Well, his background would lead to that."

Music and the arts didn't seem to captivate Stephenson imeasurably. Dahl said Stephenson pointed at one painting he had in his New York flat, by well-known Canadian painter Cornelius Krieghoff, and said, "Look at that. Look at that." "That's the only painter's name he'd ever heard of, I think. No, he was a totally uncultivated man. And, ah … not a pleasure to talk to, really. In private, socially. If you met him socially he never had any conversation at all, really. He talked to Max Beaverbrook about business. I think they probably had a ball talking about which companies they were going to take over, or bust or whatever. To ordinary people like us, no, he had no conversation at all. Absolutely none.

"He's an enigma all around. This man is an enigma. He was interested in business. And to him SIS was a business, but he was not interested in any of the arts at all. He was intrigued by writers, and he tended to hire writers to work for him. And you know perfectly well, quite a few writers were working for him in New York."

Former members of BSC, and the official history of the organization, indicate the spy agency curried favour in the American media and playwrights such as Eric Maschwitz, Benn Levy and historian Gilbert Highet worked for Stephenson. The playwright and author Robert Sherwood was present when Stephenson received his Medal of Merit from Bill Donovan. "Winchell?"

"Yeah, quite a few. Well, Winchell, he wasn't a writer, he was a fucking columnist ... Winchell. Christ."

"Well, was Fleming writing then or no?"

"No, he wasn't."

"His brother was."

"Yes, Peter was writing then. Peter was writing. But he wasn't really working for him, Ian Fleming. I mean a whole bunch of people who said they worked for Bill weren't working for him. Noel Coward kept saying he worked for Bill, you know. Bill would ask him to do the tiny little things, because he passed through New York. And Noel Coward would go all over the place saying 'I'm working for Bill Stephenson.' They all did that. I mean, Coward made a huge thing of it." Dahl lowered his voice to a whisper, "And he'd turn up in the salons in London and say 'Now, shhh, you've heard of this chap Bill Stephenson.'

"You know it's true. Any celebrity that passed through, Bill would try to see. And he'd give them some piddly little thing. 'Where are you going?' Or, 'You're going to Africa for ENSA to act for the troops, why don't you find out what so-and-so is doing and give him something' He got thrilled by it."

"How about Greta Garbo?"

"No, it's bullshit. The whole thing is bullshit. All those stories are bullshit. It's a very funny thing that a man with that kind of character is intrigued. It's a weakness. It's a weakness to be intrigued. Rich people are the most seductive of all. To most people. Most people are totally seduced by rich people ... I mean look at Churchill and all those pricks. Rich. Purely rich idiots."[11]

Stephenson never flaunted his wealth, the writer said, and he was one of the first people to spot the West Indies as a tourist resort. After the war he bought a house in Jamaica, told Beaverbrook about it, and eventually Noel Coward and Ian Fleming also bought there.

"How about his relationship with Fleming? Do you know anything about that?"

"Yes, because I knew Fleming very well indeed. And there wasn't much, I'm quite sure."

"Fleming liked him though."

"Yes, of course, Fleming. Very well. Anything to do with secrets Fleming would like to use himself.

"This man is a total enigma," Dahl continued. "And that's the interesting thing. He is an enigma. And how much wool did he pull over people's eyes, and how much truly good work did he do? But there's no question he did some truly good work."

Stephenson told Dahl during the war that his greatest achievement was the Destroyers for Bases deal with Franklin Roosevelt. He recounted flying from New York to Washington to see FDR virtually every day, and he negotiated the proceedings "on behalf of Winston." "He said he did personally with FDR. Well, I always doubted myself if you want to know, whether he had met FDR. I did."[12]

Stephenson had an extraordinary relationship with his wife, Dahl remembered. "He loved her and they had a very, very good marriage, I think. But ... she was frightened of him." Mary Stephenson would fuss and frequently bring her husband things, almost acting as a servant to him. "But they got on very well together."

Beaverbrook often talked about the women he'd slept with, but Stephenson never would. "He loved Mary." In fact Beaverbrook wouldn't talk about women the same way around Stephenson. "In a lot of ways Stephenson wasn't 'one of the boys,' as they say," Dahl said. "In a lot of ways he was a man apart."

Future advertising mogul David Ogilvy lived with Dahl for a time in Washington and Dahl thought Ogilvy would have a lot to say about Stephenson. "You'll get every sort of theory under the sun from David. You would."

Stephenson is listed in one of Ogilvy's books, *Blood, Brains and Beer*, as one of his heroes, but he doesn't go into great detail of his assignments. "He was always going on about Gallup. He said Gallup's the answer to everything."[13]

It seemed apparent the organization employed numerous good people, and many had successful careers following their stint in British Security Coordination. "That wasn't Stephenson who lifted them up," Dahl said. "He didn't give them a hand.

"He used to pick people out and seduce them away from what they were doing, and into BSC. I mean he did that to me. I was just a simple Air Attaché in Washington, and I started playing the game he played with

Winston, of sending him snippets of hot stuff. And, when I got the sack from, ah — because I insulted a lot of Air Marshals and I sent word up to him, 'Look, I'm going back home.' He said, 'Don't worry about it.' This did show power, I was impressed by the power he had then. Because I was a Squadron Leader and he said the moment you get home from seeing 'C,' or whatever it was, go and see so-and-so. And I went and saw him and this chap said, 'You're going straight back to Washington as a Wing Commander, and you're going to work for Bill Stephenson.'

"I said, 'Well, all right. Thanks. That's nice.' And I did. And the day I arrived back I was at a cocktail party in Washington and the Air Chief Marshal who sent me packing, because I insulted him or I'd actually revealed a crooked racket going on with Sir Richard Fairey, the aviation man who was running a special airplane to take his friends across the Atlantic. And so I got booted out by the big boys. And I turn up at this. And this Air Chief Marshal strode up to me and he said, 'Dahl, what the hell are you doing here? You're sent home!' I said to him, 'If you want to know what I'm doing here, you'll have to talk to Mr. William Stephenson in New York.'" He paused. "And that was it."[14]

"He had a bit of power," Dahl continued. "I don't think he was ever in touch with Halifax. They were just two totally different people. In fact any Halifax stuff, I did it. He despised him. He was a different man, Halifax was. A gentleman, a courtly English gentleman, and Bill Stephenson ..." he laughed. "And he moved very slowly indeed. And he engineered Munich and Christ knows what. He had no time for Halifax at all."

On the Moon

Roald Dahl, the writer, served Intrepid after his Royal Air Force career was cut short in a Spitfire crash. Dahl reported from Washington in 1944: "You should know that the Americans are planning to land a man on the moon ... Everyone thought that I was mad but I never heard that Intrepid laughed." About 25 years later, a telegram [from Stephenson] was delivered to Dahl's cottage in Buckinghamshire, England. It said: "Congratulations. You were right." It then quoted the serial number and date of Dahl's original memo.

— *Toronto Star*, May 27, 1979

When Dahl was questioned about the above he replied, "Your letter of July 25th. The story about me and Bill Stephenson and the men on the moon is totally true. That I can confirm." — Roald Dahl letter to author, August 3, 1990.

John Pepper

Following the publication of *A Man Called Intrepid*, John Pepper, who Dahl thought was in on Stephenson schemes, wrote to his former boss:

> Intrepid has become a household word in these Bahama Islands and I am basking in your well deserved and reflected glory. You're the most famous man I know Bill.... And I bet it's not doing your name sake any harm either. There must be a little in it for him. Will put him on the map as an author too. He should be grateful for all you have done for him, but he can't be as grateful as I am for all you did for me. — John AR Pepper[15]

When this writer was able to locate John Pepper, he was living in the Bahamas and in Switzerland. He denied he was in on all of Stephenson's schemes. After the war he was one of the vice presidents of World Commerce, but says he was not involved in all the activities. He had seen the former spy chief only a few times since the war. "I'll help you as long as it doesn't get involved with MI6," he said. A short time later he sent a one-sentence letter. "You know more about Sir William Stephenson then (sic) I do. Kindest regards, John Pepper."

Soon afterwards he seemed to have moved from his Swiss home. Unfortunately, he didn't clarify why he was grateful to William Stephenson.

David Ogilvy

David Ogilvy was involved in economic warfare during the war, and although he often visited BSC New York, he was based in the British Embassy in Washington. One of his duties was to give the OSS reports from South America, as the United States had few resources in Latin America. His American contact was Francis Miller, who had been a friend of his aunt, Zoe Fairfield. He left Washington in 1945 and bought a farm in Pennsylvania. Toward the end of the war, he suggested former members of BSC get involved in a trading company. This eventually became British American Canadian Company and then World Commerce Corporation. Ogilvy thought the trading company would be a good idea as "we all needed jobs in civilian life." Stephenson liked the idea and circulated copies of Ogilvy's paper to some of the wealthy people he worked with during the war, and some of them put up capital. "I am absolutely sure that nobody involved envisaged that the purpose of BAC was espionage," Ogilvy wrote. "I don't know who started this canard. Tripe." After a few months Ogilvy left the company, as he became bored, and with some assistance from his brother Francis he got started in the advertising business.

Ogilvy thought Stephenson became an alcoholic after the war, and as a result, some postwar publications were a "grotesque exaggeration of his achievements. It was probably booze that addled his brain."[16]

"I was devoted to WSS. A good leader. Laconic sense of humour. Ruthless. Loyal to his staff. Discreet [in those days]. More popular in Washington and Ottowa [sic] than in London."

GRACE GARNER 18

The Head Secretary Remembers

Anyone wanting to see Bill Stephenson in New York during the war had to go through his head secretary, Grace Garner. She too was from the Canadian prairies, born in Qu'Appelle, Saskatchewan and educated in Regina. Garner moved east, and for a time did some writing and editorial work for *Saturday Night* magazine in Toronto. In February 1941, after replying to a newspaper ad, she moved south and started working for the Allied war effort.

She first worked for the British Purchasing Commission at 25 Broadway in New York. The commission was brought under the Stephenson umbrella, Garner says, and a small group of people evolved into British Security Coordination. The inner core of the organization at the time was Beryl Phelps, a cashier and principal secretary, a passport control officer, and a coding clerk. In the front office was a receptionist, Willie Wilson, and an assistant, a night guard. When Garner arrived, Stephenson's inner secretariat consisted of only three or four, and there were a handful of others. Then it began to grow. "Sir William had only come over in May 1940," she said. "He had the vision, and he saw, and probably [had] a commission, as to what he was to build this organization up to." He soon moved the office to Rockefeller Center.

The Purchasing Commission had a nucleus of British people under contract to the Ministry of Economic Warfare and the Foreign Office who were in charge of contracts and contacting suppliers. There were also Canadians working there. British Columbia businessman A. J. Taylor worked for the Commission. Taylor, a business partner of Bill Stephenson, hired his daughter Kathleen to work as a secretary. Others followed from the West Coast of Canada. Vivian Jones and Elizabeth Wood, who worked for Taylor's solicitor in British Columbia, also joined the organization. "Those were the first three girls recruited. Then they began getting girls. Richard Coit's daughter, who was in the coding department came in. Ellis' wife was also in the coding department. Then they began bringing the girls down, Tommy Drew-Brook put an advertisement in, and [by] word of mouth."

British Security Coordination emerged from the supply commission and a few other British Intelligence people. Bill Ross Smith was among the first in 1940, as were Dick Ellis, Richard Coit and Walter Bell. "As far as Walter was concerned, our cover was British Passport Control," Garner said. "It was still on the front doors, British Passport Control."

Dick Ellis moved to Washington and became the senior man there. Barty Bouverie acted as the London and South American contact in the American capital. Peter Dwyer was the chief FBI liaison. Ivor Bryce was in Washington working with OSS people, but the DC group didn't get much bigger. "It was just a post office, really." The Americans were preoccupied by the Far East. "They were particularly concerned with China and Chiang Kai-shek. You see that was one of their big concerns because the war in the Pacific was very big with the States. They were involved in that. It was their area of war, really, before they started the massing of troops for the onslaught of Europe."

Doris Griffiths Hogg, a code officer, came down about the same time as Garner through Drew-Brook. Hogg, later transferred to Mexico, said her husband found a map — while he was stationed there — about proposed Japanese plans to invade the United States through Mexico. "Yes, that was quite true, because you see they moved all the Japanese on the West Coast of the States and Canada. That was very possible," she said. She also knew Hogg's husband. "He was a second generation. His family had been in the consular service there before, and he was stationed down there in Mexico."

Although BSC's Washington office remained small, the New York organization began recruiting businessmen, police, journalists, lawyers and hundreds of secretaries and coding people. BSC people worked with similar sections of Britain's Foreign Office, Americans, Canadians and others. "The intelligence was gathered on all sorts of fronts," she said. "In formulating foreign policy you need to know about economics, as well as the effects on industry, and sources of supply, and so on and so forth. Well, that's mirrored in the organization." Nearly all BSC people were from Canada. "The easiest and quickest British subjects were from Canada. That's why we were brought in." Stephenson's friend Tommy Drew-Brook did most of the recruiting; he and his wife remained active in other areas. Often their house in Toronto was used as a stopping-off point for people going to the secret Camp X in Oshawa, or over to Europe. Much later Herb Rowland did some recruiting.

Most of the BSC employees were women, and when they first came to New York many would go to the Barbizon, a women's residence. As the organization got bigger, Garner isn't sure how they were settled. "Probably Tommy Drew-Brook arranged for them — they shared flats." Recruits also came from the Canadian government. One report says Charles Vining, the president of the Newsprint Association of Canada, helped facilitate BSC connections to the Canadian government through his friendship with Defence Minister J. L. Ralston.[1] BSC placed more advertisements in newspapers as well.

"They began to get girls recruited from the civil service in Ottawa, because you see, with one advertisement, I don't know how many people answered the ad. It was really through [Lester] Pearson and [Tommy] Stone and people in the civil service in Ottawa. He [Stephenson] wanted state secretaries and people who were skilled typists and office staff."

Stephenson also worked through External Affairs, as they were his closest Canadian contacts in the United States. Eventually all sorts of Canadians were united into the Stephenson organization. "They were bringing down Canadian girls, of course. And not only that, Canadian businessmen, all sorts. [Arthur] Purvis and [A. J.] Taylor [in British Purchasing Commission]. And then of course Tommy Stone used to go down to Washington and be Canadian Embassy liaison with the British Embassy. Later on, of course, there were the [military] service personnel, and Canadian Security, and the RCMP."

If someone asked Garner what she did, she told them she worked for the British Purchasing Commission. But she was seldom out in places where people could be inquisitive. "We didn't have much time for a social life. You didn't meet many people. People who came down from Canada to New York, and friends coming shopping or that sort of thing, they weren't very interested in what you did. They just said, 'Oh, aren't you lucky, you have a job in New York.'"

When Garner arrived in New York, circumstances looked particularly grim for Britain. The United States was still not fully in the conflict, and Nazi U-boats were cutting the supply line to Europe. "You see they were used to bring over food, and there was a very severe crisis in the beginning. Late '41, '42 when we were losing so many ships it was dreadful. We had torpedoes right into the Bay of Tampa around by Florida, and the trade between New York and the South American ports, Rio and Montevideo."

"That's where Bill Ross Smith came in, because those crews, you see were South American Germans. There were an awful lot of Germans in South America, particularly in Rio and Argentina. Montevideo was quite British, but the others had a lot of Germans and German crews."

BSC faced an uphill battle in a pre-Pearl Harbor America. The United States had no corresponding intelligence network to deal with. Not only was the United States neutral, there were strong anti-British sentiments. With Stephenson's assistance, an American organization began to evolve.

"David Bruce was one of Donovan's first recruits," she remembered. "They were in the same law firm. One chose one's nearest, most trusted friends. Because at that time, you had to be very, very careful of the Americans because there was so much anti-British feeling. The America First [movement], and there was also the large [number of] Central European first-generation immigrants there. Germans, Swedes, Yugoslavs, Poles, the lot. There was a terrible anti-British feeling, the Hearst newspapers, and so on. But the irony of it is, after he [Stephenson] moved out of the St. Regis, he moved into the penthouse that Hearst had for Marion Davies on West 53rd Street.

"William Randolph Hearst and the *San Francisco Examiner* and others were terribly anti-British. Lindbergh was very anti-British. He had hero status.

"[Adolf] Berle was one of those conviction politicians. But they were only some of the people. There were these bunds, the German bunds. Middle America was largely populated by the central Europeans who went into the coal mining in central Pennsylvania and Ohio and places like that.

"Spanish [immigrants] were in pockets in California and Texas and later when they came up from Cuba, but they were not the significant racial strains that you think of in the American melting pot. So that was one of the things that you had to constantly defeat or try to alter. You couldn't bring the Americans into the war, with the strength of the anti-British feeling."

Inside the Office

Garner didn't remember any precautions taken at the office for security reasons. "Well, I wasn't given a course or anything like that. But you were pretty wary, if you had any sense." One of the rules was not to have an American boyfriend. One woman married a U.S. Marine and had to resign. In the office, however, the security seemed relaxed. "They all came through a perfectly open security thing and we had an awful lot of people in the outside office.

"But to be quite honest, we didn't think about it — it wasn't in the days of hijacking and gangsterism. No. One knew that probably you would be followed, if people knew. I dare say we were all marked people, because you went up and down. I remember the Bulova watch company had the floor above us, the 37th floor, because we had 36 and 38 and it used to amuse us because these girls were always beautifully dressed and looked like the girls behind perfume counters. They were all beautifully groomed and everything, had Bulova watches. To get on the elevators in the morning, they always won — shoved and pushed in and we would always be the last people and this would make us rather annoyed.

"It's amazing the cover for British Security Coordination was maintained for so long. The Americans were naive too. I mean they wouldn't know. I mean they must have seen this organization growing, but they didn't know what we did. They were not curious particularly. I think they'd be much more curious in Europe than they would be in the States and Canada. As I told you we had the Bulova watch company above us and we had all these girls who all worked at the Bulova watch and they all used to get into the elevators before we did. They were good tough Brooklyn cookies who could elbow their way in, you know. But I don't think it ever occurred to them that — why are all these ... [Canadians] ... what are they doing? You know, it wouldn't rouse so much suspicion. We were much the same."

Stephenson was very observant of the proceedings outside the building, and in the corridors. "Patek Philippe, the famous Swiss watch people had an office near us, and I think Sir William knew something about them. I think he might have even recognized people he'd seen in Switzerland and so on." One morning Stephenson arrived at the office and told Garner, "Get Hall". He thought he recognized a Swedish agent lingering at the foot of the elevators. "Now Hall was a New York private eye," Garner said. "He was a real Dashiell Hammett character. He was a photographer and a personal investigator, and that. A big, burly chap ... He was a very nice man, and we used to get him to do, you know, sort of discreet jobs, and he knew a lot of characters." Garner couldn't reach Hall so she took the elevator down to check out the agent herself. She hung around the window of a lingerie shop downstairs and looked for suspicious people. "I saw this chap who had dark, rather darkish skin, swarthy, and he had on a black-and-white tweed overcoat. A tall chap. He was hanging around for a while. Finally he went out the doorway that led through to the Radio City Music Hall." She returned upstairs, told Stephenson she couldn't get Hall and described the possible agent to him. "He said, 'Yes that's him,' and sent a telegram right away. He had spotted him as an agent because he'd known him.

"Although Sweden was neutral, Swedish ball bearings and Swedish ore and Swedish things were very important in the war. I always understood Sweden was much more pro-German. They were pro-market, wherever they could sell. Swedish steel is the finest. Surgical instruments are made with Swedish steel. Yes, a very high standard."

The cable Stephenson sent simply reported the Swedish agent was in New York, she recalled. Stephenson spent time in Sweden before the war. "There was an incident in Sweden, I do believe is true. Ellis more or less confirmed that, when he and a man in Sweden escaped. It was some incident about ball bearings, some shipment of ball bearings that were very crucial that were lost. It's in the midst of my memory as something I had been told."

The nimble-fingered staff of the lingerie shop downstairs were put to work by at least one BSC employee. "We had a girl who rather took things easily, and she worked with another girl in Coit's office, and her job was to wrap up the papers for the diplomatic bag, which you put in a pile in brown paper and they were wrapped up in string. They used to be sealed with sealing wax, and they had the official British Embassy seal. Dorothy Markus, that was her name, Dorothy was a girl who was mad keen on underwear and things like that. She used to spend her noon hour going down[stairs]. She became very friendly with the girls in the [lingerie] shop down there. As she couldn't be bothered doing the parcel up, she used to take the contents of the diplomatic bag downstairs and they'd wrap it up for her and she'd bring it upstairs. I mean, this innocent child. I mean, the whole thing is a hoot. That's the kind of thing ... Now it's killingly funny, I think."

One of Garner's tasks was to line up Stephenson's appointments — and many prominent people came through, "From Mountbatten down or up. We had the famous meeting of Craig, Stratton and Moll. They were MI5 officers who came over to inspect the security of the United States. That was immediately after Pearl Harbor. We had very senior personnel. Bomber Harris came over. We had a lot of Air Force personnel, Chiefs of Staff. Senior people. On their way to Washington, they would come and talk to Sir William. They went to Washington to liaise with the military people and so on who were perfectly 'en clair.' Then we had all sorts of specialist people come over. Then they began to recruit. You see we also had SOE. When they began to get these people, which was before America entered the war, they were looking for U.K. nationals or European nationals to infiltrate into Europe, and one of the heads of the department who did that was a man named Halpern. A. J. Halpern. He was a Russian, an international lawyer. In those days people worked under alias. They had two names.

"We began to get people to staff that organization; at the same time we also had various Fleet Street journalists." Journalists Sydney Morrell and Doris Sheridan, who had been with the *Daily Express,* came over to work with British Information Services. "This was propaganda, or at least putting [forward] the British case. Sheridan liaised with the Arab sections in New York, keeping in touch with foreign nationals. The English playwright Eric Maschwitz was recruited to write propaganda and scripts. University professor Bill Deakin worked for the office, as well as the philosopher A. J. Ayer. There were also bankers — Bering of Bering's Bank and Sir Charles Hambro." Stephenson also saw many people in Washington who didn't come to New York.

Garner remembered meeting Lord Beaverbrook at the Waldorf Astoria at "the end of 1943, and the beginning of the V-1s and V-2s. He was at the Waldorf Astoria with [A. J.] Balfour and [Del] Maysfield, who later became head of British Airways. Sir William seconded me to go over to his suite in the Waldorf Astoria to do some secret — to do some typing and things for them." At the time, flying bombs, the V-1s, were attacking southern England. "They used to have daily cables about how the bombs would come, and where they had landed. Beaverbrook used to be wandering in the corridors, and every time he saw me he said, 'Good evening.' No matter what time of the day it was."

After Stephenson's death, one article in the *Times* said there is no proof Stephenson ever met Beaverbrook, "let alone Churchill."[2] Garner says this is ridiculous. "Don't forget that Beaverbrook was one of the many Canadians over here, who were all in it. Their various interests, the cement, Beaverbrook's cement is where he made his fortune in Prince Edward Island. Stephenson [was] in cement and Pressed Steel. The Canadian Pacific Railways, the big banks, the stock exchange. It was a time when Canada mattered. There was a time, before the satellites and planes and that sort of thing when the CPR, the CNR, the Canadian banks, particularly the Bank of Montreal, the stock exchange, the Winnipeg Grain Exchange, was one of the great things of the world. You know those were times when Canadians had significance. To say that he didn't know Beaverbrook is like saying you don't know your own aunt or uncle. Yes, I have seen Lord Beaverbrook."

As the organization grew it handled not only the incoming of the press, the Ministry of Information and government officials, but technical people as well. The atomic scientist J. D. Bernal, a professor at Cambridge, came through the office. According to Anthony Boyle's *Climate of Treason*, Bernal was a committed Marxist.

"He could have been a Marxist," Garner said. "There was a great deal of feeling among scientists that they should change these views before the war. That science is international. You know, [Alan] Nunn May and those always made their defence that until the hostilities broke out, that what was found to be the truth was to all the scientific world. I think most of them probably were." Bernal was a dead ringer for Harpo Marx. "You could have walked him straight onto the set. Wild. He had a funny hat on, and this saggy, greeny old coat, bulging with documents." She remembers once giving him some American money, as he had none, and he insisted on going to Washington as quickly as possible.

BSC kept files on individuals and a blacklist on people to watch. Montgomery Hyde's job was very important, Garner said. BSC had people in Bermuda, Trinidad and South America linked to censorship.

When people travelled or immigrated to the Western Hemisphere by air from Europe, they flew from Lisbon and stopped over in Trinidad or Bermuda to refuel. When the planes landed, censorship offices in Trinidad and Bermuda went through the passenger lists, which were cabled beforehand from the offices in Lisbon or known departure points. The lists were cross-referenced with a watch list of suspect characters. For example, the fashion designer Elsa Schiaparelli was suspected of smuggling essential oil, Garner said. "They knew pretty well who to watch, and what they were doing. So they would be taken and interrogated ... And they [BSC] would talk to prominent business people who were coming over and so on.

"Freckles Wren, Leonard Silverston, Mary Graham and Angela Drew were in Trinidad. Those people all worked with him [Stephenson], on assessing the sensitive cable intercepts and interrogation or route, because Bermuda and Trinidad were the two transit stops for the planes."

The intelligence that was gleaned from the travellers was sent to the New York office where it was checked with registry files. They would act on the ranks of names, update the files and possibly alert people, and follow up on the new information. A section of women oversaw the files. Dall Hunty, a Briton, was the first. She brought over the original system from the central registry in England. She was succeeded by the secretary of a high-ranking air force official, who was replaced by a Canadian woman, Merle Cameron.

Stephenson was surrounded by a secretariat of Garner, Eleanor Fleming and Eleanor Little. As well, he had another group that handled much of his personal coding including Charmian Manchee, Marion de Chastelain, Elizabeth Hunter, Kathleen Taylor and Patsey Sullivan. Because of the difference in time zones, some staff worked shifts, and there could be activity around the clock. Garner didn't work shifts, although usually she came in at 7 a.m. and didn't leave till about eight in the evening. "We just worked until we more or less finished." There were also three very competent switchboard operators, Garner said, who always seemed able to make swift connections. BSC's phone numbers were unlisted, but British Passport Control was in the telephone book.

Bill Donovan was in frequent contact with Stephenson. "The Americans were supplying Chiang Kai-shek and they were taking it over the hump into China. And who knows what happened in there. So it took a lot of people to keep in touch with the Far East and that's where a branch of Donovan's organization was very active because of the Americans' interest in the Pacific. That's where we had increasingly a number of SOE people come in because they were connected with all sorts of people in the field."

Stephenson's connection with Donovan, like with Hoover, was also through Gene Tunney, she believed. "Sir William had known him anyway, but Donovan was also well known. I remember him coming, a very shy man, a very nice, very modest man, coming to see Sir William in those first early days." Tunney didn't come in but he did a lot of good work for BSC countering defeatism. "You see, after I first went there, we had the fall of Singapore, the sinking of the Prince of Wales. We had a series of the most terrible, terrible things. A series of disasters, and people felt that Britain was going to lose. And you had to try and counter that, build up confidence and get the arms. You know, as Churchill says, 'Give us the tools and we'll finish the job,' and Roosevelt's famous fireside chats. And there were these articles that were put in the press."

Garner remembers the activities of the BSC agent "Cynthia" soon after her arrival in New York. "You see Marion de Chastelain was brought in to be a liaison between John Pepper, masterminding under Sir William's direction, who was managing this "Cynthia" operation. What they wanted to get was the Italian airlines. They wanted to get them out of commission. And also we had the Free French. Don't forget we had that little problem. You see Hayes [the French ambassador] and those people were very anti-British. So Marion used to go down as a courier to Washington and deliver messages and instructions to "Cynthia," and that's how she was very useful because she could be very discreet, a very sophisticated girl." Garner's friend Elizabeth Wood also met with "Cynthia," she said.

Roald Dahl came over in about 1943, after he was injured in an air crash. For a short time he was Stephenson's personal assistant. "Then I think he got rather bored with that and moved back to Washington where he liaised in Washington for a short while. He wasn't in the New York office very much." Later he was in Oshawa to help write the [BSC] history, but he didn't write much. "I think he was too much of a butterfly." David Ogilvy was in the Ministry of Economic Warfare, attached to the embassy in Washington, and he came to see Stephenson. "He used to swing his legs on the edge of my desk and talk to me. He was a chef on the Majestic, his stories [were] of Paris restaurants and that sort of thing. He was a fascinating man. A great deal of charm." Economic warfare dealt with the constriction of supplies and contraband. "Seeing that people were keeping to the rules."

Giles Playfair did general propaganda, and he also contributed to the BSC history after the war. "He rewrote after Highet's draft was delivered to him. And Christopher [Wren] and a man called Friend were brought over during the war, because they were injured and out of the army. He first went to Trinidad as a passport control officer and censorship, and he did what Hyde did in Bermuda, and that was to interrogate these people as they crossed over. Then he came to New York, and he was in charge of that and Gladys Silverstone and Mary Graham. They used to assess the reports and sift out the names that were on the wanted list or people who were interesting. These people came from all over Europe and they would tell how conditions were and that sort thing, but also search for money and any contraband they were carrying. He returned to civilian life after.

"Peter [Dwyer] was with Friend and he was to liaise with the FBI and he would have been able to tell you not only about Bill Stephenson, he would be able to tell you about the FBI. He worked very closely particularly with the Washington FBI. He was in a bad train crash and very fussy; he always had to have a seat in the middle of the train."

Playwrights Ben Levy and Eric Maschwitz, and Bill Deakin all came at the same time. They were recruited through the Ministry of Information and worked with public relations and newspaper people. "They knew people. That's the sort of thing. We had people who could help counter things."

"Walter Winchell?"

"Oh, yes. Walter Winchell became very important. The contact for Winchell was an international lawyer [likely Ernest Cuneo] and "the mouthpiece for the CIO [the labour organization]." The lawyer was up on gossip and celebrity. "He knew everybody." Cuneo told her he once took a two-week holiday in 1935, and he missed a lot when he was away. "He could never catch up on the weeks he'd been away. He knew Walter Winchell, and the rendezvous for them was the Stork Club, this famous nightclub. Every celebrity went there. Walter Winchell used to have a table every night and at lunch time, and he would see all the celebrities and get all the gossip. He would be given stories, you see, and inside information of what was happening in Britain and so on and so forth. Very influential and a good friend.

"Drew Pearson was not a good friend. Drew Pearson was anti-British and much more critical. And Berle was definitely anti."

Garner thought stories of BSC agent Dennis Paine trying to denigrate Berle were probably true. "All sorts of things could be done to embarrass an agent. Maschwitz was writing a paper on all the things you could do." It has been referred to as Operation Vic. "Well, there was all sorts of things you could do, telephoning people in the middle of the night, sending anonymous letters to their wife. They even had a colouring, giving people something to drink and making them urinate blue. And they'd think something's terribly sick. Pranks! Yes, they were up to that sort of thing. Yeah, it was very funny. You couldn't take that seriously. These were the sort of harassing things."

She remembers Paine thought he was doing a good turn by trying to get the dirt on Berle. This ended up being an embarrassment and he was whisked, within the hour, over to Canada, because the FBI would have been after him. "I only knew he'd overstepped the markers. I could only tell you what I heard at the time, which was far as I knew, that was the case. It could have been a FBI plant. There were other things they got up to."

There was some tension between the FBI and BSC. "For no other reason than we were operating in another country, a foreign country. It was their province and the FBI was very proud. Hoover built up this huge organization. They were responsible for gangsters and security of every kind, and he was a megalomaniac anyway. He was an empire builder."

Garner didn't meet Hoover, although he was in New York all the time, she says. Stephenson usually met with the FBI's New York man, Percy [Sam] Foxworth and Garner often spoke to him on the phone. On one occasion Foxworth couldn't make a meeting with Stephenson at a hotel. The spy chief couldn't be publicly paged and Stephenson waited about a half hour before returning to the office on the subway.

Foxworth died in a Caribbean plane crash early in 1943. Garner believes he was shuttling secret information to American general Mark Clark in North Africa. The plane crash was an accident, Garner says, "but it had very far-reaching effects because it delayed the operation."

Stephenson was briefed on such overseas operations. "I think when he got that information, it didn't come through on a cable, it was when he was briefed in England, or maybe at the Embassy from the Joint Staffs. I don't know because he used to go down to these meetings, you see. But that would not be for us to pass on."

Garner met Ian Fleming, who was with the Director of Naval Intelligence (DNI), Admiral Godfrey. She also met Mountbatten a few times, who was with Robert Harling. (Harling later wrote a few books and became the editor of *House and Garden*.) "Mountbatten would not come to the office frequently. Fleming came in from time to time, and of course they were both so good-looking that just like dominoes, the girls would go down — whoosh, like that."

Mountbatten was organizing his post to South East Asia and India, she said. "They went out to Singapore and so on, after the fall, after the Americans came into the war. That's when Fleming was there, but he certainly did come into the office and I remember seeing the Minox camera [miniature spy camera] and things like that. Very affable, very amiable.

"Bill Ross Smith was very active on the Ship's Observers — especially before Pearl Harbor — because of the large number of ships, the Grace Line, and fruit boats that plied the West Coast of the United States down to South America. "They were manned by every nape — all sorts of characters, a lot of Germans, and they used to go into these German ports and so on." Garner remembers on one occasion Ross Smith attempted to get a sailor onto a ship while down the hall Richard Coit was trying to get the same man off the same ship. They were international characters." For a time, one strange thing they watched for was secret information being transmitted under butterfly wings. "They used to have magnificent brilliant blue butterflies that were native to Brazil, I think. There was quite a trade in making paper weights or framed pictures out of these beautiful butterflies ... Well somebody had the idea that the German agents were putting messages under the butterfly wings of these pictures."

Colonel Louis Frank, a Belgian banker, was brought over. "Sir William said tell so-and-so he's the greatest arbitrage expert in the world, and I never heard the word 'arbitrage,' and I thought it was 'arbitration.' So I told somebody, I think it was actually Foxworth, somebody high in the FBI, he was the greatest arbitration expert in the world. That was a boo-boo. But he was, he was famous for that. He was a great banker. He came over, he headed the SOE operation in New York. Really he was in charge of international finance. They were the people who could block bank accounts, transfer funds and all that sort of thing.

The astrologer Louis De Wohl was brought over from Britain. He had a big following in the daily papers, and propaganda people thought they could bring him over to the United States as an authority, and tell him what to predict. He didn't come to the office, but Garner was aware of his set-up in Washington. "He was very expensive. He demanded to have suites of rooms and so on. There was a very beautiful lady sent over to be his sort of hostess ... he didn't last very long. That was one of those Eton pranksters' 'think-ups.'"

"Vincent Astor was attached with OSS, just as they had David Bruce, the Rockefellers, the wealthy people that they brought in. Because they knew them and they had contacts all over the world and so on. He was not an anti- person, he was pro."

Lord Leathers was around. "He was one of Beaverbrook's people. He was in the Ministry of Supply also. He was on the Embassy side."

James Roosevelt, the president's son, did a few things in the way of propaganda for Britain, and he appeared at meetings. "He was not anything sinister or secret jobs." He could have also acted as a courier, but she doesn't recall him in the office. "I know Sir William saw him. He was in the very early days."

Nelson Rockefeller may have given BSC a break on the rent at Rockefeller Center, Garner said, but she was unaware of a formal agreement. "It could possibly be that was one of the things that was a concession to Britain. And Sir William might have very well negotiated that, because when they first came over, they were operating from this little office down on Wall Street. The Passport Control used to be on Wall Street near the docks. It was there because of passports, near the Statue of Liberty, and the shipping offices. The British Purchasing Commission was down on Wall Street and that's where Bill Ross Smith's Ships' Observers scheme — Sir Connop Guthrie used to head that. That was an MI5 proper thing, and Sir William knew that was perfectly inadequate for what he wanted, so he took this space in Rockefeller Center. The whole of the 36th floor. So it was very possible that Sir William, through his various contacts, decided this would be the move and approached them."

Herb Rowland came down from Canada as an administrator and personnel man. "He was not in any way a diplomat or engaged in agents or anything like that."

She remembered Zoltan Korda, a set designer who worked designing camouflage, but she was unaware of Stephenson's precise involvement with movie studios. "I only know that I got plane seats for [Alexander] Korda. Korda was in the office. I got plane seats and cigars for Korda. I remember one day Sir William sent me over to Dunhill to get some cigars for him. A certain kind of cigars. I came back in a panic and said, 'Sir William, they're six dollars each!' He roared with laughter and he said, 'Oh yes.' So he got a case," she laughed.

Allen Dulles moved into Rockefeller Center after Pearl Harbor. "He was one of Donovan's first appointees. He was another lawyer. Later he was to head the post-war Central Intelligence." John Foster Dulles, his brother, was on Roosevelt's staff. "He was not a great friend of England."

Tom Hill came down about 1942. He was brought in when BSC needed a lot of desk people. "They worked on various programs, either working on information with the Middle East or whatever they were doing, but he was brought in and worked with a man called Patterson."

Cedric Belfrage was brought in as one of the propaganda people. "He was a known Communist." John Paul Evans was brought in and worked for Halpern's staff. "A very nice chap. There's a chap called Dan Hedical. I always think of the two together. The recruitment of aliens. Rex Benson was the attaché in Washington. He was very nice. He was the stockbroker over here. He was a very urbane man.

"H [Henry] A Benson was SOE's second-in-command in New York. He was a nasty piece of work. He was a nasty sort of a miserable little nit-picking man.

"Gilbert Highet was again in propaganda with Belfrage, in the same offices, before Pearl Harbor. He was an historian at Columbia. A very nice man. And he wrote one of the first drafts of the history of British Security Coordination. Tom Hill compiled and administered the compilation of it. I don't think he wrote a lot of it."

When Garner started there were a few English secretaries at the office, and she didn't think they earned their pay. "I complained to Mr. Taylor one day, Kathleen Taylor's father, about the money. We were paid quite generously, but the English girls, my co-secretary and the other girl, were getting quite a lot more. And I mean, they worked sort of on the Foreign Office system. You know what I mean. They had 'Pending Baskets.' I'd never heard of a 'Pending Basket' in my life, and they'd never answer the telephone. They'd let it ring two or three times and they'd hang up. Well, anyway, so I said to Mr. Taylor, 'Look, I know it's their war but ...' Well, he fell about, he ran in to Sir William like a scalded cat and told him and the two of them were killing themselves laughing. But then, sobering down, Sir William, I think he thought, 'well, that's the attitude of these people, you see.' ... They had the feeling that the British let it happen."

"How do you mean?"

"I mean I could never understand why the British seemed to be so unprepared. If you'd read anything, you knew from the build-up of Hitler and that sort of thing, that it was going to be inevitable, and you see with the fall of Dunkirk and that sort of thing, it looked as though it were an accident waiting to happen." She was told there was British intelligence about the rise and military build-up of the Nazis, but it was either not believed or vetoed by people such as Sir Neville Henderson, Britain's Ambassador to Berlin. "Ellis was over there, and I said to Ellis, 'why did they not [know about Hitler]?' And he said, 'Oh, we sent them the reports.'

"And the other thing was the attitude of the British officers ... I don't think they put their back into it."

"In North America? Or all over?"

"No, no, no. I'm only speaking of my own organization. Some of them worked hard but a lot of it was ... well, the English work in a different way. When I came over here [to Britain], you can never go into an English office to interview somebody and start right in. You have to ask sort of how their family are, or some conversation, and then you get down to it. And they would, for instance, just a small thing, but on Sundays they would come in casual clothes. I felt some of the English secretaries didn't work the same, with the same sort of drive, should I say. They were very knowledgeable and they carried the dignity of the English office and so on. They were ladies, and people, and so on. And they weren't having any upstart girls who were a whiz on the typewriter but didn't know that Jack Barkley was the world's largest importer of Rolls Royce cars. You know. We didn't know that. After all, people weren't so well travelled.

"People only used to get two weeks' holiday. How do you come over to Europe? And you used to have to come over by boat. You see, people forget that. It wasn't within the means of people. It was a big thing.

Students, Rhodes scholars, academics, business people, and so on. But they didn't travel to that extent."

"So there was a real cultural shock."

"Not so much shock, after all, one was well-read. I remember being brought up on *Girl's Own Annual, Boy's Own Annual* and English novels and all that sort of thing, but it's not the ambience, as I said to you, people living in a very sophisticated, multi-cultural."

"So they viewed North Americans differently?"

"Yes. Because we had the North American work ethic. For instance, they used to have afternoon tea in the office when Sir William first came there, and there was a young office boy who was outside, a sort of 'dogsbody.' That's an English expression. He was the dogsbody for the Passport Control people and he used to bring around a tray of tea, and one day he dropped the tray outside Sir William's office. Crash, bang. Well that was the end of the tea. And there was no more tea. Nobody was going to have a cup of tea in the afternoon," she laughed.

Garner talked with Noel Coward on the phone a few times when he stayed at the Waldorf Astoria. On one occasion she helped him get a visa for the United States. Coward had been in Cairo and had visited American wounded at a hospital there, and officialdom were unsure of comments he was making, viewing them as possibly coded or defeatist. In Africa, Coward "talked about the American boys who were sick for home, amid the alien corn," she remembered. "The Americans didn't know the reference to that." When they received the telegram at BSC, Garner knew what Coward was talking about. "I said to Sir William, 'that's the "Ode to a Nightingale."' She and Alex Halpern decided on the poet. "I said, of course, it was Keats, and they asked me to recite it ... that's a wonderful thing, 'When the sad, sick for home, she stood in tears and stayed in the alien corn.'"[3]

"You know the poem — it's absolutely lovely. Well anyway, they took it out of context." Eventually Coward was allowed to come to the United States, and he did a few things for Stephenson. "He was a propagandist and he was used, like a lot of people, just to go around to cocktail parties and go around and spread the word. That was all. He was a glamorous figure." At the parties Coward would build up the Allied cause and try to counter defeatism. "They just go on talking to people and say 'The Germans win? Go on. Not bloody likely.' You know, that sort of thing."

Stephenson was continually seeing people. "He was a par excellent listener," she said. "You know the old saying, 'A wise little owl sat on an oak. The more he heard, the less he spoke. The less he spoke, the more he heard. Why can't we all be like that bird?' Well, that was Sir William."

External Planning

Stephenson made numerous trips across the Atlantic during the war. He was in Britain before the ill-fated Dieppe raid. One report was that the Allies tried to capture Axis radar information. "It could have been," Garner said. "It could have been to test the radar, to test the Germans, how sensitive, how good they were. You see, people forget things like Mulberry, the invention of the Mulberry docks, the invention of all that sort of thing."

Stephenson attended the Quebec Conference. "I think he was at the Atlantic Conference, but I couldn't say whether he was at Yalta or Potsdam, because I can't be sure. But I do know that he went over at, or around, the time of the conferences, to London." She knows he was in Quebec because she had to put together a number of files for shipment to Canada for it. "We took the documents to the Pennsylvania Station, [the ones] which were left on the top of the filing cabinet. They were supposed to have gone with the others, we suddenly discovered them and tore down in a taxi and Sydney Morrell came to hold the gates and they held the train until we pushed them through." Garner didn't go to the conference herself, but she went to Quebec afterwards.

Garner learned many code words during the war, but was unaware of the operations.

"You would hear the code word, but it didn't mean anything to you. I remember one was Cossac. I remember a telegram came through with the word Cossac Morgan. 'Get in touch with Cossac Morgan.'" (In the middle of 1943 the Allies set up a headquarters for the planned invasion of Europe. The head of it was General Frederick Morgan and he was known as COSSAC Morgan from the initials Chief of Staff Supreme Allied Command. The first operation of the group was planning a feigned attack on the continent.)[4] "And I said to Sir William, 'That's a funny name, a funny pen name for Morgan.' I thought it would be a pirate, or a Dead-eye Dick sort of thing, because you think of Pirate Morgan. And there was deathly silence. I knew that I stepped on a mine. But that was the operation to deceive the Germans on the exact landing of the D-Day landing."

"From Calais?"

"Cossac was the name of the operation. And Torch [invasion of North Africa] was a very secret word."[5]

Stephenson travelled across the Atlantic at least twice a year. "Well, I came in March '41. And he went over that November or December. He went over in the winter, I remember. And he went early in the spring or beginning of '42. He went at least eight times when I was there, probably more. Not all that often."

Stephenson is quoted as saying he went to Europe over forty times during the war. "Well, I don't think he went that often. He came over in '40. He probably made three or four trips before I came along … Travel to Europe was not easy. He had to go to Quebec and across by bomber." Stephenson didn't travel on regular flights, because of scheduling and security. Garner made some flight arrangements and recalled one he made with Desmond Morton and Alexander Cadogan. "They were not easy, comfortable flights. They had to have oxygen, and it was cold." Numerous couriers leaving BSC went on the regular flights with diplomatic bags.

Stephenson was in New York when the bombing of Hiroshima and Nagasaki took place.

"Would he have known that those were coming?"

"I think probably he would. He would have known about the planning. Once the Germans had been defeated in Europe, they had to concentrate on the other. And there was the question of whether they slugged it out to the last man or … I think the strategy, he would have been party to that."

"How about the Destroyers for Bases deal? Do you think Bill had much to do with that?"

"I think he had a role in that. He was in that through, I think, [A. J.] Taylor and probably [Arthur] Purvis — through the Purchasing Commission, and the deals on that. And the Foreign Office would be making deals, after the trading of the Atlantic bases, would be like the Falklands. You give away a base for 99 years. No, he certainly had an influence on what the needs were."

December 7, 1941

Stephenson's office moved twice. One move was into the Japanese consulate after Pearl Harbor. "That was a fascinating story, the day that happened, Sunday. And when we went home that night I was literally shin deep in flash bulbs from the photographers.

"They'd been standing outside and waiting for the Japanese ambassador to come down. And we went down about nine o'clock at night, because we were very busy. We had to wade through these broken flash bulbs. They got out in 24 hours, 48 hours at the most, and Sir William had arranged to have their offices, which were on the 38th floor, two floors up. In the meantime, this famous man, Professor Bayly, came over ... he was to be in charge of our communications, the coding machine and the transmission of the actual messages. Because at this time the traffic was very large. At first it was through Western Union, then it was still Western Union, but it had to be handled in a much bigger way than just writing telegrams and sending them. So Sir William had the vision to take offices on the 35th floor, with Bayly in charge. He had two or three people, a man called Maidment, a very very nice Englishman, and there were people who actually vetted the things coming in and out.

"When we went up to the 38th floor, we still retained the 35th because there were huge installations of machines. When we went up, there were stamp marks for the Japanese passport on the wall, and they even had a temple in the corner of their office, which had become our office. They had a Shinto temple built in the corner.

"It was about eleven o'clock in the morning, I remember, and Sydney Morrell, the *Daily Express* newspaperman to the last, he came in on a Sunday ... He had a long strip of the telex machine and he came in to see Bill. Bill wasn't there; he was off seeing Kathleen Taylor's father, and he didn't come back until about five in the afternoon, because they were incommunicado. He came and we had to get the two Japanese experts. It was a weekend. I had to bring them in and then, of course, that changed the whole thing. Then he was down in Washington, and of course, once the Americans came into the war it was a different ball game, because then you had quite different priorities."

One of Churchill's and BSC's wishes was to get the Americans involved in the fight against fascism, but Garner says there was no outward elation at the office. "We were very sober. It was a day of sadness, after all. It was a terrible disaster for the Americans, not only loss of life, but for their morale. And the fact they were caught napping and all this."

Certain documentaries and books imply more people knew an attack was going to take place than has been publicly acknowledged. "Oh, there are certainly things which one doesn't talk about, and there are actual recorded incidents of what happened."

"Roosevelt was pro-British."

"Yes. And Donovan was a good ally. Oh, yes, without a doubt. And the Americans became very much involved in the Far East. People in this part of the war (Britain) are blinkered. Unless people here had relations in the Far East or had fought in the Burma war over there, they didn't have much [interest] in the Pacific. It was the Americans' theatre of war. We used to read the *Herald Tribune* and the *Times* and hear about the suicide dive-bombers, the sacrifice Japanese bombers, the Kamikazes. And you had all of those things. Guam and all the way down the Pacific. Those were terrifying stories. I don't think the British over here felt the Americans were participating in that. But it was a terribly wasteful, dreadful war. And then Singapore fell, and the whole thing, and we had [General Douglas] MacArthur. I think MacArthur did come through [the BSC office]. Wilkinson was his liaison. He came through."

The Quiet Canadian and the BSC history both quote a telegram sent from BSC to England on November 27, 1941. The message read, "Japanese negotiations off. Services expect action within two weeks."

"We sent that telegram, yes," Garner said. "It was ahead of the Foreign Office intelligence.

"The significance, I remember, about the information related about the Japanese and the strength of their massing, their plans about a massive attack on Pearl Harbor was passed on to the Americans and presumably passed on to their general staff and they didn't pay any attention. This was the problem. This was the thing. And the Japanese attacked, as you know, on a Saturday night, which was because they knew that was the most vulnerable time."

"Sunday morning."

"Well, Saturday night, after they'd been having parties and so forth. Early Sunday morning. But the warning was passed on a good ten days before Pearl Harbor."

According to published accounts the Allies also received a survey regarding Pearl Harbor, information from double-agent Dusko Popov.[6] "Yes, it came from various sources, and observation, and actually watching what was happening in the Japanese Embassy in Washington. To-ing and fro-ing, and what was going on. And the intercepts. The code intercepts, this was what was happening. They knew from the code intercepts what the instructions to the Japanese fleet were, what was happening. You see, Japan and Germany were in the Axis, and the fact is, if you attack one, you attack all. I mean it was a progression. I wouldn't have thought anything was a cause for surprise there, really. You see, they didn't have to declare war on the United States. The Germans were perfectly well aware that America was arming to join."

Although BSC's principal sphere was obviously North America, Garner said they were also aware of activities in the Pacific. "They knew what was going on. Yes, in that you had your international feedback. When Mountbatten went to be South East Asian command he took one of our principal girls — in fact, two of our girls."

Bill Stephenson

Garner said Stephenson moved silently and seldom moved his arms. "He had the very dark, piercing eyes and the uncanny stillness of the man. When he walked he was very quiet and still. The man who most looked like him, and was most like him in physique, was Sir Michael Edwards, the man brought in from the motor industry. He was a very small in stature, neat man and very neatly put together, doesn't move his hands or do anything like that. A very still person."

Stephenson went by "like a panther. A black panther." And sometimes he seemed to arrive in places very quickly. "Incredible. You see he moved very fast. He really would be out of that office like a bullet. He moved fast, but it was silent and like — the only thing is like a panther. All of a sudden, he'd be in Washington. He'd get there. He used to catch planes. I don't know how he did it, but he managed. But it was incredible how fast he moved. Elizabeth Wood was to go and meet him at the airport and give him a document, and she went out to meet the appointed plane and she came back to the office, and he was in the office, sitting there laughing at her. She said, 'You weren't on that plane.' He said, 'Oh yes I was.' She said, 'Well, I looked, and I didn't see you.' He said, 'Well, you saw that lady carrying a Bergdorf Goodman bag,' or something. 'I was behind her.' You see he thought it was a great joke ... he probably saw Elizabeth there perfectly well, but he thought he'd, not teach her a lesson, but just play a trick on her. He had that quality of blending into a crowd. You wouldn't see him. You wouldn't notice him. He was not of conspicuous height or build or had any distinguishing feature. No buck teeth or anything like that. He certainly had the most wonderful eyes. Interesting eyes.

"He was so swift and so silent. He was so quick, this was the thing. And he'd put down the telephone and while the receiver was — you know, hit, he would be out of the office. And he'd be in Washington. I still don't know how he did it ... As I say, he was like Batman.

"In the most incredible way, he would catch a plane. We used to have Eastern Airlines or American Airlines or we would have to go by Pennsylvania railway. He had to get from 36th, in traffic, down to Grand Central or Pennsylvania Station for that. And he'd be in Washington. They'd have a car to meet him probably, or he'd get a taxi. But he would be there in the most incredible speed ...

"He certainly took in things in an instant, and he got to the centre of a thing. But that's what makes executives what they are. They decide. They see enough of the crux of the thing. Like Churchill. He wouldn't put up with long documents. He was supposed to have a sheet of paper, three or four by five, and he put all on it. He wouldn't stand for gobbledygook. Sir William's style, his English, was flawless, his style was terse, tense and to the point."

Garner was familiar with Stephenson's writing style, and as a result, she didn't think Stephenson wrote the foreword of *A Man Called Intrepid*. "He doesn't write like that. Incidentally, he [Stevenson] mentions he was with British Security Coordination. That was not so. None of us ever heard of him. There was no connection."

Her former boss didn't dictate letters or cables, Garner said. He would write things down to be either coded or typed. "Only later I wrote a few personal letters. People like Noel Coward and Ted Leathers and people like that. But he did not dictate cables. He wrote them out by hand.

"But it was the stealth of the man," she repeated. "I mean, I'd be typing and the first thing you'd know he'd be at your side. And it was his peculiar stillness, as I said. He didn't flail his arms around or move.

"No one has ever brought up his background. I never questioned he had the DFC. He never wore his medals. He never wore a uniform. He was not a boastful man. And he was not a generous man. He might have been a millionaire, but he didn't throw it around. I remember one time he brought me a beautiful box of chocolates, and I shared it with the girls outside. And he was mad, because he had bought it for me," she laughed. "He had bought it for me, and he was a bit annoyed. I was glad to share them. But I thought that was strange. I've never had a penny from him, nothing. There was no present. [Richard] Gambier-Parry took me lunch at the 21 Club and gave me a watch, a gold watch. And I was a bit embarrassed about it. It cost about $60 or so. But he was the one who said, 'come over [to England], you're worth your weight in gold, I'll have you at Bletchley.' You know, that nonsense, you don't pay any attention.

"He was not a man who took us all out for lunch, or never had a party for — he was not a social man at all — but he did have cocktail parties. After the war and when he was in New York he used to have people, when he saw people arriving on the ships. We used to get the ships sailing lists cabled ahead of time and he would pick off people he wanted to have invitations sent to. And he used to have cocktail parties. But he never entertained us or had us out. At Christmas time we had presents. I remember Lady Stephenson gave me a lovely dressing gown and slippers from Lorne and Taylor, and a compact. And one time he said he was going to give us all hankies and we said, 'No, Sir William, we always use Kleenex. If you pay six dollars each for handkerchiefs we'll all have a fit.' You know, $75 blown on handkerchiefs. There was nothing at all."

Garner didn't feel any curiosity about Stephenson's background. "For one thing, I was too busy. He had no family, no children — it was only his wife, and she was very much a homebody. She didn't take part. I don't think she even did things like working with some of the women who worked for the English-speaking Union. I don't think Mary ever took part. Now it might have been security reasons, you know. People asking what her husband was doing, and so on and so forth. But she was a very quiet like, little mouse thing, like that.

"She was never at the office. I'd spoken to her on the telephone. He brought over his housekeeper Nancy and she was a character. An Irish woman who was widowed. They were bombed during the war and he wrangled getting Nancy over in about '42 to run his house. When he left the St. Regis, as the organization grew and was bigger, he had to spend more time at the office, he took this apartment on 53rd street. It had been Hearst's. A love nest for Marion Davies. He brought Nancy over as his housekeeper and then he began to have people over for sandwich lunches, and he used to give cocktail parties, that sort of thing. That's when the famous martinis came into it.

"I remember they used to have a little Scotch Terrier like Roosevelt's Fala, and I remember Nancy went away for a weekend. I went over and fed the dog and that sort of thing. He once had me over for lunch and I couldn't swallow, because I just felt so ... Well, he just looked at you. And you thought he watched the piece of salmon sandwich going down," she laughed. "The only other time we met Mary [was] when we were working late, we went to the Three Crowns restaurant, which they liked.

"I don't think I've ever heard him speak of an art collection, or anything like that at all. He didn't take any interest in music or art. Never. I never heard of him going to a concert, a play. Where he got his electronic ability and that sort of thing, I don't know. I certainly know he had a very quick intelligence. He certainly saw through to the heart of a problem. I don't know if he was a very good judge of people. Not awfully good at it, I thought."

"No?"

"No."

"He got a lot out of them though."

"Oh, yes. He could do that from people. He had a feeling, that he expected a lot. And he did get a lot from people. People certainly did work very hard for him.

"... Funny enough he didn't like tall people. He said their brains were too far from their feet, you know. He had a thing about tall people. That's funny, but you know many men, brilliant businessmen, Napoleon, are small men, or short in stature. They're neat and well put together, and well, not always, I mean you take people like J. K. Galbraith, there's a man with a brain there, but you know what I mean.

"... He went through things quickly. He read quickly. And you had to get through things, and put them together, with his language sectors. He had this English girl, but she was used to the basket, the pending basket, and he had to have people who worked quickly. And funny enough, the girls who gravitated to the top were Western Canadians. Isn't that extraordinary? Patsey Sullivan came from Medicine Hat originally [sic]. I was a Western girl."

People were frightened coming in to see Stephenson, Garner said.

"Yes, because he was a very ... well, he was the head of the organization, and he was rather an intimidating man in that he could have a very cool eye. He would be obviously a man who wouldn't stand for any waffle. You would have to give him the facts straight, and no messing. He would question people on their facts, and question them on their evidence, on why they thought a certain thing. He would want to know.

"You didn't know if you had done the wrong thing. If somebody just said 'Come down to my office down on Broadway' or somewhere ... You'd be inquisitorial, should we say. It was subconscious, but there was a sort of reverence for a powerful organization. You felt you were caught up in something. You realized that it was a much bigger thing than you had...and, you see, Canadians aren't used to that kind of thing. We're not used to codes. Nor did you have agents, nor did you have ... A war was going on, and people dropped in and you heard [about] terrible things happening. I remember a wonderful man, a terribly nice man. I actually saw him packing rifles in the office on a Sunday. He was dropped into Yugoslavia and was killed. I mean, you knew the results. People disappeared."

Stephenson was knighted before the end of the war, following the D-Day landings. But knighthoods come in various levels, and he didn't receive the highest. "He didn't get any CMG. I think that hurt. But, as I say, he never boasted. He never used it. He never used DFC after his name. But I think that really hurt him, and I know that after the war he became an absolute recluse. He was the first person I know to have an answering machine, and that gave a great deal of offence to people.

"This was right in '45, because people weren't used to them and after he gave up the flat in the penthouse, he had a place on East 53rd Street and people used to ring up and get this answering machine. And it put them off. He didn't see anybody. Very quiet, and then he started this business association ... But he started out with [Ian] Fleming, [Ernie] Cuneo, and I think [John] Pepper was in it too. It was International News Media.

"It didn't last long, but he did start something up, and then he picked up his business interests. So I don't know what to account for ... he was a man of very few personal friends. He knew who they were, and that sort of thing."

Although she was close to him for a number of years, Garner knew little of Stephenson's financial affairs. "I don't know how he financed himself in Bermuda. They did live at the St. Regis in New York, but he certainly didn't throw it around. Living at the St. Regis couldn't have been cheap. It was a very expensive hotel, as it goes, and he lived there. But he had very modest tastes. He didn't eat a lot. He was not a man who was a great gourmet, or wine man, or anything. Not at all. In fact he used to have wine from California, Napa Cabernet, before California wine became a thing. We used to get our wine from Chile or from California. He said the California wine, the burgundy particularly, was very good, and this was long before it was hyped up.

"He had a wonderful sense of humour. He liked the wry side of life. I used to bring him things from the *Herald Tribune* and I remember there was a wonderful story one time about a man out in Brooklyn who phoned up police and said there was an elephant at the bottom of his driveway. And they said, 'Go back to bed, buddy, and put some water in it.' And minutes later they got another chap, and after about ten neighbours phoned — there *was* an elephant there. But the way it was written, was a marvellous story. He loved something like that ... He'd laugh at something like that and jokes, if you had a cute story, you know. Some of the things were happy. Some of the things — like the Marx Brothers in the Foreign Office, or the chap trying to get the chap on the boat and the other fellow trying to get him off. You know, those things are good for a laugh."

Garner does not know if Stephenson financed some of BSC's operation. "Hyde says he did. I wouldn't know about that. Payroll was run by a woman named Beryl Phelps, and she managed the whole thing." Phelps was the secretary of the Passport Control Officer in New York, and the money, Garner believes, usually came by courier from Washington or from one of the New York banks. They were paid cash.

"I just know about these companies he was involved in — that sort of thing. And he never, never, never used government cables for his own business. That was never done."

"Did you see any cables from Churchill or C?"

"Yes. But they're not sent like that. They're not signed, 'Yours, Churchill.'"

"How did you know where they were from then?"

"Well. I can't tell you. There were various ways in which a telegram is addressed in code."

"Stephenson's number was 48000."

"Yes, it was. It's a rather stupid thing, I would have thought. Because there were 48 states, but there you are. That was his number, yes."

The zeroes designation were similar to those used in James Bond — a licence to kill.

"I think all of that ... Bond was the name of a famous ornithologist. That book was Fleming's reading matter."

The Public Account

Garner commented on a 1952 *Maclean's* article on Stephenson, which was the first public notice of her former boss and the organization. "He was very observant?"

"Oh, yes."

"*During the war a Canadian girl secretary who pricked her forefinger and covered it with a tiny square plaster came into the office and without looking up from his desk Stephenson said, 'What have you tried to do, kill yourself?'*"

"That wasn't you?"

"I remember a girl came down, a secretary. She was in the office one day and Sir William was walking home on Broadway, and he saw her in, I think, Jack Dempsey's café, which is on Broadway, and the next day he had her sent back. He was as observant as that."

"*The pace at which he reads is also legendary. I've watched him reading a novel, says close friend Tommy Drew-Brook and it reminds you of a man rifling through an index for a reference.*" "He was a speed reader?"

"Well, he could read quite quickly, yes."

"*One girl on his war time staff handed him several sheets of closely typed manuscript, he flipped the pages, grunted and handed it back. 'Clearly,' she said, 'you haven't read it properly?' He gave her a succinct resume of its contents reciting several passages.'* Does that sound like hokum? Do you remember stuff like that?"

"No. Eleanor Fleming might have done that."

"*His New York headquarters [were] staffed with more than a thousand hand-picked Canadians. Men and women spoke of his door keeper as Peter, of his secretary as Gabrielle, and of him as God. Only a handful of them knew him by sight.*"

"Well, I think he was known as God. They used to tease you and say 'Is God at home?'"

"Who would Gabrielle have been? You?"

"Probably. Eleanor and me." She laughed. "The man who was Peter might have been John Pepper. 'Peter picked a peck of pickled peppers.' Because he was always around. He could always get an entry and nobody else. He used to have lunch with him."

"The article quotes Churchill's notation written beside Stephenson's name: 'This one is dear to my heart.'"

"Yes. That was the story that was told by him, yes."

Garner didn't believe there were any significant errors in Hyde's book, *The Quiet Canadian*. "There are things in *Camp X* that I would quarrel with." She disliked the book *A Man Called Intrepid* and thought it tarnished Stephenson's reputation. Stephenson's former secretary didn't even read it all. She commented on some details BSC may have initiated.

The magazine called *Sequel to the Apocalypse* was produced by BSC and profiled businesses in North America profiting from dealing with the Nazis. It was called the "*Uncensored story of how your dimes and quarters pay for Hitler's war.*"

"Oh, yes, that was a book that was brought out as a sort of pseudo-true thing, you know. It was just popular."

BSC came up with a bogus letter that helped get Italian airline LATI banned from Brazil.

"I remember it was going on. It was one of the things that Pepper was engaged in. That was an important thing, because it got the Italian airlines out of Brazil."

It also has been reported that BSC fabricated a map that graphically outlined the proposed Nazi occupation of South America. The map was even referred to in a speech to the nation by Franklin Roosevelt. "You thought Dorothy [Hyde] had done that?"

"Yes. That was a ruse. But that should not have been told. That was important in bringing to the United States, the threat. It was a very real threat of the Nazi plans for world domination. As I said, Latin America was stiff with Germans. There were a lot of them. Brazil particularly, and Argentina. They were not pro-British, despite the fact that in Argentina they'd been good friends. The railways, beef interests, big companies. British money built the railways, put a lot of money into

Argentina. There were a great deal of pro-Anglo Argentine families, and that's as I say, when Britain stripped its money. They never got that money back. All those foreign funds were confiscated and moved over to the British Treasury.

"The thing about the exposure of that map of South America and so on, shown to the President, that should never have been written in the book," Garner stressed. "Harford should never have done it, and this man Stevenson shouldn't have done it. It's not a need-to-know by people. You know people are going to read it 50 years later. How does it affect the thing? It doesn't."

"So before Pearl Harbor they tried to put by a few things?"

"Yes. To waken the Americans, really, to the threat."

"Would Donovan be in on it?"

"Oh, I'm not sure if Donovan was in on that. I don't think anybody was in on that at all."

A Man Called Intrepid implies BSC had something to do with the assassination of Nazi henchman Reinhard Heydrich. This has been a point of contention from many critics of the book. Heydrich was ambushed in Czechoslovakia in March 1942, and died shortly afterward. It is generally accepted that this was a European operation.[7]

"That's one [inaccuracy in the book]," Garner said. "And also a lot of it was out of context. I have to reread it but there was a lot of hyperbole. We never claimed about Heydrich. I remember things like, 'Could this man not be eliminated?' and things like that. We knew about the plot for Hitler, but so did the *New York Herald Tribune*. That came out. I don't think there was any prior knowledge of that. I don't think there was anything sinister."

Another point of contention in some criticisms of *A Man Called Intrepid* was Stephenson's reported relationship — or lack of — with the American president. Garner saw continual memoranda to and from Roosevelt regarding meetings. "Yes, there were numerous things, where he'd come back and dictate [sic] cables, after he'd seen Roosevelt and so on. Gave a verbatim account of what he'd said. He talked with Sherwood and with Donovan, of course, and later on, with Cuneo. So there were those sort of things. [If] you said, 'Did you ever see him [Roosevelt] with him?' No, I didn't. But I know he used to go down there. I don't know how much he saw him through Halifax, with Halifax, or what went on there. But you talk about 44 trips across the

Atlantic — the number of times he went to Washington was countless."

After the war, in the late 1940s, Garner crossed the Atlantic to see the Britain she'd only read about. She found the residents still shell-shocked. "When I came over here, right after the war, people were ... they were numb. And they were sort of shocked to talk about it, and it was very bad form, and [you] dare not say anything about the Prince of Wales. You could not talk about Edward VIII at all. Not the sort of people I knew. I mean, it was a terrible faux pas. They couldn't talk about it, and for a long time. I heard about people's personal stories about being covered with gas, awful stories. But a long time afterwards. They wouldn't talk."

She thought subsequently the Edward VIII story had become twisted. "Yes, it's been turned around and around, and upside down." [See Appendix.]

No one in British government or establishment circles came to Stephenson's defence following a number of negative press reports at the time of his death. Trivial details, even Stephenson's code name "Intrepid" has come into question. "I did remember the name 'Intrepid' during the war," Garner said. [See Appendix.] One of the reasons Stephenson received little recognition, and even abuse, in England, was that he was an outsider.

"I can only say he was not one of us, as Mrs. Thatcher would say. He was one of a peripheral organization. He was not in the main-stream of the British Foreign Office. He was not a career man. He was one of the many people. Many, many people had a wonderful war. I think that's part of it. I think part of it is the natural ... well, not an economy of the truth, but an economy of praise for anybody that wasn't British. Even Harford Hyde in his book does not give any praise to the Canadians. Does not single them out. He singles all the people from Britain who were names. All the big merchant bankers and British who had names. Not the unknowns."

"So it's more a nationalism?"

"It's a nationalism, yes. It's pride. It's grudging. When I came over here I was incensed at the lack of appreciation at what the Americans had done in the war. There was no gratitude for the generosity and the wealth that was spent on this country. The Bundles for Britain, the food, the things that were donated. Very little of that. There was a wave of anti-Americanism. There was a time when, 'Oh, everything from America was wonderful.' The nylon stockings, and then there was, 'Oh, it's American, is it?' And you couldn't do this and couldn't do that. And I remember, they would say, 'Oh yes, the Canadians, their boys were wonderful over here. They were wonderful. They used to give us this and give us that.' But never the fact the Canadians held their border edge at Caen. The Canadians did some of the hardest fighting. And they wouldn't want to be with the Americans, 'They're soft, they're overfed, they're oversexed, they're over here.' You know that sort of attitude. And they resented the fact they were so well fed. They were reluctant, I think, to give America credit.

"When the Marshall Plan came, after the war, when aid was given to Europe, and the French got all the building up of the ruin. And the success of Germany. The Germans after all, to give them all credit, their country was in rubble and terrible. But they built with their own hands, and their energy, and their strength. They built it up. But they had American money to re-establish themselves."

Garner chose to remain in Britain after the war. She visited Canada on a number of occasions, and she was astonished at the political conditions in her home country. She and a friend drove through Quebec after the largely French-speaking province made it against the law to have an outdoor sign in English. "We couldn't stop laughing," she said. "We laughed about it ... I despair for Canada. I really do.

"I feel strongly that Canada — Canadians would be interested [in Stephenson] because he was a Canadian, was born a Canadian, but how much ... so much damage has been done by that *Man Called Intrepid.* It's very difficult to rebut that. It only takes one big flaw like that to make the whole thing suspect.

"But what I felt about *The Quiet Canadian* is it still does not give any adequate recognition to the Canadian contribution to British Security Coordination. I know it was given the title British Security Coordination, the funds were British, the expertise, and the system was British, but it was staffed by over 400 Canadians and had contributions, as I say, from Lester Pearson, who was our Canadian High Commissioner, to eminent lawyers, to people, industrialists, and so on. Because they aren't world figures, they aren't the big bankers and those sorts of people, there's very little credit given. And they worked terribly hard."

Garner remembered seeing documentaries in 1984, the fortieth anniversary of the D-Day landings, and learning things about the war, "things they didn't tell us." Many men died right off the landing craft, weighed down in deep water, because they couldn't manoeuvre close enough to the shore. "They showed these pictures of the assault, on those landings. Well, it was absolutely devastating. I just couldn't watch it, it was so awful. We didn't know that was war ... they kept that away from us."

"The carnage," she said. "The terrible things, when the Entity Bee, the motorboat landed, the men had this heavy weight — fully armed men went into the sea, if it didn't land in the right place. Hundreds were lost like that. Now that was probably censored out of the news."

After the war Garner worked for *Harper's Bazaar*, and for Bill Ross Smith, and did public relations work in Britain. "I didn't stay with the Foreign Office. I went away like puffed rice. I wanted to get out of that."

Garner has few mementoes of the war. She still has her old typewriter with a BSC stamp on it and her security armband labelled 'CD'. The initials stood for Civil Defence — *American* civil defence. Even New York practised brown-outs during the war, she said, and in emergencies wearers of the armband would be allowed to pass through police lines. From its humble beginnings, BSC grew to be regarded as an essential component in the defence of the United States.

Garner also has a certificate from Bill Stephenson thanking her for her service.

19 BENJAMIN DE FOREST "PAT" BAYLY

The most secret member of Bill Stephenson's wartime staff was former University of Toronto professor Benjamin de Forest (Pat) Bayly. He is not mentioned in either of the Stephenson biographies, yet it seemed obvious during the course of this research that he held a senior position in the organization. Former BSC employees refer to him as the "famous Professor Bayly." Yet for much of his life, even for years after the war was over, his position was such that he could not be identified by name. There are brief references to him in material related to Bill Stephenson, but not much. The first published glimpse is in Mackenzie Porter's *Maclean's* article in 1952:

> The spider's web extended from Stephenson's BSC headquarters in Rockefeller Center to a legion of undercover men had at its core the most efficient communications system in the world. A Canadian electronics expert, whose name cannot be given, designed the equipment which coded and decoded messages in seconds, thereby saving hours of human effort. BSC business in code made up more than 50 percent of the traffic of the normal trans Atlantic cables and kept a secret transmitter in Canada operating at full capacity day and night.
> — *Maclean's*, December 1, 1952.

The first few details of Bayly's career appeared in Gordon Welchman's 1982 book *The Hut Six Story*. When Welchman, usually regarded as one of the two main conquerors of the Nazi's ENIGMA machine, started to work with Bayly, it was a promotion. A few other writers have paraphrased what Welchman said about him, but Bayly himself never spoke to anyone about what he did during the war.

No look at the extraordinary life of William Stephenson could be considered complete without reference to the mysterious communications centre that popped up, out of nowhere, that was relied on by all Allied nations. It guarded the cryptographic secrets such as ULTRA, and helped to win the Battle of the Atlantic. Bill Stephenson is considered to be a father of the CIA. Pat Bayly laid the groundwork for international cooperation in communications intelligence and cryptography. From his war work evolved the murky spheres of North America's most covert organizations — Canada's Communications Security Establishment and America's National Security Agency.[1]

The most direct route to finding Pat Bayly was through Harry Smith, Bayly's friend, a former accountant, and a Camp X alumnus. But writers who have written on BSC or wartime communications, such as William Stevenson, David Stafford and Nigel West, got no further. "As far as people contacting Bayly, ever since the war time, people who wanted to get a hold of Bayly, mostly have come through me," Smith said, "And I've pushed them off. I wouldn't give Stafford or Stevenson any clue as to how to get a hold of Bayly. I have always kept Bayly's name out of it. Nigel didn't get Bayly from me at all. It's one of the things Bayly asked when he left and moved to California."

Pat Bayly was the Deputy Director of Communications for British Security Coordination, and the second-in-charge of the entire organization. Bayly was in charge of Camp X for the duration of the war and afterwards. When Stephenson retired in 1945, Bayly became the BSC director.

David Stafford did an entire book on Camp X and did not indicate Bayly was in charge of it. "Well, he didn't know," Smith said. "You're the first person I've ever talked to that seemed to know Bayly's connection at all. No one else has ever got that deep, as far as I know, because if anyone was chasing it, and chasing it through me, they didn't get anywhere."

The First Mayor of Ajax

Benjamin de Forest (Pat) Bayly was born in London, Ontario, June 20, 1903, the son of Benjamin Moore and Alice de Forest (Seaborn) Bayly.

He grew up in Moose Jaw, Saskatchewan, where his father was a medical officer, and he always considered Moose Jaw home. For a time the young Bayly attended school in Shrewsbury, England, but he later returned to the Prairies. There he helped start a Moose Jaw radio station called 10 AB. There was no commercial radio in Moose Jaw at the time, and he and a few people began the amateur station and broadcast church services and other events. Eventually Bayly entered law school at the University of Saskatchewan in Saskatoon. He graduated at a young age in 1923, but after a period of articling, Bayly was unsure he wanted to pursue a legal career. With the encouragement and support of his Moose Jaw friend Margaret "Bun" Grant, he decided to leave the legal profession. Grant, originally from Hamiota, Manitoba, told him she didn't like a guy who didn't like what he was doing. "And I didn't like law, but I couldn't afford anything else, so she said, 'Why don't you put yourself through university and take engineering?' Bayly told her it would mean holding off their wedding for several years. "Better than wishing the rest of your life that you did," she told him. "So we did."

Bayly left the legal career alone, moved east, and entered the University of Toronto in electrical engineering. His proficiency in the field was noted by the university administration. When an electronics and communications professor left U. of T. to work in the new talking motion pictures industry, the faculty didn't look far for a replacement. Bayly was asked to teach fourth-year students while he was still enrolled in third year. "I had been a line man and I had my signals training in England." When it was time for him to graduate from U. of T., the university brass had trouble deciding how he should complete his degree. The issue eventually had to filter through the full bureaucracy. "The Board of Governors decided that I didn't have to write my [own] exam. I could give myself an 'A'," he said with a smile. "Some of the university didn't always have a sense of humour."

He continued to teach at the university following his graduation in 1930. To earn money, Bayly often played the piano, sometimes at theatres. During college, he had his own radio program on the commercial station CFCA in Toronto. However, Bayly was compelled to drop the show by Cannon Cody, the head of the university. "When I became a professor, he said he hoped I would drop the program, 'Pat At the Mike'. He didn't think it was a university professor job," Bayly laughed. Bun, nicknamed because of the rabbit-like way she used to wrinkle her nose as a child, moved with Bayly to Toronto. After six years of informal engagement, the two married, May 19, 1932. They were happily married for 54 years until her death in 1986.

Bayly stayed at the U. of T. until the end of the decade. He also acted as a consulting engineer for the Tariff Board of Canada from 1938 to 1940, and as a consultant to the National Electric Corporation (NEC). At the outbreak of war, he trained for a time in Winnipeg, and began working behind the scenes on Canada's war effort.

One of his jobs for NEC was to rig antennas onto small bombers ordered by the Free French, but France was occupied before the bombers were ready. The planes were eventually offered to the British through Lend-Lease, but since all the controls were in metric, they were given to the Russians. During the antenna installations, Bayly was asked if he could hook up bomb racks for the planes as well. He contacted American officials and was able to obtain French blueprints for the racks through covert means with the assistance of the FBI.

In 1941 Bayly was approached by Toronto stockbroker Thomas Drew-Brook, and his career was diverted into the shadowy world of espionage. Drew-Brook didn't know Bayly, but he researched his qualifications, contacted him at the university, and met him downtown for an interview. He "explained what he was doing, and would I come along, and I said I would.

"Tommy was asked to find a man who understood something about commercial communications, and who would have enough security clearance to buy top secret radio material. The point is that the English were, at the moment, developing all sorts of secret radio. Putting in the spies in Europe, and that sort of thing. They didn't want to divulge what they were buying through normal commercial channels. So I was asked to come down and do that." Later Bayly realized why the stockbroker received his unique recruiting position. "He was Bill Stephenson's best friend. They had served together in the Air Force."

Bayly travelled to England in November 1941, learned the British communications set-up and about their progress in analyzing Axis covert messages. He spent most of his time with Brigadier Richard Gambier-Parry, the SIS Communications division chief. He was introduced to Stewart Menzies, the head of Britain's Secret Service, and other top people in Britain's intelligence community. He visited the covert decryption centre, Bletchley Park, and Whaddon Hall. The professor from the harsh Canadian Prairie, "damned near froze to death in England" that November. Britain was a nation under siege, and he had to obtain a clothing ration card before he could buy warmer clothes. Eventually he managed to acquire a pair of unglamorous combination overalls to see himself through the British sojourn.

In England, progress was being made in the breaking of the Nazi cipher machine called ENIGMA. At Bletchley Park some of the best brains in Britain were at work trying to decipher the millions of variations possible from the portable coding machine. Two men in particular were responsible for the British success, following preliminary work done in Poland. Gordon Welchman is considered the man who persevered, believing the millions of statistical variations of the machine could be determined, and he figured out how to break the apparently unbreakable ENIGMA machine. Alan Turing invented the machines that helped with the solution, and in the process created the first computer.

During the war the Government Code and Cypher School, as the department was called, was headed by Alastair Denniston and later by Edward Travis. Winston Churchill knew the importance of the information produced by GC&CS, which was delivered to him regularly by Stewart Menzies. When some of the top staff at Bletchley needed more resources they wrote him personally, and quickly received the support they requested. "Action this day," the British Prime Minister demanded. Churchill referred to the scientific aspects of the conflict as the Wizard War. "This was a secret war, whose battles were lost or won unknown to the public, and only with difficulty comprehended, even now to those outside the small high scientific circles concerned. No such warfare had ever been waged by mortal men."[2]

The English quickly took to Bayly. Gambier-Parry wrote to New York to say that he was "more convinced than ever that Bayly was the right man for the job"[3]. Later Bayly thought the British were impressed for wrong reasons. While waiting in Menzies' office, he came across his personnel file on the spy chief's desk, thumbed through it, and was disappointed in its contents. They seemed overly impressed he had a portion of his education in England. "There was no mention about my present 'technical.' There was no mention of Teletype, or things that were necessary in anything I did, most of it as a lineman, before I did signal corps training. There was no mention of that at all. I'd simply gone to the right schools."

Bayly signed Britain's Official Secrets Act, and the need for secrecy was stressed. He was told how intelligence could be passed on as a result of any type of disclosure. One example he was given was David and Goliath. "I said, 'That's six thousand years ago.' And they said, 'We're telling you that to show you that time doesn't necessarily influence security. Anybody who is fighting in Arab countries knows that if you go up against a sheep herder, he can use a slingshot as accurately as a rifle, up to about a hundred yards. And the reason that everybody knows that is because of the story about David and Goliath.' I was quite impressed, because that was six thousand years ago."

• • •

The security of certain Allied ciphers was very poor at the time, Bayly discovered, and he was not impressed with Allied communications in general. When he started the job, at least one ciphering system was pitifully obsolete. "The British were still using the Playfair cipher, which they had started in 1914, and which we then could break in two minutes," he laughed. He spelled out one of the consequences of poor communication — the hasty retreat of British troops from Europe at Dunkirk, France, in 1940.

"Dunkirk happened for one good reason. I had been a signal officer in the Canadian army. Of all things, a cavalry signal officer. They only had one, and they gave it to me. I was trained in Winnipeg, and I had a radio set that had come from the First World War. It had a distance ability of 15 miles. By that time [1940], the German tanks could go 15 miles in half an hour. The British were using radio communication that had a range of 15 miles, so by the time you'd intercepted, and said 'A German tank had just gone by here'— he was already 15 miles past you," he laughed.

"The British were completely out of communication. Nobody knew where anybody else was. The tanks had come in so fast at Dunkirk that nobody knew where anybody else was. So the British finally decided 'let's get the hell out of here', and they landed at Dunkirk, and they couldn't get enough naval boats there. So everybody who had anything longer than 15 feet long tore over to Dunkirk and brought as many people home as they could. But it was entirely a complete lack of communication, and even of a decent cipher. The communication of the British army was just a disgrace — having been a communications officer in the Canadian army I knew exactly what it was, because we were taking our orders from the British."[4]

Later in the war Bayly was given British identification. He spent a lot of time dealing with British security, and this was partially to circumvent Canadian law. "The British decided if they wanted to shoot me, they didn't want to argue with Canada," he remembered. He was given the army rank of Lieutenant Colonel.

The new communications officer sailed back to North America, where his real assignment began. There were no available flights, so he returned on a converted Norwegian banana boat. Although the ship, formerly used to transport fruit to Scandinavia before it ripened, was one of the fastest on the Atlantic; it was delayed by days of strong southwest gales and his return to North America took over two weeks.

Bayly arrived in New York City on a Sunday, and he hurried to the secret office of his new boss, Bill Stephenson. He was increasing his espionage network and Bayly was to help institute secure communications. The Moose Jaw native had his plans well prepared. "I know exactly what I'm going to do," he told Stephenson, at their first meeting. "The hell you do," Stephenson curtly replied, and he handed Bayly a cable. It was from President Franklin Roosevelt and it detailed American damage in Hawaii. Bayly's first day at work was December 7, 1941. As the United States was no longer going to be neutral, his communications agenda was already changing.

But talking safely to Washington remained one of Stephenson's priorities, and Bayly made sure the spy chief stopped using the telephone for any security matters. "He couldn't do it on the telephone, because he knew that everyone would be listening. Not only the FBI, every mayor of every town in between." Telephone communication in those days was not at all private, Bayly says, and the scramblers used to conceal speech "weren't worth a darn." He told Stephenson to use a teleprinter and one-time pads.

As Bayly was working in the United States, Stephenson arranged for him to meet with American government and military officials. But first he had him checked out by Hoover's FBI. The Bureau organized an interrogation of Bayly and invited Canada's Royal Canadian Mounted Police to participate as well. The meeting made Bayly's "hair stand on end." The RCMP sent down Inspector George McClellan, and during the questioning the Mountie frequently interrupted ominously, "I know your face from somewhere." "Every time he said this, the FBI would sort of scramble for notebooks," Bayly recalled. The interview continued for a half hour, with the new recruit getting more and more nervous, thinking the Mountie's recollection was regarding some sort of illicit activity. "I don't mind saying, I was perspiring freely." Finally McClellan said, "Hell, my mother was your first music teacher." "And she was. He'd come from Moose Jaw, and Mrs. McClellan was my music teacher. And after that we got on much better."

The FBI involvement in BSC's communication at the time was extensive and in retrospect, very unusual. The American domestic police service was transmitting the Stephenson organization's secret messages to England on their channels. Not only was the foreign spy network allowed to exist in the U.S., the FBI was working for them. Bayly admits the FBI was "in a very funny position," and Stephenson had brokered the deal with J. Edgar Hoover. "The communication with England, for security reasons, they weren't carrying it through normal channels, [it] was being handled by FBI. And being handled personally by the bossman of FBI, whom I ended up liking very much, in spite of the fact that he has a reputation as being everything that is wrong in the world." J. Edgar Hoover wanted out of the communications deal, as he was unsure what would happen if Congress or the press found out what he was doing. "He finally decided it was too dangerous, and it was going to get him in wrong if it was found out, because it was still a neutral country. And he was sort of exceeding his duties."

British Embassy channels were not used, but Bayly was somewhat vague as to why. "Lord Halifax was known as Lord Holy Fox, and he was not popular in intelligence circles. Most ambassadors hate any intelligence going on in their embassy, because they are not allowed to know what is going on, and know that if it's dynamite, it could blow up in their face ... So I was brought in really to handle the communications for BSC."

• • •

"Why I didn't want to talk about these things? Let me go into detail again for a minute. Let's put it this way — all liaisons between countries is, first of all, subject to a treaty. And all the treaty says is that you may do 'this.' But from then on, the liaison is a very personal thing. If they like you, and believe you, then you have good liaison. It doesn't matter what the treaty is. If they don't like you, there's no liaison. And I was very generously treated in Canada, the States and England, and I would feel very badly if it sounds like, if in any way it appears that I was starting to shout my mouth off.

"Because these things do hang on, and they do have political repercussions. For instance, you take Hoover. If he were still alive, and it was found out he was doing BSC's communication while it was still a neutral country, politically, that would be dynamite. And there are many things like that [that] exist, so I decided that the best thing for me to do was shut up."

· · ·

Well-versed in Britain's covert communication methods and decryption successes, Bayly wanted to know what the Americans were up to. He had a book by Gilbert S. Vernam, who had worked for Bell Labs, which described encipherment of characters using teleprinters. Bayly thought this would be a good system to work with. Then he contacted Barty Bouverie at BSC's Washington office. He told him to find William Friedman.

William F. Friedman was possibly the greatest cryptographer of all time.[5] However, in the U.S., the evolution of cryptography has been somewhat staggered. American codebreaking went through periods of being shut down, or forced underground, as some politicians concluded, "gentlemen did not read other gentlemen's mail." When Bayly tried to find Friedman, he was given the runaround. "We got the story that Billy was now a librarian, and he was no longer head of the cryptographic division, because there wasn't one."

Eventually Bayly met with Friedman and explained his situation. Friedman told him to get in touch with Western Union, who had a machine called telekrypton, which was the teleprint machine that Vernam had worked on. BSC bought two of the machines from Western Union and installed one in Washington and one in New York. But Bayly knew quickly they were insecure, as the units simply ran a short rotating code tape. "After ten minutes any cryptographer could open the machine." He had both ends use one-time pads, which contained coded sheets and tables that weren't used again. "You tear it off so that there is no way it repeats itself and lends itself to statistical breaking."

The pads combined with the machines made the system secure, but the process was time-consuming and involved a lot of coding and decoding. Bayly then set about constructing the fastest, most secure cipher machine ever devised.

Cryptology vs. Espionage

"Bear in mind that the way you get an understanding of other people is to find out what they are saying — not to go and watch them and guess what they are saying. So, in other words, cryptography has taken the place of espionage." He remembered Edward Travis, the head of Bletchley Park, gave a demonstration of this when he was visiting New York. The two looked out the office window and took an interest in what was happening next door. Workers with a crane at the RCA building lifted an immensely heavy object. "It took them ages to lift it and set it down inside the building, and Travis said, 'What do you think they are doing?' and I said, 'Well, it looks as if it is heavy enough to be a vault door.'" Travis tried to find out what was happening next door and eventually, by phoning around, he found someone in an engineering office who could tell him. He was told the heavy object Bayly thought was a vault door, was a new air conditioning system they were installing. Travis said, "'Now there is the difference between espionage.' Here am I, as a perfect agent, and I've watched them putting a door on the vault, and it wasn't a vault at all. It was an air conditioning unit. And me, as a skilled watcher, watches this thing, and I don't tell them anything useful. But when you could find out what they actually were doing, by talking to the man in charge, you get so much more information. That is the difference between espionage and cryptographics, a factor of a hundred to one or something. The same piece of information, it is so easy to — even if you see it — it is so easy to misjudge what it is. But I thought that was a wonderful example."

· · ·

Although the purchased Western Union system was not secure, Bayly was convinced that utilizing punched tape and teletype was the best way to run all BSC's covert communication. It was secret, unlike telephone, and it was nearly as fast as telephone — about 68 words a minute. Bayly took off the tops of the Western Union machines and installed a long cipher tape that would run for two hours, and never be repeated. The receiving party was sent a duplicate tape to run simultaneously, and characters were added at one end of the tape, so they could be aligned with a new one. The cipher tapes were transported by courier between the two machines, often in diplomatic bags. "This was now secure because it was not using a repetitive tape." The new machine was the prototype for the machine later dubbed the Rockex. (The actual Rockex machine was different, as it could be used on commercial lines.) "It was a fine machine to be used, say, in between New York and Washington, but useless for running using commercial facilities in between," Bayly explained.

The Bayly network started from the two converted telekrypton machines and grew from there. "We started using machines to Ottawa [likely the Examination Unit] and then we used it on the cable to England." For the transatlantic communication, BSC had to have privately accessed cables, as the system was dependent on having synchronized connection, and they couldn't rely on other operators in between. The coding tapes had to be aligned properly. If the circuit was broken, the tapes were not in synch and the messages had to be started over again. As a result, BSC had to have control of the transmitting facilities. The organization leased cable and then approached the heads of ITT and had a terminal of the transatlantic cable installed in their Rockefeller Center office. "That way facilities were in our control — so there wasn't any option." With the hardware in place, the Allies began relying on BSC's resources.

"That's really what started the whole thing. This grew because we had very quick communication to England. We could send — if you went through the embassy, and had them encipher it, and the Foreign Office then decipher it — six hours was a minimum one way. That meant that to get an answer back, it took at least 12 hours. Where, with our automatic encipherment, it took a minute. Bill Stephenson and Churchill wouldn't stand for, once they had discovered that they could talk instantly, in other words you could talk to someone, and have them answer back, because there was no delay — but you couldn't take 12 hours to get an answer. So that's what started the whole ball rolling. So my original job became a non-entity. What happened then is we had to have secure communication to every place that we needed to, for Bill Stephenson. That's where I had radio circuits and cables and everything else, talking to Canada, Washington and London. Not only London but to Bletchley Park and all for Bill Stephenson's communication. When we had those facilities, we started doing other things with it."

When he arrived in New York, BSC's communication was handled by two people. "It ended up with a thousand people on the mezzanine floor of the International Building there. But this growth was just the necessities of getting on with intelligence."

The area he started in was small, on an upper floor of Rockefeller Center. He and a few other Stephenson officials had private offices there, but the rest worked in an open area. Bayly spent a lot of his time commuting between Ottawa, Camp X, London and Washington, so he approached Elizabeth Richardson, who was involved in decoding incoming messages and told her he would move out of his office, and she could have his space. "You go into the office. I don't mind moving out here," he told her. Afterwards Richardson became his "devoted admirer," he says, and when he moved downstairs to the mezzanine floor, she moved with him, and became part of his department.

The British sent over a university professor, Ken Maidment, to assist him. Maidment had no electronics background, but he understood what to look for in intercept messages. "He had a marvellous detailed knowledge about what was going on, everywhere in the world, about spies, or anti-spies." Originally he came over to show Bayly what to look for in espionage communication networks. BSC was looking for Fifth Column activity in the U.S., and if there were any connection to people in Britain. "We were still trying to find out whether the Germans were using radio amateurs in the States to communicate with England. It turned out there weren't any to speak of." Bayly's assistant then changed his focus to interception of other signals such as army, navy and diplomatic. Maidment had a tremendous mind for detail, Bayly remembered. "He could tell you what frequency, what code name, what everyone was doing."

But Bayly suspects the British shipped the university professor to North America simply because they wanted him moved. "Why he was sent over was to get rid of him, because he was a professor and people didn't trust professors, so they put him with me. Everybody in the office was from somewhere in Canada, except for Ken Maidment, who was the only Englishman in the communications division. Along with Miss Richardson."

Bayly remained convinced that utilizing punched tape and Teletype was the best way to run all covert communication. It was secret and about as fast as normal speech. It was also simple to train competent personnel, as in about half an hour a good stenographer could become a good Teletype operator. Bayly approached the U.S. government, the U.S. war production board, and the Teletype section of AT&T and persuaded them to put in two production lines of Teletype. Machines were converted and his network expanded quickly. His secret communications central, on the mezzanine floor at Rockefeller Center, became a beehive of activity. "At one time I had 105 teleprinters." It took four people to run a teleprinter round the clock — three eight-hour shifts, and one person off. The amount of heat given off by 105 teleprinters was extensive. "The operators were just about dying of the heat," he remembered. Bayly later worked out a deal to use some of the cooling system of the Radio City skating rink in the summertime to cool the area.

The top machines created by Bayly became known as the Rockex. He and Edward Travis named the devices after seeing the Radio City Rockettes out sunning one day.

The Rockex was unbreakable. At the height of the war, Bayly invented a machine that was a cryptographer's worst nightmare. Bayly's machine created no letter frequency peaks at all. "If you intercept this [enciphered message], it's completely random, in the sense that if you copied all the letters from A to Z … if you copied each of the letters, each of them would be there one twenty-sixth of the time. Which proves that it's completely random, and if it is: you could prove mathematically that this is unbreakable." If the Nazis had intercepted Rockex messages and plotted them, they would "know perfectly well it's a very high grade cipher indeed, that doesn't show peaks where letters occur."

As a result, eventually his network guarded many of the war's secrets, including ULTRA and MAGIC material. "There was no use giving the enemy back their own stuff," he said with a slight smile. "They'll spot the fact we're intercepting everything, and breaking it."

• • •

"The Rockex machine was produced quite early in the war, and it's not actually much of an invention. It's just taking what other people had done. I quote for a minute the Massey Harris binder. I asked a man one time who was an expert on patents who had patented the Massey Harris binder. And he said, 'You obviously don't know anything about developing a machine.' He said 'That goes back for five hundred years with at least a hundred people doing it.' Well, it was same as Rockex. I invented the last ten minutes of years of development of machines that did that. And they couldn't handle teleprinter communication. They could handle clear English, or they used the English alphabet. I invented a way of taking the 32 characters that you get in a teleprinter and only sending 26 characters. So we could use commercial cable companies to send them."

Roald Dahl, speaking on the radio documentary, *Tuesday Night*, recalled: "The only telegrams that didn't leak were the ones that Bill sent from New York, because I'm sure you heard he had all these fantastic ... coding machines up there. Yeah. You had to have ... whole roll of lavatory paper at one end, and another the other, and with the same size and number of holes in them (laughing)."[6]

Harry Smith recalled: "Rockex was really partly Pat's invention. There's no doubt about that. He worked on that code system, and Rockex, I guess, is used today by, I would say, all the embassies in the world — even the Russians, you know."

• • •

For security reasons Bayly's secret machines, such as the Rockex were not converted or manufactured by outside sources. "I set up a machine shop — right there in Rockefeller Center." Machinery was put on shock mounts to help curb suspicious noise. Bayly's BSC people doubled drive mechanisms on some teleprinters. "We made a whole lot of machines. For instance, we made machines which you could take Morse tape, perforated tape, which came in off the radio, and you could put that onto teleprinter code automatically, so you didn't have to have an operator doing that." (Gordon Welchman wrote, "Pat was in some way responsible for the operation of a high-speed Morse code radio link between Canada and England.")[7] "We made machines like that, so that we were just cutting down necessary manpower. We made all sorts of funny things."

Unknown even to some of the people who worked there, BSC offices were monitored and protected by plainclothes policemen of the Royal Canadian Mounted Police. "The guy sitting at the desk in my office — he looked like a hobo. He was never well dressed. He was a Mountie, and he knew who came and went."

At Camp X, Bayly put together radio linkages. "We couldn't put radio stations in the States because the war wouldn't let us, but we could put radio stations in Canada because they were licensed to me."

For security reasons large commercial transmitters weren't purchased. Amateur radio operators were approached and asked to turn in their equipment. "We couldn't go out and buy secretly $1,000 in commercial transmitters, but we could seize radio amateurs' stations, and pay for them on our own and use them 'under the table,' so to speak."

"Would not that equipment be useless on a transatlantic scale?"

"No, funnily enough, it isn't. If you take 24 hours a day, and you have a 100-watt transmitter, you could probably get through one hour of the 24. If you then went to a kilowatt you could probably get another 3 hours out of the 24, and if you went to 71 kilowatt, which is about what they use across the Atlantic, you could probably get 16 to 18 hours. You have to change frequencies, and this business of fading is quite a problem."

With the help of the RCMP and Canadian government radio inspectors, a major Allied communications link was completed. "We could get the Government inspector to say so and so has got a 500-watt radio transmitter he would probably sell you, because he can't go on the air now during the war, etcetera, etcetera. So that is what we did. We bought amateurs' and gradually increased the power so that it was something useful."

The largest transmitter they found was in Philadelphia. A newspaper owner had a radio station connected with his newspaper, and the FCC cancelled his licence. "We bought that, tore it down, and moved it up to Camp X. The whole trick of our operations was that it was fast way there and fast way back, and that we could do with ease within this continent when we wanted. To do it for England, we couldn't do it as fast as we might have liked it, but at first we were able to do it for radio and get a lot of words for free. Or you rang them. Free means that it wasn't costing us 10¢ a word or something, and that is a normal commercial rate across the Atlantic. When you've got half a million words to send, and relatively quite important, depending on the business they were about, it could cost a lot of money. Not only that, you were giving away quite a lot of facilities that people knew about. We didn't want people to know we had 100,000 words to send a day. But really at the heart of the whole thing was that we had a network of fast communications and that's what Stephenson needed," and "it was completely unbreakable."

Two-hour tapes were distributed between Camp X, Ottawa, Washington, New York and England by courier. The facilities at Camp X Bayly called HYDRA, because with OSS and SOE training going on, and RCMP and Communications people around, the place seemed to have many heads. He also arranged that radio transmissions could be adjusted for atmospheric conditions. "We had quite an installation at HYDRA. We had three transmitters and they steadily did about ten hours a day. You couldn't work them at night, mostly by day and about ten hours a day. So that we had very good communications."

Remarkably, Bayly's communications links were set up and running within months of Pearl Harbor. "That was really all I did from the beginning."

BSC's communication system had the unbreakable Rockex. It had automatic encipherment, where a stenographer could type normally and the letters would be automatically coded, and later decoded just as quickly. The cable messages could be coded automatically to radio transmitters. There were cable links, radio links, and trained staff. They all combined not only to provide communications security, they provided speed.

Meanwhile the American Army and Navy chose to focus on radio. They were impressed that radio could run at 300 words a minute, Bayly remembered, and felt Teletype was too slow for their purposes. Staffing was more of a problem, however, as it involved undulater tape and Morse Code. "It takes two years to teach a good undulater. I decided, as I had worked with both systems, that this was silly."

Soon after Pearl Harbor, the American military "discovered that running along with high speed Morse didn't work worth a darn, and they began to work with Teletype, and there was a shortage of Teletype. They discovered that I set up the Teletype production line, and got enough [U.S.] government assistance to do it. And the war production board allowed me to, because I'd done this — to have first go at the teleprinters which we wanted. The Signal Officer in the Navy, whose name I can't think of now, discovered this. He discovered also that I understood this business. He and I became quite good friends, and he made it much easier for me to deal with the cryptographic people, and this sort of thing. Navy communication." Shortly afterwards the American military decided to use Bayly's communications network as well.

As the war progressed, with a few exceptions, the Allies had increased success breaking Axis codes, as the process and machinery gradually became more efficient. But in cryptography, there can be no mistakes in a "raw" intercepted message. Often messages were recorded by hand, by relatively simple equipment, and errors were easily made. "We'd intercept in ten different places," Bayly said. "We'd intercept the German signal, and the people we had intercepting would give us ten different versions of the story. Because they were intercepting it by hand, and in small facilities and mistakes would happen. And if you are trying to bust cryptograms, you must have no mistakes, because a mistake makes a cryptogram unreadable to everybody, including machines, and so we began to need better and better communication facilities."

It was decided to funnel the raw intercepts into BSC for distribution to various countries. Signals came in from all over the British Empire, from the south of Africa to the Falklands. "Anywhere the British Empire had listening posts." The signals usually went to Camp X and then on to New York. There they were sorted and sent to the crypt bureau of the country that was working on that particular code. "The U.S. had every bit as good interception as we had, only we had it in different places. If you happened to be at the right angle from where people were going, and with this fading business that goes on with telegraph radio, we happened to be in better position than they did and they had better places than we had. But not necessarily. So frequently we could trade parts of the Pacific even with them, and they'd be only too glad to play ball with us, because we were adding to things that they didn't have. And so they would give us part of the communication, which we could to send to England to back up. In cryptography you're always trying to break fresh codes, as well as old ones, so interception, even if you're not breaking it, can be very important, so that you get accurate messages."

Many of the Axis messages picked up in North America were actually communication from Europe because of the strange bounce of short-wave skip signals off the ionosphere.

Some radio signals were picked up and analyzed in the Western Hemisphere before the message was received by the intended recipient. After the U.S. lost much of their Pacific Fleet at Pearl Harbor, the

Japanese Navy sought to assert its dominance. One of the first major objectives was the island of Midway. American cryptographers broke the instructions to the fleet, figured out the proposed plan, and took countermeasures that sank the attacking force. "At Midway we knew the Japanese admiral's instructions before he knew them. He was still asking for repeats. And we knew them. And the difference was, we were able to put our aircraft right on the top of his battleships — Bang." The Allies were searching the Pacific skies for foreign transmissions, Bayly said. "And in this case, the Japanese captain was asking for repeats, because he was listening on a little antenna on a battleship, we were looking at it with mile-wide [sic] directional antennas on shore and we had it broken out, and knew what he was saying while he was still asking for repeats."

The Japanese lost four aircraft carriers, 2,500 men, and over two hundred aircraft at Midway, which turned the war in the Pacific around. "And that was the difference between winning the Pacific and losing the Pacific, and that was done by cryptography and nothing else."

Midway was the most remarkable success for codebreakers, and the U.S. Pacific Fleet. The most infamous debacle in the region was brought on by a lack of communication and by ignorance, Bayly said.

"The whole history of cryptography and the U.S. Senate is a disgrace," he said. "The U.S. Senate decided that doing cryptographics was not a gentlemanly occupation and the United States was not going to do it. And they told the Army to quit it, and they told the Navy to quit it, and they told the Coast Guard to quit it, and they told the FBI to quit it. The Navy said, well, to hell with that, and the Army said, to hell with that, and the reason we didn't know about Pearl Harbor is the Army had half of it, and didn't dare admit they were doing cryptography, and therefore didn't tell the Navy, and the Navy got half of it and didn't dare admit that they were doing cryptographic work, in case the Senate found out, and didn't tell the Army. And the result is Pearl Harbor went on. We could have, if they were talking to each other, known exactly what Pearl Harbor was doing. Or was going to do."

Bayly said he often told the U.S. Army what the U.S. Navy was doing. Gordon Welchman says this occurred because of inter-service rivalry in Washington. (Welchman says that both he and Bayly were the go-betweens, but Welchman only was in the U.S. for a short time beginning in 1944.)[8]

During the war the American Senate wanted to know from the American military exactly which foreign codes they had, and what they were breaking cryptographically. "And the generals said, 'I have taken an oath that I will not do this, whether you're senators or you're not senators, and I'm not doing it.' That would be about the year after Pearl Harbor. Right in the middle of the war.

"Just an absolute disgrace. But Billy Friedman, because of the Senate, had to quit being a colonel in the army, resign from the army and become the resident librarian. This was the sort of nonsense. In a time of war. This isn't just a couple of kids, playing in the back street. This is a country at war, and the Senate was insisting that we shouldn't do cryptography, and they would discuss what cryptography was being done. In spite of the fact we weren't doing any."

The Plumber

Bayly had no code name during the war, but he had a code occupation. He was the plumber. His task was not to know what a particular message was. His assignment was to see that the message kept flowing. "My job was to see that there was running water, but what happened to the water was none of my business. And so I never at any time let any of my people see the breakouts of any secret documents. We just simply got coded documents and transmitted them.

"I was just myself, because I functioned almost publicly in the sense that being just a communications man, I didn't have to worry about identification, or who or why or what. Being a plumber, I didn't count in the organization for security. The joke about that was that the communications man knows who you are dealing with, how important the communication is, and what it is in the background, even if you don't know the wording, but I had no security clearance to speak of."

He had a code number, but doesn't recall exactly what it was. "It was 48 something, because Bill Stephenson was 48000 ... I wasn't allowed to kill anybody."

Few references to Bayly exist anywhere, but in the papers at the University of Regina, there is one cable from 1974 from William Stephenson to William Stevenson. It appears to refer to a book on ULTRA by Peter Calvocossi, or else comments he made on the CBS television program *Sixty Minutes* on the ULTRA Secret. It reads:

PETE [Calvocossi] SPARES NO CREDIT TO MAGIC REPT
MAGIC THE AMERICAN MACHINE ALSO TO THE FACT THAT
OUR ARRANGEMENT TO SUPPLY THEM FREE OF COST
THROUGH CANADIAN WATSON OF IBM WITH COMPUTER
OF OUR DESIGN WHICH SAVED THEM MILLIONS OF MAN
HOURS NOR ANY REF OUR TRIANGULATION U-BOATS POSI-
TIONS AND OUR TELEKRYPTON IMMENSE TRAFFIC
DIRECTED BY MY PROF. BAILEY [sic] WHOM BISON [Herb
Rowland] WORKED UNDER STOP BAILEY WAS MY RIGHT-
HAND ELECTRONICS MAN AN AUTOMATON WHO GAVE
GREAT PRACTICAL HELP TO ALL HOME COMMUNICATIONS
OPERATIONS INCLUDING ASPIDISTRA WHICH BUFFALO
KNOWS ABOUT[9]

The U-Boats
"Nor any reference of triangulation of U-boats positions ..."

"That I was concerned with, because we had now got to the point
where we could break the coding of the submarines, and Hitler had
insisted the submarines give their position reports twice a day. So if
you could break the code, you knew where the submarines were twice
a day. Every navy had to know where the submarines were, so they
could send ships [or aircraft] with depth charges. You could move a submarine completely if you could drop depth charges within so many
hundred yards of the sub; the shock was too much for the submarine.
And the timing was essential, and it was handled through the U.S.
Army, which had 30 million [letter] groups a day in their headquarters.
It was decided that this was too slow. And I was given the job of giving
submarine position reports to whatever navy could be anywhere near
that particular place, to tackle these submarines. And we were allowed
a minute and a half from the time we got the information from the
station to get it to the crypt bureau of the army or the navy or which
country could then alert the navy to where the submarine was ...

"So that was one of our things. I had devised a method, because
everything came in on punched tape. I devised a method by just punch-
ing the right holes in the tape [it] could give the code in English, so that
any operator knowing it could see that this had 'sub' or something in
front of it, and that meant a minute and a half — get rid of it. And this
method was so that inept people could code the stuff and hand it to

the next person, whether they could read the tape or not. Most of the girls could read the perforated tape as well as they could English. You get pretty experienced in that ...

"But because of this, we were given the job. And that was kind of an important job, where all these subs were. We got rid of a lot of subs that way. So that's probably what that was. Bill was very pleased with that. He thought it was proper use of our facilities." It was an "important job." Describing the importance of ULTRA and the Atlantic, in the *Sixty Minutes* interview, Peter Calvocossi said, "I would say it was the most decisive element in the Battle of the Atlantic. This was extremely important because the Battle of the Atlantic was obviously decisive about the war as a whole. If we hadn't won the Battle of the Atlantic in the winter of 1942–43 we could have been knocked out. We, I mean England. If we had been knocked out, and France had already been knocked out, what happens to the Americans? What happens to you? You can't cross the Atlantic because the U-boats are still there. If you do cross it, where do you go?"

When the Allies couldn't break the ENIGMA code, they used direction finding. Various listening stations could report the location of a U-boat as being at such and such direction, in relation to their location. The more signals that could be received, the more accurately they could zero in on a precise locale. "At first we didn't know that the subs had to report in to Hitler twice a day," Bayly said. "We only learnt that three years on, by mistakes. But up till that time we just knew that from the tones on the transmitters, and the noise that the German subs had. We could tell from the noise, the power noise, and [by] one thing and another, we could tell that was a German sub, even if we couldn't break out the communication."

From the report of only one ship or station very little could be deduced. "We wouldn't know whether it was right or wrong, but if you have ten of those, from ten different places, you've then got what we would call a 'cocked hat' which means these are places ... they all try to go through this point. Then you would say that the centre of these is the probable place."

When the codes were broken the process became easier, and if the subs were not destroyed at least convoys could be diverted. "You would then listen, and the subs would say, 'I'm at latitude and longitude so and so,' and we didn't need the DF-ing. But this came much later. But in the times that I started this, we weren't breaking the code. We just knew that this was a sub and we had to handle that as quickly as we could to give the approximate position.

"I didn't have charge of that. I was just one place where they could push the stuff in one place, and do something to it as it went by." BSC didn't plot the location of all the U-boats, they dealt with the distribution of their location messages. "We didn't organize it in any way, but we had to know what navy could be in that area, or close to that area, to make sure that everybody knew that we had this submarine reported at such and such a latitude and longitude. It wasn't much good to be twenty minutes later, because by that time he might be 10 miles further away. It had to be done as fast as possible."

The American Navy was concerned with the security of BSC's communications section, so they provided a nurse and free medical. Very few of these arrangements were formal. For example, the American Navy's top code machine was considered so secret, it was not to be even viewed by any foreigner. Bayly had one in his office. "This was just an exchange, and we did this completely unofficially in the sense that we would never admit that we could do it. I had the Navy code machine — the top code machine — in my New York office ... and if that had have been known, all hell would have broken loose. We had it sitting there so that they could send the stuff to us on that machine and we could break it out, and in turn they would have our code machine in their office. This was very practical — it worked, but it only worked because people trusted each other, and that's one of the reasons I've been quiet about writing books. When you've been dealt with that way, you feel that you would like to keep it that way. We had very good personal relationships with the people, which is the only way I've discovered anything works. It doesn't matter how many laws people pass enabling it — if you don't like each other, business just doesn't happen."

Aspidistra

"WLW radio station had obtained through political pushing around a licence for a 500 kilowatt station, at a time when 50 kilowatts was the thing. A little political manoeuvring had got the FCC to license it, and they had purchased it through RCA, and RCA had built the station. It had a front panel 200 feet long I might add, and was quite a thing. The output tubes stood 11 feet high, I think. They had enlarged the output from 500 kilowatts to a thousand kilowatts because they thought they were going to sell it to Mexico. The Americans decided they didn't want such a huge transmitter in Mexico.

"The FCC got cold feet and wouldn't license it, so RCA had this immense transmitter, the biggest transmitter that's ever been built, and nothing to do with it. And I happened to tell, of all people, the Queen's mother's brother, David Bowes-Lyon, that we had this station. And he was in charge of propaganda and he said, 'That's exactly what I want. I want a station that is so powerful it can't be interrupted with.' And he went back to England and he pulled some wires there, and they said yes, you could buy this station. RCA quoted us, I think it was $1,200,000. But in any event, we had bought the station and it was known as 79 80. In those days we were using hand-communication on the radio and mistakes happened and 79 80 would get abused and we wouldn't know what they were talking about. I said, 'Quit using a number and put a name on this thing.' And they said 'Fine. You pick the name.'

"Bun and I had been to a play with Beatrice Lilly. And Beatrice Lilly sang a song 'the biggest aspidistra in the world.' The English boarding houses always had an aspidistra. It was a sign you were nice people, if you had a big aspidistra plant. We'd listened to this song the night before and I'm having lunch at home with Bun and saying, 'I've been asked to give a name to this thing. What'll we call it?" And she said, 'Well, last night was the thing. Bea Lilly called it the biggest aspidistra in the world. Let's call it that.' So we called it Aspidistra. My wife named it.

"The first use it got was an interesting one and very rarely known. Probably most people didn't talk about it. The Germans came over with bombing raids and we had people who could speak German so fluently that they could imitate the voices of the normal people giving the bombing raids their orders. And by using Aspidistra, we could completely overcome the German orders that they were giving to the bombers and tell the bombers what to do next. A thousand kilowatts — you could smother the thing so it didn't matter what head office was telling them, we just wiped it out." On occasion the flights were so confused they went over Ireland.

Aspidistra was put underground in the south of England, and when the invasion of Europe came, the Allies were able to issue orders to the invasion troops. "They didn't want another Dunkirk, and so they wanted a transmitter big enough so the troops could get their orders without any chance of being smothered." He remembers giving his secretary, Enid Bence, a cheque for a million dollars to pay RCA. "And I can still see Enid clutching her purse to her breast," he smiled. "She had a check for a million dollars in this thing! She came back, still breathless and horrified, and all the rest of it ... But that's how Aspidistra got its name. You know, you remember the funny things."

ULTRA and Bletchley

"It was quite a thing when they released ULTRA to the general public, because it had been so secret. The reason it was so secret wasn't what was in it, but the method of production. Most of the ULTRA work was merely the results of cryptographic breaking down of German communications and Japanese. But it was secret. Very secret. Not, as I say, because of the stuff itself, but if you used anything about ULTRA in Germany or Japan, they would be certain as to where the information would come from. And we didn't want anybody to know where we were breaking their codes."

"So they said it was from a spy close to the scene?"

"Yeah, they always invented a way of defining ULTRA. But that was why ULTRA was so very secret, and I made sure that we handled it. The material was sent across in our communication, probably because of the speed of it — if you're giving something to the Americans, if it was two weeks old, the Americans would say 'Why the hell didn't we know this two weeks ago?' So they want to make it fast and so that was why I handled it. But at no time were any of my people, except the girls running the terminals, themselves in on it. So we never saw ULTRA. We didn't even know it was ULTRA."

Canadians handled Bayly's machines, even at Bletchley. "They were almost always Canadians," he said. "All the girls in England, in Bletchley, were Canadian girls they had sent over there — Bobby Griffiths was one of them."

Bobby Griffiths was from Bayly's home province, Saskatchewan. "Bobby Griffiths' father was a friend of one of the bank managers out in Moose Jaw that I knew very well. I used Bobby Griffith as the first operator of it, because I trusted her. I had known her since she was a youngster." She later married Kevin O'Neal, who was with Canada's

National Research Council, which also was involved in covert activities during the war. O'Neal subsequently became head of Canada's top secret Communications Security Establishment. Griffiths was one of the proficient operators of Rockex at the time, and Bayly sent her to Britain to handle the Bletchley connection.

Aside from trusting Canadians, Bletchley Park had trouble with the English Post Office, Bayly said. A branch of the Royal Mail handled telecommunications. This could present employee problems, and working situations dictated by postal people, not by the existing emergency in England. "And the result is that Travis and the Post Office would make arrangements, and those arrangements would become written in letters of fire. You couldn't change them," Bayly said. "It was most uncomfortable.

"It would be the Post Office which would tell us what to do, which was why I sent girls in England that would handle the ends of the cable, to keep them out of the Post Office. The Post Office was union, even through the war and the union allowed them to do this. The Post Office was most indignant when I put operators and Teletypes that they weren't allowed to go near. The English were so ... I found England's planning very uncomfortable, because it had happened long before the war, and it was now established, and you couldn't move it. Even Travis would have a hard job trying to change what went on."

Bayly knew few of the successful decrypts at Bletchley. "I deliberately kept away from that, as far as I could." But one day in England he was shown a notation from the Nazi Fuhrer to the Italian dictator Benito Mussolini. "This was a message from Hitler to Mussolini, bawling the daylights out of him for having sent some very secret stuff by courier from Italy up to Germany, and saying, 'Do not take a chance. Your courier might be intercepted. Send this by radio.' We intercepted this. I thought this was amazing, because we were breaking radio. And we could not catch couriers."

Across the Atlantic

In England, even though he was often on secret flights, Bayly had to go through customs like everybody else. However, he was what the British called "minimum interrogation," which meant the British authorities were to leave him alone and not search baggage or anything. He would contact London before going over and tell them of his expected arrival, and they would communicate with Prestwick, Scotland, or his expected port of entry. "If two people telegraph them from London or somewhere else and tell them, 'Bayly is coming in at such and such ... "Minimum interrogation" is required,' they give you pretty decent treatment. I would get Censorship, Cryptography and two other people to tell these people, 'Bayly. Minimum interrogation.' You got the royal treatment. You got red carpets and all the rest of it."

On one flight he was accompanied by the British Minister of Transport, Lord Leathers. The minister was unaware of how to coast through Customs. England was under rationing, and Leathers brought back a ham from North America. He wasn't allowed to take it into the country, and had a kerfuffle with custom officials when it was confiscated. Exasperated, he finally asked if there was anything he could do with the ham. "Give it to him," the Customs agent replied, motioning to Bayly. Stephenson's Communications head could bring anything he wanted into England, so he took the ham and gave it to the Minister of Transport later. Leathers was more surprised as they made their way back to London. Bayly had a car waiting to take him to the train station and a private carriage on the train. "He was quite impressed," Bayly remembered, "and said, 'In the next war I am not going to be a Cabinet Minister, I'm going to be a damn security officer!' He was Mr. Transportation. He could have had anything that he wanted, [but] he hadn't raised an 'advance,'" Bayly chuckled.

Late in the war Bayly found out the American OSS had a shuttle plane waiting for transatlantic arrivals in Scotland. The Americans made him a member of OSS, so he tried to hitch a lift, but he was stopped entering the plane. Why did Bayly, OSS, have a British passport? He simply answered, "You know better than to ask questions like that," and the American apologized.

Washington

Bayly was in Washington about three days a week. He was in Ottawa once every two or three weeks, which would include the trip through Camp X. "This was just liaison work, getting on with people, seeing if they had problems and weren't writing them, and that sort of nonsense. If you have four hundred girls in one place, there are lots of problems that they wouldn't write ... but if you talk to them offhand, you can quickly grasp if there is trouble."

In Washington, the American military took over a ladies' college and turned it into the U.S. Army Crypt Bureau. "And the officer commanding it had a button on his wall. It had been one of the bedrooms in the ladies' college, and the bell underneath it said, 'If You Urgently Need a Mistress Ring This Bell,'" he laughed. "The officer commanding had refused to let them take that down. He said, 'I want that in my office.'"

Bayly attended numerous meetings in the American capitol regularly, mostly to do with communications security. But some other meetings he frequented were not to talk about communications security, and that was why he was there.

"There were 57 joint committees," Bayly said, so they were known as "the Heinz." Some came and went quickly. One committee was to unify Allied phonetic names used for letters, such as "Able" for "A," "B" for "Bailey," and so on. However, certain words were viewed as being rude in England, or in the United States, and the committee soon became bogged down as they moved through the alphabet. One night the British delegation got drunk in the Mayflower Hotel, Bayly remembered, and they invented a code. "It started 'A' was for 'Arses', 'B' for 'ham', 'C' for 'colanders', 'd' for 'dung',... and 'l' for 'hell for leather,' and they presented this to the U.S. committee. The committee never met again."

Bayly also sat on the top-secret radar countermeasures committee. The Allies discovered shredded aluminum strips dropped from aircraft could confuse radar, and the code word for the project was "windows." But Bayly didn't know the details of the project. He was on the committee simply to terminate any talk about transatlantic communication and telephone security. "I was in the position, if they got mixed up in telephone security, I was to say, 'Sorry, boys. I've got order for you to stop ... can't go on any further.'" Bayly didn't enjoy the discussion. "I remember sitting as a member of the committee, and I'm bored to tears, and darned if I'm going to asked them what 'windows' is. But they kept telling me about 'windows.'"

Later he received a cable from England wanting the committee report. "'Please give us copies of the Radar countermeasures committee. We need them urgently.'" Bayly wasn't sure about that one. "So I phoned the head of G-2 [Military Intelligence] in the States and said, 'Can I get on this darn radar counter committee? There's a guy in England who wants it,' and Carter Clarke said, 'I can get it for you. But it will take months, because that is a "limited." We just cut that down to the minimum. But I'll phone you back.'"

Clarke returned the call soon afterwards, laughing. "He said, 'Hell, you're one of the 13 people that gets that damned thing.'" Bayly regularly received all the information of the committee, but he hadn't read the reports and simply stored them in a filing cabinet. He then walked across his office and retrieved them from his files. "Carter Clarke was one of the top men in G-2, with a rare sense of humour. I was glad it was him. He was a friend of mine, and not somebody else more official. Did I feel like a chump! This was the most secret 'holy of holies.'"

Gordon Welchman and British scientist Henry Tizard also sat in on some of the Allied committees, Bayly said. But not all the scientific ideas were used or were as useful as radar or "windows." He also came across Geoffrey Pike in Washington. The Allies were losing a lot of shipping in the Atlantic, and Pike had the idea that a frozen ship could be constructed using water, wood chips and a mould. The ice vessel would last long enough for a voyage across the Atlantic, and then it would be unloaded. "Pike was a screwball if there were ever one," Bayly remembered. "You just froze the ship. You had a special dry dock, which froze the ship, and you loaded it up with what you wanted, and shipped it across. Then it would melt. That was Pike's idea."

Pike didn't make a full-sized model, but he constructed something that was big enough to impress people. "But it came too late in the war to actually get used."

Bayly met a number of prominent people travelling between New York and Washington. He worked with many more. "You find that people that are famous and important treat you like a human being," he said. "But people who think they are important are regular S.O.B.s."

People
Mountbatten
Several people Bayly worked with during the war impressed him. He considered Stephenson and Hoover as two of his heroes, and another was Mountbatten, who stopped off in New York on his way to Asia. "This fellow had been a communications officer in the British Navy. He went from that to the captain of a destroyer and then kept on moving up."

Lord Louis Mountbatten was assigned to Asia, and he wanted to use Rockex while he was there. He toured BSC's secret communications centre to learn about it. He told Bayly, "I want to know about Rockex. I'm going to use that, and I'm going to depend on it. I'm a communication man and I want to know about it."

Bayly showed Mountbatten a terminal for a teleprinter cable to London, and his guest sat down beside the operator and said, "Okay dear, move over, and show me how to run this one." Mountbatten spent the day there learning all about Rockex in one way or another, and made quite an impression on some of his employees. He was with an aide-de-camp, who was there to see that everything went well, and afterwards Bayly asked some people on his floor about him and they said, "What aide-de-camp?" "They just saw him," Bayly laughed. Mountbatten's assistant had been a captain in the British Navy, but didn't register at all with them.

Mountbatten was a man he took to immediately, he said. "He was a real guy. You couldn't meet him for two minutes without being impressed that he was just a hell of a nice guy, who did his job to his best. So he was one of my heroes of the war."

Stephenson arranged a lunch for Mountbatten, Noel Coward, Brooks Atkinson (of the *New York Times*) and Bayly, soon after Noel Coward's film *In Which We Serve* was released. It was the story of a virtuous British naval captain and loosely based on Mountbatten. During the lunch Atkinson commented on the film. "Brooks said to Noel Coward, 'I liked everything about your picture immensely, except the speech the skipper gave on the deck of that sub [sic] before going into action. That was so corny! I'm quite sure that no captain would have said that.' And Mountbatten said, 'Well! I'm sorry you feel that way, because that is the speech I made on that occasion, verbatim.'" There was dead silence around the lunch table. Bayly glanced over at Stephenson. He was keeled over laughing. "Bill Stephenson was just about busting a gut. He knew the whole circumstance. The English gentry were really something," Bayly said. "They really were. But there's nothing left. Two world wars have killed them all off."

Colonel Barty Pleydell-Bouverie

"Barty Bouverie was a fine English gentleman, proper order, and one of the nicest men I knew. He'd been with the Coldstream Guards and his hobby was needlepoint. And if you'd see him, with rows of medals, going on the plane to England... American officers were sitting there staring while Barty was doing needlepoint."

John Pepper

"Pepper did a good job of work, but his motto was kiss people on all four cheeks." According to Bayly, he was not in on all of Stephenson's activities, as Roald Dahl thought. "His job was office manager. He might have handled some of the other, in preparing reports for Bill to submit. But his job really was office manager. There were two of them. He was one of the two. There was a lot of office managing to do. You had salaries, clearances.

"He was in on everything in the sense he was sort of Stephenson's personal assistant. Garner knew more than he did, but Garner wouldn't go out and interview people, and that sort of thing. If there was anything like that, Stephenson would probably pick on Pepper.

"Bill Stephenson trusted him implicitly. He was never particularly observable."

Dick Ellis

"Dickey Ellis was MI6 and the only professional, the long-term professional in the business. He had been for years and years in MI6. He's the one they thought must be a Russian or German agent, I regard as entirely unproved, because I had known him quite well. He visited us in our apartment in New York quite often. He was a musician and he just didn't ever give an indication that he was that way concerned.

"I played the piano and he would talk about things and he had a marvellous knowledge of classical music. And I think he played the cello or the viola. He never played it in my presence but he knew the scores of the viola and the cello. And I liked him very much. I liked Dickey Ellis immensely. And if he could have been a spy, I wouldn't have known the difference.

"And as I say, we're very lucky we didn't have a breach of security, a bad breach of security, and I'm quite sure if Ellis had been a spy [we would have] and I'm suspicious of the people who said he was."

Eddie Hastings

Eddie Hastings did liaison work for Government Code and Cipher in Britain and was an assistant of Edward Travis. He was frequently in

North America. "I'll tell you about Eddie Hastings, Eddie was a gentlemanly confidence man. He had been to Eton, Oxford, he had come from a good Old English family and he was a captain of the British Navy. And I didn't trust him an inch. He made his living riding horses for his gentleman friends, and he was a complete confidence man.

"Gouzenko always said that there was another man in the British [security organizations] who he called 'Elli,'[10] and I'm quite sure that what he was trying to say was 'Eddie,' and I'm sure this guy was it, and I've never had enough information that I dare say that, but I wouldn't trust Hastings as far as I could pitch him by the ears."

Part of the problem, Bayly said, was the English seemed to screen people using schooling and background as parameters. "Because they'd been at Cambridge, and therefore they were safe, and they were almost known German agents at that time. I think Eddie Hastings was probably Russian. Bill didn't like him at all," Bayly continued. "And Eddie did things that Travis finally decided he didn't trust and kicked him out."

When the war was over, Bayly gave Hastings a few accounting problems. "I had borrowed three transmitters which I used in Camp X, because the original transmitters, which we had bought from amateurs, were sloppily put together. They were running 24 hours a day. They just didn't stand up too well. I got talking to one of the [U.S.] Air Force communication officers at one stage in the war and told him the problem and he said, 'Hell, we've got a lot of those 71.5-kilowatt transmitters that we aren't using. I'll sent three of them down.' So he sent me three of these and we set these up in Camp X." The transmitters were acquired through Lend-Lease, and under those terms, the British had to pay the American Treasury the dollar value specified for each item they had used, or given away. Following the war, Hastings was to help arrange the transfer of any English wares at Camp X to Canadian government control. Hastings simply gave away the transmitters. "Eddie discovered these transmitters, I think were $90,000 each, and Eddie discovered that he had to go to the British Treasury and say I've just given away $270,000 worth of U.S. Lend-Lease." Bayly believes afterwards Hastings was not held in such high esteem. That was what finished Eddie.

"I'm afraid I was a little bitchy about that," Bayly remembered. "Because I hadn't told him they had been on Lend-Lease. You couldn't trust Eddie as far as you could pitch him. He would tell you one story and two seconds later, he would tell somebody else a different story."

Grace Garner

"I was very fond of Grace, in the sense that I admired what she did. She was a good secretary and Stephenson didn't understand women much ... And Grace Garner was very fond of Stephenson.

"She asked him one day if he'd get her a job as an editor somewhere. And he did, and she never forgave him for it, because that meant she wasn't working for him any longer.

"It always scuttled me as to why Grace would feel so badly about Bill Stephenson letting her go."

Halifax

The British Ambassador in Washington, Lord Halifax, was one of the few people with a private aircraft. Once he gave Bayly a lift to Washington and told him that upon arrival, he would have to review a guard of honour. "So I, as a half-Colonel, had to inspect the Major Generals, and their guard of honour," he laughed. "This was in the Mayflower Hotel lobby."

Stephenson and Halifax "were two men as different as day and night." On another occasion Bayly flew with Halifax across the Atlantic. "I came back on an aircraft, BOAC, with Halifax, and we ran into a bunch of bad weather. Really, really bumpy. And Halifax got down on his knees on the floor and started praying. And the pilot came back and said, 'You get the hell off that floor, or I'll break your damned head.' Because everyone else on the plane was wondering why Halifax had to pray. He was a funny guy. He was a very sincere man, but he was," Bayly hesitated, put his nose in the air and imitated a posh English accent, "very, very English."

Carter Clarke

"I'll give you an example of the kind of man he was: British Officers did not get Army Gold Badges and if you didn't have a U.S. Army Gold Badge, you didn't get into the Mall entrance of the Pentagon Building. You went in the back entrance, which is half a mile away walking, from where you could get in. I'm late to a meeting, apologize, and explained 'not having a Gold Badge.' Halfway through the meeting, his secretary gave me a Gold Badge, and it had my picture on it. He asked me to turn it in; then he said, 'Hell, keep it, you'll be coming back.' He was quite a practical guy and if he believed in what you had to do, he would back things and keep you going."

(Later, while going through his possessions, Bayly pulled out his U.S. Army Gold Badge. It seemed to be one of his most prized mementoes of the war. "It's unheard of for a foreigner to be given a U.S. Army Gold Badge," he said.)

Ivor Bryce

"Ivor Bryce I liked. He was a nice guy. Bill Stephenson didn't trust him too much, because he was English."

Montgomery Hyde

"He was a writer and he [Stephenson] wanted writers around because he'd get them to write propaganda and what have you. And Bill wasn't too reticent about getting any publicity he could. He liked to get plenty. He was in a position at first, before Pearl Harbor, where he didn't dare get any, because we were teaching OSS in a neutral country. And you couldn't very well get a lot of publicity about the fact they were breaking every law that you could think of."

J. Edgar Hoover

"I am certain that he wanted one thing. He wanted the best federal police force that there was in the States. And he would talk about this, if you were talking to him. He would explain the Secret Service, which now just looks after the President's safety, had once been a police force, until Congress had pulled it apart to nothing and Treasury then became one of the top secret things, and Congress pulled that to nothing, and they now look just for counterfeit money. He went on pointing out all these things, and he said, 'I've decided that if they want to play dirty, I'll play dirtier than they do. But I am going to have the best police force in the United States, in spite of Congress. Congress doesn't want good police forces around.' So it ended up ... I kind of liked him.

"I liked this guy just as much as Sir William. He was very sincere, in spite of all the stories about him now. At the time I knew he was a sincere guy who was going to have the best federal police force in the United States. And it was going to be over the dead bodies of Congress. And he liked Sir William.

"Hoover, I'd discovered, had bought machines. We were then using a thing called the telekrypton, which was a background of my later Rockex. But telekrypton was an automatic code machine that was pretty high grade, hard to use, but high grade, and we used that for all our communication, and we heard from Western Union that Hoover had ordered two of these machines." The machines would not have worked without the proper code tapes and synchronization, but Bayly viewed the situation with concern. "So I went in to Bill Stephenson, and I said, 'Hoover's going to, he can't do it because he can't break our codes, I'm sure, but Hoover's ordered two telekrypton machines and he's going to intercept [our messages]. What do you want me to do about that?' And Bill laughed and said, 'Well, why don't you take two of our code tapes, the latest ones, and hand them to Hoover and say, "Okay, you wanted these. Here they are." I know perfectly well what Hoover will tell you, but try it and see.' So I went over to Hoover and I said the machines are no good without these tapes. Here are the code tapes we are currently using. He said, 'Well, thanks very much.' And I'm just halfway out of the office and he says, 'To hell with you.' He said, 'if I have those code tapes I am agreeing to everything you people say to each other. This is something I don't want any stake of. Goodbye!' And he sent the telekrypton machines back to Western Union. He wasn't going to be stuck with Congress knowing he knew exactly what we were saying.[11]

"He and Bill were very close, but they were very discreet about it, because he didn't want to be mixed up with Donovan's outfit. Hoover was in a delicate position — from a U.S. government, I mean from Congress. If Congress could have tied Hoover to any illegitimate or touchy thing like the educating of OSS, they would have hung him on it like a million dollars. They hated his insides for obvious reasons."

"Back then they hated him too?"

"Yeah. Well, he saw to it that they did. In my opinion, I went into a little hero worship in regards to Hoover. He sincerely wanted to have the best federal police force there was and he would let nothing get in his way and he used any means he liked to ensure that. And when you talked to him you realized he really meant it."

"Including blackmail?"

"Including blackmail and anything else. You just name it," he laughed. "Well, there was no straightforward way of doing it. There isn't any now. He didn't like a lot of people around, because he didn't trust them. But he was, to my knowledge, because I dealt quite a lot with him, in the beginning, a very, very sincere, dedicated man, and that's rare in high policemen."

One reason BSC and the FBI got along well was Stephenson helped with U.S. security, Bayly said. At one point Stephenson found out information about German spies landing in the United States. "He gave all the details to Hoover and then let the FBI take all the credit. The FBI thought that was very nice of him."

Menzies and Leadership

Bayly eventually got to know the head of British SIS, Stewart Menzies, quite well. Menzies once told him, "It's the most amazing thing. You speak like an American. But you think like an Englishman.

"My trouble was not 'getting on' with the Americans. I had no trouble with the Americans at all. They sort of felt the British Secret Service was something to be coddled, so I had no trouble with them. I had trouble with the English people who came over. I had to tell them how to get on with the Americans, which meant I was entertaining the English people lavishly in order to keep them quiet and happy. I had to entertain the Americans, but I didn't have to mother them."

Bayly spent uncounted hours commuting overseas, and on one occasion, when stranded in Labrador waiting for a plane across the Atlantic with England's Minister of Transport Lord Leathers, they started discussing Stewart Menzies. The MI6 chief did not impress Bayly with his knowledge of the field, and he expressed some surprise that he was in charge during a world war. "I said, 'How in the name of fortune did Stewart Menzies,' who knew nothing about espionage, or counter-espionage, 'how did he get to be the head of SIS?'" Leathers replied, "'For one reason. He was a Scotch gentleman who everybody trusted.'"

"That's how you pick a leader," Bayly said. The leader of anything.

"Someone that everyone trusted. The head of a covert material thing is somebody you have to trust. The English would not put a man in charge that wasn't allowed to have his own way, and that everybody would back him. I thought that was an interesting thing. The Americans never found that out. They never found out that was the way to pick the head of something."

Igor Gouzenko

The Soviet defector Igor Gouzenko lived at Camp X for a few years in a farmhouse, but he was handled by the RCMP and Bayly kept out of it. "I had a deal that he didn't know who I was. He probably did, but I never addressed him in any way or gave him any orders. I just simply turned this place over to the RCMP and they ran it."

There was a lot of false information floating around that disguised Gouzenko's whereabouts. On one occasion Bayly and his wife heard on the radio, as they were driving from Oshawa to Camp X, reports that Gouzenko was likely staying somewhere in the Laurentians, north of Montreal. "Everybody was heading there. And here's Gouzenko sitting on a deck chair outside the house, just as we drove up. I thought that was quite amusing. Poor old Gouzenko. He had no more brains than a peanut."

"How did he write that book then?" [Gouzenko's *Fall of a Titan* won the Governor General's award.]

"I think his wife did it. She was quite a girl. It was his wife who advised him what to do. The military attaché at the Soviet embassy got Gouzenko to decode one of his messages because he didn't feel like doing it himself. When Gouzenko decoded it he saw it was instructions for him to be sent back to the Soviet Union, because he wasn't trusted." He'd be bumped off on landing," Bayly said, "the way the Russians were running things in those days." Bayly says Gouzenko then asked his wife for advice. "'What do I do now?' And so she told him, 'Go into the vault and steal every secret thing you can put your hands on, and change the combination on the vault and lock the door. It'll take six weeks for the Russians to send somebody over to chisel the door of the safe open to find out you've taken all these things. Turn yourself over to the Canadians.' So at the time the Canadian Prime Minister, King, said he wasn't going to be mixed up in that kind of Russian politics, and gave strict orders to the RCMP. Norman Robertson, who was the Secretary of External Affairs, told this story to Bill, and what King was doing with this one. So Bill Stephenson headed up to Ottawa, borrowed my Buick from Camp X, and drove it up to Ottawa and arrested Gouzenko, military arrest, and said, 'If you don't want to try him, we'll try him over in England. How would you like that?' King said, 'No, I don't want that,' so they gave this guy protection, and when he went back to his apartment, the Russians were just breaking into his apartment. They had finally got somebody over.

"Norman Robertson was behind it all," Bayly said. "And Bill was protecting Norman Robertson." There was no easy way for Robertson to overrule his boss, the Prime Minister, so he contacted the only person he thought could — Bill Stephenson. "King was his boss, and Norman Robertson could hardly have been the one that turned Gouzenko in. So Bill Stephenson invented a story leaving Norman Robertson out of the thing.

"Bill was up because Norman Robertson tipped him off … he wanted to get around and there wasn't a car available … so he took my Buick from Camp X and pinched Gouzenko. It was quite a thing."[12]

Although Gouzenko was at Camp X for an extended period, and Bayly controlled the camp until 1948, he didn't want to have anything to do with him. "I got out of that as fast as I could, because the Russians were looking all over for Gouzenko, who spent the last two years at Camp X. I didn't want to get mixed up in that one. The Russians, for years afterwards, would have gladly bumped him off."

Beaverbrook & U.S. Security

A visit by Lord Beaverbrook to New York was particularly memorable to Bayly. The Canadian-born British minister knew the transatlantic passage of the Queen Mary had been interrupted by a huge thump. Wanting to know what the ship had hit, Beaverbrook contacted his friend. Stephenson, however, didn't want to deal with any more questions from Beaverbrook, so he sent Bayly over to the Waldorf with instructions not to tell him. The Queen Mary struck a U-boat, Bayly was told, and the Americans were gleaning information from it.

"I almost perspire when you mention U-boat and I think of me spending the afternoon with Beaverbrook and not telling him what the Queen Mary had hit."

A lot of information was obtained from the Nazi submarine and it helped with ENIGMA deciphering. "They couldn't destroy their documents. It was all they could do to save their own lives, and get on deck because the battery acid had spilt and when battery acid and salt water reach together — bang! There was chlorine all over the place and they could just get topside. They just rose suddenly and everyone came above, and they didn't have anything. They couldn't destroy the documents, they couldn't get back down or anything. The U.S. Navy took it to port and blew the chlorine out of it, and found all her papers intact, all the navy ciphers and everything else. That was why it was so secret, because if we had told the Germans that this had happened they would have changed the ciphers before we could have worked some more stuff out."[13]

"Beaverbrook was just curious. He was a newspaper man and also had been very, very busy with the British government. So he just wanted to know, and Bill Stephenson didn't dare tell him. Sicced me on to it. Actually Beaverbrook was quite nice about it. He was a little irritated for a minute, then he kind of grinned and said, 'How are you? I see I've run into something I should keep my mouth shut about.'"

"He was even in the war cabinet."

"Oh yes, he was a very important individual. He didn't suffer fools gladly I can tell you."

"It's strange the way the security works."

"Well, this wasn't our security," Bayly said. "If it had been British security, or any secret in the world, everybody could hand it to him and gold-plate it. But this was U.S. security. We weren't even supposed to know this ourselves. Somebody had broken this to us. You didn't monkey with U.S. security. I mean, if we had blown U.S. security, we'd have been very wrong with everybody."

Bayly dealt with the security of three nations. He was a member of America's OSS, a director of British Security Coordination, SIS, and the head of Canada's Camp X. He even put his own people into Bletchley.

"I was as international as a person can get. I was a Canadian who had done business with FCC in the States, and in the English government at the moment. Because of that I was very lucky, and could do the job because the Canadians didn't resent me and the Americans — I talked with an American accent for all intents and purposes. The only person, as I say, was Stewart Menzies, who said to me one time, 'I just can't understand you; you talk like an American, but think like an Englishman.' But I was lucky in that way that I'd been to an English school, so they would accept me as an English person. We ran a very international [apartment] ... practically a bed-and-breakfast place."

Turing and Welchman

Two frequent guests at Bayly's B&B were his friends Gordon Welchman and Alan Turing, the two men most responsible for solving the Nazi ENIGMA machine. When Welchman came over, Bayly familiarized him with the American organizations. "I introduced him to the Navy and the Army Cryptographic bureaus, [as] they were interested in knowing what he had done with the ENIGMA machine, and how he had done it and that sort of thing, and the bombe, which was their way of breaking ENIGMA. They had several bombes in the Army and the Navy, and Welchman wanted to see their design and compare it to his, et cetera. The Americans had an entirely different mechanism, but doing the same thing, and Welchman wanted to see whether their particular drives were better than his."

When the Churchill-Roosevelt link via telephone scrambler was compromised, Turing was sent to New York to devise a method to fix it. During that time Stephenson's BSC was his home base, and he lived with the Baylys for a number of weeks, while working out a solution at the Bell Labs.

"That was Turing's job. He came over and lived with us for a while and one of his jobs was to redesign that telephone link, so that it was secure. He was able to [fix it]. He spent six months in the Bell Labs, and they tightened up that line so that it was secure. Apparently they knew that the Germans were intercepting it." There was always a voice scrambler on the line, but telephone scramblers were never as secure as enciphered messages. "The trouble with scrambling telephone conversations, is that if you get it right on anything — it suddenly makes sense. You hear a man say 'Yes', and if he says 'yes', that must be right, that part of it. But on a enciphered message and the man says '3-5-2', you don't know that is real, true encipherment or actually '3-5-2.'"

Most scrambled calls are gibberish to the ear but, "the minute you break any part of that gibberish, even if it's just a guess, you can see immediately that you've done something useful. You may only see for a moment that you've done something, but you can recognize that as language. But with encipherment all you get is a bunch of figures and you can't tell if those figures you get are true."

Turing, one of the great minds of the century, was at times a confusing house guest. He stuttered, but apart from that, Bayly thought there were also times when his brain seemed to be working so fast, he couldn't speak at all. Turing would try to talk, but only strange clicking sounds came out. On other occasions Turing cranked himself up to talk and, "he'd put his finger up to his throat and say 'peep peep'. And then you could talk, and he'd wave his fingers and say 'peep peep.' This is the way he taught himself to talk, and we used to just scream with laughter when Turing would be at the dinner table and want to talk, he'd say, 'peep peep' and away he'd go. He was a complete mad man. But he was very brave."

Alan Turing committed suicide in England in 1954. Gordon Welchman eventually moved to the United States after the war and remained involved somewhat in top-secret research and development. He published, in 1982, *The Hut Six Story*, a book about some of the activities he initiated at Bletchley Park and the breaking of the ENIGMA machine. He thought he could publish the book, and checked with what he thought were the proper authorities, but as a result of the publishing of the book he lost his American security clearance and his consulting job with the Mitre Corporation.

"Welchman was a great friend of mine indeed. Welchman's book got him thrown out from Mitre Corporation because he hadn't cleared it. He'd cleared it with the English and hadn't realized he hadn't cleared it in the States. They just cancelled his security. So he couldn't work for the Mitre Corporation." Welchman was hurt financially as a result. "In fact, he died really hard up."

Turing and Welchman, two eminent people — instrumental to the winning of the war — lived in anonymity in England with no financial or employment security. Churchill's wizards were not rewarded.

"I'll explain something else. Turing and Welchman were extremely important, because they had broken the German ENIGMA, and most of our intelligence was coming from the German ENIGMA. It was really important. So he and Turing were highly regarded and very important people. After the war the best thing that Turing could get was an assistant professorship at a third-rate, Birmingham or something, engineering school. [It was Manchester.] Everybody says he committed suicide because he was gay, which as far as I'm concerned, is just so much nonsense. He committed suicide because you couldn't go from being one of the most important people in England to just nothing at all. And Welchman felt the same way."

"Is that why he came to the States?"

"Yeah. And he had quarrelled with the people. They had moved from Bletchley to whatever city it was, and he was quarrelling with people, because he had been their senior, and by this time the ENIGMA was past history, and he wasn't getting on very well. He came over to the States where he had a much more responsible position. And it's a funny thing. If you've been important, it doesn't do you any good psychologically to become unimportant."

Bayly thought Stephenson suffered a similar post-war void.

BSC Security and Planning

"There is one thing I'd like to say. The females of BSC kept their mouths shut better than any group I have known anywhere. They were first class. We never had a breach of security right through the whole blooming war. Men know better. They don't live up to the rules, because they know this won't hurt, or that won't hurt. But the girls, if you told them not to talk about things, they just don't. Which is surprising in the female. But I have the greatest regard for the personnel we had there in New York.

"Almost everybody else did [have a breach of security]: the British Office in Ottawa, the British High Commissioners office had a bad one, the embassy in Washington had a bad one, and I think the embassy, or whatever you called it in New York, had a bad one or at least thought they did. But I was very fortunate; we didn't have anybody. The people who did the recruiting for us in Canada were pretty good.

"There was very little planning at any time. You planned by what happened, rather than deciding this would be the smart way to do it. Something worked easier done today, or something had to be done today, and that became part of the routine. It was the most unplanned thing you ever saw in your life.

"You didn't plan and go down and have elaborate meetings to decide this week we will do this, and do the other, it was just that some need would come up and somebody said, 'Could you do this for us?' and we'd say, 'Well, we'll think it over — let's try it out,' and suddenly it became routine. This applied to both Canada and the States."

Bill Stephenson

"You've cleared up ... something that always puzzled me," Bayly said. "I was the only Canadian, really, of position on his staff. And because of this he trusted me. Bill didn't trust the English. I don't know why. And he would talk about things to me. He'd just be talking out loud for somebody to talk to, if he had something on his mind. But he never ever, if I got on the subject of his early upbringing in Winnipeg, he would close up like a clam. Just change the subject. Obviously didn't want to discuss it at all. I couldn't understand this, because he was so forthcoming in everything else. He would talk about anything, without hesitation. Not Winnipeg. So you've rather solved that one.

"I worked for him for two years before I realized he knew anything about radio at all. The first two years, he thought he'd get on better with me if he pretended he didn't know anything about radio, because that was what I was doing for him. I mentioned it, and he just put it off. Laughed, and we never discussed it again. He was keeping it under his hat so that he could check up on me, if I advanced funny things.

"I trusted Stephenson implicitly. I liked him as a person, and as a boss. There's one thing about a boss. If he backs you your play, and gives you a say, and gives you a fair hearing, he's a good boss. If Bill told me something he didn't like, he'd say 'No, don't do that,' and that would be that. But if he liked it, he'd back you and if you got in trouble he'd still take. I liked him. He was good.

"He'd back you, even if you got in trouble. If you annoyed somebody and stepped on somebody's toes and annoyed people, you'd explain to Bill why, and if he liked it, he'd back you."

Bayly thought Stephenson's major contribution to the war effort was not a specific achievement, but the friendships he created and nurtured with many people across the international spectrum. "The fact that he got along [with people]."

"Bill would always have me over for cocktails. At five o'clock he'd be entertaining these people. So I met everybody from soup to nuts, and you met so many of them.

"You'd meet almost anybody. Bill knew an awful lot of people, especially in the same line as Walter Winchell, because he was using them for propaganda stories and what have you. And Bill entertained lavishly when he entertained those people. You met admirals, generals, heaven knows what ... Not only American, but French, Canadian and British.

"He liked propaganda. And propaganda was really one of the important things he did. He saw to it, before even Pearl Harbor, that the anti-British feeling there was squelched by writers. He got all sorts of people to write things that helped that. And I know. Because I met them at cocktail parties."

Bayly met people like *Time* and *Life* head Henry Luce, Walter Winchell, and playwright and Roosevelt speech writer, Robert Sherwood, at Stephenson's place.

"Winchell was a man who actually got a reputation for being a very straightforward person, and he did a lot of propaganda work for Bill Stephenson. If Bill could sell him on why the U.S. should do this, and if it did that, then Winchell would be your man. He thought very highly of Winchell.

"Robert Sherwood was about six foot four, and I once heard him say after a cocktail, 'If I have another cocktail, I'll just call timber and fall on my face.'... Sherwood would be there all the time. Bill liked Sherwood.

"And as I say, it's amazing how many people, and good people, that he had working for him on that," Bayly said. "And he'd sell them on the idea, that it was a good thing to do. He didn't pay them to do it. It was just a question of ... He was a good salesman."

One person who didn't come to Stephenson's gatherings was Bill Donovan, the head of the OSS. "Because he didn't want the public to know that Bill was educating OSS. It was touchy in those days, because the U.S. until Pearl Harbor was a neutral."

Stephenson worked without a salary, Bayly believes, and contributed some of his personal fortune into the running of the organization. "I'm quite sure that he put some of his own money in here and there, because in those days he was extremely wealthy. And his wife, too.

"On a couple of occasions I wanted to do something, and he said 'The Treasury will raise hell about that, but I'll fix.' That didn't mean that he was actually going to pay for it. But I suspect that's what happened.

"I had for all practical purposes an unlimited expense account. Bill Stephenson fixed that for me, so I never gave detailed expense accounts, I just told them $900-$1000 for a month or something like that, and that was that. Bill Stephenson realized that I couldn't put down expenses for entertaining English people, but I obviously had to do the job. The easiest way was not to account for expenses but just to estimate them."

Stephenson's deputy was told his former boss made a lot of money through his Earls Court investment once the can opener stopped making money. He didn't think Stephenson was made rich through wireless photography, as Montgomery Hyde has written. "Hyde was very impressed with that, but I don't think it made that much. There wasn't much of a market for it, really."

There were many squabbles at the multi-headed Camp X, and Stephenson's financial clout helped smooth out the supervision. When he got irritated at some of the bickering, Stephenson shut the training camp down. SOE were putting up some of the money for the operation of the camp and thought they ran it, Bayly said. "Bill Stephenson just got mad one morning and cancelled the whole thing and said, 'Now you are in charge.' And Cuthbert Skilbeck wasn't going to have that. He said, 'We put up some of the money for this place,' so he went down to New York, and he burst into Stephenson's office and he said, 'This is quite a deal, and I've told Bayly he has to get out,' and Stephenson said, 'Oh, you did?' And he said, 'Well, just wait a minute.' He phoned me downstairs, and I came upstairs and he said, 'Cuthbert Skilbeck, I'd like to introduce you to your boss.'" Bayly smiled. "And this is me.

"Bill was putting up a lot of the money for these things. I never did find out how much. But he never had to worry about Treasury. He could tell them to go jump in the lake, and they would jump. So I figured that Bill was financing a lot of that deal."

Following the war it was imperative the Communications Centre at Camp X was kept in operation, but it was uncertain who would be paying for it. Bayly was actually in charge of the remains of BSC, but he had no money. "When I took over, because he had closed up the BSC, I took over because I had to go on running the radio station for a while, to live up to some of our obligations in Canada and the States. So Bill guaranteed the expenses. I found that I'd taken over a payroll of $5,000 and I had about $2 in the bank. I had to tell Bill, and he said, 'Well, that's okay,' and he sent the money up."

Bayly felt no one knew exactly what Stephenson's link was to espionage before his New York posting. "I don't think the British had any idea of what his connection had been with that, in the past, because ... MI6 was in a great deal of trouble with the British Government for many years before World War II. Just in the same way that the CIA is in trouble with the politicians who just don't like having it around. It embarrasses them to have it around and it embarrasses them to think that their country is doing things that are covert. Therefore they must be wrong, or they would tell Parliament about it. I think the same thing existed to a certain extent in England."

Stephenson's relationship with SIS was "perfect," Bayly said. "Stewart Menzies and he got along very well. I think there was a little jealousy, because I have a suspicion that somebody else, probably Churchill, saw to it that Bill Stephenson took the job. I have a feeling he was sort of wished on Stewart Menzies. But I never heard Stewart Menzies give him anything but praise, and on a couple of occasions, when I had a fight on my hands in England, I called up Bill Stephenson on the cable, and I'd tell him to put in a word, and it always worked. When he said something ought to happen, it happened. He really had a lot of power."

"Why, do you think?"

"He knew an awful lot of interesting people ... at his house you'd meet any number of people you didn't expect to meet in such a place. He was liked by people, and they had an immense regard for his influence. On top of that, I expect he was very rich."

Bayly chose a quote from a John Pearson biography of Ian Fleming and read it aloud. For Fleming, "'Stephenson was almost everything a hero should be. He was very tough. He was very rich. He was single-minded. Patriotic, and a man of few words.'[14] That, in spite of the fact I don't believe in Fleming one inch, is a very good description of Stephenson.

"Very tough. Very rich. Single-minded, patriotic, and a man of few words. That's what I think of him. Yeah. That's how I'd sum him up."

Toward the end of the war Stephenson wanted Bayly to document the evolution of BSC's Communications division. Bayly didn't think he should. "I got in very wrong with Bill Stephenson, because he wanted me to write up my division of the thing, Communications, and I wasn't having any [of that]. Because I had been treated extremely well by Canada, the States and England — far beyond what was necessary. I was welcomed into places where it was absolutely necessary that I be, and everybody's been very kind. And doing so, we'd go out and have a couple of drinks and they'd tell me political things that really shouldn't be free, and they were really quite outspoken and I came to the conclusion at the end of the war that the best thing I could do was shut up. Because if I did, if I spoke all the things I would unwittingly mention, things that would have political ..."

He gave an example of his preferential treatment. In BSC's office they had an American stamp from the U.S. War Production Board which could print "high priority" on BSC's orders. Bayly often met with the American head of the board. "I was asking for directives, and 'high priority' for things, and he would give them to us. He said to me one day, 'Look. I ordered two of these darn stamps' that stamp priorities in coloured ink — stamp it right over the document so you can't forge it. He said, 'Here. You "store" this. If we want it back, if this one gets destroyed, bring it back. But you just "store" it, and you just stamp any damn priority you want on your stuff.' That's what we did."

BSC's purchasing department was covert, and it didn't go through the English. "We had a purchasing department there that bought everything we needed, and was supposed to be secret, and didn't go through the British Supply Commission. So this was a harmless enough thing, because we were buying so little in comparison, that the War Production Board didn't give a hoot what priorities were put on the thing. But that sort of thing, if you told about it, might still cause a lot of political trouble. They'd say, 'That guy had no business giving out that.' Now that's just one example of the sort of silly thing that you can talk about. So I just decided that I wouldn't write a book. Most of the books that got written irritated me, because they were incorrect."

Subsequently Bayly was not involved in the compilation of the BSC history at Camp X at the end of the war. "Tom Hill I knew very slightly, because he was concerned with the "Bible," as it was called, and I wasn't. I didn't have any part of it, or want any part of it. And I arranged it with the people in England that I not be cleared for publication in any of those. Nobody could write histories of my section officially, without going to England and getting their permission specifically."

He said Gordon Welchman was not aware of this arrangement and that was why Bayly's name appeared in the *Hut Six Story*. There is a communications section in the BSC history, but Bayly couldn't vouch for its accuracy as he submitted nothing to it.

"No. No, I had nothing to do with it. I didn't approve of it, like it, and didn't want to be part of it. I didn't want to be mentioned in it. Bill Stephenson believed in propaganda. If you didn't talk about things, then nobody was going to, so it should be talked about. And he used it with a fair amount of discretion. But I have a feeling that the powers that be must have screamed blue murder knowing that volume exists."

Bayly thought Hyde's *The Quiet Canadian* book was accurate. "There were some exaggerations in there ... but in the main, not exaggerating seriously. Bill believed in propaganda. He wasn't one who wouldn't advertise, although he was very closed mouthed. He saw that the right people knew the right things." Bayly did not think Stevenson's books were accurate. The "Intrepid" books left him, "colder than learning to ride a horse at 40 below at Fort Osborne." He thought David Stafford's *Camp X*, "made an attempt at accuracy, writing under difficult situations. He made several mistakes or omissions, but I think pardonable under the conditions." One major mistake in the book was the date the Camp opened, as "it was in full operation before Pearl Harbor."

Activity at Camp X continued long after BSC New York shut down. "What happened was BSC quit. We closed up for all intents and purposes. And Camp X was still actively sending communications, because we were still intercepting a lot of material that was going through there and rather than set up commercial channels I just kept on handling it."

"From who? From the Russians?"

"From all over. Just anything that we wanted to intercept."

"Just spying on everybody?"

"Well, you had to, for a very good reason. The top people, in other words, if the Germans were talking to someone they liked, they used very high-grade ciphers. In fact they used my encipherment, the Rockex."

"After the war?"

"Yes. Japan was still going, but the European thing had folded. Some of the original messages would be unbreakable, but if the original message was sent to other locations, it was usually sent in a less secure cipher. So the way you could break the original message was to wait until the people who received the high-grade message passed it on to the next one, and then you knew from the serial number and the ratings and so on what the original message was. So we were intercepting stuff from all over the place, and my communication network had three radio channels at Camp X, and we had two leased cables across the Atlantic and were running about a million and a half words a day."

"You sent it to SIS?"

"Yeah. Or the cryptographic bureau there, or whatever bureau we were running. Canada and the States had two big bureaus and a third smaller one and our job was simply to distribute this material to whoever could use it. What they were currently interested in, and what they could break. So that was highly specialized."

"So do they still do that, I wonder?"

"Yeah. Canada took over Camp X."

Following the war Bayly was asked by the British government to stay involved with covert communications on a development contract. He convinced a number of Canadian engineers to quit their jobs and work with him on the five-year deal. Bayly's task was to transform the success of the Rockex into a coding machine not just between two people, but for portable multiple use. However the whims of Britain's government changed, and the agreement was terminated.

Although it was a multi-year agreement, it was abruptly cancelled at the end of one year. Bayly was dismissed with five days' notice. "It ran for five more years, and the Labour Party got in and said, 'Sue us if you like, but you're finished as of next week.' They got into some sort of a cook-up or other, and I found myself facing a government that hadn't hired me, and didn't want to hire me and weren't willing to. It was a very dirty deal. But I wasn't in a position to argue with them." The unbreakable machine for multiple use was never completed. "It still isn't done. Nobody else has [done one] either. It was going to be a horrible machine to use. It had 21 rotating cylinders."

Finding work wasn't a problem for Bayly after the cancellation — he was still a professor at the University of Toronto — but he was concerned about all the people he had hired. "I had persuaded a whole lot of people to stay and work for me, who had finished their war leave of absence. They couldn't go back to their jobs, and that's why I formed Bayly Engineering. Because I had to employ these guys."

Bayly Engineering worked on numerous electrical and mechanical devices, many of them top-secret. "Just anything we could get our hands on." The company started out in Oshawa, and then moved to Ajax.

One man Bayly eventually hired previously worked for Germany during the war. He hid nothing, and he told Bayly what he had been doing. He said, "'I've been doing counter-espionage work in Germany, and I've heard that you would know about this sort of thing,'" Bayly remembered. "And he said, 'I'd love a job. I'm a good maintenance man, and good with electrical equipment.'" Bayly hired him. Afterwards the new employee started to tell Bayly about a few things he worked on during the war. He mentioned sonobuoys, and Bayly said 'We get them in here for repair. You'd better do those.'

The sonobuoys were microphones attached to a radio beacon, which were dropped into the ocean and used to detect U-boats. The U-boats were rather noisy underwater and if a trio of sonobuoys were dropped in a triangle around a sub, the engine noise would be louder in one than the others. The buoys beamed the sounds up by radio to passing aircraft. "German subs were noisy, and we didn't want them to care whether they were noisy or not," Bayly said. "So the sonobuoys were still pretty top-secret, even after the war was over." But his new employee knew all about them. The Germans had recovered them early on and taken them apart. "He got the first one the Germans had, and recovered the circuit, and had redrawn it and all the rest of it." Canadian security officials arrived at Bayly Engineering one day and said the German couldn't work on the top-secret buoys. However, the new employee stressed, 'I knew about these things before you people did,' Bayly remembered, "and he was quite right." The security officials eventually backed off.

Bayly left the University of Toronto in 1951, as Bayly Engineering was doing well and was taking more and more of his time. It expanded in an abandoned Shell plant in Ajax, near Toronto. He lived in Montreal for a time doing contract work, but made the Ajax area his home base. Bayly Engineering was the largest business enterprise in the district and he began to get involved in municipal affairs. Eventually the locals decided to incorporate into a new town. Pat Bayly was elected the first mayor of Ajax, Ontario. Later he sold the company and retired to southern California.

Bayly felt some of his contemporaries were not nearly as fortunate as he was following the war, and he frequently referred back to them.

"Poor old Turing had been one of the most important people during the war. This is a tough thing, psychologically. He and Welchman had been extremely important people during the war. They had broken the ENIGMA machine and everybody thought highly of them, and they were working their fool heads off. And when the war was over, Turing could only get an assistant prof's job at a second-rate university. And it really hurt."

"Why was that?"

"His mathematical genius applied to one job that they weren't interested in. The same thing happened to one of the top men in the U.S. bureau."

"Not Friedman?"

"No. Billy Friedman was a good friend of mine. But he ended up all right. This guy was in the Navy, and he had been the Dean of Mathematics in a very good university, and when the war was over he just couldn't find a job that pleased him at all. He just went downhill right and centre.

"Tension. It [war work] is tension. A flap occurred every ten minutes. I can't think of anything more nerve-racking than that sort of job. And when you work at that for years, and then you go back, and go to a faculty meeting, and somebody spends an hour deciding whether you put in a 'semicolon' or a 'comma' there. It gets you down."

From the government of Britain, Bayly received five days' notice before being fired, and at approximately the same time, the Order of the British Empire [OBE]. He received the OBE in 1946. Press reports said he was "of an organization working with the Foreign Office," who was awarded the OBE, "for reasons unspecified." He didn't think much of the honour, and never used the designation.

The American government wanted to award Bayly with a medal, but were told by British officialdom that they couldn't. "Colonial officers" could not receive foreign decorations, the Americans were told. When U.S. officials wondered what else they could do for him, Bayly said he would like to become a fellow in the Institute of Electrical Engineers. He received a fellowship shortly after the war. It was presented by Herbert W. Armstrong, often considered the inventor of radio.

From Canada, his own country, Bayly received no recognition or form of thanks whatsoever. In 1989, the University of Toronto contacted him about appearing at an alumni function, but he couldn't attend for health reasons and heard nothing more about it. But in the spring of 1991, Bayly received a plaque in the mail, completely out of the blue, from his alma mater. It reads:

Membership in the Hall of Distinction is accorded to Benjamin Deforest Pat Bayly, Class of 1930, Electrical Engineering

His useful radio hobby helped co-found a Moose Jaw station, and led to phenomenal communications feats during World War Two. From Law, University of Saskatchewan, 1923, he came to U. of T. and such was his expertise that in his third year he lectured to the fourth year. He was on the staff until 1951 with war leave. In 1941 under the close association of the British Director of Security Coordination, Sir William Stephenson, he became assistant director with the British army rank of Lieutenant Colonel. He set up communications centre HYDRA at secret agent Camp X near Oshawa and designed special equipment to link New York, Washington, Ottawa and Britain. To handle confidential traffic he invented the cipher machine Rockex now used worldwide for diplomatic communication, and his activity influenced Canada's radar development. Acknowledgment came through the award of OBE '46 and fellowship in the institute of radio engineers '47. Bayly Engineering Limited established [in] 1946 in Oshawa, moved to Ajax in '48 where his municipal leadership led to incorporation, with him as first mayor, 1955.

It was dated 1989 and signed by the president of the university, the dean of the faculty and the president of the alumni association.

"They'd done a lot of research," Bayly said about the award. But there was not even a cover letter with it, and he received it in the mail two years after it was dated. He had no idea who was behind the plaque, or why it was sent. Bayly wrote to the university, thanking whoever was responsible, but he received no response, acknowledgment, or further details. He concluded someone may have found it in a closet somewhere, and decided to send it down.

Bayly Engineering, now Bayly Communications Incorporated (BCI), is still in Ajax, Ontario, designing and manufacturing, according to a company release, "state-of-the-art digital multiplex equipment for access to voice and data transmission services." One of the main thoroughfares passing through Ajax and adjoining Pickering, Ontario, is Bayly Street. It's likely few citizens of those communities know the many reasons why.

Final Words
While visiting Grace Garner at her home outside London, she pulled a red-covered book out of her bookcase. "This book was written a long time ago, but a lot of what's in it still relates today," she said. "You should read it." It was from 1942.

"... for we are of two worlds, the Old and the New, one foot in each, knowing England, knowing America, joined to each by blood and battle, speech and song. We alone are the hinge between them, and upon us hangs more than we know."
— Bruce Hutchison, *The Unknown Country*

The end of any journey is a period of reflection, and so too the completion of this book. It is difficult to conclude a book that encompasses so many separate threads. The course of research that began with biographic intentions became more of a compilation of information, that intruded and strayed. Discovery lead to more questions. Although this author obviously has opinions on subjects raised, and the course of events, it would be presumptuous to point fingers or attempt answers. I have tried to step away from the material and will continue to do so here.

The bulk of this material was roughed together at the end of 1996. As this is being written, March 1998, somewhat negative stories about Bill Stephenson, based on previous books, still appear in British newspapers.[1] Some recent histories now refer to what the British were doing to sway the United States from neutrality.[2] I believe this research shows it was truly a multi-national Allied effort with a lot of independence from London. Also BSC's success could not be accomplished without the help and benevolence of many Americans such as Franklin Roosevelt, Robert Sherwood, Bill Donovan, and J. Edgar Hoover.

When this research began, and it was discovered Stephenson's biographical information was incorrect, this writer seriously questioned whether BSC ever existed, or was some sort of strange, exaggerated, propaganda balloon. It existed. Also the rapid transition of William Stephenson, can opener salesman, to William Stephenson, "brilliant scientist" seemed an unplausible leap. For a time, on one trip to England, newspaper death listings of "William Stephensons" were checked with address indexes, to see whether he had somehow died and someone else had assumed his identity. (This presented a rather unlikely scenario of a potential biographer — trying to decide if his subject had actually died sixty years earlier than he thought.) Eventually Stephenson's relatives, friends, various newspaper clippings, and pictures of him in England supplied by Margaret Jamieson of Winnipeg, proved it was the same person.

Winston Churchill titled his last book on the war *Triumph and Tragedy*. Perhaps an appropriate title for this volume would be *Triumph and Anonymity*. British Security Coordination, and individuals such as Stephenson, Bayly, Turing and Welchman secretly accomplished much and then disappeared further. This was part of the profession I was told: "We don't acknowledge anything." There are no bugles for spies. I think a more appropriate response is that of former SOE Chief Colin Gubbins when he was told a book was being done on Stephenson, "honour where honour is done." It seems we have been poor caretakers of history when heroes of humanity's greatest tragedy are neglected and forgotten. Certainly these were lives of triumph that could be celebrated. Yet Bayly, the only one of the above people I met, seemed unaffected. It is easy to pass off anonymity, but when it looks you in the face, it can be a bit unsettling. (For example, Bayly didn't mention his role in the Allies U-boats success until I raised the subject.)[3] Here truly was a man of accomplishment without ego. Perhaps he was what ancient Chinese texts describe as a "man of calling," and his career could be summed up not by the *Art of War*, but a passage of the *I Ching*:

"If a man is free of vanity he is able to conceal his abilities and keep them from attracting attention too soon; thus he can mature undisturbed. If conditions demand it, he can also enter public life, but that too he does with restraint. The wise man gladly leaves fame to others. He does not seek to have credited to himself things that stand accomplished, but hopes to release active forces; that is, he completes his works in such a manner that they may bear fruit for the future."[4]

What of William Stephenson? The true "Intrepid"? A definitive story of Stephenson is unlikely, but perhaps this book is at least a step in the right direction. Marion de Chastelain, when asked to sum up her war experience stressed Bill Stephenson was the only person who could have accomplished what he did, when he did. Pat Bayly thought his former boss's greatest contribution was that he got along with people. With the help of many, anything was possible. In 1989, a California-based journalist lamented about the life and death of Stephenson. "Were it not for William Stephenson, there might not be a Western world today. And yet when he passed away, there was little tribute paid to him. Untold thousands, perhaps millions, owe their lives to Stephenson. He is a genuine hero in an age largely without heroes."

K. L. Billingsley's commentary fretted whether there were any "Intrepids" left.[5] It's hard to imagine anything much more unlikely than the story of this unsuccessful can opener salesman, born to a family so poor he was given away. Today, would even Stephenson be able to rise from such a circumstance?

In retrospect, it seems for Stephenson World War I became somewhat of an equalizer. He left his insular preoccupations and he travelled. His medals and bravery in battle helped grant him, almost immediately, a certain status. World War II enhanced it. For a world hopefully without war, perhaps Stephenson himself had an appropriate vision:

"What seems poignantly evident to me is that humankind already has awesome enemies to engage — poverty, disease and ignorance for example — and in such common cause there is reward and glory enough for all."[6]

The Windsor Letters

In 1987, a former MI5 officer broke his code of silence, and published a book dealing with his exploits with the service. The British government tried, in vain, to ban the book's publication. Peter Wright called his book *Spycatcher*.

When Wright was with section D-3, the known Soviet agent Anthony Blunt became his responsibility. Before he met Blunt, Wright had to attend a briefing with Michael Adeane, the Queen's Private Secretary at Buckingham palace, as Blunt had been employed as the Queen's Surveyor of Pictures.

"The Queen," Adeane told him, "has been fully informed about Sir Anthony, and is quite content for him to be dealt with in any way that gets at the truth."

But Wright remembered there was one caveat. "From time to time," said Adeane, "you may find Blunt referring to an assignment he undertook on behalf of the Palace — a visit to Germany at the end of the war. Please do not pursue the matter. Strictly speaking, it is not relevant to considerations of national security."

Wright says he spent hundreds of hours with Blunt but never learned about his secret mission to Germany. "But then," he concluded, "the Palace had several centuries to learn the difficult art of scandal burying. MI5 have only been in business since 1909!"[1]

Wright's statement in 1987 was one of the first confirmations from an MI5 source that Blunt spent the last months of his wartime service on a highly secret personal mission for the Royal Palace. The story that Blunt had been sent by King George VI after the war to recover incriminating letters between the former King (the Duke of Windsor) and Nazi leaders had been circulating for years. The Duke and his wife travelled to meet Hitler in October 1937, and he was widely considered to be sympathetic to the Nazi cause. "Secret papers have disclosed his pro-Nazi perfidy which, of course, I was perfectly aware at the time," Noel Coward recorded in his diary in 1962. "Poor dear, what a monumental ass he has always been."[2]

"Blunt was emissary for King George VI" the *London Sunday Times* reported on the front page, November 25, 1979, soon after Blunt was outed as a Soviet agent. According to the *Times*, Blunt travelled to Schloss Kronberg Hessen, a Hesse family castle near Frankfurt, with Owen Morshead, the then librarian of Windsor Castle. King George thought Prince Phillip of Hess was an intermediary, through the Duke of Kent, between the Duke of Windsor and Hitler, and the family kept the related papers in his palace, which was taken over by the American military. According to the paper, Blunt and Morshead met with members of the Hesse family after the war in a nearby village, and then proceeded to retrieve the archive, but the American officer in charge of the castle refused to release the documents to them. However, the two persisted and covertly smuggled out the papers into a truck, and off to Windsor Castle. Blunt, a distant cousin of the Queen, was hired by the Royal family in 1945, and knighted in 1956. Morshead was knighted in 1958. Strangely, Blunt had been suspected of being a Soviet agent as early as 1951, and by 1964 he had confessed. The Soviet agent did quite well after confessing. (For example, he fared much better than Dick Ellis, who lost his intelligence job at about the same time, soon after he tried to publicize the career of William Stephenson.) Not only was Blunt never prosecuted — he continued his position with the Palace. He wasn't stripped of his knighthood until 1979, when he was publicly exposed as a Soviet agent through the work of journalists.[3]

Blunt's escapades in Europe seem to be confirmed in the diary of Sir Alexander Cadogan. "King fussed about Duke of Windsor file in captured German documents. Promised to look into it," he wrote October

25, 1945.[4] Highly regarded British espionage historian Christopher Andrew also seems to think the story of Anthony Blunt carries a bit of establishment baggage. When questioned about Blunt, the name didn't immediately equate "treason" or "treachery," but Whitehall and "ancient secrets."[5]

According to the *Times* story, sections of recovered Nazi files dealing with Windsor had a habit of disappearing. One part of the Berlin file dealing with Windsor was removed "by higher ups," and later returned. About 400 tons of documents were transferred to Britain and examined at Whaddon Hall, near Bletchley. Donald Watt, later a professor at the London School of Economics, said sections of the Windsor file appeared to be missing and he doubted they had seen all the material. "Of course it is quite possible the Windsor material had been sifted before it reached Whaddon Hall," Watt was quoted as saying. "The royal archivists have proper historians to advise them these days but at that time they were very secretive."[6]

The *Times* article also mentions the ubiquitous Hugh Trevor-Roper. He was unaware of the Windsor files in connection to Blunt, but he knew of the Soviet agent's trip. Blunt's assignment, according to Trevor-Roper, was to retrieve letters Queen Victoria sent to her daughter Vicky, who had married Frederick III of Prussia in 1858, and became the mother of Kaiser Wilhelm II.[7] Trevor-Roper's version of events was echoed in the official biography of the Duke eleven years later.[8] Edward's authorized biographer calls the Windsor file stories, "legend," "picturesque," and "fantasies." But, Philip Ziegler concludes, "Lack of evidence rarely inhibits the more venturesome biographers."[9]

How did the noted historian Trevor-Roper become an expert on the travels of Anthony Blunt? According to the journalist John Costello, Trevor-Roper told a Sunday *Times* reporter he simply ran into Blunt at MI5 St. James headquarters, while he was reporting to Guy Lidell on his mission,[10] which seems to contradict "need-to-know."

There is another version as to how Trevor-Roper became aware of Blunt's mission. According to the British writer Anthony Cave Brown, Trevor-Roper accompanied Blunt on one of his reconnaissance trips to the continent. He was apparently seconded in 1945 by Dick White to his counter-intelligence group at SHAEF and his familiarity with captured German records enabled him to write *The Last Days of Hitler*. "There were rumours that actual correspondence between Windsor and

Hitler were recovered by Professor Trevor-Roper and Anthony Blunt, the Queen's picture master and that Kim Philby was the case officer for the operation."[11] Brown also maintains similar stories assert that Philby's and Blunt's knowledge of the letters, their recovery, and their contents gave both men a degree of power over "C," the palace, and the British government, when it seemed they were about to be exposed. Brown seems to conclude the secrecy on the issue and possible treason was unavoidable. "If the entire matter of the Windsor letters appears medieval in its mystery, it must be remembered that no British government, Socialist or Conservative, would like to find itself required to provide evidence for a hanging charge against a royal prince who had once been King of England."[12]

Ironically, if Trevor-Roper and Blunt were partners on a shadowy trip to Europe after the war, their fortunes went in completely opposite directions at the same time. In November 1979, Hugh Trevor-Roper was heralded into Britain's House of Lords — as Lord Dacre of Glanton. Days later, Prime Minister Margaret Thatcher announced in the House of Commons that the Queen's Surveyor of Pictures Sir Anthony Blunt was a Soviet agent. In December 1979, Trevor-Roper was appointed master of Peterhouse at Cambridge which freed him from his professorial duties at Oxford.[13]

"The Electrolux Man"

The Electrolux man was Swedish industrialist Axel Wenner Gren (1881–1961). He formed Electrolux in 1921 to manufacture vacuum cleaners. Shortly afterwards he obtained plans, for $500,000, for the electric refrigerator. He was quite successful with these two business ventures. By 1938 he was one of the wealthiest men in the world, and he plied the world's waterways on his large yacht, *Southern Cross*. He had large land holdings around the world, including the Bahamas. The *Southern Cross* transported the Duke and Duchess of Windsor to the United States in December of 1940.

In 1935, Wenner Gren bought up a large part of Bofors Munitions from German interests, and he was known to have had close ties to Nazi Germany. "If there should happen to be a stalemate and a negotiated peace, I might be of great use. I have good standing in Germany," he was quoted as saying during the war. In 1941, he visited Rio de Janeiro as part of a Swedish-German consortium and attempted to buy up rich iron ore deposits in a rural state of Brazil.[14] This plan was thwarted through a move of the U.S. Export-Import bank.

Shortly afterwards he moved to Mexico, dealt in various investment enterprises and tried to interest his friend, the pro-Nazi General Maximino Camacho, the brother of the Mexican president, in a program of road building. He also became involved with a Mexican telephone company. He parked the *Southern Cross* in Mexico, gave it Mexican registry, and let the Mexican government use it. "If I took it out, people would say I was fuelling U-boats," he said.

In January 1941, Sumner Welles sent a confidential memo to the U.S. State Department that said, "The most recent information I have regarding Mr. Wenner Gren indicated that he is in constant and close touch with the Duke of Windsor," and Wenner Gren was "anxious to participate in an American consortium planning the investment of a considerable amount of capital in Mexico."[15]

In January 1942, Wenner Gren was put onto a U.S. government blacklist of people who were doing business with Nazi countries. A short time before this, Chrysler Corporation obtained licenses for the famous Bofors anti-aircraft gun and began mass production.

In March 1941, about a dozen Mexicans, including Camacho, visited the Duke of Windsor in the Bahamas. The Mexicans were escorted to the Governor's mansion by multimillionaire Harry Oakes, a former prospector who made a fortune in Canada's gold industry. Oakes moved to the islands in 1935, and he was killed in July 1943, the victim of an unsolved murder. When the Mexicans visited the Duke, he had a visitor.

Alfred de Marigny, Oakes' son-in-law, who was charged and acquitted of murdering him, points out the first indications of surreptitious dealings between Mexico, Oakes and Windsor came from "the famous British spy, H. Montgomery Hyde, who served on the staff of Sir William Stephenson ... A Man Called Intrepid."[16] Hyde was visiting the Duke to discuss the security of the Bahamas at the time, and theorized the Wenner Gren conference involved a scheme where the Nazis and others could launder foreign money through Mexican banks. This was "highly irregular" for the Duke, Hyde says, as Mexico had recently broken off diplomatic relations with Britain and expropriated all British oil companies without offering compensation.[17]

Rudolf Hess

At the time of his arrival in Scotland, Rudolf Hess was a deputy leader of the Nazi party. He took part in the Munich uprising in 1923, and shared imprisonment with Adolf Hitler. It has been reported that Hitler dictated *Mein Kampf* to Hess.

In May of 1941, Hess flew solo in a small plane to Britain on a mysterious peace mission. His arrival prompted Churchill's comment, "The maggot is in the apple." Hess asked to meet with the Duke of Hamilton, but he was essentially kept under wraps, imprisoned, and eventually received a life sentence at Nuremberg in 1946. He died in 1987 of an apparent suicide, the only remaining prisoner of Spandau prison in Berlin.

About a month after Hess's flight, the Nazis attacked the Soviet Union. The entire quixotic sequence of events has inspired numerous conspiracy theorists. Hess's sortie also concerned many of the principals of the time.

Before visiting the Soviet Union, Lord Beaverbrook was one of the few who met with Hess following his imprisonment. When the Canadian born British minister met with Stalin, the Soviet leader wondered what to make of Hess's flight. He asked Beaverbrook if Britain was going to make peace with Germany, as he considered Hess a possible line of communication. If the British were not dealing with the Nazis, he wondered, why wasn't Hess shot? Beaverbrook told him that Britain didn't shoot people without a trial. Stalin asked why Hess came to England and Beaverbrook said, "To persuade Britain to join Germany in making an attack on Russia."[18]

One of the chroniclers of Hess's career noted Hess's secret mission astonished the British, bewildered the Americans, horrified the Germans, and struck fear in the Russians. Apparently Washington was left in the dark. "Puzzled at the time by Churchill's silence, FDR remarked to an aide: "I wonder what is *really* behind this story," and continued to believe that there remained in Britain a small but potentially powerful minority who wanted peace conversations and were in fact having them."[19]

This may have been close to the truth. The disgraced former King Edward VIII and his wife Wallis Simpson dined twice at the home of Rudolf Hess during the thirties. According to Hess' son, Wolf-Rudiger Hess, they discussed the prospects of a "new world order," with Edward returned triumphantly to the British throne.[20]

Hess also appears in *Eclipse*, a book of fiction following the "Intrepid" sagas by William Stevenson. One premise of the book is when Hess arrived in Britain he wasn't alone. It also supposes that aerial photographs during the war revealed the Nazi extermination camps, but they were not bombed. One character in the novel concludes, "the truth about Hess" was "that he negotiated with both the British and Soviets to let Hitler have his Jews."[21]

Edward VIII

Sun Tze's: The Use of Spies

10. Having INWARD SPIES, making use of officials of the enemy.

11. Tu Mu enumerates the following classes as likely to do good service in this respect: *"Worthy men who have been degraded from office, criminals who have undergone punishment; also, favourite concubines who are greedy for gold, men who are aggrieved at being in subordinate positions, or who have been passed over in the distribution of posts, others who are anxious that their side should be defeated in order that they may have a chance of displaying their ability and talents, fickle turncoats who always want to have a foot in each boat. Officials of these several kinds,"* he continues, *"should be secretly approached and bound to one's interests by means of rich presents. In this way you will be able to find out the state of affairs in the enemy's country, ascertain the plans that are being formed against you, and moreover disturb the harmony and create a breach between the sovereign and his ministers.*

The love story of King Edward VIII and Wallis Simpson, the twice-divorced American, is one of the most publicized relationships of the century. Less well documented is the former King and his partner's role leading up to, and during the World War II. The couple, in the words of one writer, have been misplaced by society, or history.[22]

The possibly treasonous activities of the former English king likely influenced William Stephenson's endeavours in the late 1930s. His 1940 "exile" from Europe, as Governor in the Bahamas, brought him directly under Stephenson's security umbrella.

Following the war, the Duke penned his memoirs but they end with his abdication in 1936, and don't detail his activities afterwards.

The Duchess of Windsor's tale is a bit more forthright and in subsequent years more and more information has emerged about the couple's later activities. Soon after resigning the British throne for the woman he loved, Edward and Wallis married at the French home of Charles Bedaux, a known Nazi sympathizer. Bedaux, who later committed suicide after being arrested as a Nazi collaborator, helped arrange a visit for the newlyweds with Adolf Hitler. The Royal couple met with Rudolf Hess and Hitler at Berchtesgaden. When Britain declared war on the Nazis, the Windsors were relaxing by a pool in the South of France. According to the Duchess, a servant appeared to tell the Duke the British ambassador was on the phone from Paris. The Duke then reported to his wife: "'Great Britain has just declared war on Germany, and I'm afraid in the end this may open the way for world communism." Then there was a splash; he had dived into the pool."[23]

Later the Duke took a military posting on the continent and met with French and English troops in France and Belgium. His personal position was "delicate and difficult," the Duchess wrote, as he was a former monarch with a subordinate rank. Windsor visited the Belgian front and met his brother, the Duke of Gloucester, there. When some British troops presented arms, Windsor took a salute meant for his higher-ranking brother. Windsor was later "coldly notified" that he violated military etiquette. This was particularly "galling" to him as he always had a gift for dealing with troops, his wife reported. Surprisingly, in the same paragraph, she equates their perceived status problems with World War II. The couple "had two wars to deal with — the big and still leisurely war, in which everyone was caught up, and the little cold war with the Palace, in which no quarter was given."[24]

The "leisurely war" eventually forced the Duchess to move south from Paris, to the coast near Spain. When she moved to Biarritz her hotel and room number were reported on German radio, which she describes in her book as an unchivalrous trick, "suggesting that Fifth Columnists were everywhere." This didn't deter her husband however, who gave her war updates from Paris. "Edward phoned every day. Through his guarded language I was made to realize that Paris was almost certainly doomed."[25]

Windsor left Paris and the couple ended up in Spain. In Madrid the couple were looked after by the British Ambassador Samuel Hoare. The well-known appeaser and friend of the Duke was not popular with the new Churchill government. The Under Secretary of Foreign Office Alexander Cadogan's diary for Sunday, May 12, 1940, reported, "S. Hoare now to go to Madrid! I suppose they want him safely out of the country!" Hoare moved to a post as Spanish ambassador in Madrid, and he arranged accommodation for the Windsors at the Ritz Hotel. "The slippery British ambassador conveniently suspended all activities of the Secret Service in the Spanish capital for the duration of the Windsors visit. They were thus free of surveillance."[26] The Windsors continued to meet with many pro-Nazi people at the Ritz. One Spanish general was full of information on German military might, Wallis wrote later. Another woman "completely disconcerted Edward and me by rendering the fascist salute."[27] British intelligence picked up information that the Windsors were to be kidnapped by the Nazis and reinstalled on the throne following the invasion of Britain. Churchill ordered the royal duo to return to England, but the couple refused. The Prime Minister became increasingly agitated and pointed out in one cable, "Already there is a great deal of doubt as to the circumstances in which Your Royal Highness left Paris."[28] The Duke was serving in the military at the time, and in most democracies he would have been court-martialed for desertion.[29]

It was then decided that the Windsors could go to the Bahamas where he would become the Governor. The couple moved to Lisbon and prepared to leave the continent. On July 22, 1940, it was reported a secret message was sent to the German minister Joachim Ribbentrop from London saying the Duke was urging King George VI to appoint a new pro-Hitler appeasement cabinet that would replace Churchill. Amongst those involved would be Lloyd George, Lord Halifax, Sir John Simon, and Sir Samuel Hoare.[30] There is also strong evidence that Windsor was more than an appeaser. In a July 11, 1940, cable to Berlin, the German ambassador to Portugal, Oswald Baron von Hoyningen-Huene wrote that, "The designation of the Duke as Governor of the Bahamas is intended to keep him far away from England, since his return would bring with it strong encouragement to English friends of peace, so that his arrest at the insistence of his opponents would certainly have to be expected. [The Duke] is convinced that if he had remained on the throne, war would have been avoided, and he characterizes himself as a firm supporter of a peaceful arrangement with Germany. The Duke believes that the continued severe bombings would make England ready for peace."[31] The author Charles Higham has pointed out not long after the telegram was received in Berlin, some of the heaviest bombing of England began.[32]

Eventually the Windsors agreed to leave Europe, but the duo reportedly planned on going to the United States, not the Bahamas. On July 20, 1940, the U.S. ambassador to Portugal, Herbert Pell, cabled Cordell Hull in Washington that the "Duke and Duchess of Windsor are indiscreet and outspoken against British government. Consider their presence in United States might be disturbing and confusing. They say that they intend remaining in the United States whether Churchill likes it or not, and desire apparently to make propaganda for peace." He suggested cancelling their visas.[33]

To compound the problem Britain's ambassador to the United States, Lord Lothian, was lobbying President Roosevelt to permit a visit from the Windsors. When the royal couple finally arrived in the Bahamas, they wanted to head to the U.S.A. Lord Lloyd sent a note to then Foreign Secretary Halifax that complained "I have just got the Duke, as I thought, clamped down securely in the Bahamas for awhile, and now Lord Lothian is stirring up the waters again."[34] Lothian died suddenly not long afterwards, in December 1940. (He was a Christian Scientist, and is said to have refused treatment that would have saved him.) Britain was without official representation in the United States at a pivotal point in its history.

Also in December 1940, Wallis Windsor had a serious dental problem and arranged to travel to Florida for treatment. They sailed on Swedish industrialist Axel Wenner Gren's yacht, the *Southern Cross*. The couple was greeted by thousands of people in Miami. Following the death of Lothian, the Duke flew from Miami to meet with Roosevelt aboard the presidential cruiser, *Tuscaloosa*. He returned to Miami and sailed back towards the Bahamas on December 17.

Soon afterwards the Duke met with another American, Fulton Oursler, the editor-in-chief of *Liberty*, a popular American weekly magazine. Oursler died in 1952, and a decade after his death, his son discovered he worked as a liaison between the FBI and agents in South America. Neither he nor others in his family knew anything about it. While going through his father's papers, Oursler Jr. discovered a seventeen page memo in one of his notebooks. The memorandum, dictated to a secretary at the time, described what he saw and heard at the end of December 1940.

"There was a huge dichotomy between the public's perception, and what many British and American officials knew about Windsor," Fulton Oursler Jr. later wrote in *American Heritage* magazine. When the Windsors arrived in the Bahamas aboard the *Southern Cross* on December 19, 1940, Oursler was in Nassau waiting to interview him.[35]

In their meeting, the Duke amazed Oursler with his pro-Nazi sentiments. Hitler, he said was the right and logical leader for the German people. "It would be a tragic thing for the world if Hitler were overthrown."

After the interview Oursler was taken aside by an aide of the Duke's. A Captain Drury told Oursler to relay a message to the U.S. president. "Tell Mr. Roosevelt that if he will make an offer of intervention for peace, that before any one in England can oppose it, the Duke of Windsor will instantly issue a statement supporting it, and that will start a revolution in England and start peace."

Oursler and his family returned to the United States and he arranged to see Roosevelt himself, at the White House. On the morning of December 23, 1940, he met with Roosevelt in the Oval Office, but the editor was somewhat stunned that the president already seemed to know what he was about to say. Roosevelt told him, "Why do you know that I amazed to find some of the greatest people in the British Empire, men of the so-called upper classes, men of the highest rank, secretly want to appease Hitler and stop the war?"

Roosevelt related to him a sequence of events following the abdication of Edward VIII. The Duke subsequently went to a castle in Austria and associated with German friends. Some people in Britain began to feel suspicious about it, Roosevelt said. When the war came, Windsor became a liaison officer between the British and French armies. He was present during the secret discussions of the Commanders-in-Chief of the two armies, and he was aware of everything that was going on. Periodically he would return to Paris for a few days.

"Now I have nothing to prove what I am going to say but I do know that there were nine short-wave wireless sets in Paris constantly sending information to the German troops, and no one has been able to decide how such accurate information could be sent over these stations," Roosevelt told the *Liberty* editor.

The president said it was suggested that the Duke go to the south of France to be with his wife. "... Finally he and his wife went to Madrid where they mingled with the wrong people."

The president dictated a letter to Oursler to send to the Duke's assistant Drury which said "everything is on a twenty-four hour basis and no one is able to read the future." Roosevelt also told the editor that in the thirties, confidential documents were brought to the King daily from Downing Street. The secret papers were found strewn around Fort Belvedere where Mrs. Simpson often socialized with the "Ribbentrop Set."

Oursler feared for his life with what he knew. Windsor's aide Drury told him, if what he knew about the Duke became public, "the lid would be blown off the British Empire." The *Liberty* editor confided everything to Walter Karig, a journalist who often worked with him "in case I should die too suddenly on the way home from Washington." When he started to talk to Karig, he found three chambermaids from the Willard Hotel were listening outside the door to their conversation.

Oursler's son considered publishing his father's memo for a 1963 biography, and he consulted Louis B. Nichols, then third-in-command of the FBI. Nichols knew the entire story and hypothesized that British Intelligence must have known about the Windsors and their exploits. Nichols warned that even twenty years later, the memo was still explosive and it was never printed.

Oursler Sr. presumed at the time that certain agents must have kept tabs on the Duke, and his household in the Bahamas, and the British Embassy must have passed on his information to Roosevelt. (He was perhaps forgetting the ambassador had recently died, and embassy business was likely in a slight state of turmoil). There was, of course, one other unpublicized communications route between the Western Hemisphere and the anti-Hitler forces in Europe — Bill Stephenson. The memo the *Liberty* editor dictated about the Duke on December 26, 1940, concluded as he stepped outside Roosevelt's White House office into the hall. He wrote:

"As I walked out I found a little man sitting in a chair just outside the door. I stopped and looked at him. He kept his head down so I could not see his face. Who was he? Only God and Franklin Roosevelt know."

General Reinhard Gehlen

General Reinhard Gehlen joined the German secret service in 1942 and was the chief of the section responsible for Eastern Europe on which the "Organization Gehlen" was based. He established a network of saboteurs behind Russian lines and at the end of the war Gehlen surrendered to the Americans. He is said to have made copies and hid all his files as he saw the end coming.

Gehlen's elaborate espionage organization interested the U.S., especially since the revelations of Igor Gouzenko alerted them to Soviet penetration of Western democracies. The Americans funded his spy network until the government of West Germany took it over in 1955. He retired in 1968. Even decades after the war, his spy organization was regarded as "remarkable", and he accurately predicted the date of the six day Arab-Israeli war, and the Soviet invasion of Czechoslovakia in 1968.[36]

For years he refused to be photographed, and he was known as the man without a face. He changed his cars and identity frequently and carried a loaded gun. During the Cold War, reportedly there was a million marks reward on his head from the Eastern bloc.[37] In his memoirs, Gehlen said that Martin Bormann, Hitler's top aide, was a Soviet agent and died in the Soviet Union in the late sixties. But he offered no proof.[38]

Gehlen wrote in *The Service* that during the Cold War the Soviets thought an important part was played "in the continuing struggle," by swaying opinion. Through "psycho-politics and *desinformatsiya*, or disinformation — a targeted stream of information deliberately designed to influence the recipient in a certain, predetermined manner," he wrote, one result the old Soviet Union tried to secure was "an indirect political gain from the penetration of the enemy mind."

"It was Marx who stated that the idea becomes a political force as soon as it penetrates the mind of the masses. If we accept the Communist theory of the absolute interdependence of all that happens, it follows that ... every political action carries within it the means of penetrating the mind: conversely, every mind-penetrating action both can and should lead to political consequences."[39]

In the West, according to Gehlen, Soviet psycho-political lobbying was done by "influencers." "In many cases the work of the influencers is not even punishable; it is this feature and their completely unsuspecting character, that makes it impossible even to estimate how many influencers there are, let alone pinpoint and neutralize them. In West Germany, it has not proved possible to identify more than a few isolated cases, and these influencers have been prevented from doing further harm.

"How welcome it must be for their Communist controllers to find that their own training and subtlety are actually aided by our guilelessness (which verges on downright rashness) and political ineptitude."[40] In his memoirs Gehlen quotes Sun-Tse's *Rules for Political and Psychological*

Subversion from about 500 BC which he said still held true.

"There is no art higher than that of destroying the enemy's resistance without a fight on the battlefield. The direct tactic of war is necessary only on the battlefield; but only the indirect tactic of war can lead to a real and lasting victory.

"Subvert anything of value in the enemy's country. Implicate the emissaries of the major powers in criminal undertakings; undermine their position and destroy their reputation in other ways as well, and expose them to the public ridicule of their fellow citizens.

"Do not shun the aid of even the lowest and most despicable people. Disrupt the work of their government with every means that you can.

"Spread disunity and dispute among the citizens of the enemy's country. Turn the young against the old. Use every means to destroy their arms, their supplies, and the discipline of the enemies' forces. Debase old traditions and accepted gods. Be generous with promises and rewards to purchase intelligence and accomplices. Send out your agents in all directions. Do not skimp with money or with promises, for they yield a high return."[41]

THE NAME "INTREPID"
Igor Gouzenko lawyers

> Gouzenko always had a theory that before the Russians would kill him they had to destroy his credibility, because they never kill anybody unless they destroyed their credibility first — any person in the public eye.
>
> — Nelles Starr, Gouzenko's lawyer
> *Gouzenko: The Untold Story* p. 122

Following the Cuban revolution, the United States pondered what to do about their socialist neighbour. In the years following the revolution there were reports the CIA considered many ways to discredit Cuban leader Fidel Castro, including slipping him chemicals that made his beard fall out, and exploding cigars. According to some accounts, assassination was also considered.

In the early 1960s U.S. President John Kennedy played host to Ian Fleming, whose writing he was a fan of. He invited the English spy writer to the White House and during the course of the evening he asked the former naval intelligence officer what to do about Cuba and Castro. Fleming, according to his biographer, told Kennedy the U.S. was making too much fuss about Castro, "Inflating him instead of deflating him." Applying one or two ideas would "take the steam out of the Cuban," the author told him. Kennedy wondered how this could be accomplished. 'Ridicule, chiefly,' said Fleming."[42]

• • •

There has been much conjecture about some details of Stephenson's career and the validity of what has been written about him. Even Stephenson's supposed code name, "Intrepid," has come into question. It was not Stephenson's official code name, the author Nigel West has written, but a name that referred to a cable address of the entire organization.

The writer Mary S. Lovell has pointed out it would be natural for a person sending a cable to BSC New York to say, "Send this to Intrepid," and the name would stick to the head of the organization. In the same manner, if a message to "Intrepid" was intercepted, it is likely those who intercepted the message would not assume it referred to a huge espionage agency hidden in the heart of New York. They would assume it referred to simply one man. A man called Intrepid. It appears the name of the book was actually based on a message.

> Report AS/783/25X to Red Army Intelligence Hq, Znamensky 19, Moscow, USSR, dated 23.1.1944, concerning Hermina Rabinovich and the assistant Soviet Military Attaché (cover name Lamont) in Ottawa: "Funds were delivered to William Helbein of the Helbein Watch Company of 6, West 48th Street, New York, NY, the firm known to 'Hermina' when she was stationed in Geneva. This completes SMERSH Plan Destruct..."
>
> Report AB/3/97X to the Fuhrer of the Third Reich, Adolf Hitler, from SS-General Heinrich Mueller, otherwise known as "Gestapo" Mueller: "Liquidation of the man called INTREPID is now assured."

The date on this file recovered from wartime German archives is exactly one month before the Soviet intelligence report quoted above. The above reports are followed by a narrative that says orders for the destruction of the Intrepid "Anglo-American" secret operations were first issued by "Gestapo Mueller" when Hitler and Stalin were still bound by their peace pact and Hitler was about to invade Britain. According to the narrative, Mueller — actually working for the Soviet Union — reported to Moscow on Hitler's plan to combine the new German Empire with the old British Empire to dominate the world. Hitler's future collaborators in Britain were named. "The laws of libel prevent their publication except in the case of the British Ambassador to Franco Spain of that time, Sir Samuel Hoare, now dead."

> "The biggest single obstacle to Anglo-German imperialism apart from the public hatred of Hitler in Britain was INTREPID. He was thus described in the Mueller dossier and this story is taken from the strangest manhunt in modern times."

Intrepid, the narrative continues, virtually unknown outside a small collection of people who ran the world's affairs in 1939, was sent to North America by Churchill, "to build up the largest secret operation in history" and the first American intelligence agency, which later became the CIA.

Intrepid was Bill Stephenson, a fourth-generation North American who was the sole link between Churchill and President F. D. Roosevelt when the two leaders conspired to preserve freedom from both the threat of Nazi conquest and Soviet subversion.[43]

What is this synopsis?

It is the original outline of *A Man Called Intrepid*, dated June 5, 1973, and in the files of William Stevenson at the University of Regina.

It's a challenge to confirm whether or not aspects of this outline were in fact true. The first document quoted refers to the Canadian Royal Commission into the espionage activities of the Soviet Union following the defection of Igor Gouzenko, headed by Robert Taschereau and R. L. Kellock. In the formidable mound of transcripts of the 1946 inquiry, there is a reference to a cable dated January 23, 1944. There are also references to details such as Hermina, Heilbein Watch Company, Lamont and Znamensky 19. "Hermina" was Hermina Rabinowitch, who for a time was stationed in Geneva with the International Labour Organization. The contents of that specific cable are not spelled out in the released papers, although any money being delivered seems to have been destined for Switzerland. The Gouzenko transcripts weren't widely released, in any form, until years after the publication of *A Man Called Intrepid*.[44] No reference could be found to the second report AB/3/97X, and an official at the Imperial War Museum in London could not place the quotation.

In *A Man Called Intrepid*, "Gestapo" Mueller is not even mentioned. Soon after the first outline was composed, the author decided there was a "basic story which is filled with political intrigue in high places," and "It does not seem necessary to complicate matters with cutaways to what the Germans were doing to stop Intrepid." He says it has not been proved that Mueller was a Soviet agent, although Stephenson believed this on the basis on his own files, and it was best to leave Mueller out of the book.[45] In later letters it seems Stevenson the writer is perhaps justifying a pro-British slant in the American-published book. In a July 24, 1974, letter to Stephenson he wrote, "It should be said that all Julian's [Muller] comments have been within the context of his own admiration for Britain and his anxiety that an American audience be captured by the fact an Anglo-American alliance saved the world from tyranny."[46]

Gestapo stands for Geheime Staats Polizei or Secret State Police. In Nazi Germany, the ss became almost a state within a state, duplicating almost every aspect of state administration. The Gestapo was its spearhead. Lt. General Heinrich Mueller reported directly to Reinhard Heydrich, and the organization dominated all of occupied Europe, and contained numerous sections and subsections over a wide range of areas.[47] There do appear to be Soviet influences, if not connections.[48]

Following Rudolf Hess's flight to England, Mueller carried out a purge of those around him. Even his chauffeur was arrested. Mueller disappeared at the conclusion of the war, much like Martin Bormann. He was possibly seen in Moscow and died there in 1948.[49]

Soviet military counter-intelligence during World War II consisted of two successive organizations, the Special Departments of the NKVD (OO/NKVD) until April 1943, and after that date, the Third Main Directorate for Counter-intelligence of the People's Commissariat of Defence (GUKR-NKO). The latter organization was given the nickname SMERSH, or Smert Shipionam (Death to Spies) by Stalin himself (Soviet Military Encyclopaedia). Stalin thought the organization should not deal only with German spies, but the intelligence services of other countries as well.[50]

The existence of SMERSH became widespread public knowledge in the 1950s, in a somewhat unique fashion. The possibility that elements of Soviet Intelligence were in favour of attacks on Western Intelligence figures following the war was revealed in the same manner. An author's note refers to names, numbers and places.

"Not that it matters, but a great deal of the background to this story is accurate.

SMERSH, a contraction of Smert Shipionam — Death to Spies — exists and remains the most secret department of the Soviet government.

At the beginning of 1956, when this book was written, the strength of SMERSH at home and abroad was about 40,000 and General Grubozaboyschikov was its chief. My description of his appearance is correct.

Today the headquarters of SMERSH are where in chapter 4, I have placed them — at No. 13 Sretenka Ulitsa, Moscow. The Conference Room is faithfully described and the Intelligence chiefs who meet round the table are real officials who are frequently summoned to that room for purposes similar to those I have recounted."

A Soviet intelligence meeting is reconstructed in the fourth chapter. A selection of Soviet officials engage in a roundtable discussion about future plans and how to possibly weaken foreign intelligence organizations.

"It is not just a question of blowing up a building or shooting a prime minister," one concludes. "Our operation must be delicate, refined and aimed at the heart of the Intelligence apparatus — hidden damage which the public will perhaps hear nothing of, but which will be the secret talk of government circles ..."

The intelligence services of the Swedes, Italians, Spaniards and French are rejected. The Americans are dismissed as well. Although they are often technically superior, and have had successes, they have no understanding of the work, and do everything for money, is the conclusion. "Good spies will not work for money alone, only bad ones, of which the Americans have several divisions," was the analysis.

The consensus concludes the English service would be the target of a terrorist action, not because of an overt superiority, but because of underlying factors. "Of course most of their strength lies in the myth — the myth of Scotland Yard, of Sherlock Holmes, of the Secret Service. We certainly have nothing to fear from these gentlemen. But the myth is a hindrance, which it would be good to set aside.

"... And now for the target within that organization. I remember Comrade General Vozdvishensky saying something about a myth upon which much of the alleged strength of this Secret Service depends. How can we help destroy this myth and thus strike at the very motive force of this organization? Where does this myth reside? We cannot destroy all its personnel at one blow. Does it reside in the Head? "

"... He is an Admiral. He is known by the letter M. We have a zapiska on him, but it contains little ... The public does not know of his existence. It would be difficult to create a scandal around his death. And he would not be easy to kill. He rarely goes abroad. To shoot him in a London street would not be very refined."

"... But we are here to find a target who will fulfil our requirements. Have they no one who is a hero to the organization? Some one who is admired and whose ignominious destruction would cause dismay? Myths are built on heroic deeds and heroic people. Have they no such men?"

There was silence around the table while everyone searched his memory,

"... It was Colonel Nikitikin of the MGB who broke the embarrassed silence.

He said hesitantly, 'There is a man called Bond."

—Ian Fleming, *From Russia With Love*

GLOSSARY AND CAST OF CHARACTERS

Aiken, Max (Lord Beaverbrook) (1879–1964): Canadian-born newspaper owner, adviser and friend of Winston Churchill and friend of William Stephenson.

America First: American anti-war, isolationist organization targeted by BSC.

Astor, Vincent (1891–1959): Close advisor and friend of Franklin Roosevelt. Helped run a private intelligence service.

Ayer, Alfred Jules (1910–89): Philosopher attached to SOE and BSC.

Bell, Ulric (1891–1960): Washington correspondent of *Louisville Courier-Journal*; worked with BSC ally, Robert Sherwood, and at Office of War Information.

Baldwin, Stanley (1867–1947): British prime minister (1923–29, 1935–37).

Belmonte letter: Phony letter created by BSC. Researched by Harford Hyde, the letter supposedly implicated Bolivia's military attaché in Berlin in a plot to overthrow the Bolivian government. The letter — with a signature forged by BSC's Dorothy Hyde and Betty Raymond — led to arrests in Bolivia and the German minister was thrown out.

Bedson, Derek: Canadian political mandarin, a good friend of Stephenson's after the war and regular visitor to Bermuda.

Berle, Adolf (1895–1971): American State Department Official, who wanted to stay out of European conflict and to keep close tabs on BSC. Wary of a foreign intelligence service operating in the U.S.

Bruce, David (1898–1977): Head of OSS London during the war; later became American ambassador to Britain and to NATO. He wrote the foreword to the first book written about Stephenson, *The Quiet Canadian.*

Bryce, Ivar: Worked for BSC and OSS in Washington. Brother-in-law of American columnist Walter Lippmann, close friend of Ian Fleming, and wrote a book about the friendship and the war, *You Only Live Once.*

Cadogan, Sir Alexander (1884–1968): Permanent Under Secretary at Britain's Foreign Office during the war. He was also British representative at the UN Security Council (1946–50) and chairman of the BBC (1952–57).

Camp X: Wartime espionage training and communications centre at Oshawa –Whitby, Ontario.

Chamberlain, Neville (1869–1940): British prime minister (1937–1940). He advocated the appeasement policy towards Italy and Nazi Germany. He returned from Munich in 1938 claiming "peace for our time." He resigned as prime minister in 1940 and was succeeded by Winston Churchill.

Clarke, General Carter: Assistant head of American Army intelligence (G-2).

COI : Coordinator of Information. American intelligence group set up by Roosevelt in July 1941, and headed by William Donovan. It was the precursor to Office of Strategic Services (OSS).

Coit, Richard "Dickie": One of the early members of BSC.

Cuneo, Ernest (1905–1988): A lawyer and journalist, Cuneo was also a Roosevelt insider. The solicitor for American columnists Drew Pearson and Walter Winchell, Cuneo did liaison work for Stephenson. He married Margaret Watson of Winnipeg from Stephenson's staff.

CSIS: Canadian Security and Intelligence Service. Canada's domestic intelligence organization that deals with counter-espionage.

De Chastelain, Marion (1910–2000): American-born member of Stephenson's inner office. Worked as a cipher clerk and as a courier/translator for BSC/OSS operative "Cynthia" Elizabeth Pack.

Donovan, William (1883–1959) ("Wild Bill," "Big Bill"): Soldier, lawyer, public official. Donovan was chosen by Roosevelt to set up America's first all-encompassing intelligence service. He was first named Co-ordinator of Information and then headed up the U.S. Office of Strategic Services (1942–1945). He was a friend of Bill Stephenson and set up an OSS office in Rockefeller Center. He later said, "Bill Stephenson taught us all we knew about foreign intelligence."

Evans, Jean Paul: British-trained BSC agent. Assignments included the Gouzenko case.

Ellis, Dick: Australian-born, British-trained intelligence agent. Was one of the first members of BSC. Wrote a history of BSC after the war and a foreword to *A Man Called Intrepid*. After his death was accused by some British sources of working for either the Soviets or the Germans or both.

DNI: Director of Naval Intelligence.

Drew-Brook, Tommy: Toronto stockbroker, one of William Stephenson's best friends since serving together in World War I. Toronto house became a stopping-off point for many people headed to Camp X.

Dwyer, Peter: British-trained BSC agent. Assignments included the Gouzenko case.

ENIGMA: Portable German cipher machine, which until the end of the war Nazi leaders thought to be to be unbreakable . It was broken by Allied codebreakers and provided invaluable intelligence — code named ULTRA — that saved lives and shortened the war.

Fleming, Ian (1908–1964): English-born writer and journalist. Fleming worked for British naval intelligence during the war and was a frequent visitor to BSC New York. He worked for the Kemsley group of papers after the war. He later retired to Jamaica and created the master-spy James Bond. Fleming wrote the foreword to *Room 3606*.

Friedman, William (1891–1969): Renowned American cryptologist broke Japanese "purple" code.

G-2: American Army's intelligence organization.

Gouzenko, Igor (1922–1985): Soviet cipher clerk stationed in Ottawa embassy came over to the West in 1945 with his wife Svetlana. Documents smuggled out by Gouzenko exposed large Soviet espionage operations in the West. The revelations and the resulting repercussions are often regarded as being the start of the Cold War. His novel *Fall of a Titan* won Canada's Governor General's literary award in the 1950s.

Halifax, Lord (Edward Wood)(1881–1959): Foreign secretary under Neville Chamberlain (1938–1940), Halifax helped implement his appeasement policy. He was ambassador to the United States (1941–46).

Hoover, John Edgar (1895–1972): American lawyer took over the Bureau of Investigation in 1924, and built up the FBI into America's national police force. He was director of the FBI for 48 years.

ICI: Imperial Chemical Industries.

IRD: Intelligence Research Board, a division of MI6.

Ismay, Hastings Lionel "Pug" (1887–1965): English soldier, served as Winston Churchill's Chief of Staff (1940–46). Later he became secretary-general to NATO (1952–57).

Knox, Frank (1874–1944): Journalist and cabinet member, Knox was the owner of the Chicago Daily News (1931–1940). Although he was a Republican, Franklin Roosevelt made him Secretary of the Navy (1940–1944). Was highly regarded by BSC.

Korda, Alexander (1893–1956): Hungarian-born filmmaker and British intelligence agent. He was a friend of Bill Stephenson and a favourite of Winston Churchill. He was knighted in 1942.

Lothian, Lord (1882–1940): British ambassador to the United States During the 1930s he did not seem too concerned about Nazi expansionism.

MAGIC: intelligence derived from the decryption of Japanese coding machine.

MI5: Britain's domestic security service, similar to the FBI.

MI6: Britain's foreign intelligence service, similar to the CIA. Sometimes referred to as SIS (Secret Intelligence Service). Usually foreign operatives had cover occupations, often related to Britain's Foreign Office. During the war the frequent cover was Passport Control.

Menzies Stewart (1899-1974): Head of Britain's MI6 (1939–1952). Known by the initial "C."

Morrell, Sidney "Bill" (1912–1985): British journalist and advertising man.

Maidment, Ken: British university professor who became Benjamin de Forest Bayly's right-hand man. He later moved to New Zealand.

Ogilvy, David (1911–1999): Born in Surrey, England. Ogilvy had a varied career. He settled in New York in 1939 and worked for the British embassy and BSC New York. Following the war he helped found the advertising agency Ogilvy and Mather.

ONI: Office of Naval Intelligence (U.S.).

Sherwood, Robert (1896–1955): Playwright and author. He began as a reviewer of books and movies and then worked on some screenplays in Britain. He later became Roosevelt's speechwriter. Was the head of the American Office of War Information (OWI) (1942–1944).

SOE: Special Operations Executive. British-run wartime operation that supported and collaborated with resistance movements in Occupied Europe.

Station M: BSC Department used to concoct phony documents.

Turing, Alan (1912–1954): British mathematician. Turing was a major part of the Bletchley Park success in cracking Axis codes. Helped design the "bombe," a high speed calculator, and "Colossus," one of the first electric programmable computers.

ULTRA: Intelligence derived from the breaking of Nazi codes. It was the highest security level intelligence and many of its recipients were unaware of its source.

VENONA: Code name used for the U.S. Signals Intelligence (forerunner of National Security Agency) secret effort to collect and decrypt the text of Soviet messages from the 1940s. Begun in 1943, the messages had become accumulated by the Signal Intelligence Service (often referred to as "Arlington Hall" after the Virginia location of its headquarters).

NOTES

Preface

1. When the British double agent Kim Philby was suspected of being a triple agent by Moscow, they demanded over and over that he write out long, detailed biographies of himself. It seems no one got a biography out of Stephenson (cited in James Bamford, "The View From the KGB," *New York Times*, January 29, 1995).
2. He wrote, for example, that he knew of the date of the Arab–Israeli war of 1967 before it occurred (William Stevenson: About the Author, *90 Minutes at Entebbe*, 1976).
3. Joseph P. Lash, *Roosevelt and Churchill*, p. 140.
4. *South* magazine, February 1991, no. 119, p.78.
5. Stephenson quoted in *CBC Times*, September 7–13, 1968.
6. William Stevenson, *The Bormann Brotherhood*, p.21.
7. Joseph Lelyveld, "Le Carre's Toughest Task," *New York Times*, March 16, 1986. The first novel not offered for clearance was his eleventh, *The Perfect Spy* in 1986.

Introduction

1. *Manchester Guardian Weekly*, February 1989.
2. Stevenson, *A Man Called Intrepid*, p.4.
3. Gislasson later said he was referring to a picture of Stephenson in a defunct Icelandic paper run by a relative. Subsequently another Stephenson picture was located, headlined "Islenzkur Flugmadur — Icelandic Flyer."
4. Unfortunately Derek Bedson died suddenly that week, so was unable to further discuss Stephenson.

Chapter 1 A Boy from the Prairies

1. Lutheran funeral #427, First Lutheran Church, Winnipeg. Death of, Funeral Service records.
2. Heber had previously interviewed a Mrs. Davies, who lived on Sutherland Street in Point Douglas, who knew the families, and was over a hundred years old when she died in 1986.

3. In 1912, Thorarinn, Kristjan and Gudmindur bought the general store in the Interlake town of Lundar, Manitoba. Because the brothers had different fathers, in the Icelandic tradition, they had different last names. They created a common surname, Breckman, after Klungubrekka, the Icelandic town they were from, and they named the Lundar store Breckman Brothers."

4. George Johnson interview, May 1989.

5. *Winnipeg Free Press*, November 26, 1952.

6. Alan Artibise, *Winnipeg: An Illustrated History*, p. 55.

7. *Op. cit.* p. 104.

8. James H. Gray, *Red Lights on the Prairies*, p. 68.

9. Artibise, p. 105.

10. *Ibid.*

11. *Manitoba Free Press*, November 12, 1910.

12. *Winnipeg Telegram*, November 17 & 18, 1910.

13. Artibise, p. 106.

14. *Ibid.*

15. *Manitoba Free Press*, January 12, 1914.

16. *Op. cit.*, December 9, 1913.

17. *Op. cit.*, January 22, 1914.

18. *Op. cit.*, December 11, 1913.

19. *Op. cit.*, January 15, 1914.

20. *Op. cit.*, January 12 & 13, 1914.

Chapter 2 Wartime Hero

1. Attestation paper, Canadian Overseas Expeditionary Force.

2. It is not known why this is the case. Stephenson was perhaps concerned about being at least twenty to be sent overseas. One report in the Icelandic Manitoban paper *Logberg Heimskringla* (March 10, 1989) indicates when he enlisted he was one year under age. A later newspaper story on his RAF flying exploits in the Icelandic Manitoban *Votgorold*, May 14, 1918, has Stephenson's correct age, 21. Stephenson's relatives have records of his actual birth date. It is a strange anomaly.

3. Stephenson to Stevenson, August 21, 1975, U. of Regina 83-7 801.1-1

4. *Manitoba Free Press*, September 9, 1919; also Hyde file photographs, Churchill College, Cambridge (CCC).

5. Stevenson, *AMCI*, p. 5; Anthony Cave Brown, *The Last Hero Wild Bill Donovan*.

6. Regiment records indicate it may have been later in 1917.

7. Hyde, *The Quiet Canadian*, p. 7.

8. Drew-Brook to Hyde, December 12, 1961, CCC, Hyde papers 1/5.

9. *The Great Canadian Spy* radio transcript, U. of Regina 1/5.

10. Intrepid to Steverite, July 15, 1974, U. of R., 83-7 801.1-1.

11. *Gazette*, September 21, 1918, p.1125522/ 3/ 18 one, RFC communique No. 132, 83-7 box 9. Marteville, offensive patrol, 2 Vickers guns, Sopwith Camel No.B7502. 305 p.m. 5000 feet March 24, 1918 Sopwith Camel D6421 10:40 a.m., offensive patrol, 1000 feet 8–14 April 1918 Military Cross 2 Lt. William S. Stephenson (second lieutenant). p. 37 Royal Air Force 1918 Military Cross to 2nd Lt ... for conspicuous gallantry and devotion to duty. When flying low and observing an open staff car on a road, he attacked it with such success that later it was seen lying in the ditch

upside down. During the same flight he caused a stampede amongst some enemy transport horses on a road. Previous to this he had destroyed a hostile scout and a two seater plane. His word has been of highest order and he has shown the greatest courage and energy in engaging every kind of target. (*Gazette* 22, June 1918, p. 7423) 3 /5/ 18 p.58 Lt W., Stephenson, 73 sqn, in a general engagement between his patrol and a formation of EA triplanes and scouts, singled out one EA scout and fired about 250 rounds into it. The EA went down and was followed a short distance by Lt Stephenson who watched it going down and eventually nose dive into Ploegsteert Wood. July 9 18 Sopwith Camel No. C8296, Moncheaux, 10500 feet one July 10 1918 Sopwith Camel C8296 one shot down, one out of control p.134 July 14 1918 Enemy aircraft were also brought down during the period under review by 73 Lt W S Stephenson (one) p. 138 July 21 73 Lt W. S. Stephenson July 21 shared Fokker triplane p. 143 22-28 July 1918 73 Lt W S Stephenson (3) July 22 1918 Bazoches, 2, Fokker Triplane and biplane July 25 1918, Camel C8296, St. Thibaut, 10000 ft, Fokker biplane July 25 1918 same Camel, near Cohan, LVG two seater, (shared) p. 158 Honours and Awards DFC Lt WS Stephenson MC July 28 1918, NW Fere-en-Tardenois, General Flying, at least one Fokker biplane Lieut Stephenson is missing after this engagement. Distinguished Flying Cross to Lt William Samuel Stephenson, MC "This officer has shown conspicuous gallantry and skill in attacking enemy troops and transports from low altitudes, causing heavy casualties. His reports have also contained valuable and accurate information. He had further proved himself to be a keen antagonist in the air having during recent operations accounting for six enemy aeroplanes."

12. Translation of extract from French paper *Avion*, CCC Hyde 1/1.
13. The *Avion* passage, and the fact that Stephenson was likely brought down by friendly fire demonstrates the difficulty assessing dog fight reports and 'kills' during World War I.
14. Tommy Drew-Brook to Hyde, December 12, 1961 Hyde CCC 1/5.
15. Hyde 1/6 CCC.
16. *Winnipeg Tribune* Canadian Press wire story, July 7, 1954
17. Hyde 1/6 CCC.
18. *Manitoba Free Press* September 6, 1919.
19. Cited in *Manitoba Free Press*, August 28, 1923 (refers to recent article in leading London newspaper).

Chapter 3 International Success

1. *Manitoba Free Press*, August 28, 1923. (For some reason this clipping is dated in the Hyde file at CCC as September 1924).
2. Current Biography, 1940. Beaverbrook.
3. Interview with Margaret Jamieson. Wilf Russell continued to visit Winnipeg regularly and visited with the Jamieson family, as he had been engaged to her mother's deceased sister.
4. *The Times* (London), January 1, 1926.
5. Hyde, *The Quiet Canadian*, p. 14. Hyde remembers Lord Londonderry, then Air Minister, bought one for his private use and Hyde frequently flew with him in it.
6. London Street indexes, 1934, Stephenson was #19, and Hambro #18 New Cavendish.
7. *The Times*, May 4, 1936.

8. Thomas Troy, *Wild Bill and Intrepid*, p. 166–68.

9. *The Times* index for June 20, 1927, indicates there was a story in it where someone named Stephenson spoke on a cinematograph film bill. I could not locate this in the paper.

10. *The Financial Times* (London), July 7, 1939.

11. *Daily Telegraph*, February 3, 1989.

12. U. of R. 83-7 Box 9 801. 3-1 passage titled Lady Mary. Frank Whittle died in 1996. His association is in *Daily Telegraph*, February 3, 1989, and other sources. Stephenson cabled to William Stevenson that he helped recruit BTH and GEC Labs to search for a high speed steel alloy that would remain hard even at red hot temperatures. (U. of R. 83–7 801.1-6). It is apparent from the correspondence that Stephenson knew Whittle, and the writer Stevenson met with Whittle during the writing of *A Man Called Intrepid*. Stephenson says in one cable, "Give my regards to Frank."

13. Letter, William Stevenson to Lester B. Pearson, October 25, 1972, U. of R. 83-7 Box 9 801.7-2. Stephenson's or Churchill's attendance at a Fabian gathering could be initiated through their mutual friend Beaverbrook, whose top *Evening Standard* columnist, Arnold Bennett (1867–1931) was a well known Fabian. Beaverbrook was known for tolerating a wide spectrum of political views, and Bennett accompanied him on a trip to Russia in 1929.

14. Hyde, *The Quiet Canadian*, p. 15.

15. Hyde, *Secret Intelligence Agent*, p. 80.

16. Interview with Victor Bryant, January 1991.

17. Anthony Cave Brown, *C*, p. 262.

18. *The Times*, November 3, 1936.

19. *Op. cit.*, November 13, 1936.

20. *Op. cit.*, February 6, 1937.

21. *Op. cit.*, June 18, 1936.

22. *Op. cit.*, November 13, 1936.

23. "Turning the Pages of History," publication supplied by Earls Court.

24. *The Globe and Mail*, May 20, 1982.

25. Ellis, in *A Man Called Intrepid*, CBC television documentary (1974 broadcast).

26. Interview with Dick Ellis, *Tuesday Night*, Roll C Take 1, U. of R.

27. Ibid.

28. Stevenson, *A Man Called Intrepid* p. xxvii.

29. *Op. cit.*, p. 32.

30. Hyde, *The Quiet Canadian*, p. 14.

31. *Britain Between the Wars*, p. 592; also Lord Londonderry's *Ourselves and Germany*.

32. Harold Nicolson, Vol. II, *Diaries and Letters, The War Years 1939–1945*, p. 458–59.

33. F. W. Winterbotham, *The Nazi Connection* p. 133.

34. Ibid.

35. Robert Goralski, *World War II Almanac*, November 28, 1934, p. 30.

36. Winterbotham, *The Nazi Connection*, p. 157

37. *Op. cit.*, p. 158, 159.

38. If England was sleeping, Kennedy's father Joe, the American ambassador in England, was probably in a coma.

39. John F. Kennedy, *Why England Slept*, p. 92–93.

40. Winterbotham, *The Nazi Connection*, p. 163–164.

41. Martin Gilbert, Richard Gott, *The Appeasers*, p. 28, citing Lord Londonderry, *Ourselves and Germany*, p. 97, February 21, 1936).

42. Stephenson cable to Steverite, November 2, 1975. U. of R. 83-7 801.1-6.

43. Interview with Dick Ellis, *Tuesday Night*, Roll C Take 1, U. of R.

44. Brown, *C*, p. 195.

45. Intrepid to Steverite, August 23, 1974. U. of R. 83-7 801.1-4

46. Brown, *C*, p. 195.

47. Hyde, *The Quiet Canadian*, pp. 20–24. There are numerous other references to this including an interview with Stephenson in the CBC television documentary, *A Man Called Intrepid*.

48. *Tuesday Night*, Interview with Dick Ellis U. of R. Roll C Take One.

49. Intrepid to Steverite cable, September 12, 1974, U. of R., 83-7 801.1-1

50. Winston Churchill, *The Gathering Storm*, pp. 196–97.

51. Robert Sherwood, *The White House Papers of Harry L. Hopkins*, pp. 151–152.

52. Beaverbrook to Churchill, December 13, 1940. Beaverbrook Archives (cited in Lovell, *Cast No Shadow*, p. 337)

53. Brown, *C*, p. 7.

54. R. G. Grant, *MI5 MI6 Britain's Security and Intelligence Services* pp. 48–49.

55. Alvin Finkel and Clement Leibovitz, *The Chamberlain–Hitler Collusion*, p. 286.

56. An edited version of Cadogan's diary was published by David Dilks. The actual diary of Alexander Cadogan is at Churchill College, Cambridge. Cadogan, CCC.

Chapter 4 Assignment: New York

1. Martin Gilbert, *Winston S. Churchill*, vol. 6, p. 358.

2. *Great Canadian Spy* radio transcription, U. of R. 83-7 Box 4 500.

3. Tunney to Thomas Troy (CIA) August 6, 1969, U. of R. 83-7 Box 9 801.9 Later Stephenson thanked Tunney for the role he played. "Sir William sent me a very charming letter thanking me for what I had done and telling me that I would be very proud to have played the part of mediator, though I would expect no information about the affair. Sir William did refer to me in the book, *The Quiet Canadian* as having played the part I did ... which was still of course secret."

4. Tunney to Stephenson, August 6, 1969 letter, U. of R. 83-7 Box 9 801. 7-1 Tunney died in 1978. In 1975, Troy completed a history of the CIA, produced in two volumes, "aimed at satisfying the need of the employees of the Central Intelligence Agency". It was classified SECRET. Later, in 1981, the work was reproduced as a single volume called *Donovan and the CIA: A History of the Establishment of the Central Intelligence Agency* — "released for leisurely reading outside the office." The history was reclassified, after it was re-edited, and shorn of a total of about six pages. The Tunney references are not in the released text, although his letters appear in the sources. Tunney is mentioned in Troy's later book, *Wild Bill and Intrepid*. Numerous publications mention the Stephenson–Hoover meetings. None mention that British government officials were not to know about it.

5. Hyde, *The Quiet Canadian*, p. 26.

6. Curt Gentry, *J Edgar Hoover: the Man and his Secrets*, p. 265, citing an interview with Ernest Cuneo.

7. Letter from Ernest Cuneo to William Stephenson, December 15, 1975, U. of R. 83–7 Box 10 801 10-4. Thomas Troy reports that Cuneo didn't remember being the

go-between at this early stage and a more likely conduit was Vincent Astor. Cuneo is quoted in Gentry's *J. Edgar Hoover the Man and his Secrets*, and didn't contradict the story.

8. Cuneo wrote the introduction to a book by Winchell, *Winchell Exclusive*.

9. Stephenson cable to Steverite December 20, 1975, U. of R. 83-7 801.1-6

10. Hyde, *The Quiet Canadian*, p. 26.

11. Anthony Cave Brown, '*C*', p. 262.

12. There has been some controversy about the date — that is the exact day of the week — of Beaverbrook's dinner outing decades ago, and incredibly, this has been used to question Stephenson's achievements, and whether he even knew Churchill or Beaverbrook. Following Stephenson's death, an article in *The Times* of London by their Defence correspondent (*The Times*, February 18, 1989) highlighted the concerns of an assortment of British "scholars," "historians" and "distinguished figures." "The meeting with Churchill at the centre of historian's arguments," read a subhead line. "Stephenson chose the silliest of all dates (May 10, 1940) to claim his dinner session with Churchill. It was the one day everyone knew where Churchill was," Sir David Hunt commented in the story. *The Times* story also quotes from A. J. P. Taylor's Beaverbrook biography, which says Churchill and Beaverbrook lunched and dined alone together on May 10, 1940. (The Taylor biography also says Beaverbrook's immediate task at the time was to advise Churchill on appointments, p. 410.) A cable from Stephenson to the writer Stevenson, October 25, 1973, years before *A Man Called Intrepid* was published or there was any controversy, is the earliest mention of the meeting in available papers. In the cable, Stephenson says he can't recall the exact date of the Beaverbrook dinner, thirty-three years before, but it was probably May 12, 1940.(U. of R. 83-7 801.1-1). The centre of the historical argument seems a bit donut-like. The same article in *The Times* mentions intelligence files remain closed. The story continued, "*I've [Hunt] also spoken to Alan Taylor* [A. J. P. Taylor, Beaverbrook biographer] *and there is no evidence Stephenson even knew Beaverbrook, let alone Churchill.*" There was evidence in the files of H. Montgomery Hyde, before they were closed by the British government. As cited earlier, in May 1940, the month Stephenson was appointed to America, Churchill told his son, "I shall drag the United States in." (Gilbert, *Winston S. Churchill*, vol. 6 p. 358) It is well documented that Churchill met, and knew William Donovan, Roosevelt's intelligence coordinator and the head of the OSS. It is rather ludicrous to suggest that Churchill would not know his own intelligence representative in the U.S. Apart from other references to the Stephenson and Churchill relationship in this book, Stephenson's working relationships with Franklin Roosevelt, and Winston Churchill first became public in the 1950s. *The Quiet Canadian* mentions meetings between Churchill and Stephenson. The facts were never questioned by Churchill, who was still alive at the time. *The Sunday Times* of London, the sister paper of *The Times*, printed a syndicated version of *The Quiet Canadian* in 1962 , which told readers of the Stephenson–Churchill association. It seems somewhat strange that *The Times* would later publish a story that questioned whether the relationship existed. If Churchill had been still alive, it is unlikely such revisionism of history would have been allowed to occur.

13. Hyde, *Secret Intelligence Agent*, p. xv, foreword, signed by Stephenson.

14. Intrepid to Steverite, March 19, 1974, 83-7 801.1-3 Later discussing his relationship with Lothian and Roosevelt, Stephenson cabled *"lothian christian scientist was deathly ill gave me every ounce of cooperation his health allowed until his last days when i sitting by his bedside holding his hand in farewell being en route urgent visit london stop* (December 1940*) he died whilst i was en route and my meetings thereafter* (with Roosevelt*) strictly duo except son james occasional appearance and later donovans when knox stimson and hull were enlisted by donovan to implement franklin's edicts of acquiescence to urgent american moves of statesmanship and self interest intrepid*

15. Joseph Lash, *Roosevelt and Churchill,* p. 140. Lash's book deals with correspondence between Roosevelt and Churchill, but he does not specify the source. The passage is also in *A Man Called Intrepid.* A paraphrased vision of the passage appears in *The Quiet Canadian* (pp. 26–27).

16. Intrepid to Steverite, May 16, 1974, U. of R. 83-7 801. 1-1 24.

17. Cited in the *Toronto Star,* September 19, 1989 (*Washington Post* Syndicated story based on the 'BSC History' leaked to the paper by William Stevenson and verified for authenticity by CIA historian Thomas Troy).

Chapter 5 The Secret Expansion

1. Hyde, *Secret Intelligence Agent,* foreword by Stephenson, p. xv.

2. National Archives and Records Administration (nara) RG59 702.4111/1608.

3. Certificate of Admission in Troy's *Wild Bill and Intrepid,* p. 35.

4. Hyde, *The Quiet Canadian,* p. 31-32.

5. Ellis in *A Man Called Intrepid,* CBC television documentary, 1974.

6. John Tracy, *Winnipeg Tribune,* Canadian Press Wire story July 7, 1954.

7. *The Two Bills,* Bermuda Island Press, April 1968. U. of R. 83-7 Box 4 500. 1–7.

8. Lash, *Roosevelt and Churchill,* p. 113, reporting comments of Harold Ickes.

9. Robert Goralski, *World War II Almanac,* July 1, 1940 p. 125.

10. *Op. cit.,* September 27, 1940, p. 133.

11. Quoted in *The World At War 1939-42* documentary.

12. Richard Dunlop, *Donovan, America's Master Spy,* p.vii, foreword by Stephenson, dated May 1, 1982.

13. *The Two Bills,* Bermuda Island Press, April 1968, U. of R., 83-7 Box 4 500. 1-7. Some of the Americans contacted at an early stage were Gene Tunney, Junius Morgan, Ernest Cuneo, Vincent Astor, Errett Cord, Henry Stimson, Frank Knox, Cordell Hull, Ben Cohen, Wendell Wilkie and Edward Stettinius. Troy, *Wild Bill and Intrepid,* pp. 166–67 on meeting Donovan. "Stephenson was very fortunate in reestablishing contact with Donovan. He knew Donovan [had] known him in the past, he had not any official connections with him, but he knew him quite well. And it was through Donovan that he was able to meet people in high places in Washington ..." (Dick Ellis in *Tuesday Night* documentary transcription. U. of R. Roll C Take 1).

14. Anthony Cave Brown, *Wild Bill Donovan: The Last Hero,* p. 148.

15. Dunlop, p. viii, foreword by Stephenson.

16. Stephenson, "The Early Days of OSS (COI)" p. 4 cited in Troy, *Donovan and the CIA,* Hyde, *The Quiet Canadian,* p. 36.

17. Troy, *Donovan and the CIA,* p. 55. The preface pages refer to the volume as the

"product of official research," but not the official position of the Central Intelligence Agency.

18. Morton to Colonel E. I. Jacob, September 18, 1941, Churchill Papers CCC, Box 145, Folder 463, item 2; also quoted in CIA paper entitled, " Studies in the history of intelligence, p. 109. Printed in 1974. Cited in Lovell p.339. Lovell infers the "British officer" involved was Stephenson, as does Troy.

19. *The Great Canadian Spy*, Roll 3 of 4 83-7 box 4 500.1-7 p 3/1-2.

20. Conyers Read's "Pre-COI Period" transcript, OSS records, Wash-Hist-Off-Op.23, cited in Troy, p. 146.

21. Dunlop, p. viii, foreword by Stephenson.

22. Pforzheimer Collection cited in Dunlop, p. 206.

23. Lee, cited in Dunlop, p. 210.

24. What was the best defense against air attack? Could the war be won by air power and blockade alone? Which types of ordinance were proving effective, and which types ineffective? How could intelligence operations be improved? What were the principal problems the British had in mobilizing economically for the war? The British were expanding their armed forces with the greatest possible speed and the United States would probably have to undertake a similar expansion; in what ways could we profit from the British experience?" (Extract from a biography of Donovan — NARA source unknown.)

25. "I note that Arthur Schlesinger makes it clear," Stephenson said later, that neither Churchill's "direct appeals, incidentally through me, nor the King's letter, moved FDR on the destroyers and it would tend to confirm that it was clearly only our clique including W. J. D., Stimson, Knox, Hull, Ben Cohen Wendell and Stettinius and other private and administrative citizens gathered with me to ease FDR into legal reasons and explanations that finally achieved the destroyers okay from FDR fearing a reluctant Congress to overcome and our group of lawyers found the way to the great advantage of the Allies and indeed the whole world." Intrepid to Steverite, August 31, 1974, U. of R.83-7 801.1-1 Stephenson also said of the deal, "DESTROYERS BASES DEAL HYDE PAGE 37 WORKED BY LEGAL FORMULA WITH DONOVAN AND LAWYER FRIENDS AND MINE INCLUDING SECRETLY WILKIE (Wendell) AFTER WINSTON'S DIRECT AND PUBLIC APPEALS TO FDR HAD FAILED TO PRODUCE THIS VITAL LIFELINE PRODUCTION AS EARL M OF B SAID LATER TO YOU STOP — Intrepid to Steverite, July 15, 1974, U. of R.83-7 801.1-1

26. Stephenson in *The Two Bills*, transcript of an interview by Shaun Herron, Bermuda 1968, U. of R. 83-7 Box 4 500 1-7.

27. *The Great Canadian Spy*, Roll 2 of 4, 83-7 box 4 500.1-7 p 2/8-9

28. Dunlop, p. ix, foreword by Stephenson.

29. *The BSC history*, 'Procurement', pages 10, 11, 14, 17, 27, 334, 335, 352, 393–399.

30. *The Great Canadian Spy*, Roll 3 of 4, 83-7 box 4 500.1-7 p 3/1.

31. *The Sunday Star* (Toronto) October 8, 1989, based on BSC history, and CIA study released in 1974.

32. Intrepid to Steverite, April 6, 1974, U. of R. 83-7 801.1-3.

33. Herb Rowland, resume U. of R. 83-7 Box 9 801. 7-1. He was kept on after the war at the request of Britain's Foreign Office, employed by the Super Security Agency of British Foreign Office in Washington, and was in continual liaison with the FBI and the CIA.

34. Stephenson was unsure he would live through the war and Hill's brother-in-law, Canadian lawyer Glenn McPherson became executor of a new will.

35. *Canadians at War, Reader, Digest* Vol. 2, p. 512.

36. Ibid.

37. Hyde, *The Quiet Canadian*, p. 178, p. 181.

38. Stevenson mentions Tommy Drew-Brook, Charles Vining, Herb Rowland, Ernest Bavin. "I reduced the Canadian content simply because it shrinks within the larger picture ..." Stevenson explained to R. S. Malone, then editor-in-chief of the Toronto *Globe and Mail*. (June 4, 1974, letter) " You can see how the balance could come down rather heavily on U.S.–U.K. aspects," continued the British-born journalist. "On the other hand, Sir William is the central character and I have emphasized how vital his Canadian background was throughout BSC's history." 83-7 Box 9 801.4.

39. Thomas Troy, *Donovan and the CIA*, 1981, p. 34.

40. Tracy, Canadian Press wire, *Op. cit.*

41. *The Two Bills*, cited in *Winnipeg Free Press*, September 23, 1989, *Washington Post* Syndicated, based on BSC history.

42. Cited in *Winnipeg Free Press* September 23, 1989, *Washington Post* Syndicated.

43. Cited in *The World at War 1939-42*, "On Our Way," producers Jeremy Isaacs, Peter Batty, Thames.

44. Cited in *Winnipeg Free Press*, September 23, 1989, *Washington Post* Syndicated.

45. Ibid.

46. Ibid.

47. *Toronto Star*, September 19, 1989 (*Washington Post* Syndicate story — citation from BSC history).

48. Donald Downes, *The Scarlet Thread*, p. 59–60.

49. *Op. cit.*, p. 60–61.

50. In early April 1941, Brig. Gen. Sherman Miles, the Assistant Chief of Staff Intelligence wrote to the Chief of Staff warning of Donovan, "In great confidence ONI tells me that there is considerable reason to believe that there is a movement on foot, fostered by Col. Donovan, to establish a super agency controlling all intelligence. This would mean that such an agency, no doubt under Colonel Donovan, would collect, collate and possibly even evaluate all military intelligence which we now gather from foreign countries. From the point of view of the war department, such a move would appear very disadvantageous, if not calamitous." Memo, Miles to Marshall, April 8, 1941. Records of the Army staff, Army Intelligence Decimal File Record Group 319, File 310.11, Washington National Records Centre, Suitland Maryland, cited in Troy, *Donovan and the CIA*, p. 42.

51. William Donovan to Adjutant General War Department, through Joint Chiefs of Staff, Recommendation for Award of Distinguished Service Medal to William Stephenson, July 19, 1944, attached to Memorandum for the President, from Donovan, of same date.

52. *A Man Called Intrepid* CBC television documentary, executive producer William Harcourt, 1974.

53. Historical notes written by Dick Ellis (said to be given to Whitney Shepardson) undated CCC Hyde 1/12. Also *Tuesday Night* transcript , Roll 3, U. of R.

54. June 19, 1944, William Donovan memorandum to Adjutant General War

Department, through Joint Chiefs of Staff, with copy to Roosevelt, Donovan Papers, "OSS Reports to the White House 1942–1944," Carlisle, Penn.

55. Stephenson, speaking in *A Man Called Intrepid*, CBC television documentary, 1974.

56. Noel Coward, *Future Indefinite*, pp. 271, 275.

57. Ingall to Shaun Herron, U. of R. 83-7 Box 9 801.7-2

58. William Donovan to Adjutant General War Department, through Joint Chiefs of Staff, Recommendation for Award of Distinguished Service Medal to William Stephenson, July 19, 1944, attached to Memorandum for the President, from Donovan of same date.

59. "Appointments and telephone calls, August 9. 1941–Sept 29, 1945," Donovan papers, cited in Troy, *Donovan and the CIA*, p. 83.

60. Cited in Dunlop, p. 327, not footnoted — says message relayed by diplomatic pouch.

61. Ian Fleming, "Memorandum to Colonel Donovan," June 27, 1941, OSS records, Wash-Dir-Op 125. Fleming sent copies to Admiral Godfrey and WS Stephenson. (Lovell and Troy) According to Ellis, Fleming "had nothing to do with it," and the main structure was established long before Fleming visited the U.S. *Tuesday Night* transcript Roll 4 p. 4 U. of R.

62. Historical notes written by Dick Ellis (said to be given to Whitney Shepardson), undated. CCC Hyde 1/12

63. Bradley F. Smith, *The Ultra Magic Deals*, p. 88, citing October 19, 1941. Lee to Washington, file 10/16/41, Box 247 Entry 59, R.G. 319, Suitland, NA.

64. Historical notes written by Dick Ellis (said to be given to Whitney Shepardson), undated. CCC Hyde 1/12

65. *The Great Canadian Spy*, Roll 1 of 4, 83-7 box 4 500.1-7 p 1/9

66. *New York Times*, December 6, 1940, Dunlop, p. 232.

67. Nadya Gardner Letteny to W. S. S. March 19, 1976. U. of R. 83-7 Box 11 801. 17-1 When she retired she wrote a history of her cases, which was to be deposited in the National Archives for use as a training manual in the event of future hostilities. She was told it would be available only on a direct Presidential order.

68. Interview With Dick Ellis, *Tuesday Night* Roll 3 Page 1, U. of R. According to *A Man Called Intrepid*, they were prepared in Toronto.

69. *A Man Called Intrepid* — blurb, and other sources. This quote is also used in a summary of the career of William Stephenson, which was printed by the veterans of the Officers of the OSS, indicating the veterans do not consider this quote or the episode as nonsense.

70. Winston Churchill, *The Grand Alliance* ,p. 163

71. Winston Churchill, *The Grand Alliance*, p 166–167

72. Letter from Acting Secretary of the Treasury to Secretary of State. 841.011 B11, August 11, 1942.

Chapter 6 The Transatlantic Link

1. Lovell, *Cast No Shadow*, p. 330.

2. Gubbins to Ellis, August 16, 1972, U. of R. 83-7 Box 9 801.6.

3. U. of R. 83-7 Box 10 801. 10-12.

4. Gubbins, foreword, U. of R. 83-7 Box 10 801.10-9

5. Stephenson tells of another meeting with Churchill in a cable to the writer William Stevenson. Churchill was in bed reading reports at seven in the morning with Stephenson and Bill Donovan. Churchill asked if they knew the French resistance leader Charles De Gaulle. "Bill replied 'Oh yes. I have known him since his St. Cyr days. [De Gaulle graduated and taught at St. Cyr, a French military school.] He is a very difficult and obstinate man with a Jean D'Arc complex. Requires tight hold on a short leash.' Winston grunted, 'Oh, I suppose I have handled more difficult men in my time — garumph.' But you will recall his subsequent admission, 'Of all the heavy crosses I have had to bear the double-cross of Lorraine.' et cetera." Intrepid to Steverite, August 29, 1974. U. of R. 83-7 801.4.

6. Cuneo to Stephenson, December 15, 1975. U. of R. 83-7 Box 10 801.10-4.

7. In his letter to Stephenson, Cuneo says,"My war record is obscure, in the nature of things, and I should like a written document to indicate that when my days are over ... As the tontine works, you are the only high authority who is in a position to describe my services." *Ibid.*

8. *Maclean's*, December 1, 1952.

9. Handwritten note, Colin Gubbins to Dick Ellis, August 16, 1972, U. of R. 83-7 Box 9 801.6.

10. Studio history provided by Shepparton Studios. The studios re-opened for filmmaking business at the end of 1945 with six stages. One stage was a casualty in the second of three air raids on the studios.

11. Hyde to Harrington, June 15, 1942. CCC 3/22.

12. Hyde, CCC 3/22.

13. In September 1942, Hyde met with the FBI director to discuss the premature release of information regarding German agents in Trinidad who were sending wireless messages. Hoover thanked Dorothy Hyde for the instruction she gave to FBI, and said eight German saboteurs captured in July '42 broke down quickly. BSC was used to exchange information. Hoover was interested in preparations Axis nations were making for the use of bacteriological weapons, as the FBI had little information on the subject. There is a record of a January 20, 1944, meeting between Hyde and Hoover, as Hyde was leaving the U.S. Hyde, CCC 3/30.

14. Hyde, CCC 3/13.

15. Letter to "Herbert" from Stephenson, Hyde CCC 3/13.

16. The scope of North American security measures can be determined from this security executive paper marked "Secret" in Hyde's files. It lists (a) Port Security (b) Alien's Policy (c) Subversive Activities (d) Anti-sabotage (e) Control of Entry (f) Colonial Security (g) Security in South America. (1) Espionage (2) Sabotage (3) Subversive Activities (4) Other Fifth Column Activities (5) Aliens (6) Control of Information and Communication (7) Identity cards, passes and permits (8) Security of SpecIal Localities (9) Control of Entry Exit Travel Facilities (10) Shipping Security. Hyde, CCC 3/13.

17. U. of R. 83.7 801.1-3.

18. Troy, *Donovan and the CIA*, p. 83.

Chapter 7 Clandestine Success

1. Stephenson to Stevenson, April 18, 1974. U. of R. 83.7 801. 1-3.

2. BSC History, p. 155.

3. *Op. cit.*, p. 165.

4. Intrepid to Steverite, February 22, 1974. U. of R. 83-7 801.1-3.

5. Stephenson to "Bison," Toronto, (Herb Rowland) October 15, 1973, U. of R., 83-7 Box 9 801.8. Also *Intrepid*, p. 461.

6. Outline U. of R. 83-7 box 9 801 .3-1.

7. Intrepid to Steverite, December 30, 1975. U. of R. 83-7 801.1-6.

8. Intrepid to Steverite, U. of R. 83-7 801.1-1 According to Stephenson, Tizard was at the Shoreham Hotel when he received a phone call from the FBI about security of his possessions; Stephenson contacted Hoover who didn't know about it. Later the call was traced through Sam Foxworth to the German Embassy.

9. *The Great Canadian Spy*, radio transcript, U. of R. 83-7 Box 4 500.1-7 Roll 2 of 4.

10. British Embassy to Department of State, January 21, 1941. NARA 841.01B11/185. Hoover is said to have thought of the name British Security Coordination.

11. Hyde, CCC 3/23 October 30/42 (November 7/42 message).

12. February 6, 1941, letter from special agent Bannerman to Clark. NARA 841.01 B11/191.

13. State Department, copy of letter from British Embassy, July 15, 1941. NARA 841.01 B11.

14. Berle to Welles, March 31, 1941, R.G. 59 State file 841.20211/23

15. FDRL, February 5, 1942, Berle letter to Roosevelt.

16. Berle diary, February 4, 1942.

17. February 4, 1942, letter from Sherwood to Roosevelt.

18. See "Bill Ross Smith."

19. Biddle memorandum, February 26, 1942, Hyde Park, New York.

20. Berle diary, March 5, 1942, NARA RG59, 841.20211/36.

21. Berle diary, March 10, 1942, NARA RG59 841.20211/36.

22. David Ogilvy to W. S. S. February 25, 1963. Hyde CCC 1/10.

23. Intrepid to Steverite, April 6, 1974, U. of R. 83-7 801.1-3.

24. A January 22, 1944, letter from Cox, the US Assistant Solicitor General requested from BSC: (1) list of employees (2) supplemented with additional information (3) BSC will conduct and limit its activities (a) conduct no investigations of any kind without the written approval of the Director of the FBI (b) all information obtained about the Western Hemisphere should be transmitted to the FBI (c) if transmitted to another US agency should be transmitted simultaneously to the FBI (d) BSC will maintain no arrangements with informants whether or not with compensation (e) BSC will maintain liaison with the Combined Chiefs of Staff only through the British Joint Staff Mission ... (f) BSC will maintain no liaison with the United States Civil Service. "While we are required under the Act to keep a record of the activities in which your organization may engage, we wish to do so without any unnecessary requirements or inconvenience to you and we shall be glad at any time to discuss with you questions that may arise." Stephenson's response isn't recorded.

25. Hyde, *Secret Intelligence Agent*, p. 232.

26. Stone to Stephenson letter, June 18, 1943. Hyde CCC 3/30.

27. *Tuesday Night* transcript, pp. 2–3 U. of R. Roll 8.

28. Spruille Braden, *Diplomats and Demagogues* p. 247.

29. Braden, *Op. cit.*, p. 252.

30. Hyde's later version admits the forgery. See Hyde, *Secret Intelligence Agent*, p. 154–155.

31. Braden, *Op. cit.*, p. 251.
32. Cuneo, cited in *Desperate Deception*, p. 14, CIA file.
33. Sir Bede Clifford to Hyde, July 5, 1963, Hyde CCC 1/11 (After reading Hyde's book, Clifford thought the search may have had something to do with the smuggling of industrial diamonds, *The Quiet Canadian*, p. 132).
34. Letter, Hoover to Stephenson, March 30, 1945 Hyde CCC 1/1.
35. Carlisle Papers, June 19, 1944. Memorandum for the President from Donovan: recommendation for the award of Distinguished Service medal to Mr. William S. Stephenson.
36. Carlisle Papers, September 25, 1946, letter Donovan to Cadogan.

Chapter 8 A Final Case

1. BSC History, foreword by Stephenson.
2. Interview with Grace Garner, London, February 1990.
3. Interview with Tom Hill, March 10, 1993 (and subsequent Hill quotations).
4. Lovell, *Cast No Shadow* (for MI6 classification), p. 346. A version of the history was published by British writer Nigel West in 1998.
5. *Washington Post*, September 17, 1989.
6. August 15, 1973 cable, U. of R. 83-7 801 1-2.
7. October 10, 1945, cited in *Spy Wars*, p. 47.
8. King diary cited in *Spy Wars*, p. 56.
9. Intrepid to Steverite, April 13, 1974. U. of R. 83-7 801.1-3.
10. A history of the VENONA project released by the National Security Agency says Gouzenko's efforts had no bearing on the actual VENONA breakthroughs, but they "were important to Allied counterintelligence efforts."
11. Intrepid to Steverite, December 20, 1975. U. of R. 83-7 801.1-6.
12. John Sawatsky, *Gouzenko the Untold Story*, pp. 122, 202.
13. Peter Worthington, *Looking for Trouble*, p. 431.
14. U. of R. 83-7 Box 9 801. 3-2 January 9, 1976, letter to W. S. S.

Chapter 9 Island Retirement

1. William Stephenson letter to the editor, *Globe and Mail*, following Malone's death (undated in author's files).
2. *Maclean's*, December 1, 1952.
3. *Evening Standard*, "Londoners Diary," January 21, 1951.
4. Smallwood to Stephenson letter, October 27, 1952. U. of R. 83-7 Box 9 801.7-3.
5. Rothschild to Stephenson letter, April 2, 1976. U. of R. 83-7 Box 9. 801. 9-1.
6. *Time*, June 6, 1939.
7. Interview with Tom Hill, March 1993.
8. Caribbean Cement Co. Ltd. annual report, 1960, and W. S. S. speech, April 29, 1961, in Hyde file.
9. "CARIBCEMCO WILL REQUIRE TWENTY MILLION FOR PRESENT EXPANSION WHICH I SUPPOSE I WILL HAVE TO FINE [*sic*] FOR IT," he cabled William Stevenson in 1973. Cable to Steverite, August 15, 1973 U. of R. 83-7 801 1-2. According to Hill, some of the work was transferred to a company called Cement General which was changed to Canadian General.
10. *Kingston Daily Gleaner*, November 18, 1961.

11. *Winnipeg Free Press*, December 23, 1954.
12. Interview with Douglas Campbell, March 1989.
13. January 11, 1974, MC Fulton, MD letter. U. of R. 83-7 Box 10 801. 10-4.
14. *Toronto Star,* May 27, 1979.
15. Dahl to Stephenson, June 28, 1972. U. of R., 83-7 Box 9 801. 7-1.
16. Letter from Rothschild to Stephenson, May 25, 1976. U. of R. 83-7 box 9 801.9-1.
17. Noel Coward, *The Noel Coward Diaries*, March 21, 1949, p. 125.
18. *Op. cit.,* November 12, 1956.
19. Stevenson, *A Man Called Intrepid,* p. 505.
20. Intrepid to Steverite, March 14, 1975, U. of R. 83-7 801.1-5.
21. Robert Collins, *Who He?*, p. 179.
22. Intrepid to Steverite, March 16, 1975. U. of R. 83-7 801.1-5.
23. Thomas Troy, *Wild Bill and Intrepid*, p. 15.
24. *Toronto Star*, May 27, 1979.
25. Intrepid to Steverite, August 8, 1974, U. of R. 83-7 801.1-4.
26. *Winnipeg Free Press*, July 9, 1954.
27. *Toronto Star*, May 27, 1979.
28. October 25, 1972. U. of R. 83-7 Box 9 801.7-3
29. *Toronto Sun*, December 13, 1973; December 26, 1973, Worthington columns.
30. Intrepid to Steverite, December 27, 1973. U. of R. 83-7 801.1-2.
31. *Toronto Sun*, August 26, 1974.
32. *Toronto Sun*, August 17, 1975.
33. *Winnipeg Free Press*, July 8, 1980.
34. Radio interview in possession of Stefansson family.
35. Interview with Bina Ingimundson, June 1989.
36. Interview with Irv Stefansson, June 1989.
37. Interview with Mackenzie Porter, March 10, 1991.
38. Interview with David Young, April 1992.
39. Interview with Dr. Philip Hall, Winnipeg, March 1997.
40. Interview with Derek Bedson, May 9, 1989.
41. Interview with Irv Stefansson, May 1989.
42. Carolyn Rickey, producer to W. S. S., referring to April 20, 1977 broadcast, May 17, 1977, U. of R. 83-7 Box 11 801. 17-1.
43. "Wells' (1866–1946) preoccupation with Utopian ideals — a belief that the millennium was coincident with the onward march of science — led to [his] scintillating dissertations. But, as he began to see that science could work for evil as well as good, his faith deserted him, and declined into pessimism." G. B. Shaw (1856–1950) often promoted the merits of individual virtue. "... Shavian morality of individual responsibility, self-discipline, heroic effort without thought of reward or atonement, and the utmost integrity," Chamber's Dictionary.
44. Quoted in *The Royal Gazette* (Bermuda), February 3, 1989.
45. *Winnipeg Free Press*, February 3, 1989.

Chapter 10 "A Mysterious Millionaire"
1. Interview with Mackenzie Porter, March 10, 1991.
2. See *Maclean's*, December 1, 1952.
3. *Logberg Heimskringla*, March 9, 1989.

4. Tim Naftali, "Intrepid's Last Deception," *Intelligence and National Security* 8.

5. Napier Moore story on Cuneo, *Financial Post*, February 18, 1956.

6. Noble information, August 25, 1975 cable, Intrepid to Steverite.. U. of R. 83-7 801.1-6

7. Porter interview, *op. cit.*

8. See Chapman Pincher's *Their Trade is Treachery* (1981), Peter Wright's *Spycatcher* (1987).

9. W. S. S. to Ellis, August 24, 1959, CCC Hyde 1/11.

10. Porter interview, *op. cit.*

11. August 23, 1962, letter. CCC Hyde 1/6.

12. Interview with Bill Ross Smith February 11, 1990.

13. Naftali, "Intrepid's Last Deception," p. 93.

14. Hyde, *Secret Intelligence Agent*, p. 119.

15. *The Times*, August 12, 1989. Hyde had a dispute with the British authorities when he left his university position. The British Council "had an interest in his job in Pakistan," Hyde wrote to Stephenson in 1963. When Punjab University released him to pursue the Stephenson book, it "was not satisfactory" to the Council and they reneged on helping Hyde with moving expenses from Asia. As a result Hyde took the Council to court. Hyde, *Ibid.*

16. *The Sunday Times*, October 21, 1962.

17. *New York Times*, clipping undated p. 18 CCC Hyde 1/1.

18. Ellis to Hyde, letter. CCC Hyde 1/10 9-1.

19. May 28, 1963, letter. CCC Hyde 2/14.

20. Mary Stephenson to Hyde. CCC Hyde 1/9.

21. July 30, 1963, letter to Stephenson, CCC Hyde File 1/11.

22. Hyde File 1/5, CCC.

23. *The Sunday Times*, October 21, 1962.

24. Letter to Hyde, January 9, likely 1963, CCC Hyde 1/10.

25. July 30, 1963, Hyde to Stephenson. CCC Hyde 1/11.

26. Hyde's file, CCC, also Mary Lovell's, *Cast No Shadow*, p. 376.

27. Drew Brook letter to Hyde, December 12, 1961. CCC Hyde 1/5.

28. Rosalyn Hyde interview, February 1990.

29. Cables addressed from Intrepid, March 13–15, 1963 CCC Hyde 1/11.

30. *Ibid.*

31. Naftali, p.96.

32. August 24, 1959, letter Stephenson to Ellis, CCC Hyde file 1/11.

33. *Winnipeg Tribune*, July 7, 1954.

34. Ellis, *A Break in the Silence*, p. xxiv.

35. Stevenson papers, October 20, 1975. U. of R. 83-7 801.1-6. It seems Stephenson did not want the Ellis passage used.

36. *New York Times Book Review*, February 28, 1976, p. 2.

37. Cited in March 16, 1976 cable from Stephenson. U. of R. 83-7 801. 1-7.

38. Lovell, *Cast No Shadow*, p. 376.

39. Numerous books chronicle Philby's career See *Spyclopedia* pp. 358, 359 for Philby bibliography.

40. Ducas interview, 1990.

41. Mahl, *Desperate Deception*, p. xii.

42. Mahl, *Ibid.* p. xiii, citing L. B. Kirkpatrick's review of Hyde's *Quiet Canadian* in

Studies in Intelligence 7, the CIA's in-house journal, Summer 1963.

Chapter 11 A Man Called Intrepid

1. September 12, 1975, David Bruce to Julian Muller. U. of R. 83-7 Box 10 801.13.
2. Gubbins to Ellis, August 16, 1972.U. of R. 83-7 Box 9 801.6
3. *Ibid.*
4. Stephenson to Stevenson, September 11, 1972. U. of R. 83-7 801 1-2.
5. Chapman Pincher, *Their Trade Is Treachery*, p.204.
6. October 20, 1975. W. S. S. cable to Stevenson. U. of R. 83-7 801.1-6.
7. Kildare Dobbs book review of *A Man Called Intrepid, Globe and Mail*, reprinted in *Winnipeg Free Press*, March 9, 1976.
8. March 22, 1976, "I dropped reference to an association with you from the manuscript of *AMCI* ... Kildare Dobbs may have picked something from the HBJ press release," explained Stevenson in a letter to the puzzled Stephenson. U. of R. 83-7 Box 9 801 3-2 52.
9. Stevenson, *Zanek!*, About the Author.
10. Stevenson, *90 Minutes at Entebbe*, About the Author.
11. *New York Times*, February 18, 1976, U. of R. 83-7 Box 9 801.9
12. August 26, 1975. U. of R. 83-7 Box 9 801 3-2 p. 2
13. August 26, 1975. U. of R. 83-7 Box 9 801. 3-2 p.3
14. Stevenson to Stephenson, January 27, 1976 U. of R., 83-7 Box 9 801. 3-2
15. For example :"... the fact is that I am still wading knee deep through *AMCI* material. But a quick run through it today has given me the sense at last that it is right. For example one copy editor suggested we should give more space to the Battle of Britain to explain why certain things were done — and I've finished what is really a brief insert, but what seems to me to be a moving summary of that Spitfire summer. It not only gives substance but puts that battle into new perspective — and a welcome counterbalance to these tales of the Mafia–CIA plots put out by the KGB Disinformation Bureau. July 24, 1974, p. 6 letter Stev to W. S. S. U. of R.; "... we are faced with a task of psychological warfare fought on behalf of democracy, far more complex than anything experienced before. The Russians have learned from the Nazi mistakes. The communist subtleties are such that the masses are easily mislead ... The situation within the media adds to the problem — not all newsmen by all means are willing dupes, but many have a social conscience and unwittingly advance Russia's long term interests by championing small causes that on the surface appear to have no communist inspiration or connection." Letter Stev to W. S. S. 83-7 Box 9 801.3-2. August 23, 1975; "I am satisfied the chief Russian objective is to subvert the media here, and in general to diminish the confidence between English speaking countries." August 23, 1975, letter to Stephenson. U. of R. 83-7 Box 9 801.3-2 (In 1993 Oleg Kalugin, former head of foreign counter-intelligence for the KGB did say he publicized information of the RCMP's illegal activities in the 1970s to stir up trouble. "We always considered it our duty to fan discord among the allies of the United States, among the citizens and the structures of the government, among those who are our enemies at the time." *Canadian Press* wire based on CBC *Fifth Estate* interview, cited in *Winnipeg Free Press*, March 30, 1993).
16. Letter to Stephenson, August 25, 1975. U. of R. 83-7 Box 9 801.3-2.

17. Interview with Ron Robbins, May 19, 1992.
18. Letter to Malone, June 4, 1974. U. of R. 83-7 Box 9 801.4.
19. Letter to Ogilvy, August 9, 1974. U. of R. 83-7 Box 9 801.4.
20. Letter to Stephenson, October 9, 1975. U. of R. 83-7 Box 9 801.3-2.
21. Stephenson to Stevenson, October 20, 1975. U. of R. 83-7 801.1-6.
22. Stevenson, *Zanek!*, p. vi.
23. Stevenson, *A Man Called Intrepid*, p. 481.
24. There are references to Bohr's departure from Europe in correspondence between Stevenson and Stephenson, and with S.O.E. chief Colin Gubbins before the publication of *AMCI*. There are also, in the files of William Stevenson, copies of message sent to 'Justitsraaden,' a Danish government department purporting to describe the location of microfilm hidden in a key with an "important message from the British government." (It seems that although Stephenson's sphere of influence was North America during the war, he was aware of some of major clandestine activities on the continent. If not, what is this paper?) Stephenson says in a cable that Bohr was "aboard one of the several fast subchasers I wangled from USN for SOE he then [*sic*] shipped to me and I handed him over to Admiral Strauss of the Manhattan Project." In the television documentary, *A Man Called Intrepid*, Stephenson's recollection is similar. He says the "torpedo boats" were usually used to ship ball bearings from Sweden, and "they got him, flew into London, and put him on a ship to New York, where he was picked up and taken to the offices of the Manhattan Project." Stephenson doesn't mention waiting for Bohr in a Scottish field. Gubbins wrote that Bohr was shipped out on a fishing boat to Sweden, and then onto the U.K. He remembers Stephenson's subchasers were a "Godsend" and invaluable shuttling agents ("How we and our Norwegian crews blessed 'little Bill'"), but from his letter to Stevenson, it seems he doesn't remember them in relation to transporting Bohr. Stephenson, in his correspondence with the writer, recalled the banker and former SOE chief Charles Hambro arranged, through a branch of his bank, to alert Bohr's son, "to ready and accompany Niels to boarding point off Copenhagen for trip to Scotland." In Stevenson's account Charles Hambro is not mentioned, and Stephenson tells "a young officer who joined him" in Scotland about the need to airlift out Bohr's son, as he was familiar with his father's work. July 30 (1972?) letter Gubbins to Stevenson. U. of R. 83-7 Box 9 801.6.
25. Letter to Stephenson, June 4, 1973. U. of R. 83-7 Box 9 801. 3-1.
26. Stevenson to W. S. S. July (1974?) U. of R. 83-7 Box 9 801.3-2 p. 2.
27. Sir David Hunt, *Times Literary Supplement*, May 28, 1976, review.
28. David Ogilvy letter to author, January 28, 1990.
29. Stephenson to Rowland, July 23, 1973. U. of R. 83-7 box 9 801.8.
30. Letter Stevenson to W. S. S., January 27, 1976. U. of R.
31. Letter to W. S. S., March 22, 1976. U. of R. 83-7 box 9 801.3-2.
32. Letter Stev to W. S. S., March 16, 1976. U. of R. 83-7 box 9 801.3-2.
33. W. S. S. cable to Stev, March 16, 1976. U. of R. 83-7 801. 1-7.
34. Stev letter to W. S. S., July 2, 1976. U. of R. 83-7 Box 11 801. 17-1.
35. Cable W. S. S. to Stev, August 21, 1975. U. of R. 83-7 801.1-1.
36. Letter to Stephenson, August 25, 1975. U. of R. 83-7 Box 9 801.3-2.
37. Stevenson, *A Man Called Intrepid*, pp. 114, 310.

38. ITT had numerous holdings in Germany, and Behn met with Hitler in 1933 with the assistance of the American embassy in Berlin, as would be normal course of events. By the end of the decade ITT had lost control of its operations in Nazi Germany, and Behn was not allowed even to visit the ITT plants there. Currency controls were in effect, and there was no way of bringing funds out of Germany. Behn helped bring out scientists from occupied France in 1940, and their work helped Allied advances in radar and high frequency radio direction finding. ITT supplied radio and telephone equipment to Allied forces, secured land lines, and later reorganized communications labs in France and Belgium to produce portable radio equipment. Behn was awarded the Medal of Merit by President Truman after the war, the highest honour the United States could give to a civilian. Behn was buried in Arlington National Cemetery in 1957. U. of R. 83-7 Box 11 801.17-2.

39. William Stevenson to Edward J. Gerrity Jr. June 2, 1976. U. of R. 83-7 Box 11 801.17-2.

40. Richard Deacon, *Spyclopedia*, p. 229, and other sources.

41. J. C. Masterman, *The Double-Cross System*, p. 80.

42. Nicolas J. Cull, *Selling War*, p. 186.

43. Thomas Troy, 'The British Assault on J. Edgar Hoover,' *International Journal of Intelligence and Counterintelligence.* Volume 3, No. 2. Summer 1989.

44. Intrepid to Steverite, November 16, 1974. U. of R., 83-7 801.1-4. Montagu was friendly with Stephenson. His wife Iris worked for BSC. Montagu to W. S. S. U. of R. 83-7 Box 9 801.7-1.

45. August 23, 1975, letter Stevenson to Stephenson. U. of R. 83-7 Box 9 801.3-2.

46. August 25, 1975, letter Stevenson to Stephenson. U. of R 83-7 Box 9 801.3-2.

47. Anthony Summers, *Official and Confidential: The Secret Life of J. Edgar Hoover*, p. 128.

48. Montgomery Hyde, *The Atom Bomb Spies*, p. xi.

49. Robert Collins, *Who He?* p. 182.

50. Gubbins to Stevenson, February 6, 1976. U. of R. 83-7 Box 9 801.6.

51. Mountbatten to W. S. S. February 2, 1976. U. of R. 83-7 Box 11 801. 17-1 In early 1976, Stephenson cabled the author indicating he wanted this quote to be used on the book flap of future editions. It doesn't appear to have been used. Cable to Stevenson, February 9, 1976. U. of R. 83-7 801.1-1.

52. Gilbert Highet to Stephenson, March 7, 1976. U. of R. 83-7 Box 9 801. 9-1.

53. Letter Bruce to Muller, September 12, 1975. U. of R. 83-7 Box 10 801.13.

54. *New York Times Book Review*, February 29, 1976.

55. There was some controversy when Trevor Roper was appointed Regius Professor of Modern History. Others on staff, such as the historian A. J. P. Taylor, had an edge in published work. He was quite well known for written attacks on fellow historians, such as R. H. Tawney, Lawrence Stone, and Arnold Toynbee. He was particularly hard on Toynbee. Reviewing Toynbee's *A Study of History*, Trevor-Roper wrote Toynbee was trying to establish himself as a prophet, and he compared him to Hitler. When Trevor-Roper was established as Regius Professor in 1957, the *Observer* reported that some were "wondering about the influence on undergraduates of a man capable of writing a considered article with such elaborate violence and personal hatred." Politics were thought to be involved. The appointment was " widely represented as an act of political partisanship by [former Prime Minister and publishing magnate] Harold Macmillan, and the appearance of

jobbery was enhanced when Trevor-Roper organized the campaign for Mr. Macmillan's election to the Chancellorship of Oxford in 1960," John Grigg wrote in *The Guardian* in 1964. Trevor-Roper's *The Last Days of Hitler* was published by Macmillan. Citations in *Current Biography* 1983. *The Guardian*, January 23, 1964. In April 1983, Trevor-Roper's haughty reputation as a war expert put himself in the glare of publicity. The German magazine *Stern* acquired 60 volumes of diaries, supposedly those of Adolf Hitler, that were written between 1932 and 1945. The London Times offered $400,000 for excerpts of the diaries and Trevor-Roper, who had been a director of Times Newspapers Ltd. since 1974, was sent to check their authenticity in the safe of a Zurich bank. On April 23, after a quick examination, Trevor-Roper announced that they were genuine. On May 6, 1983, it was proved by chemical tests that the diaries were forgeries.

56. John Costello, *Mask of Treachery*, p. 381. Trevor-Roper acknowledged that he "knew of Philby's communist past" before it was widely known. But it "never occurred to me, at that time, to hold it against him, because our superiors were lunatic in their anti communism." That Trevor Roper did not expose Philby, one writer concluded, owes as much to his own hostility to MI6 as an institution. He determined from his espionage career that the British services were flawed organizations. "When I looked coolly at the world in which I found myself, I thought that, if this was our intelligence system, we are doomed to defeat. Sometimes I encouraged myself by saying such an organization could not possibly survive, unchanged, the strain of war: it would have to be reformed. In fact I was wrong both times. We won the war and SIS at the end of it remained totally unreformed." Trevor Roper, cited in *"C"*, Anthony Cave Brown, p.229.

57. Peter Worthington, "A Particularly Canadian Trait," *Ottawa Sun*, March 5, 1989.

58. *The New York Review of Books*, May 13, 1976. He says, for example, he remembers Stephenson as number 38000. Stephenson was 48000. "All SIS agents were known by their numbers and those in America had five figure numbers beginning with '3.'" He implies that this was where the author got the large estimated number, 30,000, of BSC employees.

59. *Sunday Telegraph*, February 19, 1989, "Death of an Intrepid Fraud."

60. Montgomery Hyde, *Secret Intelligence Agent*, foreword by Stephenson.

61. *The New York Review of Books*, May 13, 1976.

62. Heinz Hohne & Hermann Zolling, *The General was a Spy* (also called *Network*) 1971, p. xxxiii.

63. *Sunday Telegraph*, February 19, 1989, "Death of an Intrepid Fraud."

64. David Stafford resume, Hyde CCC 5/4.

65. Stafford, *Camp X*, p. 289.

66. *The Sunday Star* (Toronto), October 8, 1989 and private information.

67. *Saturday Night*, October 1990.

68. *Winnipeg Tribune*, April 24, 1973.

69. "Miserable cockroaches" is in the Toronto *Sunday Sun*, April 10, 1988; "antisemitic" and "Canadian-of-convenience" in *Toronto Sun*, October 1989. "Lies are their only ammunition."

70. Stafford article in *Saturday Night*, "The Defector," November 1984.

71. *New Statesman*, March 26, 1976.

72. *Times Literary Supplement*, May 28, 1976.

73. *The Times*, February 18, 1989.

74. *Toronto Sun*, July 17, 1981. The information refers to Coville's book, *Winston Churchill and his Inner Circle.*

75. Winston Churchill, *Their Finest Hour*, p. 229.

76. *The Times* (London), February 18, 1989.

77. Richard Cleroux, *Official Secrets* (1990), p. 117.

78. John Bryden, *Best Kept Secret* (1993), p. 335.

79. Naftali, *Intelligence and National Security*, July 1983.

80. *The Royal Gazette* (Bermuda), February 27, 1989.

Chapter 12 BSC Recruits

1. FitzGerald also wondered about the shabby way history had treated the story of William Stephenson. Later she wrote to the author, "I have been rereading parts of *Intrepid's Last Case*. The last paragraph on page 251 jumps out at me. Re-read it!" The page reads "When told that [Kim] Philby after all was a Soviet agent, [former British Prime Minister] Harold Macmillan commented, "You should never you know, catch a spy! Discover him and then control him, but never catch him. A spy causes far more trouble caught than uncaught." It seems Stephenson was aware of the conversation. In the mid-seventies he wrote to the author Stevenson "Assume you refer to Harold's comment as Foreign Secretary to Security head after giving him drubbing. Quote Such are the contradictions strangely of security in a democratic system." Stephenson to Stevenson, July 28, 1975. U.of R. 83-7 801.1-6.

2. Cited in December 30, 1990 letter, Patsey Sullivan to author.

Chapter 13 "Cynthia" and Marion

1. Deacon, *Spyclopedia*, p. 171.

2. Hyde says she did, (*The Quiet Canadian* p. 106–7), but he was later was sued in Italian court. Lais died in the fifties.

3. Cited Lovell, *Cast No Shadow*, p. 326.

4. Interview with Mary Lovell, January 1991. Also in her book, *Cast No Shadow*.

5. There were apparently other sources in the embassy as well. The BSC History and related documents allude to a Ms. Cadet at the Vichy Embassy: "For the past year she has been receiving $300 monthly from Mr. Howard of the British Intelligence division." January 7, 1943.

6. It is possible the New York trips were before de Chastelain worked with her, as Cynthia is quoted as remembering New York meetings. "The routine never varied, I always stayed at the same hotel on Madison, awaited Marion or Mr. Howard. They debriefed me, gave me assignments and acted as paymasters. They were my only contacts."

7. Letter cited in Hyde's *Cynthia*, p. 7.

8. November 15, 1962 letter to Hyde. Hyde CCC 2/7.

9. December 22, 1942 NARA RG 59 701.5111/12-2242. Donovan letter to an assistant of Berle's: "A certain young lady be permitted to go to Hershey and proceed with the French to France."

10. John Coville, author and a Churchill secretary for a short time wrote that he didn't remember Churchill talking about Stephenson. Hyde, *The Quiet Canadian*, p. 138.

Chapter 14 Bill Ross Smith

1. Kim Philby, *My Silent War*, p. 120.
2. David Stafford, *Camp X*, p. 123-124.
3. Richard Dunlop, *Behind Japanese Lines: With the OSS in Burma*, p. 84.
4. Bill Ross Smith on the Ellis Affair. Charles Howard Ellis, known everywhere as Dick Ellis, was accused first of all by Chapman Pincher and following him, by Nigel West in various books. Chapman Pincher in *Their Trade Was Treachery* accused him of being a spy for the Germans and the Russians. Chapman Pincher's source on this was undoubtedly Peter Wright because Peter Wright tells virtually the same story in *Spycatcher*. Chapman Pincher published *Treachery* in 1980, five years after Ellis' death. And he tells the story of Ellis being sent to Paris by SIS in 1923 and he recruited as a subagent his brother-in-law Alexander Zolinsky, a White Russian with considerable connections both in German and Russian intelligence. According to Pincher, for the next 15 years Zolinsky had a high old time selling British secrets to Germany and Russia and vice-versa. This cumulated in, according to Pincher, the actual selling of the British order of battle to the Germans [sic]. He was further accused of giving the Germans the benefit of information the British had obtained by tapping into the hot line which Ribbentrop had installed in the German embassy when he came there in about 1936. "All of this is manifestly untrue because firstly Alexander Zolinsky did exist and was indeed Ellis' brother in law. But in 1923 when Pincher has him as a high-powered spy with connections throughout the hierarchies, he was in fact ten years of age. Secondly, Ellis never served in France at all and in the years 1923 to 1938 he was serving in the British consulate in Berlin, later in the British Chamber of Commerce in Vienna and in the years '35 to '38, I'd have to check the exact years he served as an accredited correspondent to the League of Nations in Geneva, where he was supplied with a nice flat and a chauffeured car. In fact he didn't even join the service proper until 1938. The story therefore by Wright given to Pincher and taken up by the others is sheer fabrication. Thirdly, he could not have given the order of battle to the Germans for the same reason and he could not have given the benefits of the Ribbentrop telephone line to them because it ceased to exist when Ribbentrop returned to Germany at the end of his Ambassadorship before 1938. Therefore the subsequent statement that he had given this evidence up to the outbreak of war is chronologically false. Wright had also said he was a very senior SIS officer having being in charge of SIS operations in the Far East before returning to England in about 1938 to take up as chief of western hemisphere intelligence. This is quite erroneous because he had just entered the Service proper in 1928 and he actually became chief of Far East operations in Singapore after the war in 1946. He was never chief of western hemisphere intelligence. One could only assume therefore that Peter Wright made up these stories about a dead man in order to make a good story for his book and for the information which he sold to Pincher for his book, *Their Trade Was Treachery*. You see what happened on that was that he was brought together. Lord Rothschild asked Peter Wright. I'll go back a bit further. "The story of Peter Wright is that he had worked for fifteen years for navy intelligence as a scientist during which he came into contact with MI5 a lot. He told MI5 he wanted to join them. MI5 said they didn't poach on other services but anytime he was free if he would like to talk to them again they would be pleased to speak to him. Some while later he left Naval intel-

ligence and joined Marconi. Again in that capacity he came in contact with MI5. And after a couple of years with Marconi he proposed and was accepted as an employee of MI5. At that time he asked them to assume his fifteen years on Navy pension. They refused. When at the end of his service he again raised to question of fifteen years of navy pension and named it MI5 again refused saying that they had hired him from Marconi and they had not had him transferred from the Navy to them, therefore they had no responsibility for his pension. He was very embittered about this and said that he would one day get even. He then left the country and went to Tasmania where in due course he had written about a ten thousand words of a biography. Somewhere about 1978, '79 Lord Rothschild invited him to come to England to write officially what Lord Rothschild had done for MI5 during Rothschild's service and afterwards as a protection against any possibility he might be named under the general scandal following the Blunt affair. While he was in England as Rothschild's guest he said to Rothschild he'd like to meet somebody who could write a book. Rothschild called Chapman Pincher and put them together. Wright and Pincher agreed to cooperate on this book, but it was decided to keep Wright's name right out of it and his financial part should be handled through a Swiss bank, supposedly set up by Rothschild. And his part of the royalties should be paid directly there, but his name would never appear. This is supposed to have netted Wright 30,000 pounds or more. He handed the ten thousand words to Chapman Pincher who used them as the basis of *Their Trade Was Treachery*. Subsequently Wright wrote his own book called *Spycatcher* and much of the same wording appears in it, particularly about the Ellis affair.

5.   NARA RG 59 701.6511/1028.
6.   Hyde, *Cynthia*, p.117.
7.   NARA RG 59 701.6511/1037.
8.   *New York Times*, May 8, 1941.
9.   *New York Times*, May 8, 1941.
10.   Beck cable, May 13, 1941, NARA RG59 701.6511/1050.
11.   After July 1940, it was never possible again to read the main Italian naval book codes, except for a few brief intervals as a result of captures after the middle of 1941, he wrote in *Code Breakers The Inside Story of Bletchley Park*. "Fortunately however the Italians began from December 1940 to put more and more of their naval traffic on to a medium grade Swedish cipher machine; this traffic was designated as C 38. It was broken into in the summer of 1941, and read almost continuously afterward. The sinking of the Axis convoys that resulted probably turned the scale against Rommel in North Africa."

Chapter 15 Betty Raymond

1.   Hyde, *The Quiet Canadian*, p. 79.
2.   Hyde, *Secret Intelligence Agent*, p. 150.
3.   Hyde, *Secret Intelligence Agent*, p. 154. Raymond was told the forged signature was checked by the FBI.
4.   *New York Times*, July 24, 1941.
5.   *New York Times*, July 24, 1941.
6.   *New York Herald Tribune*, July 30, 1941.
7.   Hyde, *Secret Intelligence Agent* p. 160; Sumner Welles, *Seven Major Decisions*, p. 101.

Chapter 16 Astley and the Service

1. Intrepid to 'McEwen Toronto,' May 3, 1973, telegram U. of R. 83-7 Box 9 801.8.
2. Astley, *The Inner Circle*, p. 64.
3. Astley, *The Inner Circle*, p. 31.
4. Brown, *Bodyguard of Lies*, p. 687, citing Wingate interview.
5. Duff Hart Davis, *Peter Fleming*, p. 266.
6. Astley, *The Inner Circle*, p. 49–50.
7. Anthony Cave Brown, *"C"*, p. 606.
8. Bell accompanied the ambassador Lord Inverchapel [Clark Kerr] to Washington in May 1946 as a special assistant. At the time the First Secretary at the British Embassy was the infamous Donald Maclean, the Soviet double agent. In 1950 the Bells visited Maclean and his wife Melinda in Cairo in response to his "warm and repeated invitations." The Macleans led a busy social life in Egypt and even hosted a party for the Duke of Edinburgh. However Donald Maclean had a reputation as a bit of drinker. On one occasion he tried to strangle his wife at a party, and was forcibly dragged off by fellow partygoers. Later Maclean in a drunken stupor grabbed the loaded rifle of an Egyptian guard and threatened to smash his head. A Foreign Office colleague, Lees Mayall, tried to stop Maclean and in the ensuing struggle broke his leg. One evening during the Bell's trip, Maclean, the Head of Chancery, went on a drunken binge with a reporter from the *Observer,* Philip Toynbee. The Bells received repeated phone calls to join him for a drink but they declined and Katie noticed Maclean sounded very angry that evening. During the night Maclean broke into the vacant apartment of an employee of the U.S. Embassy in Cairo, drank her liquor, smashed her furniture, broke her bath tub in two and threw her underwear down her toilet. Soon after the U.S. ambassador to Egypt filed a formal complaint about the British representative of HMG. The FBI is also said to have inquired into Maclean's conduct. Maclean returned to England two days later, because as one writer put it, "people began to talk." Maclean took some sick leave in Britain, but apparently faced no disciplinary action. In November 1950 he was appointed head of the Foreign Office's American department.
9. Major General Carl Spaatz was the Commander-in-Chief of the United States Air Force in Europe during World War II. He was honored for heroism in World War I and between the wars he performed in the Army's Flying Circus. In 1929 Spaatz spent a world record 150 hours in the air and was awarded the Distinguished Flying Cross. In the summer of 1940 Spaatz was sent to England as a 'special military observer.' This was the same time as Bill Donovan's infamous trip to Britain in which, according to Intrepid legend, the English were told to 'bare their hearts' by William Stephenson, and the red carpet was rolled out to convince Donovan and the Americans of Britain's resolve to withstand the Nazi assault. At an airfield outside London, Spaatz signed his name and occupation in the guest book, "Brigadier General Spaatz — Spy." (*Current Biography* 1942.) According to John Gilbert's Winant's book *Letter from Grosvenor Square* in 1940, no man in the United States had a more accurate knowledge of the strength of the German air force than Spaatz. Winant also accompanied Donovan on the British trip to give President Roosevelt his opinion on the morale of the British civil population. Roosevelt was very conscious of the fact that supplies, munitions and equipment

that had been dispatched to the continent were now in the hands of the Nazis, and he didn't want a similar fate for help — either public or private — sent to Britain. Winant wrote that American army and navy observers reported to Donovan that Britain did not have a hope. However the then Lieutenant Colonel Spaatz said he thought Britain would pull through. He talked to British pilots and flew their newest fighter planes. Spaatz thought the Germans could not beat the RAF and the Nazis would not invade until they had air superiority. Donovan returned to the United States and recommended the transfer of destroyers to Britain and further assistance to the island.

10. Intrepid to Steverite, July 15, 1974 U. of R. 83-7 801.1-1. There is a reference from Stephenson to one meeting with Ismay. "IT WAS LARGELY A RESULT BLACKETTS IMPASSIONED PLEA TO MYSELF THROUGH PUG ISMAY THAT TRIGGERED MY SPECIAL EXTRA PROCUREMENT OF HUNDRED LIBS FOR COASTAL COMMAND STOP"

11. Sir Edwin Leather, a Canadian, former governor of Bermuda.

12. The photo appears in *A Man Called Intrepid*. Many people assume the unidentified figure in the foreground is Brendon Bracken, Churchill's assistant. But the shadowy figure in a hat has also been identified as Stephenson. The famous *Times Newspaper*'s photo has also been reproduced at least twice (August 1965, July, 1991) in *National Geographic*. A November 1991 letter identifies the silhouette as Stephenson, without any editorial comments or corrections from the magazine.

13. Her responsibilities grew to include being the organizational head of Britain's delegations to the Big Three conferences. "I was on the administrative side. You needed somebody setting it up see. The trouble was, Ismay was a wise man and didn't believe in large staffs. The Cabinet Offices were very small, very hard working, and very efficient. And the same went for the conferences. It always came to the cabinet office, because we were into the service, you see. You know all the services and the civil service were represented. We could set up a special conference organization in no time at all. A Brigadier, two colonels, and four captains, and six lieutenants and a whole lot of ATS, and WACS and who knows what. You see what I mean. Parkinson's law. A naval aide, paymaster Commander Morris Knott helped with the organization in the beginning. I went to help him, and went to two or three conferences, and after he went out to sea I did it myself. I became personal manager. You take anybody from the office. You take one's self. It was very piece meal but it worked ... It was a very big set up. You can't move three or four hundred people in ..."

14. Astley, *The Inner Circle*, p. 49.

15. The telefilm was not Canadian but British according to the Internet Movie Database.

16. U. of R. 83-7 Box 9 801 7-1, April 1, 1973.

Chapter 17 Roald Dahl

1. *The Times*, November 24, 1990.

2. *Contemporary Authors*, Volume 73–76.

3. *The Cambridge Guide to Literature in English*, 1988.

4. Admiral Chester Nimitz actually became commander-in-chief of the U.S. Pacific fleet December 17, 1941. He replaced Admiral Husband Kimmel who was relieved

of his command pending the investigation into the Pearl Harbor attack. Although battleships *Arizona, California, Oklahoma* and *West Virginia* were sunk at Pearl Harbour and many other vessels were damaged, all the valuable aircraft carriers were at sea.

5. Montgomery Hyde's papers seem to indicate although Stephenson set the wheels in motion for the first book, he didn't pay to have it written about the organization. Montgomery Hyde's papers show that once the book came out Stephenson suppressed attempts to publicize *The Quiet Canadian* and refused to permit the selling of film rights.

6. In various files I could find only records of two speeches.

7. Dahl in *A Man Called Intrepid*, CBC television documentary (1974 broadcast).

8. *The Price of Vision: The Diary of Henry A. Wallace 1942-1946*, p. 385, 492.

9. Stevenson to Ogilvy, August 9, 1974, U. of R. 83-7 Box 9 801.4.

10. Hyde Papers, CCC. 3/21 February 21, 1942 memo V.W. to W. S. S.

11. After the war Churchill was often a guest of the rich and famous, and many were not former friends or associates. This irritated his wife and on occasion she refused to accompany him.

12. It is unlikely Stephenson would try and deceive Dahl about personal contact with Roosevelt when Dahl knew the president and, in theory, could verify if Stephenson was lying. In discussions with other BSC staff and through various documents, it is obvious Stephenson knew Roosevelt.

13. George Gallup was labeled America's foremost soothsayer, and an oracle during the 1930s. In 1935 he set up the American Institute of Public Opinion at Princeton which did numerous research surveys, and soon afterwards he started a similar British Centre. His new techniques flourished. By 1940 there were some objections to the possible political influence of his polls, and he was called "the most discussed man in the advertising world." Ogilvy's knowledge of Gallup's polling methods were utilized to an extent by the psychological warfare departments of the allies. Following the war advertising became Ogilvy's full time career.

14. In a later biography of Dahl, Jeremy Treglown says he could find no evidence Dahl had achieved the rank of Wing Commander. However the diaries of former U.S. Vice President Henry Wallace refer to his acquaintance with Flight Commander Dahl in 1944, and later Wing Commander Dahl in 1945. The writer Treglown, who interviewed some former members of BSC for his book said Stephenson had a thousand or more regular informants. (Treglown later refers to Dahl's work with the BSC history being compiled in Oshawa, Ontario.) Jeremy Treglown, *Roald Dahl: A Biography*, p. 67–68.

15. April 2, 1976, Pepper to Stephenson. U. of R. 83-7 Box 11 801.17-1.

16. Letter from David Ogilvy to author, January 28, 1990.

Chapter 18 Grace Garner

1. *Canadians at War*, p. 516.

2. *The Times*, February 18, 1989.

3. Thou was not born for death, immortal Bird!
    No hungry generations tread thee down;
    The voice I hear this passing night was heard
    In ancient days by emperor and clown:

Perhaps the self-same song that found a path

Through the sad heart of Ruth, when, sick for home,

She stood in tears amid the alien corn;

The same that oft-times hath

Charm'd magic casements, opening on the foam

Of perilous seas, in faery lands forlorn

John Keats, "Ode to a Nightingale"

4. Anthony Cave Brown, *Bodyguard of Lies*, p. 317.

5. The code word for the deception for Cossac's first operation was actually Cockade according to Cave Brown. Torch was the code name of the invasion of Africa.

6. Double Agent Dusko Popov was given an intelligence survey regarding Pearl Harbor by the Germans before December 7, 1941 which he relayed to the Allies.

7. The book implies the organization had something to do with the assassination. It refers to mock-ups at Camp X, and assassination discussions at BSC, but it also refers to "Icicle", the Czech parachute assassins' "Baker Street instructor." William Stevenson, *A Man Called Intrepid*, p. 382. The only reference this writer could find in available papers is a short reference from Stephenson who wrote "quietly flowed the Don since last heard of Heydrich." June 23, 1974 cable to Stevenson. U. of R. 83-7 801. 1-3. Harry Smith, who was at Camp X during the life of the training camp said, " Let's say we went through a lot of schemes with people, that could have been applied to that. But whether anything was ever used? I don't know if the people who were involved with the Heydrich assassination were ever at the camp, but it was the sort of thing that you put students through all the time."

Chapter 19 Benjamin de Forest "Pat" Bayly

1. For Stephenson's role see Troy's *Wild Bill and Intrepid*. As for a history of the NSA, former historian for the CIA Troy wrote "re: an Official NSA history, the answer is No. In fact there is no official history of any American intelligence service." Troy to author, November 1, 1994.

2. Winston Churchill, *Their Finest Hour*, p. 381.

3. Cited in Stafford, *Camp X*, p. 159. November 19, 1941, letter, Gambier Parry to Stephenson. Letter in Hyde papers at CCC. This document was censored by the British government during the author's numerous visits to CCC.

4. H. H. Hinsley's Official British intelligence history is a bit more delicate explaining the army communications breakdown in 1940 Europe. "The basic [cypher] book was captured in Norway and at Dunkirk in 1940, but it appears that the Germans had no success against British cyphers, as *opposed to* field codes and radio telephony, during their western offensive in 1940."

5. Born in Russia in 1891, the Friedman family emigrated in 1892 to America and settled in Pittsburgh. After first enrolling in Agriculture College, Friedman attended Cornell University in Science. In 1915, Friedman was hired by Riverbank laboratories in Geneva, Illinois as a geneticist. The owner of Riverbank, George Fabyan, also dabbled in language and cryptography, and he was attempting to prove the works of William Shakespeare were actually written by Francis Bacon. Friedman, and his soon to be wife Elizabeth, moved on to the study of ciphers at Riverbank. Cryptographers try to decipher communication which is in either code or cipher. Codes are letters or numbers that substitute for a whole word or a phrase. The weak-

ness of codes is that with repetition, they can't be used for long, and be considered safe. As a result new code books have to be devised and distributed. Ciphers are more difficult to crack, as every letter of a word is replaced with a different letter or numeral. In 1920, Friedman published *The Index of Coincidence and Its Applications in Cryptography*, which helped elevate the study from theory into a science of statistics. All codebreakers begin with a letter frequency count. In English, the most commonly used letters are E, T, A, O, N, I, and the least used are J, K, X, Q, and Z. Eventually, if individual characters of an intercepted message are charted and graphed, certain peaks and valleys usually occur which may indicate particular letters, and lead to breaking. Contact analysis, or the common placing of letters, and other linguistic characteristics is also used. In English for example, 'T H' is a common pairing. 'S' is often beside a consonant, 'R' is usually with vowels, and so on. Friedman moved this study of linguistic quirks into the realm of mathematics. In the late 1930s, using his theories, Friedman and his team attacked the Japanese diplomatic machine cipher, code named Purple. Simply by analysing intercepted messages, Friedman and his team were able to construct a machine which could consistently solve the foreign puzzles. The decrypts were appropriately called "Magic". Remarkably, the Japanese machine that created the ciphered messages was never seen or recovered. Friedman's accomplishments were for years shrouded in secrecy, and only after his death have his contributions to the covert world of communications breaking, and the importance of that success on the battlefield, been more fully recognized. Fifty years later, the cipher-breaking machine the Friedman team constructed to break the Japanese code is still under guard in a secret warehouse in Maryland.

6. *Tuesday Night*, Dahl; Interview. U. of R. Roll 1 page 5

7. David Stafford, *Camp X*, p. 163. Gordon Welchman, *The Hut Six Story*, p. 172. Welchman also says the transmission could be adjusted for atmospheric conditions.

8. Gordon Welchman, *The Hut Six Story*, p. 174–175.

9. December 4, 1974. U. of R. 83-7 801 .1-4. Bayly didn't remember who "Watson of IBM" was. Thomas Watson was the head of IBM.

10. The debriefing of Igor Gouzenko, the former cipher clerk, identified a number of Soviet undercover agents in Canada, the United States, and Britain. One was Kay Willsher, an employee of the Ottawa High Commission, whos cover name was "Elli". However, Gouzenko said there was another "Elli" who worked in either MI5 or 'five of MI', (section 5 of MI6) who had something Russian in his background. Gouzenko always felt the British never followed up on his findings. There has a been some question about why the Soviets would have had two people with the same code name, or a feminine name for a male agent. Some writers have guessed "Elli"could have been Roger Hollis, a former British MI5 head. Others thought it could be Dick Ellis, because of the similarity of their names.

11. Hoover wasn't known for getting along with non-Americans. According to William Sullivan, who worked for him, the FBI head "didn't like the British, didn't care for the French, hated the Dutch, and couldn't stand the Australians." There seems to be no reference of what he thought of Canadians. Cited in Curt Gentry's *J. Edgar Hoover, The Man and His Secrets*, p. 265.

12. Bayly's Buick had a licence plate that was untraceable to police. An identification search would come up simply "classified." On one occasion he was chewed out on

Parliament Hill, as a convenient parking space he frequently used belonged to the Prime Minister, and no one knew whose car it was.

13. It is difficult to ascertain the exact date or which U-boat this was. It is possible it could be U-505 which was captured by the Americans, June 4, 1944 and towed into Bermuda; U-744 boarded by the HMCS *Chilliwack*, March 6, 1944, or one of the U-boats that disappeared and was not seen again. It also possibly could have been the mysterious U-869 (also known as "U-who" or "Hitler's Lost Sub") which supposedly was sunk by the Americans off the coast of Africa in February 1945, but instead was found by divers off the coast of New Jersey in 1991. The *Queen Mary's* greatest defense against torpedoes was speed, and the ship was not allowed to stop. October 2, 1942, the ship hit the HMS *Curacao*, cutting it in two, killing over 300 sailors. The ship's bow was eventually repaired in Boston, and moored in New York. Stephenson could have been using "the need to know" to avoid the truth.

14. Cited in *Camp X*, p. 278.

Epilogue

1. *The Sunday Times*, London, March 1, 1998, in a book review referring to a new book by Nigel West.

2. See Thomas Mahl, *Desperate Deception*, or Nicholas J. Cull, *Selling War*.

3. The Bayly interview referred to was in November 1991. Bradley F. Smith's *The Ultra-Magic Deals* (1993) is the first book I could find that verifies Bayly's account. It refers to "existing British channels" used to transmit ENIGMA material sent on "high security cable routes ... used by BSC New York to carry German U-boat ENIGMA intercepts "(p. 156) David Kahn's *Seizing the Enigma* (1991) refers to keys used by the British and Americans being exchanged "through the office of British Security Coordination in Rockefeller Center, New York"(p. 239). Neither book footnotes this material. Neither book mentions Pat Bayly. Renowned American code expert Kahn, whose doctoral work with Hugh Trevor-Roper at Oxford resulted in his book *Hitler's Spies* (1978), said he'd never heard of Bayly (January 26, 1998 interview).

4. The *I Ching*, 'the Receptive,' Richard Wilhelm translation, Princeton University Press, 1950.

5. *A Tale of a Man Called Intrepid*, February 1989 (undated), *Los Angeles Times*. (Billingsley was the California Correspondent for the *London Speculator*.)

6. Stevenson, *AMCI*, HBJ, 1979, foreword by W.S. Stephenson.

Appendix

1. Peter Wright, *Spycatcher*, pp. 275–276.

2. *Noel Coward Diaries*, December 31, 1962, p. 520.

3. Notably Andrew Boyle's, *Climate of Treason*.

4. *The Diary of Sir Alexander Cadogan*, Thursday, October 25, 1945. CCC. This passage is not in the widely circulated David Dilks condensed version.

5. Andrew is considered by *The Times* of London to be "Britain's leading unofficial historian of intelligence." He has co-written a couple of books with Oleg Gordievsky who, according to the British, worked for them as a penetration agent inside the KGB since 1974. Andrew was asked the following question on a speaking tour.

"Anthony Blunt confessed in the 1960s yet nothing happened to him until a journalist found out that he had confessed, and he didn't even lose his knighthood until this journalist found out that he had confessed. What does that say about the SIS cleansing itself, and how many more do they still have hidden?" "Well, none is the answer to the last question. But I'll come back to that in a minute. Don't forget he was in MI5, he wasn't in SIS. I hope that it is reasonably clear that I don't think that Whitehall's attitude to ancient secrets is anything other than ludicrous. It's something I've said so many times, in so many places, that you must forgive me if I have forgotten to repeat it today. So nothing I say today will seek to, I hope, will give the impression that I think that the British Government is anything other than stupid in the way that it keeps so many ancient secrets. But so far as nonprosecuting Blunt is concerned, I suspect that exceptionally I insist on it, I suggest that they may have had a rather good point, the reason is this that security services all around the world, SIS included, are very shy in admitting one straightforward fact, which is that it is diabolically difficult to get the conviction for espionage. If we look at the cases which happened after World War II, they virtually all involve and that includes the British convictions Alan May and Fuchs people who are fooled into making confessions, rather than saying we never would they admitted it ..." Andrew speech at University of Manitoba, MPR, UMSU, November 1991.

6. *The Sunday Times*, November 25, 1979, story by Colin Simpson, David Leitch, and Phillip Knightley.

7. *The Sunday Times*, November 25, 1979, and Anthony Cave Brown, *"C"*, p. 406.

8. Philip Ziegler, *Edward VIII*, p. 550. Ziegler says Blunt and Morshead also travelled to the Netherlands to pick up relics of the Kaiser.

9. Philip Ziegler, *Edward VIII*, p. 552.

10. John Costello, *Mask of Treachery*, p. 406.

11. Anthony Cave Brown, *"C"*, p. 683. This information has also been referred to by the journalist Peter Worthington, *Ottawa Sun*, March 5, 1989.

12. Brown, *Ibid.*

13. *The Times*, London, December 20, 1979.

14. *Current Biography* 1942. Also *Cambridge Biographical Encyclopedia* (1994).

15. Cited in Alfred de Marigny, *A Conspiracy of Crowns*, p. 298.

16. *Ibid.*

17. Hyde, *Secret Intelligence Agent*, p. 117.

18. A.J.P. Taylor, *Beaverbrook*, p. 485. Taylor states "It is often said that Hess came to Great Britian in order to enlist British support against Russia. When he came, the German attack on Russia had not started, and it is unlikely that Hess was informed of Hitler's plans. He simply wanted to end the war between Great Britain and Germany." It is likely Hess knew of Hitler's designs on the Soviet Union. Plans for Hitler's attack on the Soviet Union, Barbarossa, were issued in December 1940. Hess arrived in May 1941.

19. Douglas Hamilton, cited in *"C"*, Anthony Cave Brown, p. 349.

20. Cited in Reuters wire story, November 13, 1995.

21. Stevenson, *Eclipse*, p. 352.

22. Alfred deMarigny, *A Conspiracy of Crowns*, p. 298.

23. Wallis Simpson, *The Heart has it Reason's*, p. 325.

24. The Duchess of Windsor, *The Heart has Its Reasons*, pp. 335–336

25. *Op. cit.*, p. 3.

26. Charles Higham, *The Duchess of Windsor*, p. 279.

27. The Duchess of Windsor, *The Heart has Its Reasons*, p. 346.

28. Cited in Higham, p. 280.

29. Cited in *The Traitor King*, documentary A&E, December 1996 broadcast.

30. Cited in Higham, p. 289 refers to still classified telegram and Italian accounts headlining the story in papers such as the *Gazetta del Popolo* of Turin.

31. Martin Gilbert and Richard Gott, *The Appeasers*, p. 324.

32. Higham, p. 385.

33. Cited in Higham, p. 288.

34. September 28, 1940, Lloyd to Halifax. Higham, p. 305.

35. *American Heritage* magazine, December 1991.

36. Charles Whiting, *Gehlen: Germany's Master Spy*.

37. *Toronto Star*, June 10, 1979.

38. *The Service: The Memoirs of General Reinhard Gehlen*, p. 70 (On September 1, 1945, the Toronto *Globe and Mail* reported that the Soviet-controlled Berlin radio had announced that Martin Bormann, Hitler's chief deputy in the Nazi party, was "in Allied hands.")

39. *The Service: The Memoirs of General Reinhard Gehlen*, pp. 299–300.

40. *Ibid.* pp. 330, 331

41. Quoted in *Encyclopédie Francaise*, 1959, and Gehlen's memoirs, p. 33.

42. John Pearson, *Ian Fleming*. An account of the Kennedy meeting also appears in *Ian Fleming* by Andrew Lycette (pp. 367–68) According to Lycette, the next day, Allen Dulles, the then head of the CIA asked to talk to Fleming.

43. June 6, 1973, letter William Stevenson to Julian Muller U. of R. 83-7 Box 10 801.10-10.

44. *The Gouzenko Transcripts*, Robert Bothwell and J. L. Granastein, 1981.

45. U. of R. 83-7 Box 10 801. 10-12 (no date).

46. July 24, 1974, letter to Stephenson. U. of R. 83-7 box 9 801. 3-2.

47. R.S.H.A. IV (1) (a) Marxism, enemy broadcasting, enemy propaganda, partisans, Russian prisoners-of-war. (b) Reaction, monarchism, pacifism, liberalism, rumours undermining moral, defeatism. (2) Sabotage, radio jamming, parachutists, commandos. (3) (a) Counter-intelligence, careless talk (b) Economics, foreign exchange (c) Frontier Controls (4) (a) Catholicism, Protestantism, Freemasonry (b) Jews (5) (a) Anti-social behavior, shirking (b) Party affairs, press (6) (a) Card Index, personal dossiers, information (b) Protective custody, concentration camps. pp. 92–93.

48. Edward Crankshaw, *Gestapo*, p. 94. "For the purpose of general supervision and repression, the Gestapo modelled itself closely on the Soviet Secret Police. Himmler had at his command an extremely able police officer, Heinrich Mueller who became known as Gestapo Mueller, a close and devoted friend of Soviet methods. Mueller was impressed by the efficiency of the internal spy system which had been perfected by the Soviet government, the effect which, ideally, was to isolate the individual by making it impossible for anybody to trust anybody else. He set to reproduce this system in Germany by more economical means."

49. Jacques Delarue, *The Gestapo*, p. 393.

50. *Journal of Contemporary History*, October 1987, Volume 22 #4. Story by Robert Stephan. "According to a Soviet history of the Special Departments, there were several suggestions at a meeting with Stalin of names for the new organization. One of the suggestions was Smernesh or 'Smert nemetskim Shipionam' (Death to German spies). Stalin replied: 'And why, as a matter of fact, should we be speaking only of German spies? Aren't other intelligence services working against our country? Let's call it 'Smert Shipionam'. Hence the nickname ' Death to Spies' was given to the GUKR-NKD."

BIBLIOGRAPHY

Alcorn, Robert Hayden. *No Bugles For Spies: Tales of the OSS,* New York: Van Rees Press, 1962.

Allen, Peter. *The Crown and the Swastika.* London: Robert Hale Ltd, 1983.

Andrew, Christopher. *For the President's Eye's Only: Secret Intelligence and the American Presidency from Washington to Bush.* New York: Harper Collins, 1995.

Artibise, Alan. *Winnipeg: An Illustrated History.* Toronto: James Lorimer & Company, 1977.

Astley, Joan Bright. *The Inner Circle: A View of War at the Top.* London: Hutchinson & Co. Ltd., 1971.

Astley, Joan Bright and Wilkinson, Peter. *Gubbins and SOE.* London: Leo Cooper, 1993.

Aarons, Mark and Loftus, John. *Ratlines.* London: Mandarin Paperbacks, 1980.

Barnet, Sylvan, Berman, Morton and Burto, William. *Nine Modern Classics.* Boston: Little, Brown and Company, 1973.

Beesly, Patrick. *Very Special Intelligence.* London: Sphere Books Ltd., 1977.

Bloch, Michael. *Operation Willi.* Toronto: Random House, 1984.

____. *The Duke of Windsor's War.* New York: Coward McCann & Geoghegan, 1983.

____. *Wallis and Edward: Letters 1931-1937.* New York: Summit Books, 1986.

Boldt, Gerhard. *Hitler's Last Days.* Lodnon: Sphere Books Ltd., 1947.

Bothwell, Robert, and Granatstein, J.L., ed., *The Gouzenko Transcripts.* Ottawa: Deneau Publishers, 1982.

Boyle, Andrew. *The Climate of Treason.* London: Coronet Books, 1979.

Braden, Spruille. *Diplomats and Demagogues.* New Rochelle, NY: Arlington House, 1971.

Brinkley, David. *Washington goes to War.* New York: Ballantine Books, 1988.

Brody, Iles. *Gone with the Windsors.* Toronto: The John C. Winston Company, 1953.

Brown, Anthony Cave. *Bodyguard of Lies.* New York: Harper & Row Publishers, 1975.

____. *C: The Secret Life of Sir Stewart Graham Menzies.* New York: Macmillan Publishing Company, 1987.

____. *The Secret War Report of the OSS.* New York: Berkeley Publishing Corporation, 1976.

____. *Wild Bill Donovan: The Last Hero.* New York: Times Books, 1982.

Bryan III, J. and Murphy, Charles J.V. *The Windsor Story*. New York: William Morrow & Company, Inc., 1979.

Bryce, Ivar. *You Only Live Once: Memories of Ian Fleming*. London: Weidenfeld & Nicolson, 1984.

Bryden, John. *Best-Kept Secret*. Toronto: Lester Publishing Ltd., 1993.

Casey, William. *The Secret War Against Hitler*. Washington: Regnery Gateway, 1988.

Chambers Biographical Dictionary, Edinburgh: W&R Chambers Ltd., 1984.

Chisholm, Anne, & Davie Michael, *Beaverbrook A Life*. London: Hutchinson, 1992.

Churchill, Winston S. *The Gathering Storm*. Boston: Houghton Mifflin Company, 1948.

_____. *Closing the Ring*. Boston: Houghton Mifflin Company, 1951.

_____. *Their Finest Hour*. Boston: Houghton Mifflin Company, 1949.

_____. *The Grand Alliance*. Boston: Houghton Mifflin Company, 1950.

_____. *The Hinge of Fate*. Boston: Houghton Mifflin Company, 1950.

_____. *Triumph and Tragedy*. Boston: Houghton Mifflin Company, 1953.

Cleroux, Richard. *Official Secrets: The Inside Story of the Canadian Security Intelligence Service*. Ontario: M&S Paperbacks, 1990.

Collins, Robert. *Who he?* British Colombia: Greystone Books, 1993.

Colvin, Ian. *Chief of Intelligence*. London: Victor Gollancz Ltd., 1951.

Costello, John. *Mask of Treachery*. New York: Warner Books edition, 1990.

_____. *Ten Days to Destiny*. New York: Morrow, 1991.

Coville John. *Winston Churchill and His Inner Circle*. New York : Wyndam, 1981.

Coward, Noel. *Future Indefinite*. New York: Doubleday, 1954.

Cull, Nicholas John. *Selling War: The British Propaganda Campaign Against American Neutrality in World War II*. New York: Oxford University Press, 1995.

Deacon, Richard. *Spyclopaedia*. London: Futura Publications, 1987.

_____. and West, Nigel. *SPY!* London: British Broadcasting Corporation, 1980.

Delarue, Jacques. *The Gestapo: A History of Horror*. New York: Dell Publishing Co. Inc., 1964.

De Marigny, Alfred. *A Conspiracy of Crowns*. New York: Crown Publishers, 1990.

Donaldson, Frances. *Edward VIII*. Philadelphia and New York: J.B. Lippincott Company, 1974.

Downes, Donald. *The Scarlet Thread*. Verschoyle, 1953.

Dunlop, Richard. *Donovan: America's Master Spy*. Foreword by William Stephenson. New York: Rand McNally & Co., 1982.

Farago, Ladislas. *Aftermath*. New York: Simon and Schuster, 1974.

_____. *Burn after Reading: The Espionage History of World War II*. New York City: Pinnacle Books, 1961.

_____. *Burn after Reading*. New York: Macfadden Books, 1961.

_____. *The Game of the Foxes*. New York: David McKay Company, Inc., 1971.

_____. *Spymaster*, New York: Paperback Library Inc., 1954.

Finkel, Alvin and Leibovitz, Clement. *The Chamberlain-Hitler Collusion*. Halifax: James Lorimer & Company (Merlin Press, UK), 1972.

Fleming, Ian. *From Russia With Love*. London: Gildrose Productions, 1957.

Fromm, Erich. *Escape from Freedom*. New York: Holt, Rinehart and Winston, Inc., 1941.

Gehlen, Reinhard. *The Service*. New York: Popular Press, 1972.

Gentry, Curt. *J Edgar Hoover The Man and the Secrets*. New York: WW Norton & Company, 1991.

Gilbert, Martin, and Gott, Richard. *The Appeasers*. London: Weidenfeld & Nicolson, 1963.

Goldston, Robert. *The Road Between the Wars: 1918-1941*, New York: Fawcett Crest, 1978.

Goralski, Robert. *World War II Almanac: 1931–1945*, New York: G.P. Putnam's Sons, 1981.

Gouzenko, Igor. *This Was My Choice.* Toronto: JM Dent, 1948.

Government of Canada Veterans Affairs, *Uncommon Courage.* Ottawa: Minister of Supply and Services Canada, 1985.

Granatstein, J. L. & Stafford, David. *Spy Wars.* Toronto: Key Porter Books Ltd., 1990.

Granatstein, J. L. & Bothwell, Robert, *The Gouzenko Transcripts.* Ottawa: Deneau Publishers, 1982.

Grant R.G. *MI5 MI6 Britain's Security and Intelligence Services.* London: Bison Books, 1989.

Gray, James H. *Red Lights on the Prairies.* Toronto: Macmillan, 1971.

Greene, Graham, & Greene, Hugh. *The Spy's Bedside Book: An Anthology.* London: R Hart Davis, 1957.

Halter, Jon C. *Top Secret Projects of World War II,* New York: Julian Messner, 1978.

Higham, Charles. *The Duchess of Windsor: The Secret Life.* New York: McGraw-Hill Book Company, 1988.

Hilton, Stanley E. *Hitler's Secret War in South America 1939-1945,* New York: Ballantine Books, 1981.

Hinsley, F. H. et al. *British Intelligence in the Second World War.* Vols 1–5. HMSO, 1979-1990.

____. and Stripp, Alan, ed. *Codebreakers: The Inside Story of Bletchley Park.* New York: Oxford University Press, 1993.

Hodges, Andrew. *Alan Turing: The Enigma,* London: Vintage, 1983.

Hohne, Heinz and Zolling, Herman. *The General was a Spy: The Truth about General Gehlen and his Spy Ring.* London: Pan Books Ltd., 1971.

Hyde, H. Montgomery. *The Quiet Canadian.* London: Hamish Hamilton, 1962.

____. *The Atom Bomb Spies.* London: Hamish Hamilton, 1980.

____. *Cynthia.* New York: Ballantine Books, 1965.

____. *Room 3603.* Toronto: Farrar, Straus-Giroux, 1962.

____. *Secret Intelligence Agent.* foreword by William Stephenson. New York: St. Martin's, 1983.

Hutchison, Bruce. *The Unknown Country.* Toronto: Longmans, Green & Company, 1942.

Irving, David. *Churchill's War.* New York: Avon Books, 1987.

____. *Hess: The Missing Years, 1941-1945.* London: Grafton Books, 1987.

Jones, R. V. *Most Secret War.* Great Britain: Hamish Hamilton Ltd., 1978.

Kahn, David. *The Codebreakers.* New York: MacMillan, 1967 (Signet 1973).

____. *Hitler's Spies: The Extraordinary Story Of German Military Intelligence.* London: Arrow Books, 1978.

____. *Seizing the Enigma.* Boston: Houghton Mifflin, 1991.

Keegan, John. *The Battle for History: Refighting World War Two.* Toronto: Vintage Books, 1995.

Kennedy, John F. *Why England Slept.* New York: Dolphin Books, 1961.

Lash, Joseph P. *Roosevelt and Churchill.* New York: Norton, 1976.

Lovell, Mary S. *Cast No Shadow : The Life of an American Spy Who Changed the Course of World War II.* New York: Pantheon, 1992.

Lycett, Andrew. *Ian Fleming.* London: Weidenfeld & Nicolson, 1995.

Mahl, Thomas E. *Desperate Deception: British Covert Operations in the United States. 1939-44.* London: Brassev's Washington, 1998.

Masterman, J. C. *The Double-Cross System in the War of 1939 to 1945.* New Haven and London: Yale University Press.

Neal, Patricia. *As I Am.* London: Arrow edition, 1989.

Nicolson, Harold. *The War Years: Volume II of Diaries and Letters.* New York: Atheneum, 1967.

Ogilvy, David. *Blood, Brains and Beer.* London: Hamish Hamilton, 1978.

Payne, Graham, and Morley, Sheridan (eds). *The Noel Coward Diaries*. London: Weidenfeld & Nicolson, 1982.

Pearson, John. *The Life of Ian Fleming*. New York: McGraw Hill, 1966.

Philby, Kim (Harold Adrian Russell). *My Silent War*. London: MacGibbon, 1968, Grafton, 1989.

Pincher, Chapman. *Their Trade is Treachery*. London: Sidgewick and Jackson, 1981.

____. *Too Secret Too Long*. New York: St Martin's Press, 1984.

Popov, Dusko. *Spy Counterspy*. Greenwich Conn.: Fawcett Crest, 1974.

Reader's Digest Association, *The Canadians at War*. 1939/45. Volume 1 & 2, Montreal: Reader's Digest Association, 1969.

Rusbridger, James, and Nave, Eric. *Betrayal at Pearl Harbor*. New York: Simon & Shuster.

Sherwood, Robert. *Roosevelt and Hopkins*. New York: Harper & Bros., 1948.

Sklar, Dusty. *The Nazis and the Occult*. New York: Dorset Press, 1977.

Sigmundsson, Elva. *Icelandic Settlers in North America*. Winnipeg: Queenston House Publishing, 1981.

Smith, Bradley F. *The Shadow of Warriors: OSS and the Origins of the CIA*. New York: Basic Books, 1983.

Speer, Albert. *Inside the Third Reich*. New York: Macmillan, 1970.

____. *The Ultra – Magic Deals*. Novato: Presido Press, 1993.

Stafford, David. *Camp X*. Toronto: Lester & Orpen Dennys Limited, 1986.

____. *Churchill and Secret Service*. Toronto: Stoddart, 1997.

____. *The Silent Game*. Toronto: Lester & Orpen Dennys Limited, 1988.

Stevenson, William. *The Bormann Brotherhood*. New York: Bantam, 1974.

____. *Eclipse*. New York: Doubleday & Company, 1986

____. *Intrepid's Last Case*. New York: Villard Books, 1983.

____. *A Man Called Intrepid*. New York: Harcourt Brace Jovanovich, 1976.

Summers, Anthony. *Official and Confidential: The Secret Life of J. Edgar Hoover*. New York: GP Putnam's Sons, 1993.

Swatsky, John. *Gouzenko: The Untold Story*. Toronto: MacMillan of Canada, 1984.

Sweet-Escott, Bickham. *Baker Street Irregulars*. Methuen, 1965.

Taylor, A.J.P. *Beaverbrook*. New York: Simon and Shuster, 1972.

Treglown, Jeremy. *Roald Dahl: A Biography*. London: Faber and Faber, 1994.

Troy, Thomas F. *Donovan and the C.I.A.* New York: University Press of America, 1981.

____. *Wild Bill and Intrepid*. New Haven: Yale University Press, 1996.

Wallace, Henry A. *The Diary of Henry A Wallace 1942-1946 The Prince of Vision*. Boston: Houghton Mifflin, 1973.

Welchman, Gordon. *The Hut Six Story*. New York: McGraw-Hill, 1982.

West, Nigel. *GCHQ*. London: Weidenfeld & Nicolson, 1986.

____. *MI5: The True Story of the Most Secret Counterespionage Organization in the World*. New York: Stein and Day, 1982.

____. *Unreliable Witness*. London: Weidenfeld & Nicolson, 1986.

____. (ed) *The Faber Book of Treachery*. London: Faber & Faber, 1995.

Whiting, Charles. *Gehlen: Germany's Master Spy*. New York: Ballantine Books, 1972.

Winant, John Gilbert. *Letter From Grosvonor Square*. Boston: Houghton Mifflin, 1947.

Windsor, The Duchess of. *The Heart Has Its Reasons*. New York: Award Books, 1956 (1974 edition).

Windsor, The Duke of. *A King's Story: The Memoirs of the Duke of Windsor*. New York: GP Putnam, 1951.

Winterbotham, F. W. *The Nazi Connection*. New York: Dell, 1978.

_____. *The Ultra Secret.* London: Collins, 1990.

Winterbotham, F. W. *The Ultra Secret.* London: Weidenfeld & Nicolson, 1974.

Wright, Peter. *Spycatcher: The Candid Autobiography of a Senior Intelligence Officer.* New York: Viking, 1987.

Ziegler, Philip. *King Edward VIII: The Official Biography.* London: Collins, 1990.

Selected Articles and Reviews

Collins, Robert. "Master of Intrigue," Champion of Liberty, *Reader's Digest,* December, 1984.

Cavendish, Anthony. "Inside Intelligence," *Granta 24* Summer 1988.

Evans, Michael. "The Enigma of a Man they Call Intrepid," *The Times,* February 18, 1989.

'Mandrake.' "Death of an Intrepid Fraud," *The Sunday Telegraph,* February 12, 1989.

Fleming, Ian. "Intrepid Silhoutte of a Secret Agent, " *The Sunday Times,* October 21, 1962.

Le Carré, John. "England's Spy in America." *New York Times Book Review,* February 29, 1976.

Naftali, Timothy J. "Intrepid's Last Deception: Documenting the Career of Sir William Stephenson," *Intelligence and National Security 8* (July 1993): 72–92.

Oursler, Fulton Jr. "Secret Treason: The Shocking Truth about the Duke of Windsor," *American Heritage,* Volume 42, Number 8, December 1991.

Portor, McKenzie. "The Biggest Private Eye of All," *Maclean's Magazine,* December 1, 1952.

Saturday Night. Letters. "The Case For Intrepid," October 1990.

Stafford, David. "A Myth Called Intrepid," *Saturday Night* October 1989.

Trevor-Roper, H. R. "Superagent," *New York Review of Books* 13, May, 1976.

Troy, Thomas F. "The British Attack on J Edgar Hoover: The Tricycle Case," *International Journal of Intelligence and CounterIntelligence,* Intel Publishing Group Volume 3, No. 2.

Adeane, Michael, 341
Aitken, Maxwell. *See*
  Beaverbrook, Lord
Allied radio link, 299–301
Alpha Cement, 48
America First, 74, 75, 166,
  190–91, 360
anti-American sentiment,
  282–83
anti-British sentiment, 161,
  255–56
Argentina, BSC in, 218–20
Armour, Lester, 106
Aspidistra radio transmitter,
  306–8
Astley, Joan Bright, 226–36
Astor, Vincent, 360
Ayer, Alfred Jules, 360

Baker, T. Thorne, 44
Baldwin, Stanley, 54–55, 260
Banks, Brooks, 214
Baptiste, Elizabeth, 109, 118, 156, 183

Baptiste, Rhys, 109, 118
Basque intelligence, 89, 194–95,
  196–97
Bayly, Benjamin de Forest "Pat,"
  72, 179, 285–335
Bayly Engineering, 332–33, 335
Beaverbrook, Lord (Maxwell
  Aitken), 45, 58, 104, 242,
  258–59, 321, 346, 360
Beck (American agent), 205–6
Bedson, Derek, 108, 112, 114, 360
Behn, Sothenes, 138
Belfrage, Cedric, 203
Bell, Katie, 229–31
Bell, Ulric, 96, 360
Bell, Walter, 229–31, 233
Belmonte, Elias, 216–18, 360
Bence, Enid, 308
Bensaude, Jose, 189, 201
Benson, Rex, 106
Berle, Adolph, 92–95, 193, 361
Bermuda mail intercept station,
  80, 85

Bernal, J. D., 259

Biddle, Francis, 93–94

Bletchley Park decryption centre, 288, 289, 308–9

Blunt, Anthony, 143, 341–44

Bohr, Niels, 82–83, 135–36

Bolivia, intelligence in, 97

Bonham Carter, Sir Maurice, 51

Bouverie, Barty, 253, 313–14

Braden, Spruille, 96–97

Breckman, G. K., 39

British American Canadian Company, 106, 251

British Censorship Bureau, 85

British Information Services, 164

British intelligence service, 59, 62–64, 66, 71

British Pacific Properties, 48

British Pacific Trust, 48

British Passport Control Office, N.Y., 63, 65–66, 155

British Security Coordination (BSC), 71, 74, 79, 87, 155; Canadians in, 73, 254, 283; coding and code-breaking, 154, 157, 160–61, 176; communications, 295, 306–8; filing system, 90–91, 190; financial administration, 201–2, 329–30; foreign operations, 88, 95–97, 160, 218–20; forgery, 97, 216–18, 280–81; history of, 100–101, 123–28, 243–44; New York offices, 154, 190, 221, 325, 256; propaganda, 158–59, 189, 265, 326; recruiting, 72, 153, 162, 187, 254; reunion, 156, 185;

secret agents, 78, 88–89, 173–78, 205, 214–15, 261; staff, 153–69, 187–88, 214, 230, 266–67

Brousse, Charles, 88–89, 173, 175–76

Bruce, David, 361

Brunner, Sir Felix J. M., 51

Bryce, Ivor, 253, 361

Bryden, John, 103

Burgess, Anthony, 128

Cadogan, Sir Alexander, 60, 361

Calais deception (WWII), 227–28

Camacho, Maximino, 345

Cameron, Merle, 100, 260

Camp X, 77, 100, 102, 198–201, 243, 286, 299–300, 327–28, 330–31, 361

Canadians in British intelligence, 254, 283, 308–9

Caribbean Cement Co. Limited, 107

Chamberlain, Neville, 59–60, 361

Churchill Falls hydro development, 105

Churchill, Sir Winston, 52, 53–54, 57, 158, 183, 349

Clarke, Carter, 316–17, 361

Clifford, Bede, 98

code names, 269–70

codes and ciphers, 154, 157, 160–63, 165–66, 176, 178, 181, 233, 289, 290, 293–95, 301, 302–3, 306, 308–9, 311

COI. See Coordinator of Information

Coit, Richard "Dickie," 361
Cold War intelligence, 102, 112
Cook, Betty, 167
Coordinator of Information (COI), 76–78, 361
Cottenham, Earl of, 59
Colville, Sir John, 148
Coward, Noel, 77, 104, 110, 247, 268
Cox Cavendish Electrical Company, 45
cryptography. *See* codes and ciphers
Cuneo, Ernest, 62–63, 83–84, 122, 246, 362
"Cynthia." *See* Pack, Elizabeth

Dahl, Roald, 100, 108–9, 237–50, 261
Deaguirrie Quobre, Hosio Antonio, 196
de Chastelain, Alfred Gardyne, 174–75, 181
de Chastelain, Marion, 174–86, 261, 362
Degener, Claire, 125
Delasota, Manu, 195–97
Delasota, Ramon, 196
Denham, G. C., 95
Des Graz, Charles, 85
Destroyers for Bases, 70–71, 248
Domville, Sir Barry, 59
Donovan, William "Wild Bill" ("Big Bill"), 21, 32–33, 67–71, 76–81, 113, 130–31, 155, 201, 215, 260–61, 362
Downes, Donald, 74–75
Drew-Brook, Thomas "Tommy,"

33, 36, 72, 122, 127, 254, 288, 362; prisoner-of-war, 36
Dunkirk, 290
Dwyer, Peter, 102, 253, 362

Earls Court Limited, 49, 50, 51–52
Edward VIII. *See* Windsor, Duke of
Einstein, Albert, 90
Eliscu, W. K., 106
Ellis, Charles Howard "Dick", 52, 124, 126, 130–31, 135, 203, 314, 362
ENIGMA, 289, 321, 322–23, 363
Evans, Jean Paul, 102, 362
Evenson, Dorothy, 162–65

Fairbairn, William Ewart, 198–200
Fairey, Sir Richard, 249
Farquar, Charles, 46, 178–79
Farquar, Margaret, 46
FBI, 93–94, 193, 215, 220, 263, 317–19
Ferguson, Marjorie, 153, 154
Ferguson, Ruth, 154
Fish, Hamilton, 74
FitzGerald, Janet, 159
Fleming, Eleanor, 100, 202–3
Fleming, Ian, 78, 104, 121–22, 125, 363
Forester, C. S., 237–38
Forgan, Russell, 106
Foxworth, Percy [Sam], 263
Franck, Louis, 86, 264
Franco-British Supply, 36
Friedman, William F., 293, 363

Friend (FBI agent), 262
Fuchs, Klaus, 102
Fulton, Maurice, 108

Gardner, Nadya, 212–13
Garner, Grace, 72, 100, 178, 186, 252–84, 316
Gehlen, Reinhard, 352–53
General Aircraft Limited, 48
General Radio Company Limited, 45
German rearmament, 53–55
German submarines, 304–6
Gerrity Jr., Edward, 138
Gestapo, 357
Gislasson, Hjalmar, 23–24
Gislasson, Ragnar, 15–16, 23–24, 43
Glyn, Sir Ralph, 51
Gouzenko, Igor, 101–3, 133, 147, 166, 319–21, 363
Gouzenko, Svetlana, 102–3
Government Code and Cypher School, 289
Graham, Brian, 118
Grand, Lawrence, 227
Great Canadian Spy, The (radio documentary), 129, 145
Green, A. M., 84, 104, 224
Griffiths, Bobby, 308–9
G-2, 363
Guatemala, BSC office in, 160
Gubbins, Colin, 77, 82–83, 130–31

Halifax, Lord (Edward Wood), 56, 88, 94, 316, 349, 363
Hambro, Sir Charles, 48, 106
Harris, Alan, 103

Hart, John, 90
Hastings, Eddie, 314–15
Heber, Elly, 15
Henman, Jim, 197
Herron, Shaun, 90, 129
Hess, Rudolf, 227, 346–47
Heydrich, Reinhard, 203, 281
Highet, Gilbert, 90–91
Hill, Tom, 72, 100–101, 106, 115
Hiss, Alger, 102
Hitler, Adolf, 56, 57–58, 209
Hoare, Sir Samuel, 348–49, 356
Hogg, Doris Griffiths, 170, 253
Hoover, J. Edgar, 62, 94, 98, 139–40, 292, 317–18, 363
Huggard, John, 39
Huggins, Sir John, 107
Hunt, David, 147–48
Hunty, Dall, 260
Hut Six Story, The, 324
Hyatt, Gilbert, 100
Hyde, Dorothy, 86, 195, 212
Hyde, Harford Montgomery, 53, 84–85, 100, 124–27, 211, 212, 218, 345
Hyde, Rosalind "Robbie," 41
HYDRA, 300

Industrial Intelligence Centre (IIC), 53
Ingimundson, Bina, 37
intelligence services: American, 58–59, 363; Basque, 89; British, 59, 62–64, 66, 71
intelligence training, 199–200. See also Camp X
International Documentary Center, 131

International Telephone Telegraph Corporation, 138
Intrepid code name, 355–57
Intrepid's Last Case, 141
Ismay, Hastings Lionel "Pug," 227, 229, 363
isolationism, U.S., 73–75, 92–93, 190–91

Jacques, Ronnie, 122
Japanese negotiations, 179–80
Johnson, George, 16, 118
Jones, Vivian, 253

Karig, Walter, 352
Kellock, R. L., 103
Kelly, Clarence, 140
Kennedy, Joseph, 58, 67, 69
Knox, Frank, 191, 364
Korda, Sir Alexander, 104, 223–24, 364
Korda, Zoltan, 77
Krafchenko, John, 28–30

Lais, Alberto, 88, 204–6
Leathers, Lord Fred, 57, 310
Lee, Raymond, 69
Lend-Lease deal, 315
Lewis, F. R., 51
Lindemann, Charles, 90
Lloyd George, David, 349
Londonderry, Lord, 53, 55
Lothian, Lord (Philip Kerr), 88, 350, 364

Mack, Margaret (Breck), 116
Mackenzie King, William Lyon, 102

Maclean, Donald, 128
McCloy, J. J., 106
McCormick shipping line, 189
McGibbon, Pauline, 109, 150
McKellar bill, 92–93
MAGIC, 364
Maidment, Ken, 163, 296, 364
mail interception, BSC, 80, 85–86, 195, 211–13, 219–20
Malone, R. S., 134
Man Called Intrepid, A (book), 130–50, 156, 207–8, 223, 232, 274, 281–82
Man Called Intrepid, A (television documentary), 132
Manchee, Charmian, 157–58
Markus, Dorothy, 257–58
Marques del Comillas, 205–6
martial arts at Camp X, 198–99
Maschwitz, Eric, 206, 258
Mason-McFarlane, F. N., 56
Masterman, John, 139
Mellon, Richard, 106
Menzies, Stewart, 21, 51, 144, 319, 328, 364
Mercier, Amedée, 47–48
Merton, George, 106
Midway (island), 302
Monckman, Walter, 52
Moore, Napier, 123
Morrell, Sidney "Bill," 364
Morshead, Owen, 342
Morton, Desmond, 53–54
Mountbatten, Lord Louis, 70–71, 312–13
Mueller, Heinrich, 355–57
Muller, Julian, 136
Murray, Gladstone, 77

Musa, Jean-Louis, 88

National Electric Corporation
  (NEC), 288
Nazis, 53–55, 74, 75, 80–81,
  344–52, 357
Newfoundland and Labrador
  Corporation, 105
newspapers and intelligence, 188
Noble, Marjorie, 123
Nunn, Alan, 102
Nye, Gerald, 74

Oakes, Harry, 345
Office of War Information
  (OWI), 158–59
Ogilvy, David, 106, 134, 191,
  250–51, 261–62, 364
Ogilvy, Francis, 211
Operation VIC (harassment),
  200, 263
Order of Canada, 112–13
Oursler, Fulton, 350–51
Oxford Group, 159

Pacific, war in, 272
Pack, Elizabeth "Cynthia"
  (Thorpe), 88–89, 173–78, 205,
  261
Passport Control Office, N.Y.,
  63, 65–66, 155
Paine, Dennis, 93, 193–94
Peacock, Jean, 165
Pearl Harbor, 139–41, 180,
  238–39, 270–73, 302
Pearson, Drew, 102, 241
Pell, Herbert, 350
Pepper, John, 106, 245, 250, 314

Phair, Molly, 17, 153–56
Phelps, Beryl, 201, 278
Philby, Kim, 127–28, 132, 143, 344
Pincher, Chapman, 203
platinum trade, wartime, 188
Playfair, Giles, 100, 262
Pleydell-Bouverie, Barty. See
  Bouverie, Barty
Point Douglas, 24, 25–27
Popov, Dusko, 139–41
Porter, Mackenzie, 115, 121–23
Pressed Steel Company, 48
propaganda, 74, 158–59, 326,
  353–55

Quebec Conferences, 233
Quiet Canadian, The, 123–28

radar countermeasures commit-
  tee, 311
radio interception, 301–2, 331–32
radio link, Allied, 299–301
Raymond, Betty, 197, 211–25
Reagan, Ronald, 113
resistance activities, 82–83
Ribbentrop, Joachim Von, 53, 55,
  57
Richardson, Elizabeth, 158, 296
Rimmer, Reg, 114, 137
Robertson, Norman, 101, 320–21
Rockefeller Center, 71–72
Rockefeller, Nelson, 106
Rockex teleprinter, 297–98
Rollaston, Gwen, 160–61
Roosevelt, Franklin Delano, 58,
  244, 351–52
Ross Smith, Bill, 187–210
Rowland, Herb, 72

Royal Canadian Mounted Police (RCMP), 90, 153, 159, 298
Russell, Charles Wilfrid "Wilf," 36, 38, 40
Russia, Nazi invasion of, 80–81
Ryan, Frank, 106–7

Sassoon, Sir Victor, 106
Schiaparelli, Elsa, 89–90
Schreyer, Edward, 113
Scott, Ted, 202
secret police, European, 357–58
Shepparton Studios, 48–49, 50, 84
Sheridan, Doris, 258
Sherwood, Robert, 93, 365
shipping activity, Axis, 189–92
Ships' Observers Scheme, 189–92, 195, 198, 202
Siddiqui, Rahman, 56
Simon, Sir John, 349
Simpson, Wallis (Duchess of Windsor), 344–45, 347–51
SIS headquarters, 71–72
Smallwood, Joey, 105
SMERSH, 357–58
Smith, Harry, 286
Smith, Ross, 218–19
SOE. See Special Operations Executive
sonobuoys, 332–33
Sound City Films, 48–49, 104
Soviet secret police, 357–58
Special Operations Executive (SOE), 82–83, 365
Spycatcher, 341
Spy/Counterspy, 139
Stafford, David, 145–47, 183–84

Stagg (BSC agent), 96–97
Stalin, Joseph, 346
Stanger, Sarah (Johnston), 22–23
Stanger, William Hunter, 22–23
Stanger, William Samuel Clouston. See Stephenson, William
Starr, Nelles, 103
Station M, 365
statistics, BSC, 161
Stefansson, Irv, 115, 116
Stephenson, Julianna, 46
Stephenson, Kristin, 22, 23, 24, 50
Stephenson, Lillian, 115–16
Stephenson, Mary, 109, 248, 275
Stephenson-Russell Limited, 39–40, 44
Stephenson Taylor holding company, 47
Stephenson, Vigfus, 22, 23, 24, 38, 50
Stephenson, William: attempts to discredit, 143–49; awards, 34, 35, 38, 98–99, 186; business ventures, 36–37, 38–40, 44–51, 84, 104, 106, 107; and Churchill, 52, 57, 63, 83, 158, 183; death of, 13–14, 118; and economic development, 105, 107, 108, 109, 185; employee impressions of, 155–56, 168, 170–71, 222–25, 273–82; and espionage, 51–59; family, 24–25, 37–38, 42, 50, 114–16, 137; finances, 39–40, 47, 182, 327; martini legend, 109–10, 168, 184–85, 224, 276; publicity,

121–23, 146; scholarship endowment, 109; stroke, 108–9; in WWI, 31–36; youth, 15–31
Stettinius, 107
Stevenson, William, 41–42, 112, 131–41
Stone, Tommy, 95
submarines, German, 304–6
Swedish neutrality, 257

Taschereau, Robert, 103
Taylor, A. J., 47, 72
Taylor, A. J. P., 147
Taylor, Kathleen (Kay), 72, 157, 253
telekrypton machine, 154, 293
telephone security, 291, 323
teleprint machines, 293–95, 297–98
Thompson, Nancy, 161–62
Thorpe, Amy Elizabeth. See Pack, Elizabeth
Till, Kenneth, 108–9, 246
"Tiny" (BSC agent), 214–15
Tizard, Henry, 90
Trevor-Roper, Hugh (Lord Dacre), 143–45, 184, 343–44
Troy, Thomas, 139–40
Tunney, Gene, 33, 61–62
Turing, Alan, 289, 323–24, 365
Turner, Ron, 108
Type X machine, 163

U.S. intelligence service, 58–59, 75–76, 363
U.S. Navy, 162, 300–301, 306
U.S. neutrality, 92–93

U-boats. See submarines
ULTRA, 230, 305, 308–9, 365

VENONA, 102, 365
Vichy French, 88–90, 173
Von Ribbentrop, Joachim, 53, 55, 57

Wallace Affair, 240–41
Walsh, Marion. See de Chastelain, Marion
Walton, George William, 47
weapons, covert, 220–21
Webb, William "Steam Kettle Bill," 211
Weinberg, Sidney, 106
Weizmann, Chaim, 90
Welchman, Gordon, 289, 322–23, 324
Wenner Gren, Axel, 89, 344–45
West, Nigel, 149, 235
West Indies, intelligence in, 97, 220
White, Harry Dexter, 102
Winchell, Walter, 262, 326
Windsor, Duchess of. See Simpson, Wallis
Windsor, Duke of (Edward VIII), 342, 344–45, 346–52
Winterbotham, Frederick W., 54, 59
wireless photography, 44–45, 47
wolfram, 97, 216, 217
Wood, Edward. See Halifax, Lord
Wood, Elizabeth, 170–71, 253, 273
Woolley, Helen, 159–60

World Commerce Corporation,
106–7, 251
Worthington, Peter, 103, 112
Wren, Marjorie, 214–15
Wren, Walter "Freckles," 194
Wright, Peter, 341–42

Young, David, 109, 115
Yugoslavian revolution, 80–81

ACKNOWLEDGEMENTS

This work was completed with the assistance of many people such as: Irv Stefansson, Mary Jane Stefansson, Kris Stefansson, the late Steena Stefansson, the late Ragnar Gislasson, Margaret Rimmer, the late Norma Feller, Joan Morrison, Brad Stephenson, Kay Germaine, Elly Heber, Margaret Jamieson, the late Derek Bedson, Joy (Bedson) Grant, Gerald Stephenson, the late George Johnson and the late Douglas Campbell.

Former members of British Security Co-ordination also assisted: Molly Phair, Georgie McCance, Ruth Ferguson, the late Marjorie Ferguson, Patsey Sullivan, Mary Taylor, Enid Bence, the late Bill Ross Smith, the late Roald Dahl, the late Pat Bayly, the late Tom Hill, Kathleen Taylor Cockburn, Walter Bell, Betty Raymond, Doris Hogg, Charmian Manchee, Helen Wooley, Janet FitzGerald, Gwen Rollaston, the late Nancy Thompson, Dorothy Evanson, Jean Peacock, the late Marion de Chastelain and the late David Ogilvy. Grace Garner's help was invaluable.

Also, thanks to: the late Harry Smith, Eric Adams, Norm Delahunty, Hugh Whitney Morrison, Eddie Chow, George Carothers, Thomas F Troy, Mary S Lovell, Anthony Cave Brown, Mark Jaffe, Ron Robbins, Monica Jensen-Stevenson, Andrew Lycett, Peter Worthington, Peter Chapman, McKenzie Porter, Rosalyn Hyde, Joan Bright Astley, Pauline McGibbon, Churchill College (Cambridge), Elizabeth Bennett, Patricia Ackerman, Sheila Claire, University of Regina, Shelley Sweeney, Selina Coward, First Luthern Church (Winnipeg), Gregg Calkin at the

Canadian High Commission London, Cross and Cockade, Dr. Rodney Hunter, David Young, Dr. Phil Hall, Ken Reddig, James Hutchison and Vaughan Baird.

Many people from many places provided assistance with such things as transcribing hours of interview tapes, indexing, introducing me to various books and helping with transportation and overseas research. From Australia: Jane Brockhouse. From Germany: Karen Kosmider, Andreas Hertz. From Switzerland: Nicole Ramseier. From the United States: Renee Johnson, James Bell. From Malaysia: Daljit Singh. From Great Britain: Sarah Betts, Garry Norris, Jule & Kate, Gail Thompson. A special thanks to Mike McNabb in London for his hospitality and assistance. Ross Green, Bruce & Gwen Roberts, Lance Barber, Rick Jost, Tim Dirks, Bill Lawrence, Peter Heese, Bruce Benson, Kim Wright, David Becket, Marcus Wolfe, Emma Kroeker, and Rod Brecht.

The Manitoba Arts Council provided a trip grant. The excerpt taken from *From Russia With Love* is reprinted by permission of Glidrose Publications Ltd.

In 1994 an Intrepid Society founded by Winnipegger Syd Davy, was formed to remember the life and work of William Stephenson. In 1997 a Winnipeg library was named after Stephenson. A statue of Stephenson by renowned sculptor Leo Mol was unveiled by Princess Anne near Manitoba's Legislative Grounds in 1999.

And finally, I would like to thank my immediate family, Joan and especially Claire, without whose help this book would not have been possible.

A teacher and journalist, Bill Macdonald lives in Winnipeg.

Weird Sex & Snowshoes (and Other Canadian Film Phenomena)
by Katherine Monk
With the discerning eye of a critic, the enthusiasm of an insatiable cinephile and the passion of a proud Canuck, Monk delves into the guts of Canada's cinematic tradition — where it came from, what it looks like and what's going on beneath the surface of the frame. She pulls Canadian film apart at the splice marks, rips open its subtext, and exposes not just the beating heart of one very plucky cinematic species, but the hidden soul of a nation.
1-55192-474-9 · $26.95 CDN/$18.95 US

The Presumption of Culture
by Tom Henighan
Will Canadian culture survive into the new century? Institutions such as the CBC, the Canada Council, the National Film Board and the National Ballet have been hit by repeated funding cutbacks and lurch from one financial crisis to the next. In this important book, Henighan explores Canada's past and present cultural psyche, demonstrates just how far we have advanced since the 1950s, reminds us of what we stand to lose, and suggests a plan of action for the future.
1-55192-013-1 · $15.95 CDN/$11.95 US

The Maclean's Companion to Canadian Arts and Culture
by Tom Henighan
What separates Canadian culture from the cultures of other nations? How does a nation as vast and diverse as Canada define its culture? What is Canadian culture? Henighan ponders these and many other questions about our nation's artistic personality. A one-of-a-kind reference, a basic primer and an informed assessment of Canada's artistic scene — in short, a book that should be read by anyone who cares about Canadian culture.
1-55192-298-3 · $24.95 CDN/$18.95 US

A Pour of Rain: Stories from a West Coast Fort
by Helen Meilleur
This reissue of an out-of-print treasure of BC history is one of the best histories we have of a West Coast community. Port Simpson is located just south of the Nass River, an area largely inhabited by the Nisga'a people. In the 1920s, Meilleur attended a one-room school on the Native reservation here, where her father ran the general store. A Pour of Rain combines personal memoir with a well-researched, carefully reconstructed history of the fort in the mid-nineteenth century.
1-55192-422-6 · $24.95 CDN/$18.95 US

Scientific Canadian: Invention and Innovation from
Canada's National Research Council
by Roy Mayer
Since its inception nearly 75 years ago, the NRC has created an exceptional environment in which diversely talented and creative men and women have made lasting contributions, not just to Canada, but to the world. From the space shuttle's Canadarm in outer space to the canola fields of the Prairies, from Internet technology to marvels of medical diagnostics, Mayer tells the story of these unsung Canadian heroes and their inventions.
1-55192-113-8 · $19.95 CDN/$15.95 US